D1227268

LITERARY
JOURNALISM
ON TRIAL

LITERARY JOURNALISM ON TRIAL

Masson v. New Yorker and the First Amendment

Kathy Roberts Forde

University of Massachusetts Press

AMHERST

Copyright © 2008 by Kathy Roberts Forde
ALL RIGHTS RESERVED
Printed in the United States of America

LC 2008003493
ISBN 978-1-55849-653-8 (paper); 652-1 (library cloth)

Designed by Steve Dyer
Set in Minion by dix!
Printed and bound by The Maple:Vail Book Manufacturing Group

Library of Congress Cataloging-in-Publication Data
Forde, Kathy Roberts.
Literary journalism on trial : Masson v. New Yorker and the First
Amendment / Kathy Roberts Forde.
p.   cm.
Includes bibliographical references and index.
ISBN 978-1-55849-653-8 (pbk. : alk. paper)—ISBN 978-1-55849-652-1
(library cloth : alk. paper)
1. Masson, J. Moussaieff (Jeffrey Moussaieff), 1941—Trials, litigation, etc.
2. Malcolm, Janet.—Trials, litigation, etc.   3. Trials (Libel)—United States—History—
20th century.   4. Interviewing in journalism—United States.   5. Journalism—
Objectivity—United States.   I. Title.
KF228.M3747F67 2008
342.7308'53—dc22
2008003493

British Library Cataloguing in Publication data are available.

An earlier version of chapter 4 appeared as "Libel, Freedom of the Press,
and the New Yorker," American Journalism 23, no. 4 (Winter 2006): 69–91.
Reprinted with permission.

Source materials used in chapter 4 include the New Yorker Records,
Manuscripts and Archives Division, New York Public Library,
Astor, Lenox and Tilden Foundations. Courtesy of The New Yorker /
The Condé Nast Publications Inc. www.newyorker.com.

For Jack and Zada James Forde
and
Lynne and Buck Foster

A word is not a crystal, transparent and unchanged; it is the skin of a living thought and may vary greatly in color and content according to the circumstances and the time in which it is used.

Justice Oliver Wendell Holmes,
Towne v. Eisner (1918)

CONTENTS

ACKNOWLEDGMENTS

OUR ACHIEVEMENTS ARE RARELY THE RESULT OF SOLITARY ENDEAVOR. This book is no exception. I wish to thank a number of people for helping me think through complex legal and historical issues raised in this book. The first among these is Ruth Walden, James Howard and Hallie McLean Parker Distinguished Professor and former Associate Dean for Graduate Studies at the School of Journalism and Mass Communication at the University of North Carolina at Chapel Hill. As an adviser and mentor, she taught me—through the example of her own intellectual rigor and generosity toward her students—what it means to be a professional academic. I am a better scholar, teacher, and person for knowing her. Others have made valuable contributions to this work, including Fitzhugh Brundage, Frank Fee, John Hartsock, Jane Kirtley, Lloyd Kramer, Cathy Packer, Norm Rosenberg, and Michael Stamm. Any errors that have found their way into this work are mine alone.

I am grateful to the knowledgeable and helpful staff of the Park Library, Davis Library, and Law School Library at UNC–Chapel Hill; the Law Library at Duke University; various libraries at the University of Minnesota; the Manuscripts and Archives Division of the New York Public Library, where the *New Yorker*'s records are housed; the U.S. District Court Library of Northern California; and the National Archives and Records Administration in San Bruno, California. Kate Edenborg, a graduate student at the University of Minnesota, provided valuable research assistance. Working with the intelligent, engaged, and unfailingly pleasant editors and staff of the University of Massachusetts Press has been a special pleaure. Clark Dugan, senior editor, gave me and this book a chance; Amanda Heller copyedited the manuscript with close attention; and Carol Betsch and Mary Bellino kept the project (and me) on schedule and helped tie up loose ends. My heartfelt thanks to all of them.

I am grateful to Jeffrey Masson, his lead counsel in *Masson v. New Yorker*, Charles O. Morgan, and assistant counsel Paul Kleven for discussing the case with me and contributing to this historical record. Early in our conversation Jeffrey Masson told me that the episode about which I was asking him to speak was deeply distressing. If he could revise his life, he said, he would erase the two articles at the center of his dispute with Janet Malcolm. Given his unpleasant memories of the dispute, I am especially grateful to him for agreeing to discuss it with me. I was able to contact Janet Malcolm only indirectly through Gary Bostwick, one of her lawyers in the *Masson* case, and she ultimately declined to speak with me. He was, of course, obliged to follow her lead. Although I am sorry not to have had their oral histories as primary sources, I am grateful to them nonetheless for considering my request and responding graciously. Finally, I thank James Wagstaffe, who served as counsel for the *New Yorker* at various stages in the life of the case. He has thought deeply about the matter, and our conversation broadened my understanding of key legal issues and strategies in litigating libel cases with First Amendment implications.

This book could not have been written without the people who give my life happiness, meaning, and stability. Thank you, all, especially my family in North Carolina, Alabama, and California, and my friend the poet Leigh Anne Couch, whose interest in and wise counsel regarding my work and life have never flagged.

Jack and Zada James, you are a special case. Your hijinks and playfulness fill our home with laughter and surprise. You distracted me from my work when I was most in need of distraction and reminded me daily what is most important. You are my everything.

LITERARY
JOURNALISM
ON TRIAL

Introduction

Journalism, Libel Law, and the Problem of Facts

IN LATE NOVEMBER 1984, JEFFREY MASSON FILED A LIBEL SUIT AGAINST Janet Malcolm, the *New Yorker* magazine, and the publisher Alfred A. Knopf, Inc.,[1] initiating a dispute that would make its way to the U.S. Supreme Court and occupy the federal court system for almost twelve years. Masson accused Malcolm of libeling him by fabricating quotations attributed to him in a profile she wrote for the *New Yorker* about his career as a Freudian scholar and administrator of the Freud Archives.[2] Malcolm denied fabricating any quotations. Both maintained their positions throughout the long, tumultuous life of *Masson v. New Yorker* and beyond.[3] Although the courts ultimately absolved Malcolm of legal wrongdoing, the case raised ethical issues about the practice of journalism and led to interpretations of libel law that remain controversial.

The substantial legal documentation of the case, as well as Malcolm's own writings, suggests that the two principals had irresolvable conceptions of appropriate journalistic methods in the representation of truth, particularly the use of quotations. Furthermore, the lower courts understandably had trouble applying the falsity element of the "actual malice" standard—a constitutional protection of expression in the area of libel law, erected in 1964 in the landmark case *New York Times v. Sullivan*—to the previously unexplored instance of the libel of a public figure through alleged misquotation.[4] The competing conceptions of truth in *Masson v. New Yorker*—both legal and journalistic— required not only the Supreme Court's further interpretation of actual malice but also, finally, resolution before a jury.

Masson spent more than forty hours with Malcolm over seven months in 1983, talking about his short, controversial tenure as projects director of the Freud Archives and his life in general.[5] The *New Yorker* published Malcolm's profile of Masson as a two-part series in December 1983.[6] When Masson read both articles just days before the first was published, he was shocked.[7] He had expected a profile discussing his psychoanalytic theories and critiques of Freud's seduction theory. The articles did that and, unexpectedly for Masson, much more: they explored his personal and professional life, and in the process, Masson claimed in his libel complaint, falsely portrayed him as "unscholarly, irresponsible, vain, lacking in personal honesty and moral integrity," largely through what Malcolm presented as his own words.[8] The articles also portrayed him as a once sex-obsessed womanizer. The *New York Times* reported that Masson "hit the ceiling" when he read them.[9] Alfred A. Knopf published a book version of the *New Yorker* articles called *In the Freud Archives* in 1984. The publishing house soon found itself embroiled in one of the most contentious libel suits of the late twentieth century.

Masson v. New Yorker originated in a federal district court in California, which in 1987 granted summary judgment in favor of Malcolm, the *New Yorker*, and Knopf, finding that all the contested quotations were protected under the First Amendment.[10] Masson appealed the decision. In 1989 the Ninth Circuit Court of Appeals affirmed the lower court's decision.[11] Masson then appealed to the U.S. Supreme Court, which in 1991 reversed the lower courts' rulings, established a further interpretation of the actual malice standard in the instance of altered quotations, and remanded the case for additional proceedings consistent with its findings.[12] *Masson* then returned to the Ninth Circuit, which ruled that the case against Malcolm and the *New Yorker* should go to trial but affirmed that Knopf, as established in the district court's grant of summary judgment in 1987, was in the clear.[13] In 1993 a federal jury found that Malcolm had indeed libeled Masson, but the trial ended surprisingly when the jury could not reach consensus on the question of damages. The judge declared a mistrail and subsequently dismissed the *New Yorker* from the case because the jury had cleared the magazine of liability.[14] A second federal trial took palce in 1994, with Janet Malcolm as the lone defendant. This time around, a second set of jurors found in favor of Malcolm.[15] In 1996, the Ninth Circuit affirmed the jury's findings in the second trial.[16] Almost twelve years after Jeffrey Masson filed his original complaint, *Masson v. New Yorker* had finally exhausted itself.

But the story of the case begins well before there was even a legal dispute. Janet Malcolm was first drawn to Masson as a profile subject after reading a *New York Times* article about his tenure as projects director of the Freud

Archives.[17] According to *Times* reporter Jane Gross, what originally attracted Malcolm was Masson's speaking style: "If his discoveries about Freud were correct, Mr. Masson said . . . then all psychoanalytic patients since 1901 would have to be recalled 'like the Pinto.' "[18] Ironically, it was in attempting to capture Masson's speech that Malcolm inadvertently set the stage for a libel suit that would follow her into the next decade.

What Masson called fabrication, Malcolm called ordering his often "chaotic, contradictory" speech.[19] When she altered his exact wording and compressed quotations from several interviews into one monologue, she was attempting, she testified at trial, "to present [Masson's speech] in logical, rational order so he would sound like a logical, rational person."[20] Although she was not reporting verbatim, stenographic quotations, she was not fabricating either, she claimed throughout the court documents and federal trials as well as in her own writing.[21] Although the *New Yorker* writer claimed she had presented a truthful portrait of Jeffrey Masson and defended her narrative techniques, many press observers found her reporting methods in the Masson profiles ethically suspect. A firestorm of criticism, from practicing journalists to press critics to press scholars, surrounded the Masson-Malcolm dispute almost from the beginning.

To understand the dispute, it is helpful to review a contested quotation that survived all the way to trial—what was known in the court opinions as the "sex, women, fun" quotation. In her articles and book Malcolm quoted Masson describing Maresfield Gardens, the Freud family home in London which then housed the Freud Archives and which Masson expected to direct as a Freud museum after Anna Freud's death: "It was a beautiful house, but it was dark and sombre and dead. Nothing ever went on there. I was the only person who ever came. I would have renovated it, opened it up, brought it to life. Maresfield Gardens would have been a center of scholarship, but it would also have been a place of sex, women, fun. It would have been like the change in *The Wizard of Oz*, from black-and-white into color."[22] Although Malcolm's tape recordings of her conversations with Masson contain statements with similar themes, they do not include the references to "sex, women, fun" and *The Wizard of Oz*. In its *Masson* opinion, the Supreme Court referred to two recorded statements in its assessment of the quotation in dispute. In one Masson says: "It is an incredible storehouse. I mean, the library, Freud's library alone is priceless in terms of what it contains: all his books with his annotations in them; the Schreber case annotated, that kind of thing. It's fascinating."[23] In an earlier interview Masson referred to the Freud house in speaking of meeting a London analyst and came much closer thematically to the "sex, woman, fun" quotation: "I like him. So, and we got on very well. That was the first time we ever met and you know, it was buddy-buddy, and we were to stay with each other and [laughs] we were going to pass women on to each other, and we were going to have a great time together when I lived in the Freud house. We'd have great parties there and we were [laughs] . . . going to really, we were going to live it up." [24] In his final complaint, Masson disputed the "sex, women, fun" passage in Malcolm's profile as false and defamatory. The dispute over the quotation survived throughout the life of the case.

Malcolm claimed all along that the "sex, women, fun" statement occurred in a conversation she had with Masson over breakfast when he was her houseguest in New York City near the end of their time together. Because her tape recorder was broken, Malcolm said, she took notes by hand and later typed them out. [25] All that was left in the record of this conversation was Malcolm's typed transcript of the handwritten notes that she claimed to have lost. According to Masson, this conversation never took place. [26] In the federal district court (1987) and Ninth Circuit (1989) opinions granting summary judgment to Malcolm and the other defendants in the case—and in the Supreme Court opinion (1991) reversing the lower courts' decisions and remanding the case for possible trial—Malcolm's typed notes were never considered as evidence. This exclusion was a requirement of the Federal Rules of Civil Procedure: when a court examines a case for summary judgment—that is, when a court determines whether it can issue a judgment without moving the case to trial—it must consider all facts in a light that is favorable to the plaintiff. [27] When Masson disputed the authenticity of Malcolm's typed notes, the courts could not consider them in their review of the facts.

Well before the case made its way to the Supreme Court, Malcolm had defended her narrative techniques in the Masson profile by referring in her own public writing to the nonfiction writer's duty to "actuality": "The writer of non-fiction is under contract to the reader to limit himself to events that actually occurred and to characters who have counterparts in real life, and he may not embellish the truth about these events or these characters." But the exact translation of spoken speech to written speech often demonstrates "how the literally true may actually be a kind of falsification of reality." It is up to the writer, she asserted, to perform the filtering function for the written word that the ear provides for speech: "Only the most uncharitable (or inept) journalist will hold a subject to his literal utterances and fail to perform the sort of editing and rewriting that, in life, our ear automatically and instantaneously performs."[28]

In the contested articles Janet Malcolm told Masson's story using a range of techniques, including explanation, analysis, and narrative. Although narrative techniques do not alone convey the unflattering portrait of Masson that emerges in the profile, they were the techniques solely at issue in Masson's complaint. Every passage he identified as false and defamatory was a direct quotation attributed to him. Accordingly, *Masson v. New Yorker* focused on one particular legal issue: determining whether the allegedly altered quotations constituted libel within the established constitutional framework. In the tortuous judicial proceedings in the case, however, the courts examined more than the contested quotations. They examined in exhaustive detail Janet Malcolm's narrative journalistic strategies and techniques: her immersion strategy of reporting, which yielded more than forty hours of taped interviews; her compression of multiple interviews into one crafted conversation; and her method of transcribing spoken speech into written speech. The case became, in many respects, an investigation into—and an evaluation of—Malcolm's narrative reporting. And the courts were not investigating alone.

The press followed the case closely, evaluating Malcolm's methods and ethics against what it considered to be standard journalistic practices and principles. Press coverage of *Masson v. New Yorker* thus became a means for the institutional press to discuss among itself, and to share with the public, the cultural norms and ethical standards of the profession. Because some of Malcolm's methods contravened these norms and standards, the case became a cause for the press to celebrate and reify its professional practices. The result was a nearly unanimous vilification of both Janet Malcolm and literary reporting.

In the press discourse about the Masson-Malcolm controversy, the dominant voice belonged to the *New York Times*. The *Times* published nine stories about the Supreme Court iteration of *Masson v. New Yorker* and provided day-by-day, front-section coverage of the first federal trial in the case, which lasted more than three weeks before ending in a mistrial. Three of these stories made the front page. Although such intense coverage of the *New Yorker*'s and Janet Malcolm's tribulations may be attributed to the economic and social competition between important news media that play defining roles in the public life of the same major city, or perhaps merely to New York's perpetual fascination with itself, the coverage was also a reflection of a significant cultural and institutional divide between the *New York Times* and the *New Yorker*. By repeatedly highlighting the Masson-Malcolm case, and by devoting so much attention to assessments of Malcolm's journalistic methods and the *New Yorker*'s editorial processes, the *Times*, one of the most influential daily newspapers and journalistic outlets in the United States, was attempting to define the difference between the traditional report and the literary report and between established codes of journalism ethics and standards and Malcolm's challenge to the conventional journalistic practice of quoting speakers.

To the *New York Times*, the case provided an opportunity to tout its own high standards of professional ethics and reporting—and to construct narrative literary journalism as some *other* kind of journalistic expression practiced by *other*, presumably less judicious and trustworthy publications. But the *Times*'s coverage of the *New Yorker*'s legal problems represented more than just professional turf-staking and revealed more than just competitive gloating. It ultimately made public a major epistemological problem animating then-current debates in intellectual and scholarly circles: Was it possible to offer through language an "objective" representation of the world, or did the inherent ambiguity of language ultimately make all reports "subjective" interpretations? In the world of human experience and expression, what was knowable as "fact" as opposed to "interpretation" or "opinion"? When the conventions and practices of the traditional report collided with those of the literary report in the Masson-Malcolm dispute, the resulting firestorm reflected not only tensions between two different journalistic traditions but also the incendiary emergence of postmodern thought into public life.

Masson v. New Yorker is the only U.S. Supreme Court case that directly addresses the First Amendment dimensions not just of altered quotations but of narrative technique in journalism. It thus dramatizes the largely modern clash between two contrasting notions of what constitutes, as James Carey put it, "an adequate report of the world": on the one hand, the traditional journalistic report, characterized by its inverted pyramid structure, focus on facts, and objective point of view,[29] and on the other, the literary, or narrative, report, characterized by its narrative structures, immersion of the writer in the subject's world, and subjective point of view.[30] The definitional boundaries of literary, or narrative, journalism are much contested, as is the appropriate terminology to use in categorizing the form.[31] In this book I use the terms "literary journalism" and "narrative journalism"—as well as "the literary report" and "the narrative report"—to refer to those nonfiction forms that depend on information gathering and, to appropriate and slightly adjust historian John Hartsock's working definition of the form, read "[in part] like a novel or short story" and make "a truth claim to phenomenal experience."[32] I am not comfortable with a definition of literary journalism that does not acknowledge the newsgathering that supports all journalism and insists that all literary journalism must read throughout like a novel or short story. Narrative is a key element in such works, but it need not be the only representational or discursive strategy employed.

I use the admittedly inexact term "traditional journalism" to indicate the daily newspaper journalism that so largely dominated and defined the American press throughout the twentieth century. Naming a current or tradition in any social institution as complicated as the press is deeply problematic. The American press changed substantially throughout the century in terms of its institutional structures, business management, and increasing attention to professional ethics, so in a sense, calling the dominant journalism in American press expression "traditional," given the institution's acknowledged change across time, is misleading. In addition, American journalism is hardly as monolithic as the term "traditional journalism" might suggest. There are many traditions and movements within modern journalism in the United States, including alternative, advocacy, precision, and public journalisms. Even so, and even given the criticisms of objectivity that have repeatedly been raised in press discourse since the 1930s, a form of journalism tied to the ideal of objectivity and the conventions and standards of the daily newspaper has emerged as the dominant model in the American press. As technically inadequate as the term "traditional journalism" may be, it is nevertheless useful in identifying this dominant model: the documentation and explanation of current events through the emphasis on facts, the frequent use of the inverted pyramid form, and the assumption of an objective and neutral stance. The term also serves a necessary role in identifying the dominant form of American journalism alongside which literary journalism developed.

Masson v. New Yorker crystallizes the foundational issue that has driven debate in the scholarly literature about the roles of traditional and literary, or narrative, journalism in public life: the degree to which the literary report is a legitimate vehicle for delivering the news.[33] One purpose of this book is to analyze the Masson-Malcolm controversy, including its contextual legal, journalistic, and scholarly debates, as a reflection of broader social and cultural issues pertaining to the American press since the beginning of the twentieth century: What have been the roles and functions of both traditional and literary journalism? What are the historical connections and ruptures between professional standards of American journalism and both the narrative and traditional report? How do these traditions of American journalism conceptualize the role of truth in press expression? What are the social and cultural patterns of libel law and its relationship to traditional and literary journalistic traditions in the United States? These issues are worth exploring, especially given the ever-increasing interest in and prevalence of narrative reporting in the American press.

As an expression of contemporary free press theory, *Masson v. New Yorker* allows us to address a much broader range of issues concerning the current state of the institutional press and its self-asserted role as the Fourth Estate in American social and political life. Although the *Masson* case does not concern political speech or the speech of a public official, its Supreme Court decision is the progeny of *New York Times v. Sullivan* and thus further articulates the boundaries of First Amendment protection for all speech about public officials, figures, and private persons. What matters for First Amendment jurisprudence and its theory of the role of free expression in the proper functioning of democratic government is the degree to which the Supreme Court's *Masson* ruling, placed in the context of the long line of other Supreme Court decisions staking out the meanings of actual malice and the scope of protections for expression, expands or diminishes *Sullivan*'s promise of protection and challenges or embraces the democratic theory supporting this promise.

To get at this issue is my broader concern in this book and requires the exploration of a series of related issues implicated in the *Masson* case: What are the theories of the First Amendment articulated in the line of constitutional libel cases running from *Sullivan* to *Masson* and their implications for press freedom? What are the attendant judicial conceptions of truth and their role in this jurisprudence—and what are their epistemological sources? What are the relationships among these various First Amendment theories and their assumptions about the ideal nature of American democracy, the actual nature of American democracy, and the role of the press in the public sphere?

My final concern is to map the particularized ideas and cultural issues of the Masson-Malcolm dispute onto the larger terrain of American intellectual history. This project suggests that the *Masson* case is historically conditioned and specific—that is, *Masson v. New Yorker* is the highly visible and public product of what began as a volatile academic debate about the nature of reality, the role of language in representing that reality, and the degree to which truth about such reality is knowable. This debate emerged fully in the academic disciplines in the 1970s and moved into public consciousness in the 1980s, when literary theory (particularly deconstruction) became a favorite topic of cultural critics. The debate took a new shape in the public arena in the 1990s, when history took its place in the culture wars.[34] As the historian David Paul Nord puts it, "The postmodern notion that human reality exists as a kind of text or discourse, that everything is interpretation, struck critics as a philosophy of 'anything goes.'"[35] It was just this postmodern notion, and the charges of relativism that critics leveled against it, that found expression in the culture wars over the legal and journalistic issues raised in *Masson v. New Yorker*.

A complex and distinct American press culture ultimately produced and supported the Masson-Malcolm dispute and its accompanying debates. The historical forces shaping this culture were multiple and varied in nature, not the least of which were the philosophical debates marking twentieth-century American social thought about the actual and ideal nature of democracy, the press, and free expression, and the interrelation of all three. Journalism began to develop professional standards at the turn of the century, and, as the years passed, a variety of press organizations formed that helped to professionalize the press as never before.[36] The concerns and needs of daily journalism and its most long-standing institution—the newspaper—dominated this professionalization. The results were ethical codes, press standards, and legal norms tied to the deadline structure, newsgathering techniques, and editorial procedures of the newspaper institution and the genre conventions of the newspaper report. Of all the press standards, the standard of objectivity was perhaps the most important in shaping social and cultural expectations about what constituted a news story, the parameters of press freedom, and the responsibilities of the press.[37]

The *New Yorker* has been a significant player in the creation of a distinctive American literary journalism, a journalism that did not develop in lockstep with the standards and conventions of newspaper journalism. Not long after its inception in 1925, the magazine began to distinguish itself through its factual reporting, profiles, and literary aspirations.[38] Many newspaper writers joined the staff, and after adjusting to the much longer lead times the magazine afforded over the daily deadlines of newspaper writing, began to fashion a distinctive long-form literary journalism.[39] Defining exactly what made this journalism literary is a nearly impossible task because different writers used different techniques. But the common thread is the use of storytelling techniques—such as scene setting, dialogue, characterization, emplotment, and narrative points of view such as first person and limited third person—to tell stories about contemporary events and people. The degree to which a "fact piece"—*New Yorker* jargon for the journalism its magazine published—used narrative conventions varied from story to story. And the literary quality of the journalism often inhered in qualities beyond narrative conventions, such as tone and word choice and departure from the standard of objectivity. Despite the epistemological problems in defining the *New Yorker*'s brand of journalism, the magazine has been recognized as an influential contributor to sustaining an American literary journalism tradition that preceded it.

The narrative techniques Janet Malcolm used in her Masson profiles were in keeping with historic practices at the *New Yorker*. As Ben Yagoda notes, styles of storytelling that blurred the line between fact and invention developed at the magazine and in the broader arena of American literary journalism and nonfiction in the years preceding *Masson v. New Yorker*.[40] The use of composite characters and the techniques of compressing and revising quotations were accepted. Brendan Gill, a staff writer at the *New Yorker* for more than sixty years, called the first piece of writing he published in the magazine "an unambitious little bastard of a piece—neither fact nor fiction." It was what the *New Yorker* called a "casual," generally a short fact piece, and it told the story of "an encounter between the genuine Sinclair Lewis and an invented Dr. McGrady," based on Gill himself, who had encountered Lewis at a performance of one of his plays.[41] Joseph Mitchell and A. J. Liebling, who joined the *New Yorker* staff in the 1930s along with Gill, also crossed borders in their fact writing. Mitchell used composite characters; Liebling compressed quotations and likely even embroidered dialogue.[42] Alastair Reid, who began writing for the magazine in 1951, had long used composite characters, invented settings, and embroidered dialogue in his fact writing. But in 1984, only a few months after Malcolm's Masson profile was published, he became the subject of a press scandal when he told the *Wall Street Journal* about his techniques.[43]

Janet Malcolm did not create composite characters in her profiles of Jeffrey

Masson and would not characterize her use of quotations as a blurring of "fact and invention." She appeared to understand herself as an objective reporter working within the unique literary tradition of the *New Yorker* magazine. But she did alter quotations and compress events in a way that many in the traditional press believed disregarded established standards of ethical journalism. Yagoda suggests that Malcolm simply got caught in the crosswinds of historical change.[44] The standards of daily journalism had long been on a collision course with those of American nonfiction—and the *Masson* case was part of the inevitable wreck.

Jeffrey Masson's libel complaint against Janet Malcolm and the *New Yorker* was, at least in part, the result of increasing tension between what had come to be considered traditional journalistic reporting and the narrative reporting that emerged at the turn of the century, was incubated at the *New Yorker*, and was reborn in the 1960s New Journalism movement. In the Masson-Malcolm dispute, the literary culture of the *New Yorker* and the American tradition of literary journalism clashed with the professional culture of daily journalism in what seemed an irreconcilable confrontation. The media scholar James Carey wrote in the early 1970s: "Journalism is essentially a state of consciousness, a way of apprehending, of experiencing the world. The central idea in journalism history is the 'idea of a report' and the changing notions of what has been taken to be an adequate report of the world."[45] As the robust historiography of American journalism attests, the objective, fact-centered inverted pyramid–style report has dominated press expression for the better part of a century.[46] Alternative ideas of the report developed alongside it, however, most notably the narrative or literary report, which surfaced repeatedly in moments of social crisis to challenge the hegemony of traditional reporting.[47] That hegemony is the result of social and cultural patterns that emerged during the late nineteenth and early twentieth centuries, when journalism gradually became a profession. Professional standards of both journalism and modern First Amendment jurisprudence have thus taken shape in a social, cultural, and legal context dominated by the traditional report, and both in turn have served to reify its legitimacy as the dominant form of press expression in the United States.

This tension between the traditional and literary reports only partially accounts for the cultural salience of the Masson-Malcolm dispute and the significant public attention it received during its long life. In the 1970s and 1980s, the law of libel experienced a cultural resurgence under the post-*Sullivan* constitutional regime. There were many contributing influences, including the rise of the critical culture in the 1960s, the growth of investigative and advocacy journalism, an increased valuing of reputation in an image-conscious culture, public disdain for corporate media power, and declining public opinion of the press.[48] The explosion of high-profile libel cases during this era resulted from this potent mix of cultural forces, and *Masson v. New Yorker* was no exception.

Perhaps the strongest historical factor in explaining the context of the Masson-Malcolm dispute—and why the dispute was so explosive—was the trenchant postmodern critique of the objectivist epistemology that emerged in the years preceding the dispute and gained strength during its long public tenure. Up until the 1960s, a belief in objective knowledge had structured academic disciplines and the public's understanding of what constitutes reality. As an intellectual project, postmodernism called into question the Enlightenment's legacy: modernity's seemingly inviolable distinction between fact and value, an understanding of truth as that which corresponds to reality, a belief in the determinacy of meaning in language, and a faith in the progress of all inquiry toward revelatory and stable knowledge.[49] Postmodernists insisted that language necessarily expresses indeterminate meanings, that the word is not the thing itself, and that language can thus never represent anything beyond human descriptions of reality, not reality itself. As Peter Novick suggests in *That Noble Dream*, his masterly exploration of the ideal of objectivity in the American historical profession: "The notion of a determinate and unitary truth about the physical or social world, approachable if not ultimately reachable, came to be seen by a growing number of scholars as a chimera. And with skepticism about that telos, the meaning of 'progress' in science and scholarship became problematic. The objectivity question, in one form or another, moved to the top of the disciplinary agendas."[50]

This critique of objectivity, with roots in American pragmatism, emerged during the broad cultural and social transformations of the late 1960s and 1970s. By the early 1980s, when Jeffrey Masson filed his libel claim, the critique was roiling the disciplines, and postmodern notions about the nature of knowledge, language, and truth had spilled over into American public life. By the 1990s, when the case came before the Supreme Court and then went to trial, the culture wars over the new sensitivity to the nuances of language and its resistance to determinate meanings had fully emerged, as evidenced broadly in the public debates over "politically correct" language and more narrowly (and absurdly) in President Bill Clinton's much-mocked grand jury testimony, "It depends on what the meaning of the word *is* is."[51] This new understanding of language and its relationship to the meaning of human events was widely acknowledged but deeply contested in every realm of American public life, from the academic disciplines to the newsroom to the courts. The Masson-Malcolm dispute was one of many expressions and workings out of this shift in both the academic and popular understandings of the nature of knowledge and truth.

The central intellectual issue in the dispute was the difference between fact and interpretation, while the central legal issue in the Supreme Court's consideration was determining at what point an altered quotation becomes libelous. Though a fairly narrow concern, it was a First Amendment issue, and thus the resulting rule and theoretical justification extended far beyond the unique fact pattern of the case.[52] In 1964 the Court revolutionized libel law in *New York Times v. Sullivan*, pulling into the constitutional penumbra all expression that allegedly libeled a public official.[53] To prevail in a libel suit, the Court said, a public official had to prove actual malice, that is, that the allegedly false and defamatory statements were published with knowledge of their falsity or reckless disregard for the truth. Before *Sullivan*, the common law of libel often demanded that the defendant prove the truth of a disputed statement, a strict liability standard that substantially delimited the freedom of the press to criticize public officials.[54] In *Sullivan*, the Supreme Court repudiated such presumptions against freedom of expression and for the first time articulated a theoretical justification for this First Amendment freedom. The democratic experiment at the heart of American government and public life demanded that "debate on public issues should be uninhibited, robust, and wide open," the Court wrote.[55] This is the theory of the First Amendment that has since guided the Court's further interpretation of the fault standards that protect expression about public figures and private persons involved in matters of public concern.[56] It is the theory at the very heart of modern First Amendment jurisprudence.

In *Masson*, the Supreme Court said that the alteration of a speaker's words would not constitute knowledge of falsity unless the quotation was substantially different in meaning from the speaker's actual words.[57] The so-called material alteration test further extended the Court's interpretation of the actual malice standard, clarifying the substantial truth doctrine as the foundation of the standard[58] and establishing the conditions under which an altered quotation would be false and constitute actual malice. "Minor inaccuracies do not amount to falsity," the Court wrote, "so long as 'the substance, the gist, the

sting, of the libelous charge be justified.'"[59] In the instance of altered quotations, courts must assess the meaning of the words and punctuation in a disputed statement to determine whether the statement is substantially true and
thus not libelous.[60] In *Masson v. New Yorker*, the Court collapsed the traditionally separate judicial determinations of falsity and the existence of actual malice. The *Masson* test required the fact-finder to compare the meaning of the
actual words spoken with the meaning of the altered quotation as published. If
the differential in meaning between the two was substantial, the Court suggested, both falsity and knowledge of falsity (that is, actual malice) would exist.

According to the *Sullivan* decision in 1964, the First Amendment demands
that an allegedly false and defamatory statement must be factual to be actionable in a libel suit. In other words, only factual statements can be proved true or
false, according to the Court's philosophy of language. But as the *Sullivan* case
line grew, the distinction the Court had erected between actionable factual language and non-actionable language that was somehow not factual began to
fragment. In time the Court found itself not only determining how *Sullivan*'s
actual malice standard ought to be applied but also interpreting the meanings
of expression that was not presumably factual. That is, the Court was deciding
whether the *meanings* of contested statements existing somewhere on a continuum between factual utterance and language that resisted characterization
as "fact" were true or false. As a result, the Court sometimes expanded and
sometimes restricted the kinds of speech offered wholesale protection by the
First Amendment. As the last cases in the *Sullivan* line make clear, including
Masson, the Court ultimately moved toward restriction.

The endgame was a philosophical and practical retrenchment on the press-
protective spirit of *New York Times v. Sullivan*. In *Sullivan*, the Supreme Court
articulated a vision of the First Amendment that permeates the social and legal
fabric of America's democratic system. Our system of free expression depends,
the Court wrote, on the protection of "debate on public issues [that is] uninhibited, robust, and wide-open, and . . . may well include vehement, caustic,
and sometimes unpleasantly sharp attacks on government and public officials."[61] As the legal scholar Lee Bollinger has observed, the *Masson* Court did
not emphasize this bedrock function of the First Amendment in its refusal to
extend "First Amendment protection to speech because in its view to do so
would undermine the *character and quality of public discourse*."[62]

At least for the development of journalism, a defining element of American
culture was the charged conflict between two distinct philosophies of the pub-

lic sphere and democracy that competed for dominance throughout much of the twentieth century. In their well-known debate in the 1920s about the role of the public and the press in democratic government, John Dewey and Walter Lippmann did more than any other public intellectuals to articulate these competing philosophies. Dewey spoke for a participatory democracy, the vigorous education of the public in the affairs of the day, and a news form based in social science inquiry but animated by a literary, even artistic, presentation. Lippmann spoke for a limited democracy in which elites, conducting and absorbing social science research within nonpolitical administrative units, made the bulk of the necessary decisions of government.[63] To Lippmann, the public, hampered by lack of knowledge and understanding, simply was not capable of making these decisions in the rational, informed, disinterested manner necessary to effective government. And because news was suited for the relaying of facts but not truth, newspapers could never provide the public with adequate knowledge.[64] The facts of the news thus should be discovered through a rigorous objective method and presented with the utmost objectivity in order to provide the public with enough knowledge to vote the elites in and out of office. But the press, Lippmann asserted, had only a limited role to play in American democracy.[65] Entrenched in the metaphysical tangle of the Dewey-Lippmann controversy was a distinctly modernist preoccupation with, and a deep anxiety about, the role of truth in human affairs, including scientific inquiry, philosophical and political systems, and perhaps most fundamentally, the expression central to these affairs.

In the end, Lippmann's vision of professional journalism came to dominate daily newspapers and public culture while Dewey's vision of journalism as art lived on in niche publications, muted and chastened. One such niche was the *New Yorker*, a magazine born in the same era as the Lippmann-Dewey debate about the role of news in public life. Early in its existence, the *New Yorker* implicitly answered Dewey's call for a new kind of journalism attuned to artistic expression. When Janet Malcolm found her journalistic methods and practices under siege in the wake of Jeffrey Masson's libel suit, she had been working in a journalistic tradition that had long honored literary expression perhaps as well as the objective method of gathering and evaluating information.

The Dewey-Lippmann debate was as much about democracy as it was about the press. Although we can look at America's contemporary administrative state and know that Lippmann's limited democracy carried the day in history,

Dewey's luminous belief that a fully participatory democracy is the means not only to a "good society" but also to individual self-fulfillment and self-realization has endured. His vision illuminates the landmark Supreme Court case *New York Times v. Sullivan*, which marks the beginning of First Amendment jurisprudence in the area of libel. In the same tumultuous decade, American society, in response to the cultural dislocations of the civil rights movement and the Vietnam War, began questioning the received terms of life in America, including the limited, administrative democracy that had come to be its government, the objective journalism that dominated its media, and the parameters of free expression promised its citizens.[66] The results were, at least in part, the constitutionalization of American libel law, along with the Supreme Court's fullest assertion yet of a guiding First Amendment theory for its jurisprudence; a student-led movement to replace administrative democracy with participatory democracy; and the challenge posed by the so-called New Journalism's narrative reporting to traditional journalism. At stake was the philosophical foundation of the American democratic system and the press institutions that claimed to support it. The elemental contested value in this clash of ideas was the nature of truth, its accessibility through the vehicle of language to the public, journalists, and administrative experts, and its role in democracy, journalism, and the law of libel.

These events and cultural trends of the 1960s were intellectually rooted in late-nineteenth- and early-twentieth-century America. The pragmatist philosophy born of this age rejected classical philosophy's insistence on finding truth and first causes through metaphysical inquiry. Instead, pragmatists understood the individual's participation in democracy, the essential expression of what John Dewey termed "associated living,"[67] as the necessary means for working out a set of contingent truths by which society might live.[68] These truths were thus not universal, monolithic, or static. They were always open to reinterpretation by the public as cultural and political situations changed. But this pragmatic conception of truth was itself historically contingent. World War II and then the cold war came to define the political and cultural terms of American life, and pragmatic philosophy was, as Louis Menand has so aptly observed, incompatible with a battle fought on uncontested principle: "The notion that the values of the free society for which the Cold War was waged were contingent, relative, fallible constructions, good for some purposes and not so good for others, was not a notion compatible with the moral imperatives of the age."[69] Despite the profound cultural critique the New Left launched against American political and social institutions in the 1960s, as well as *Sullivan*'s expression of faith in free speech and participatory democracy in the same decade, there was ultimately ideological space only for existing institutions, ensconced within what had become a full-bodied administrative state. But it nonetheless remains true that the philosophical foundations of the role of the press in American democracy were contested, muddled terrain in the 1960s, and as *Masson v. New Yorker* and its predecessors in the *Sullivan* line of First Amendment doctrine make clear, they are no less muddled today.

In telling the story of *Masson v. New Yorker*, I make three closely related historical arguments that outline an intellectual history of twentieth-century American journalism. First, the professional and disciplinary divide that emerged between traditional and literary journalism beginning in the early twentieth century has produced an often intractable debate about the promises and limitations of journalistic forms, methods, and language in representing "reality" and "truth." The *Masson* case grew out of this divide and expressed these debates. Second, the postmodern critique of objectivity, which insisted on the instability of language and knowledge and the rejection of unitary, determinate truth in human affairs, developed increasing traction from the 1960s on. Violent backlashes surfaced in the academy, in the profession of journalism, and in American public life at large. The Masson dispute occurred in this cultural and intellectual milieu—and the backlash in journalism pitted literary journalism against more traditional forms of reportage. Third, the *Masson* case not only dramatized the competing conceptions of truth at stake in these debates but also forced a highly problematic judicial resolution of these conceptions in the constitutional arena of libel law. The Supreme Court's decision in *Masson v. New Yorker* embraced traditional journalism's valuing of fact and objectivity and rejected a broader conception of truth. In choosing this path, the Court turned away from the First Amendment theory animating *New York Times v. Sullivan*, opting to emphasize the protection of the so-called quality of public discourse more than the protection of free expression.

When considered broadly, the story of *Masson v. New Yorker* shows us that traditional journalism, with its emphasis on objectivity, both dominated American press expression throughout the twentieth century and may have been one of the historical forces that constrained a broader range of expressive forms from developing in public discourse. The result in part was the condemnation of literary journalism in the *Masson* discourse, both journalistic and legal.

A close reader of this book will discover that conflict serves as an organizing principle in the discussion of the *Masson* case and the legal, social, and cultural issues it raises. These issues ineluctably fall into the same adversarial pattern: traditional journalism versus literary journalism, Lippmann versus Dewey, administrative democracy versus participatory democracy, the social responsibility of the press versus press freedom, fact versus opinion, objectivity versus subjectivity, and so on. In many ways the logic of the legal case, pitting plaintiff against defendant, prefigures analysis of the Masson-Malcolm dispute and its attendant issues. The categories constructed around the case are useful and convenient, but it is important to recognize that the concepts and phenomena they represent are not nearly as neat and tidy as the categories suggest. There is not, in fact, always such a sharp distinction to be made between traditional and literary journalism. A brief review of any issue of the *New York Times* will find plenty of narrative techniques at work in daily journalism. And a review of the *New Yorker* will reveal fact pieces that comport more with purportedly objective analysis than with the various techniques of literary journalism. Both Lippmann and Dewey believed in the public value of social science inquiry and the scientific method in knowledge-seeking, and both were significant contributors to the *New Republic* in their day. A more participatory American democracy, were it to come into being, would likely not survive without the many contributions of administrative governmental agencies. And it is entirely possible that the contemporary American press, increasingly lodged within large corporate entities, needs to learn social responsibility as much as it needs the protection of the First Amendment. Finally, despite profound anxiety within the twin professions of journalism and history over the postmodern insight that reality is a social and cultural construction, "radical postmodernism" has found little traction in either. Empiricism and objectivity still structure professional practice in both endeavors, but as a result of the postmodern challenge, both journalists and historians have become much more circumspect and thoughtful about the nature of the truths they claim to have discovered.[70]

Legal cases and trials inherently invoke the language and epistemology of dichotomy. We see this logic in case names—*Masson v. New Yorker*—and in the competing narratives lawyers construct in briefs and memoranda, in oral arguments, and at trial in the service of their clients. One narrative uses evidence to defend the accused and dilute or obliterate the plaintiff's claim; the other uses evidence to expose the defendant's alleged wrongdoing and the plaintiff's rights. The very form and language of court cases and trials pose human action in the polarized terms of conflict and as susceptible to the clear judgment of *right* and *wrong, liable* and *not liable, legal* and *illegal.* When paired with the deeply embedded American impulse to choose sides—to root for one team or the other—the dichotomous logic of the court case and trial profoundly pre-figured press coverage and public thinking about the issues in the Masson-Malcolm dispute. What is rarely acknowledged in our public discourse about judicial conflicts is the generally misleading nature of the dichotomy structur-ing the issues. What actually happened—the truth of the disputed events—rarely locates itself cleanly at one side of an either-or proposition. The meaning of contested language—a determination often demanded in libel cases where the defendant's state of mind is an issue—may even be beyond measuring as truth or falsity. And yet such measurement is what our judicial system demands.[71]

The historian of a legal case is forced to work within the law's logic of di-chotomy and the historian of journalism within the characteristic language of journalism's objectivist claims to knowledge and representation. But to work within an established epistemology and its vocabulary is not necessarily to be trapped within them. What makes *Masson v. New Yorker* ultimately so interest-ing is not the clear logic of its many dichotomies, for in the end they are simply convenient categories. Its interest lies rather in the murky territory between the poles of dispute, that place where the "reality" of the case, as contingent and in-scrutable as it may be, makes its home. In this book I attempt to map and to make sense of that territory.

Journalism history has yet to engage in a sustained way the postmodern cri-tique of objectivist knowledge that has influenced the broader discipline of history.[72] This lack of engagement is a problem I try to address by tying the in-tellectual debate over objectivism to actual institutions, events, and material processes. The cultural historian investigates texts and contexts together, inter-preting the thick description of cultural expression to make sense of the past. Texts and contexts—including institutional structures and practices, as well as the discourses operating within and beyond these institutions—push and pull at one another, in all directions and with constantly shifting points of contact. Ideas find expression in the process, and the intellectual historian is at pains to locate and explain, however provisionally, the meanings and historical import of those ideas. In this study of *Masson v. New Yorker* I attempt to work as both cultural and intellectual historian within an established historiographic and cross-disciplinary movement of the past several decades: the rise of cultural history and the related postmodern insights about the limits of objectivist knowledge.[73] In doing so, I do not pitch a tent either with the logical positivists or with the thoroughgoing postmodernists. To be a historian or legal scholar (or journalist) is to believe that the past and the world itself are at least partially knowable. I thus join with those scholars who have identified pragmatism as the *via media*.[74] Pragmatists believe that communities create a consensus of meaning out of their shared experiences and languages, and that truth— provisional, contingent, and indeterminate though it may be—is located in that consensus. The story of *Masson v. New Yorker* is, finally, a story about the nature of truth and its role in public expression and public life.

The chapters that follow shift between telling the specific story of *Masson v. New Yorker* and exploring important elements of the cultural context that gave rise to, and constituted the home of, the dispute. The book proper begins in medias res; chapter 1 tells the story of the first federal trial in the case in order to familiarize the reader with the issues and personalities of the case. Chapter 2 documents and explores the social and cultural history of two different notions of the report that have coexisted throughout the modern history of American journalism—the traditional and the narrative—as well as the role of the *New Yorker* in that history. Chapter 3 examines the broad history of American libel law and its transformation and constitutionalization in *New York Times v. Sullivan* in 1964 as well as the changing conception and role of truth in libel law and the meaning of the First Amendment. It also connects this history to America's transformation into an administrative democracy and the contextual debates about the proper form American democracy should take and the role of the press in that democracy. Chapter 4 tells the story of the *New Yorker's* experiences with libel law prior to *Masson* and documents the magazine's editorial policies and legal strategies regarding libel threats from the magazine's inception in the mid-1920s to the post-*Sullivan* years. Chapter 5 returns to the early years of *Masson v. New Yorker* and charts its path to the Supreme Court; it also explores the cultural forces contributing to the explosion of libel cases in the 1970s and 1980s of which *Masson* was a part. Chapter 6 analyzes the *Sullivan-Masson* line of Supreme Court cases and documents the Court's struggle not only to define actual malice but also to determine when allegedly false and defamatory speech is sufficiently factual as to be actionable in a libel suit. The changing conception and role of truth in libel law comprehended in the First Amendment is central to this analysis. Chapter 7 documents and discusses the judicial and extrajudicial resolution of *Masson v. New Yorker*. The concluding chapter establishes the case's ultimate meanings.

CHAPTER ONE

———— ⚬✧⚬ ————

Masson v. New Yorker
Goes to Trial

IN A FEDERAL DISTRICT COURTHOUSE IN SAN FRANCISCO, PARTICIPANTS
in the libel trial of *Masson v. New Yorker* waited for the jury's verdict.[1] Journalists and spectators crowded U.S. District Judge Eugene Lynch's seventeenth-floor courtroom, some standing in the back, others sitting in the aisles.[2] It was Thursday, June 3, 1993—the third day of jury deliberations. The high-profile trial, held more than nine years after the first complaint in the case was filed, had lasted almost a month. It was contentious from the beginning, as a prominent New York City libel attorney had predicted. "The charges are so stark and the protagonists are so intriguing," Robert D. Sack told the *New York Times* several days before the trial began, "that it should be a hell of a show."[3] It was.

For almost a decade, a group of elite players in American culture had closely followed the charged conflict between *New Yorker* writer Janet Malcolm and Jeffrey Masson, former project director of the Freud Archives and subject of the two-part profile Malcolm published in the magazine in 1983.[4] Masson accused Malcolm of libeling him by misquoting him and fabricating words she attributed to him and placed in quotation marks. The charge struck a nerve in legal, journalistic, and academic circles. Thus began the epic of *Masson v. New Yorker*. Had a successful Freudian scholar actually called himself an "intellectual gigolo" and "the greatest analyst who ever lived"?[5] Or had a respected writer for the *New Yorker* knowingly placed false, self-damning words in her subject's mouth? Writers, journalists, media institutions, psychoanalysts, libel lawyers, and press organizations all waited to see how Masson's $10 million libel suit against Malcolm would finally play itself out in court. Many chose sides as they waited, evaluating and commenting on Malcolm's journalistic methods and ethics and the validity of Masson's claims in news stories and scholarly articles published during the life of the case.

The institutional press sensed from the outset that the case augured nothing good for American journalism. In a culture in which public resentment against the press ran strong, a plaintiff's charge that he had been defamed through fabricated quotations could only spell trouble, no matter how the claim was ultimately resolved. It became clear early on that Malcolm had, in fact, altered Masson's exact words in her articles, although she insisted that these changes were minor and in no way altered the truth and accuracy of the quotations.[6] But in a profession that prides itself on accuracy and sanctifies the verbatim quotation in its professional standards,[7] a journalist's attempt to defend her alteration of a speaker's quoted words—an alteration that may have damaged the speaker's reputation—could only hurt the already tarnished reputation of the press. The *Masson* case was journalism's bête noire. And like all dreamers of the horrific, journalists could not resist retelling, dissecting, and analyzing the nightmare.

For the journalism community, the case presented an unpleasant mix of free press issues and what many considered to be offensive journalistic practices. For the legal community, the case presented a novel First Amendment question: Do fabricated or altered quotations necessarily reach the level of knowing or reckless falsehood that is required by the "actual malice" standard of libel law?[8]

For at least two people in the courtroom that Friday, the case presented not just theoretical questions but personal issues that a jury was charged with resolving. For almost a decade Jeffrey Masson had pursued his libel claim against considerable odds. When a federal district court granted summary judgment for the defendants in 1987, he appealed.[9] When the Ninth Circuit Court of Appeals upheld the summary judgment in 1989, he appealed again.[10] When the U.S. Supreme Court agreed to review the case in 1990, six years after he filed his original complaint, Masson received his first judicial affirmation that his case had merit. A year later the Court reversed the lower courts' decisions, articulated a test for determining when an altered quotation would constitute actual malice, and remanded the dispute for trial, resurrecting a case that on several occasions had appeared to most observers to be past saving.[11] Whatever human emotion or reasoned argument animated Masson's crusade against Malcolm over all those years, it was a powerful, unyielding force. And

Malcolm's motivation for resisting Masson's claim—a desire to vindicate her journalistic methods, perhaps, and thus preserve her professional reputation—was just as powerful.

Most libel cases do not proceed like the legal case of *Jarndyce and Jarndyce*, the tragicomic property dispute stretching over generations in Charles Dickens's *Bleak House*—a literary analogy made by more than one observer of the *Masson* case, including Malcolm herself.[12] Often one of the parties tires of the slow-moving and expensive litigation. The plaintiff drops his complaint. The defendant settles out of court. A court grants summary judgment.[13] But in the Masson-Malcolm dispute, both sides held fast. Masson appealed two summary judgments. Malcolm refused to settle. The other media defendants in the case, the *New Yorker* magazine and Alfred. A. Knopf, publisher of *In the Freud Archives*, the book version of Malcolm's articles, stood behind their writer. Masson and Malcolm both fervently proclaimed the rightness, even the righteousness, of their opposing positions during the nine years that passed between the filing of the first complaint and the 1993 trial. Masson claimed that his scholarly and personal reputation had been unjustly tarnished by a journalist's unorthodox methods of quoting and reporting. Malcolm claimed that her quotations were accurate and her journalistic methods sound. In the spring of 1993, in a federal courthouse in San Francisco, a jury of their peers was meant to decide, finally and for the record, who was right in the eyes of the law.

The seeds of the Masson-Malcolm dispute were planted as early as 1981, when Janet Malcolm read about Jeffrey Masson's dismissal from his post at the Freud Archives. In a speech that offended Kurt Eissler, the head of the archives at the time and a major figure in the psychoanalytic community, Masson suggested that Freud had suppressed his original theory of childhood seduction in order to please his peers. According to Masson, Freud dismissed this early theory, which attributed adult neurosis to sexual abuse suffered in childhood, in an effort to join the mainstream scholarship of the Victorian era and thus escape what had become a painful isolation. In his new theory Freud suggested that repressed memories of sexual abuse in childhood were more likely the result of fantasies resulting from infantile sexuality. Eissler, who had planned to appoint Masson as the next director of the Freud Archives, reportedly called Masson's ideas "plain nonsense."[14] He viewed Masson's speech as a heretical attack on Freud and urged his removal from his position at the archives. The archives board acquiesced.[15]

When Janet Malcolm read about Masson's scholarship and his dismissal from the Freud Archives in the *New York Times*, her interest was piqued.[16] The daughter of a well-known New York neurologist and psychiatrist, Malcolm had written about psychoanalysis in the past.[17] Because of her long-standing interest in the profession, news coverage of Masson's revision of Freudian scholarship and his ultimate dismissal captured her attention as a journalist. But she was also attracted to Masson's lively, imaginative speaking style.[18] The new understanding of Freud's seduction theory would, Masson claimed, alter psychotherapy forever.

Lawyers commenting on the Masson-Malcolm dispute in its early days believed that Malcolm's interview tapes would easily resolve the conflict.[19] Resolution proved more complicated, however, than a simple comparison of allegedly libelous quotations with transcripts of tape-recorded interviews. When the case finally went to trial, five quotations were at issue. Of these, three were recorded in Malcolm's typed notes from the conversation she claimed to have had with Masson over breakfast when he was staying with her in New York: the disputed "intellectual gigolo" and "sex, women, fun" quotations she attributed to him, as well as one in which Masson claimed that, after the publication of his book *The Assault on Truth*, the psychoanalytic community would regard him after Freud as "the greatest analyst that ever lived." The fourth quotation, not recorded on tape or in Malcolm's notes, has Masson saying, "I don't know why I put it in," referring to the concluding sentence of a conference paper in which he denounced the sterility of modern-day psychoanalysis.[20] The final quotation is based on tape-recorded comments Masson made about Kurt Eissler's request that he accept his dismissal from the Freud Archives quietly. Malcolm reported the following exchange between Eissler and Masson: "'You could be silent about it. You could swallow it. I know it is painful for you. But you could just live with it in silence.' 'Why should I do that?' 'Because it's the honorable thing to do.' Well, he had the wrong man." On tape, Masson renders the exchange somewhat differently: "'Why should I do that? Why? You know, why should one do that?' 'Because it's the honorable thing to do and you will save face. And who knows? If you never speak about it and you quietly and humbly accept our judgment, who knows that in a few years if we don't bring you back?' Well, he had the wrong man."[21]

Whether the case would have made it to trial in the first place had the courts been able to consider Malcolm's typed notes is uncertain. What is certain is that Malcolm did alter Masson's exact wording at times and compressed quotations from several separate interviews into one long monologue she represented Masson as having delivered during a luncheon at Chez Panisse, a restaurant in Berkeley. And it is also certain that the "sex, women, fun" remark, which, Malcolm testified at trial, Masson had actually made at her New York City home,[22] was included in this lunch monologue, as well as the "intellectual gigolo" quotation.[23]

In Malcolm's writings about the dispute and in her trial testimony, she attempted to establish a case for the writer's necessary transliteration of a subject's words from the medium of speech to the medium of the printed page. "The transcript [of an interview] is not a finished version, but a kind of rough draft of expression," Malcolm has written. "When a journalist undertakes to quote a subject he has interviewed on tape, he owes it to the subject, no less than to the reader, to translate his speech into prose."[24] There is a certain disconnect, of course, between Malcolm's argument about the writer-reader contract and her cobbling together of different interviews into a monologue Masson delivers during lunch at a café. In part, the disconnect is due to the substantive difference between "translating" speech into prose and combining purportedly thematically related quotations (or translated quotations) from different moments in time into a single prose monologue. Malcolm and Masson *did* have lunch one day at Chez Panisse, as the articles suggest. But Masson testified at trial, before a gasping courtroom, that he did not order the baked goat cheese appetizer and striped bass with fennel as Malcolm reported. Malcolm testified heatedly that he did.[25] If one assumes that Malcolm's memory is correct, she seems to have felt that the elements of an event that must not be embellished include the time, place, and menu of a luncheon—but not the exact conversation, which instead needed to be "translated" for the reader through her technique of compression so as best to render the truth of what Masson said. Analyzed in this way, her argument about the nonfiction writer's contract with the reader holds together (even if one disagrees with it). If one assumes that Masson's memory is correct, things fall apart.

In her profile of Masson, Malcolm employed a range of nonfiction techniques, but the only technique implicated in Masson's libel complaint was narrative, in particular, the use of direct quotation as a means of storytelling. The profile painted a somewhat negative portrait of Masson, and that portrait did not emerge merely from Malcolm's rendering of his own words about himself. Nevertheless, the only passages in the profile that Masson disputed as false and defamatory were direct quotations Malcolm attributed to him. The question of libel law that *Masson v. New Yorker* presented was a novel one: at what point does the alteration of a quotation constitute both falsity and actual malice under the First Amendment?

"Actual malice" is a term of art used in libel law at least since the 1920s, but it did not have a standard meaning—and constitutional status—until the landmark Supreme Court case *New York Times v. Sullivan* in 1964.[26] Before *Sullivan*, the falsity of a defamatory publication was often presumed under common law, and no proof of fault on the part of the defendant was needed; in other words, the defendant in a libel case generally had to prove the truth of a contested defamatory statement in order to prevail at trial.[27] After *Sullivan*, the burden of proof was shifted to the public official plaintiff, who had to prove falsity and, more to the point, fault in order to prevail. This new fault standard mandated by the First Amendment was "actual malice"—that is, knowing falsity or reckless disregard for the truth on the part of the defendant. In time, the Supreme Court expanded the category of plaintiffs who would have to prove actual malice in order to prevail in a libel suit to include public figures.[28] Jeffrey Masson was such a plaintiff. When the Supreme Court granted *certiorari* in the *Masson* case, it was faced with articulating whether and when altered quotations constitute actual malice. An altered, defamatory quotation would not equate with knowing falsehood, the Court determined, "unless the alteration results in a material change in the meaning conveyed by the statement."[29] This was the First Amendment test the jury was called upon to apply to the five contested quotations at issue in the trial.

"This is not a case about a mistake," the First Amendment attorney Floyd Abrams told *Time* magazine during the trial. "Someone is lying."[30] Was Masson lying about not having said what Malcolm quoted him as saying about himself? Was Malcolm lying about the occurrence of the breakfast conversation at her New York City residence involving three of the disputed quotations? Abrams may have been right, but even now, many years after the case was finally put to rest by the Ninth Circuit Court of Appeals in 1996, it is still not clear who was lying, if indeed anyone was. As James Wagstaffe, one of the lawyers representing the *New Yorker* in the trial, has noted, the Masson-Malcolm dispute "was a case of memory about memory."[31] And memory and truth are not necessarily synonymous.

In many respects, this was a dispute about two opposing ways of understanding knowledge claims regarding human experience. Throughout her many articles and books, Malcolm has chronicled the elusiveness of truth, the contingency of language. "Trials are won by attorneys whose stories fit," she has written, "and lost by those whose stories are like the shapeless house-coat that truth, in her disdain for appearances, has chosen for her uniform."[32] In Malcolm's view, the genre of journalism rents space in what she called the house of "Actuality": the journalist "may bring in his own furniture and arrange it as he likes . . . [b]ut he must not disturb the house's fundamental structure or tamper with any of its architectural features."[33] Malcolm's metaphor suggests that truth in journalism—and the law, for that matter—is not always best understood as a one-to-one correspondence between language and reality. For his part, Masson emphasized an objective reality that is knowable and primary in human experience. In explaining his basic disagreement with orthodox analysts to Malcolm, Masson suggested that these analysts stressed the importance not of what actually happened in a patient's life but of the patient's feelings about what happened. "Which is not reasonable," Masson told Malcolm, as she reported in her profile. "There's an enormous difference between whether you were beaten within an inch of your life and whether you imagined you were. There's an enormous difference between whether you actually were in Auschwitz and whether you dreamed you were in Auschwitz. And it's not the fantasies that we have to look at first; it's the reality."[34] In a discussion about his withdrawal from the psychoanalytic profession, also recorded in the profile, Masson declared that the members of the Freud Archives board were boring. "They didn't have anything interesting to say," he told Malcolm, who responded: "Nothing *is* interesting. We invest certain things with interest." But Masson did not agree: "*No*. Certain things *are* objectively interesting, and certain things are *not*."[35] This difference in worldview became, in time, profoundly meaningful, for it was the philosophical foundation of the *Masson v. Malcolm* legal dispute: two differing and irreconcilable conceptions of what constitutes truthful quotation.

Before the 1993 trial began in earnest, Judge Lynch assigned weekend homework to the seven women and one man serving on the eight-person jury: they were to read Malcolm's two-part *New Yorker* article about Masson.[36] At 48,500 words, "Trouble in the Archives" was no small assignment. As a reporter dryly observed in *Newsweek*, "They're the first folks constitutionally required to actually finish one of those things [a multipart *New Yorker* feature]."[37] The portrait of Masson the jurors encountered there was somewhat at odds with the portrait Masson's lawyer, Charles O. Morgan Jr., painted in his opening arguments the following Monday. Masson was, he said, "a gifted, brilliant researcher" who had challenged Freud out of a desire to protect women and children from a psychoanalytic theory that devalued the reality of childhood sexual abuse.[38] Morgan's portrayal was more in line with what Masson had expected the articles to be about—not so much his life as his scholarship and the reality of child sexual abuse. Masson admitted to talking at length with Malcolm about his personal life, but "if you look at the tapes," he noted in an interview, "most of what I talk about is child abuse. And that played a very small role in her book. But that's where I felt, that was, to me, the real betrayal, that she was not taking that issue seriously." [39]

The question of the degree to which Malcolm engaged the reality of child sexual abuse in her articles and book is probably a value judgment. She did explain and explore Masson's revisionist Freudian scholarship. And she seems to have found his views misguided. "Although Freud came to believe that many or most of the seductions reported by his patients were 'wishful fantasies,'" she wrote, "he never doubted that seductions and rapes and beatings of children sometimes do take place. It is simply that as he grew more and more fascinated and preoccupied by his universal psychology he grew less and less interested in the special plight of the people to whom unspeakable things happen." [40] But while her narrative acknowledged Masson's position on Freud's seduction theory as a key explanation for his dismissal from the Freud Archives, that position was hardly the only—or even the main—subject of her articles. Near the end of the second and final article, after interviewing several analysts whose relationships with Masson had gone sour, Malcolm observed, "In every case, it was a personal issue—not ideology—that had caused the breach." [41] Malcolm was not interested in the material he had found to support his revision of Freud, Masson has contended. "She was interested in me. And that's where we were at deep cross-purposes. And she won in a way because I let myself loom larger than I should have." [42]

It is precisely this focus on the personal that became, at least in part, the subject of the trial, for the issue at hand was whether Malcolm altered Masson's own words about himself so as to change and falsify his meaning materially and thus unfairly damage his reputation. And there were other troubling facts of the case that had nothing to do with the contested quotations but everything to do with the damaging nature of some of Masson's self-revelations. Consider, for example, Masson's statement that he had slept with about a thousand women in his younger days, which Malcolm duly recorded in her profile. At trial, Masson and his lawyer clearly had a strategy: confront early and head-on the basic truth of an undisputed but perhaps prejudicial claim that had already been well covered in news reports on the case. On the first day of testimony, Jeffrey Masson, then forty years old, said he had become interested in psycho-analysis when, as a young man, he sought to overcome a promiscuous lifestyle. Believing that his promiscuity was a kind of illness, Masson received help from the well-known analyst Erik Erikson. "I was promiscuous with women and I wanted to get married and have children," Masson testified. Although Masson did not challenge Malcolm's portrayal of his previous sexual promiscuity, he did claim that Malcolm had falsely quoted him as saying his peers believed he was an "intellectual gigolo." Whatever that term meant, Masson and his lawyer must have sensed that his sexual history might have something to do with the jury's interpretation of the term's meaning and damaging nature. This testi-mony seemed designed to suggest that while Masson may once have been sexu-ally promiscuous, he was no longer, and he had never claimed to be a gigolo of any kind.[43]

In his opening statements Malcolm's lawyer, Gary Bostwick, portrayed Masson more in the way that Malcolm had in her articles. Masson was, Bostwick claimed, a chronic complainer given to careless exaggeration. "Put a mike in front of him—boom, he's off. Accidents happen that way." Malcolm was different, he said. She was quiet and careful. "She doesn't have great pres-ence," he explained. "She has great absence." She avoided interviews and speak-ing engagements because she was uncomfortable in the spotlight. "If we had the time, when I asked her questions, she'd write eight drafts before answer-ing," he continued. "Being on the stand makes her nervous. It is not her best way of expressing herself." Bostwick also defended Malcolm's journalistic method of compression, which involved using quotations from different inter-views in a single narrative scene. "People in the *New Yorker* don't talk the way you and I do," he told the jury in explaining why such a method was neces-sary.[44] He was stating the obvious to anyone who had read the *New Yorker*—and the jury had. As *Newsweek* asked its readers during the trial, "Does anyone believe the subjects of classic New Yorker profiles really talked in those per-fectly cadenced paragraphs?"[45]

Bostwick would vigorously defend Malcolm's translation and compression methods later in the trial when she took the stand. (Interestingly, Bostwick had defended the alleged murderer Jeffrey MacDonald in the case Malcolm wrote about in *The Journalist and the Murderer*. Malcolm met him while researching the case.) It would be an important strategy in defending against Masson's libel claim. The techniques had been the subject of much damning discussion in the pages of the press, and Bostwick and Malcolm would have to make them seem innocuous as well as necessary to her story if they were to survive Morgan's claim that Malcolm's journalism was unethical and, more significantly for the trial, had resulted in knowing or reckless falsification. But first Bostwick cross-examined Masson, attempting to show that he did not have a reliable memory of what he had and had not said to Malcolm during their many months of conversations. One by one, Bostwick ran through quotations Masson had contested in a series of early complaints and memoranda he had filed in his libel suit before he gained access in 1986 to Malcolm's tape recordings of their interviews.[46] (Of the nine quotations Masson contested in his initial complaint, five turned up verbatim on tape, according to a defense lawyer for the case.)[47] Using large placards placed on an easel to allow jurors to read what they were about to hear, Bostwick played tape recordings intended to demonstrate to the jurors that Masson had indeed made statements he formerly claimed not to have made.[48] One such disputed statement was Masson's claim in Malcolm's profile that he was able to speak fluent German after only a six-month sojourn in Munich. Another was his claim that his discoveries about Freud would allow him to "bring down" the profession of psychoanalysis "single-handedly." Bostwick's point, of course, was to establish that Masson had a hard time remembering what he had said—and what he had not said—during the more than forty hours of conversation with Malcolm. If he had not remembered the statement about fluent German, Bostwick implied, wasn't it likely that he didn't remember saying that Kurt Eissler and Anna Freud thought "him to be like an intellectual gigolo—you get your pleasure from him, but you don't take him out in public"?[49]

Janet Malcolm finally took the stand the morning of the fourth day of testimony before a packed and silent courtroom. Morgan, Masson's attorney, began his examination by reading from the afterword of another controversial book Malcolm published during the life of the *Masson* case, *The Journalist and the Murderer*. "The idea of a reporter inventing rather than reporting speech," he quoted Malcolm as writing, "is a repugnant, even a sinister one." Malcolm had in fact invented Masson's speech, he implied, though even she condemned such a practice. Morgan relentlessly questioned the authenticity of Malcolm's typed notes containing three of the contested quotations as well as the rigor of the *New Yorker*'s professional standards. While Masson had been comfortable on the stand, Jane Gross of the *New York Times* reported, Malcolm was "stiff, edgy," speaking "in a tentative, whispery voice, with the slight accent of her native Prague." Malcolm described tape-recording her interviews with Masson, taking handwritten notes, and transcribing tapes and notes by typewriter. She also described her technique of compression, which incorporated bits of separate conversations held across a period of time into one monologue like "sketches incorporated into one painting." She discussed selecting representative expressions from her many conversations with Masson, choosing those that she felt characterized him well. The technique was a convention and a tradition at the *New Yorker*, she said, and as long as compression did not change the speaker's meaning, it was an acceptable method for dealing with the vagaries and sloppiness of speech. Morgan disagreed, citing a 1984 staff memorandum that *New Yorker* editor William Shawn circulated after Alastair Reid, a writer for the magazine, became the subject of a media frenzy when he discussed his reportorial techniques with the *Wall Street Journal.* "We do not permit composites, we do not rearrange events, we do not create conversations," Shawn insisted.[50] (His memorandum was not circulated, of course, until after Malcolm's profile on Masson had been published.)

Responding to her own lawyer's questioning in subsequent testimony, Malcolm described Masson's speech as exuberant, "full of images and force." But "things came out in a rather chaotic, contradictory way," she explained. "He's trying to tell too many things at the same time. You had to work hard to get the story straight because he was all over the place." She might have paraphrased his speech rather than rearranging and quoting it, she said, except that his idiosyncratic style of speaking was so essential to his character. "It was really the only way to tell his story . . . to choose among the many things he said and put them in a logical, rational order." As for the typed notes, they had been turned over to *New Yorker* lawyers in 1984, long before Masson had identified either the "sex, women, fun" or "intellectual gigolo" quotations, both contained in the notes, as libelous.[51]

Except for Janet Malcolm's final testimony, the rest of the trial focused on other witnesses and other evidence. Very little of it was boring. Nancy Franklin, the fact-checker at the *New Yorker* in charge of reviewing Malcolm's articles, who by 1993 had become a nonfiction editor, contradicted Masson's claim that he had objected to any of the disputed quotations in a telephone call. The fact-checking conversation, during which she asked Masson between fifty and seventy-five fact-based questions about his life, was, she testified, "perfectly friendly" throughout.[52] She also testified that Malcolm had asked her not to verify certain statements in the articles. Jurors saw the galley proofs of the articles with the fact-checker's marks, including the notation "OA"—"on author"—above such statements. This notation meant, Franklin said, that the writer has taken responsibility for the information.[53] The *New York Times* interpreted this information as proof that the *New Yorker's* much-heralded fact-checking department was not as exacting as it portrayed itself. With seeming relish, the *Times* reported that the *New Yorker* had long been a "writer's haven . . . where established writers could propose ideas, set off for months without supervision and then write book-length pieces that were lightly checked and gently edited." Janet Malcolm's husband, Gardner Botsford, took the stand next, not in his role as spouse but as that of Malcolm's editor at the magazine. Such an arrangement—one spouse serving as editor for the other—would not be allowed at many publications, the *New York Times* noted. Botsford testified that, against the advice of a lawyer for the *New Yorker*, he had allowed the words "sex" and "women" to remain in the disputed "sex, women, fun" quotation. Yes, he knew the quotation was not on the tape recordings. "Janet showed me her notes, which was good enough for me," he said.[54]

In one of the more unusual moments of the trial, an actor read from a sworn deposition of William Shawn, the former editor of the *New Yorker*. Shawn had died the previous year, but in a deposition taken in 1986 he told Masson's lawyers that Malcolm had informed him that she had tape-recorded all her interviews with Masson. Malcolm testified at trial that she had never made such a claim to Shawn. In the deposition, Shawn said that he would believe Janet Malcolm's assurance that she had not fabricated quotations even without the benefit of tape recordings. "She has been writing for us for 20 years and I have known her for 30 years. If I didn't trust her she wouldn't be writing for us." He further defended Malcolm's technique of compression as long as no deception or distortion was involved. "It is not a [*New Yorker*] policy to do that [but] if it is done . . . to make something coherent . . . or for literary reasons and not to in any way violate the truth of the situation or of what the person is saying . . . it is a practice that has been followed in many instances."[55] The complete invention of a quoted statement, he also said, would be unacceptable.

In the course of the trial, Malcolm's lawyer argued that the academic and analytic communities had recognized what he characterized as Masson's controversial scholarship and problematic social behavior before Janet Malcolm published her profiles. He was no more a pariah after the articles were published than before, Bostwick suggested in his opening and closing arguments. Furthermore, Masson's celebrity had only increased as a result of press coverage of the case throughout the years, a factor that contributed to the financial success of a number of books he had written since initiating the suit. Bostwick's point was to establish that Masson had not suffered damage as a result of the articles, injury being a critical element in a libel suit. But Masson's former girlfriend, who had been involved with him for six years at the time of publication, testified that the articles caused Masson such anxiety that his resulting behavior ruined his relationships with her and a number of friends. (Masson's fiancée in 1993, the well-known feminist law professor and lawyer Catharine MacKinnon, attended the trial with Masson.[56] The two never married.) An anthropology professor testified that she and other academics she knew had shunned Masson after reading the "intellectual gigolo" passage in Malcolm's article. They interpreted the phrase to mean that Masson was a man "who sleeps with every convivial idea but is loyal to none."[57] The first lawyer Masson consulted after reading the articles also testified. James J. Brosnahan, a prominent San Francisco attorney, said that he was convinced, after listening to Masson's complaints about Malcolm's portrayal of him, that the quotations were largely accurate and Masson had little basis for claiming libel.[58] In a file memo written after his meeting with Masson, Brosnahan wrote that Masson had "confirmed that the quotes were by and large accurate."[59]

Malcolm, who had already appeared on the stand as part of Masson's case, was the final witness to testify in the trial. She again unequivocally denied fabricating quotations. "I don't know how to make up quotes," she said. "That's why I write in this form. I would have been crazy to make up quotes. This man is such a wonderful talker. He leaves you with an embarrassment of riches."[60]

On the day of closing arguments, Judge Lynch's courtroom was full to overflowing.[61] Masson's lawyer argued before the jury that the disputed quotations in Malcolm's articles had transformed Masson's reputation from that of a reputable and courageous scholar to that of a "jerk" and a "buffoon." He told the jury, "In retrospect, Jeff Masson was a total fool for baring his soul and his life to Janet Malcom." But Malcolm was still at fault for making up false and damaging quotations and placing them in Masson's mouth. He also suggested that it was extremely unlikely that three of the five contested quotations actually appeared in Malcolm's typed notes. "Respectfully, I say those notes are a total fabrication." As for Masson's past promiscuity, "You may not like that," Morgan told the jury. "You may hate his guts. But you wouldn't be doing your duty if you said, To hell with him, he deserves what he gets." Morgan asked the jury to award Masson $7.5 million in damages, reduced from the $10 million stated in

Masson's complaint. In rebuttal, Malcolm's lawyer argued that the quotations in dispute had not damaged Masson's reputation and that other taped statements showed that Masson had said things that were substantially similar in meaning to the contested quotations. What is more, the fact that three of the disputed quotations were contained only in Malcolm's typed notes suggested that Masson "chose the three knowing they're not on tape." "This lawsuit was designed to complain about things that were not on tape," Bostwick told the jury. Malcolm, he insisted, did not fabricate any quotations. "I want to get it straight. We're saying he said it all." As for the typed notes, they had been held in the *New Yorker's* offices since Masson filed his first complaint in 1984, in which he did not even include the "intellectual gigolo" remark, considered by some to be perhaps the most defamatory of all the quotations. Janet Malcolm's reputation, Bostwick told the jury, hung in the balance of its decision. "The truth is he said all these things, and if he gets one red cent by coming in with only one piece of proof—'I didn't say those things'—her career is ruined." [62]

"They deserve each other," *Newsweek* quoted *New York* magazine media critic Ed Diamond as saying. "Masson is a 24-karat jerk. Malcolm looks like she should be teaching classics in some prep school. And *The New Yorker* with its holier-than-thou attitude. Can you pull for nobody to win?" [63] Published at the height of the trial, Diamond's assessment likely made great reading for those delighting in what they saw as the arrogant *New Yorker's* comeuppance. While Diamond's easy categorizations flattened the people and institutions of the case into caricatures, he captured the tone of titillating scandal that infused coverage of the case and the trial. And in the end, Diamond got what he wished for.

The jurors had been deliberating for three days when, in the late afternoon of Thursday, June 3, they sent a message to Judge Lynch. They could not come to a decision on the amount of damages to award Masson, a signal that they had found he had been libeled. Shocked, Malcolm rushed from the courtroom with Bostwick, trailed by a frenzied pack of reporters asking questions she refused to answer. Masson and his lawyer stayed to enjoy the partial verdict and its affirmation of Masson's long quest to prove Malcolm's wrongdoing. Theirs was a short-lived celebration. The very next day the trial came to an unexpected close with the jury deadlocked on damages. [64]

Despite the jury's decision that all five quotations were false and defamatory and that Malcolm had published two with knowing falsity, or actual malice, Judge Lynch was forced to declare a mistrial on what was an unusual twist in a civil case—a jury impasse on the damage award. In interviews given in the days following their finding, jurors told the press that some on their panel wanted to award Masson upwards of $1 million while others fixed the appropriate award at one dollar.[65] The problem was profound disagreement within the jury over the extent to which the disputed quotations damaged Masson's reputation. Therein lay a deep legal problem surrounding the case. Damages in a libel suit are supposed to compensate a plaintiff for the reputational harm suffered as a result of false defamatory statements. But the five quotations at issue in the Masson-Malcolm dispute were, in the end, part of a larger collection of defamatory passages in the articles, including uncontested and presumably true statements. How to parse and measure which defamatory passages—the contested or the uncontested—had damaged Masson, if any? Throughout the trial and in written jury instructions, Judge Lynch reminded jurors that they could consider only the disputed quotations in their awarding of damages.[66] In this jury's estimation, the degree to which Masson had been damaged was even more difficult to determine than whether Malcolm had committed libel.[67]

The jury found all five quotations to be false, and all defamatory, but only two published with actual malice: the "sex, women, fun" and "he had the wrong man" quotations. In an interview with Jane Gross of the *New York Times* several days after the trial, juror Patricia Brooks explained the jurors' reasoning.[68] They did not believe, as one might expect, that Malcolm had fabricated the typed notes of a key conversation in which Masson was reported to have uttered three of the disputed quotations: "sex, women fun," "like an intellectual gigolo," and "the greatest analyst who ever lived." Instead, they believed that Malcolm had misinterpreted her notes, mistakenly taking her own recorded observations to be Masson's words in all but one of the three quotations (presumably "the greatest analyst who ever lived").[69] A third party reading the notes could not distinguish Masson's speech from Malcolm's observations, or so the jury believed. Such reasoning apparently led the jurors to conclude that the quotations taken from the typed notes were false.[70]

But the jury thought that Malcolm had acted with reckless disregard for the truth (not with knowing falsity, the other prong of the actual malice standard) in the case of only two of the five quotations Masson disputed in his suit: "sex, women, fun" and "he had the wrong man." Only one quotation appearing in Malcolm's typed notes was considered to have been published with actual malice: "sex, women, fun." During the editorial process, this was the phrase that a *New Yorker* lawyer had flagged as possibly libelous, but Gardner Botsford,

Malcolm's editor and husband, had allowed the words to stay on the basis of Malcolm's assurance that they were in her notes. The lawyer's query should have caused Malcolm to review the phrase and her notes more carefully, the jurors concluded, which would have led her to realize her mistake. The second quotation the jury found to constitute actual malice occurred in a passage Malcolm had edited in such a way as to change the meaning, according to Brooks. Masson had said that the board members of the Freud Archives "had the wrong man" if they expected him to accept his dismissal silently, but in the jurors' reading the edited passage had Masson saying that they "had the wrong man" if they expected him to act honorably. When Malcolm discussed this change with her editor, she should have seen that she had altered the meaning, said Brooks.[71]

The trial ended in early June 1993. On September 9, after failed attempts to persuade Masson, Malcolm, and their lawyers to avoid more litigation and work with a mediator, Judge Lynch ordered a new trial in the dispute, noting that the issues of liability and damages in a libel suit were too interdependent to allow a trial only on damages. Finding that the jury had cleared the *New Yorker* of liability, he dismissed the magazine from the case. Because Knopf, the publisher of the book version of the articles, had been dismissed from the case before trial, Janet Malcolm now stood alone.[72]

In most ways the 1993 *Masson* trial was a bust for all involved. The jury cleared the *New Yorker* of libel, but not before the magazine's editorial and fact-checking procedures were tarnished in testimony and, more significantly, in robust press coverage of the trial. News articles republished the allegedly libelous Masson quotations countless times and criticized Malcolm's journalistic methods and repudiated them as unethical. Of the major parties involved in the suit at this stage in the life of the case, not a single reputation emerged from the trial unscathed.

The larger problem of how a trial court should interpret and apply the Supreme Court's *Masson* ruling—the material alteration test—also remained. From jury interviews it appears that the jury found Malcolm liable on the reckless disregard of the truth prong of the actual malice standard. But the material alteration test focuses on the other prong, knowing falsity. How, then, did the jury instructions articulate this test and its proper application? Did the jury apply the lesser fault standard of negligence instead of the reckless disregard standard, which requires, according to the then recently decided Supreme Court case *Harte-Hankes Communications, Inc. v. Connaughton,*[73] the purposeful avoidance of the truth rather than just a mistaken reading of one's notes? When the jury reached an impasse on the damage award, with some jurors wanting to award $1 million and others a mere dollar, it became clear that the injury element of the case was deeply problematic. Did the jury unwittingly apply the incremental harm doctrine,[74] which the Supreme Court had ruled was not mandated by the First Amendment[75] and the Ninth Circuit had ruled was not part of California libel law?[76] As this avalanche of questions suggests, the material alteration test proved highly problematic for the jury to use in determining not only the truth or falsity of the disputed quotations but also liability and damages. These are key issues in establishing the degree to which the Supreme Court's *Masson* ruling embraces or rejects *Sullivan*'s promise of press protection and the First Amendment theory that supports this promise. In later chapters we will return to these concerns. But this chapter began in the middle of the Masson-Malcolm story. At this point we now go back in time, to search for the beginnings of the case in the broader swath of American cultural and social history.

CHAPTER TWO

———— ∞∞ ————

Literary Journalism and the *New Yorker*

THE *NEW YORKER* MAGAZINE HAS LONG HAD A REPUTATION AS A STRONG-hold of literary journalism in American culture. Established in 1925 under the editorial leadership of Harold Ross, the *New Yorker* was, in the beginning, a humor magazine written primarily for a New York City audience. The magazine aimed at sophistication, interpretation, and wit in its coverage of contemporary events, people, and the arts. It also published fiction, verse, and cartoons, intending from the very beginning, before the first issue was even published, to distinguish itself with its humorous illustrations.[1] It still distinguishes itself in this area, as anyone with even a passing familiarity with the magazine knows.

But within a brief ten years it had become much more than a thin humor magazine with a New York circulation. With the intelligent writing and editing of E. B. White and Katharine Angell White, who married in the magazine's early years and were together responsible for recruiting talented writers of all genres, the *New Yorker* became, as the literary and social critic Edmund Wilson observed, elegant and literate.[2] In 1939 William Shawn became managing editor for fact writing, a broad category that included reportage, commentary, and criticism of all kinds, organized in classic *New Yorker* departments such as "Talk of the Town," "Notes and Comment," "Profiles," and "Reporter at Large." (The term "department" was the magazine's special nomenclature for its different genres and categories of writing.) He assumed the editorship in 1952 after Ross's death.[3] With Shawn at the helm, the *New Yorker* increasingly became a haven for literary journalists in the years before World War II, publishing the likes of Joseph Mitchell, A. J. Liebling, Lillian Ross, and John Hersey.[4] Most had been feature writers for newspapers, and they flourished in the literary-minded atmosphere of the *New Yorker,* where in-depth writing was encouraged. In time, these writers developed a kind of storytelling reportage that became associated with the magazine.[5]

The "Art of Fact" at the *New Yorker*

That the *New Yorker* was a clearinghouse for some of the best modern literary reportage in America is widely acknowledged. But exactly what this particular kind of fact writing should be called, and how it should be defined, has been the subject of considerable professional and scholarly debate. The form has been known in recent years as narrative journalism, a term favored and made popular by Harvard's Nieman Program on Narrative Journalism and its successful annual conference for editors and journalists. But that term has by no means gained dominance in either the professional or scholarly lexicons. The form has been known variously as literary journalism, literary nonfiction, creative nonfiction, journalistic narrative, and the New Journalism, and there are as many variations on its definition as there are on its name. Chris Anderson has called the form a hybrid text, "paradoxical, threshold, problematic" in nature, relying on the techniques and conventions of storytelling to present the news and the world of fact.[6] Phyllis Frus has persuasively argued in her foundational study of the form's theoretical basis that the separation of fiction and journalism as distinct narrative categories is not natural and inevitable but rather historically contingent. Writers of these "texts on the border," Frus notes, "have muddied these neat distinctions and questioned their basis."[7] Ben Yagoda, author of the broadest and perhaps best history of the *New Yorker,* has also written about literary journalism, or "the art of fact," which he has identified as "informed and animated by the central journalistic commitment to the truth" and "thoughtfully, artfully, and valuably innovative."[8]

Whatever it was called and however it was defined, literary journalism found a home in the *New Yorker,* and some of the most recognized and acclaimed writers of the form made their names publishing in its pages. Some of them were direct influences on Janet Malcolm, who began writing for the magazine in the 1960s and in time joined the ranks of its pantheon of acclaimed prose stylists. She has identified Joseph Mitchell and A. J. Liebling as the most influential.[9] Known for his extraordinary way of writing about the lives of ordinary

men and women in profiles such as "The Rivermen" and "Up in the Old Hotel,"
Mitchell has been called "the greatest fact writer in the magazine's history." [10]
His 1940s "Mr. Flood" profiles, featuring a ninety-three-year-old resident of a
waterfront hotel in the Fulton Fish Market area of New York City, showcase his
characteristic technique of "merging himself" with his main character and
then writing about the character in the third person. [11] It turned out, as Mitchell
explained in an author's note he wrote for the book publication of the profiles
in 1948, that Mr. Flood was a composite character, a combination of "aspects of
several old men who work or hang out in the Fulton Fish Market, or who did in
the past." [12] Mitchell said that he wanted his Mr. Flood stories "to be truthful
rather than factual, but they are solidly based on facts." [13] As Ben Yagoda notes
in his history of the *New Yorker*, not a single brow was raised in publishing
or journalistic circles over the revelation of Mitchell's composite technique.
A. J. Liebling, who became a friend of Mitchell's when both worked at the *New
York World* writing features in the late 1920s and early 1930s, wrote mainly
first-person narratives, one of the best recognized being his three-part profile
of Colonel John R. Stingo, a pseudonym for an actual horse-racing columnist.
When it was published as a book, the jacket copy informed readers that it was
impossible to know how much of the story was factual and how much embroidered. "Again," Yagoda explained, "no one complained." [14]

　　As public and journalistic non-reaction to Mitchell's and Liebling's creative
approach to fact writing suggests, in the late 1940s and early 1950s there was
room in the American public's imagination, as well as in the profession of journalism, for nonfiction reportage of this kind. It may be that the conventions of
daily journalism were not as entrenched in the culture as they later came to be,
and both the public and the profession of journalism had a more fluid understanding of the genres of fiction and nonfiction, including journalism, and an
appreciation of the borderland that exists between the two. Alternatively, it
may be that journalism simply was not the object of public scrutiny and discontent that it later came to be. Or perhaps both suppositions have explanatory value. Whatever the reason, it is clear that until at least 1984, when the
New Yorker found itself under attack for both Alastair Reid's creation of composite characters and Janet Malcolm's altered quotations and compression,
"the lines between fact and invention had traditionally been quite blurry" in
American nonfiction in general and at the *New Yorker* in particular. [15] By the
time Masson filed suit, Yagoda explained with a hint of ironic historical under-
statement, "the vocation of journalism had somehow turned into a profession,

with rather rigid standards. Composite characters and quote-doctoring were not among them." [16] Of course, traditional daily journalism had professionalized in the early twentieth century. But its "rigid standards" were not necessarily those of literary and other forms of journalism.

When Mitchell and Liebling joined the *New Yorker* staff in the 1930s, it was a time of tremendous growth for the magazine, in terms of both literary innovation and financial stability. Between 1939 and 1949 its circulation grew dramatically, with subscriptions doubling.[17] Although the magazine was a staple in the reading diet of certain New York City residents, its market was national. Flourishing in the late 1940s and 1950s, the magazine had become by the end of the Second World War "a powerful cultural agent" in the nation according to the historian Mary Corey.[18] By the early 1980s, when the *New Yorker* published Janet Malcolm's profile of Jeffrey Masson, annual profits were the highest in the magazine's history at $5.3 million.[19] Malcolm was writing not only for a financially successful publication but also within a tradition and institution at the very heart of American higher culture. "More than a magazine," it was, Yagoda suggests, "a totem for the educated American middle and upper-middle classes. It became the repository for increasingly high standards of English prose, taste, conscience, and civility." [20]

But when Malcolm acknowledged using the technique of compression in her Masson profiles—a stitching together of quotations from different moments in their many hours of interviews—the journalism community exploded with criticism. Something had changed in the professional culture of journalism, and conventions that were practically a tradition in certain kinds of *New Yorker* fact writing (though certainly not mandated or even formally articulated)—the use of composite characters and compression, for example—had become anathema in mainstream journalism.

Janet Malcolm and the *New Yorker*

When Gary Bostwick presented his opening arguments in defense of Janet Malcolm in the first libel trial of *Masson v. New Yorker*, he made an obvious point—obvious at least to many readers of the *New Yorker*. "People in the *New Yorker* don't talk the way you and I do," he told the jury.[21] The jurors had read the Masson profiles in preparation for the trial, so they knew what he was talking about. By the time the case went to trial, the quotations at issue had been winnowed down to five, most of which appeared in a long, multipage monologue Malcolm had Masson deliver over lunch at a café. It is classic *New Yorker*-style seamless speech—articulate, polished complete sentences, flowing one after the other with perfect cadence and clear logic. It is the kind of speech, of course, that few in real life ever manage to utter, the kind we imagine ourselves using at our witty, chatty best but know we never pull off. Verbatim speech is almost always not pretty, at least when it is reproduced at any length.

This was Janet Malcolm's perspective, which she explained repeatedly as she was forced to defend her use of compression and translation techniques first in the press and later at trial. In an essay published in the *New York Review of Books* and as the afterword to *The Journalist and the Murderer*, she argued that transcribed speech should not be the same as the final, written version.[22] The ear and the mind filter speech and make sense of it, she asserted, and the writer must do the same:

> Fidelity to the subject's thought and to his characteristic way of expressing himself is the sine qua non of journalistic quotation—one under which all stylistic considerations are subsumed. Fortunately for reader and subject alike, the relatively minor task of translating tape-recorderese into English and the major responsibility of trustworthy quotation are in no way inimical; in fact, as I have proposed (and over and over again have discovered for myself), they are fundamentally and decisively complementary.[23]

Malcolm's argument—that quotation, at least in literary or narrative reportage, should be more than stenographic—is compelling, at least to many who see value in the kind of nonfiction reporting found in the pages of the *New Yorker* and publications like it. But her argument was ill received in the press community. In writing about the case for the *New York Times* during the Supreme Court stage of its travels, Alex Jones contended, "By journalistic standards, if Ms. Malcolm did pipe [fabricate] the quotes, she would be guilty of dishonesty and unprofessional behavior." Journalists use quotations, Jones noted, to show the reader that "the narrative portion of an article is based on something more than the writer's opinions. And for that reason, a sort of covenant exists between reader and writer that whatever appears between quotation marks is a literal, verbatim reflection of what someone said."[24] Jones's implied point—that anything less than verbatim quotation comes dangerously close to fabrication—characterized press coverage of the case during the twelve years it worked its way through the judicial system. Again and again, Malcolm was represented as an unethical reporter.[25]

What Alex Jones, along with the U.S. Supreme Court justices in their *Masson* decision, failed to question is whether readers of the *New Yorker* actually believed that multiparagraph and even multipage quotations in the magazine's fact writing were reported verbatim. Did readers understand that some kind of convention was at work other than the daily journalism standard of reporting short, often partial verbatim quotations? The Supreme Court did not ask itself this question, although it did acknowledge that, in many genres, quotations are *not* understood "to convey that the speaker actually said or wrote the quoted material."[26] The Court gave examples, including docudrama, historical fiction, and works that acknowledge re-creating conversations from memory.[27] Malcolm's profiles, however, like most "journalistic writing," did not fall into these categories, the Court said. According to Justice Anthony Kennedy, who wrote the majority opinion in the case, the Masson profiles offer "the reader no clue that the quotations are being used as a rhetorical device or to paraphrase the speaker's actual statements."[28] Hardly anywhere in the public discourse on the Masson-Malcolm dispute—in the vast whole of court opinions and press coverage—does anyone other than Malcolm, a few supporters, and her lawyers acknowledge that different reporting standards may have developed throughout the twentieth century in daily journalism and literary, or narrative, journalism. When this historical reality was acknowledged, it was often in the context of an attack on the New Journalism or literary journalism at large as fictionalized, and therefore unethical, journalism.

Objectivity and Traditional Journalism

Literary, or narrative, journalism has a long history in the American press and has been a constant, if at times submerged, presence throughout much of the past century. It is a history in which the *New Yorker* played a major, but certainly not the only major, role.

As a kind of literary journalism, Janet Malcolm's profiles of Jeffrey Masson were part of a tradition extending beyond the magazine which blended the aspirations of literature and journalism in a single form. In its use of storytelling techniques to deliver the news, and its use of perspectives other than the objective third-person voice of traditional journalism, the form by its very nature leaned more toward the subjective than the objective. The problem for Janet Malcolm was that, by the 1980s, objectivity had become a dominant, if not the defining, value of traditional journalism. The result was that journalism not

written in objective mode, unless labeled opinion or editorial, was suspected
of not being true or legitimate journalism at all. Such reportage included
Malcolm's profiles of Masson, in which the "I" of the author, long monologues
crafted by using the techniques of compression and translation, and the development of narrative scenes revealed the author's subjectivity.

Submerged in the issues raised in *Masson v. New Yorker* is an implicit questioning of the news value of objectivity. That objectivity underpins contemporary
conceptions of the journalistic report despite the challenges of postmodernism
is hardly disputable. As the journalism historian David Mindich has memorably
noted, "If American journalism were a religion, as it has been called from time to
time, its supreme deity would be 'objectivity.'"[29] Despite the robust critique the
news standard of objectivity has received in recent decades, the contemporary
traditional journalist still begins with the assumption that objectivity is a workable ideal—in other words, that reality is, by and large, knowable, that truth
inheres in the facts of what happened and what was said, that a written report
approximates reality. But determining exactly when and how objectivity came to
define the American news enterprise—and thus the traditional report—has
been somewhat unsettled scholarly terrain.

While some journalism historians have equated the emergence of the idea of
objectivity with the advent of the telegraph and wire services, both Michael
Schudson and Dan Schiller have persuasively argued that it emerged even earlier, with the penny press in the 1830s.[30] (Of course, the term "objectivity" did
not enter the journalistic vocabulary until the early twentieth century.) They
disagree, however, about the social forces that fed the rise of objectivity. While
Schudson sees the penny papers' nascent form of objectivity as a response to a
growing middle class with a disdain for upper-crust values, Schiller traces it to
the working-class belief "that knowledge, like property, should not be monop-
olized for exclusive use by private interests."[31] David Mindich follows Schiller's
line of thinking but goes further, finding the birth of the penny press to be
more a response to the entrenched conflicts of the Jacksonian era. The hallmark features of the "pennies"—detachment and nonpartisanship—were
meant, he says, to transcend the "divisive ideology and violence" of the time.[32]

When objectivity emerged is not nearly as important as the fact that it did.
By the mid-nineteenth century, the telegraph and wire services were solidify-
ing the role of objectivity in the journalistic report. Telegraph lines were noto-
riously unreliable. To make sure that the basics of their stories reached their
newspaper offices before the line broke down, reporters developed the habit of

front-loading their dispatches with the facts of the events they were covering. The most important facts were packed into the first paragraph. Thus the journalistic preference for fact became further codified in developing news values.[33] Wire services, too, contributed to the emphasis on facts. In selling stories to newspapers displaying a range of political allegiances, wire services found it prudent to concentrate more on fact and less on opinion, thereby avoiding at least the appearance of political partisanship.[34] The traditional news report—characterized by its objective voice, neutral tone, and inverted pyramid structure—had emerged.[35]

By the turn of the twentieth century, the "objective" journalistic news story, the muckraker magazine article, and realistic fiction all conveyed "a belief that reality could be identified and objectified."[36] Dorothy Nelkin observes that during this period, "scientific values penetrated many social and political institutions," largely in the form of the principles of rationality and neutrality. In the press, these scientific values developed into the news standard of objectivity.[37] That journalism took on the values of science has everything to do with the cultural context of the late nineteenth century. In the post–Civil War years, the social problems related to industrialization were immense. In the resulting economic and social order, people were entirely dependent on one another for their lives and livelihoods. The new social realities exploded the American myth of the self-sufficient individual who made his way in life entirely on his own merits. The new order encouraged the growth of the scientific spirit in American society and the birth of the modern social science professions.[38] American universities were multiplying, modernizing, and promoting these new disciplines as the means for solving the critical social problems emerging between producers and owners, labor and capital.[39] Universities were adopting the German scientific method, which rejected the notion of a supernatural cause in the effects of phenomenal action. "Pure science," as it was known, relied instead on observation and measurement to explain the world.[40] Such an approach assumed the rationality of the scientist and the measurability of the world. These assumptions about human capacity and the nature of reality permeated American culture and led to the steady growth of the social sciences. As these professionalized, the historian Mary Furner has argued, "objectivity grew more important as a scientific ideal and also as a practical necessity" for social scientists, who "based their claims to competence in social analysis on the authority conferred by scientific methods and attitudes."[41] In practice, though, social scientists "were usually guided more by the state of existing knowledge and by their own interests than by social conditions. Ideological considerations were inevitably present, but they were ordinarily unacknowledged."[42]

In the late nineteenth century, American journalism was largely considered a trade rather than a profession, although journalists of the era were deeply engaged in debates about the purpose and role of journalism in society and the desirability of its professionalization.[43] By sometime in the early twentieth century, the newspaper industry had absorbed the social science approach to knowledge as the basis for what was quickly becoming the "profession" of the press. The journalist became the rational scientist observing and measuring the world he was reporting. Although journalism education had been introduced in America in the years after the Civil War, when newspapers first became major social institutions, its greatest stronghold was in western and midwestern state universities. With the founding of the Missouri School of Journalism in 1908 and the opening of Columbia University's College of Journalism in 1912 (funded by Joseph Pulitzer, who advocated that journalism be advanced from a trade to a profession),[44] formal journalism education came into being. By the 1920s, journalism curricula had turned toward the social sciences.[45]

By the 1930s, objectivity had become a fully entrenched professional standard in journalism, largely due to the influence of Walter Lippmann's press criticism.[46] It is important to note that the term "objectivity" as applied to news reporting is entirely an invention of the twentieth century; in the nineteenth century it was known by other names that highlighted certain ideas implicit in the larger construct, such as "nonpartisanship" and "detachment" in the 1830s and 1840s and "balance" and "facts" in the 1890s.[47] Lippmann introduced the phrase "objective reporting" in 1919 in his *Atlantic Monthly* essay "What Modern Liberty Means" and discussed its meaning the following year in *Liberty and the News*.[48] He envisioned objectivity as a quasi-scientific method for reporters to gather and report the news, a rigorous means of collecting relevant information, separating fact from opinion, and verifying the facts on which news reports were based.[49] In the years that followed, the term slowly gained traction in journalistic discourse, spread not only through intellectual debates but also in journalism textbooks and speeches given at the annual meetings of the American Society of Newspaper Editors. By the late 1920s the word "objectivity" was commonly used in the world of journalism.[50]

"As Lippmann understood the term," writes journalist and author Jeremy Iggers, "objectivity was a method, not a claim about the epistemological status of truth claims. As a method, it meant that truth claims were to be subjected to the same continuing and rigorous scrutiny as scientific hypotheses."[51] Although Lippmann's understanding of objectivity shares much with the pragmatist vision of truth as something revealed through experience and experiment rather than philosophy, his sense of objectivity as "a method of systematic doubt" became "in practice, in its institutionalized form," according to Iggers, "a sort of naïve realism."[52] According to veteran journalists Bill Kovach and Tom Rosenstiel, Lippmann called for "journalists to develop a consistent method of testing information—a transparent approach to evidence—precisely so that personal and cultural biases would not undermine the accuracy of their work."[53] For Lippmann, it was the journalist's "method [that] is objective, not the journalist."[54] But in the profession of journalism, objectivity came to be more a value than a method, an assumption about the nature of knowledge implying that a one-to-one correspondence existed between the language of a news report and the reality it was meant to represent.

Objectivity thus reached maturity as a news standard at the same time journalism education and the newspaper trade professionalized. During the rapid national economic growth of the late nineteenth and early twentieth centuries, newspapers became major players in the emerging capitalist order. Advertising filled the pages of newspapers, production costs dropped as printing technology advanced, and circulation increased along with consumerism.[55] By the 1920s the School of Journalism at Columbia was in full swing, newspaper editors and publishers had formed professional organizations, and ethical codes for journalism were coming into existence.[56] The standard of objectivity, articulated in the American Society of Newspaper Editors' first code of ethics in 1923, allowed editors to control their reporters more easily and to increase production efficiency.[57] Objectivity, writes Michael Schudson, had become "a fully formulated occupational ideal, part of a professional project or mission. Far more than a set of craft rules to fend off libel suits or a set of constraints to help editors keep tabs on their underlings, objectivity was finally a moral code."[58]

The traditional report, rooted in the professional standard of objectivity, came to dominate the American press under particular historical and cultural circumstances, and thus it is a mistake to see it as the natural form for the expression of news. As this form of report was starting to become in the post–Civil War years what it would grow to be in the twentieth century, other forms of news delivery were being practiced, including sensational yellow journalism and the narrative report.[59] By the 1890s, however, two particular strains of journalism dominated newspaper reporting—the "information" and the "story" models.[60] The former includes the traditional hard news report, the latter the narrative, or literary, report.

Narrative Journalism in the Modern American Press

To understand why the literary, or narrative, report emerged in American journalism in the 1890s is to understand the cultural context of the time. From 1860 to 1890 the United States was changing rapidly from an agrarian to an industrial society. Immigration doubled the national population, and people of different cultures and experiences were adapting to life together in America's burgeoning cities. Large class and economic disparities were widening between owners and producers, the elite and the masses. And the clash between capital and labor grew increasingly sharp and, at times, violent.[61] As John Hartsock notes, "Given such a social context, it is no wonder that the alienating nature of the information and sensational models of objectified journalism would fail to account for what was happening in people's lives."[62] The response was a more subjective journalism, as journalists took on the problematic task of helping their readers "understand *more intimately* the consequences" of these changes in American life.[63]

By the 1890s a self-consciously literary form of reportage had developed in American newspapers. Journalists adopted the techniques of the new realistic fiction: "dialogue, scene construction, concrete detail, and showing activity."[64] The traditional report eschews the journalist's own value judgments in striving for neutrality and objectivity. Traditional reports claim, Dan Schiller asserts, "that, ideally at least, they recount events without the intrusion of value judgments or symbols."[65] But objectivity "precludes the very presence of conventions and thus masks the patterned structure of news."[66] The point of the new literary journalism was to tear away this masking, "to narrow the gulf between subjectivity and the object,"[67] as Hartsock argues, and thus to engage readers in the experience.

For a variety of reasons the literary report enjoyed only a brief heyday. In the early twentieth century, literature increasingly rejected journalism and journalism increasingly rejected literature, a cultural state of affairs that was in part the by-product of increased professionalization of the reporter's trade.[68] But other historical forces drove a wedge between what the first press trade journal called in 1886 "the twin professions of literature and journalism."[69] A key aspect of social thought of the era was the belief that society should be rationally ordered if the liberal notion of American progress was to be achieved. This belief produced, in part, more rigid conceptions of class-based cultural forms. Whereas expressive culture in the early nineteenth century was conceived in broadly democratic terms—the arts, for example, were assumed to be for the consumption and enjoyment of all the social classes—by the turn of the twentieth century a new rigid hierarchy of cultural forms had emerged. To borrow historian Lawrence Levine's descriptive terms, certain kinds of artistic expression came to be understood as "highbrow," suited principally for the consumption of the socially and intellectually elite. Other kinds came to be understood as "lowbrow," suited for the masses.[70] In this dispensation, literature was "highbrow" and journalism "lowbrow." Journalists' roles as propagandists in the First World War, and Walter Lippmann's subsequent call for objective journalism to combat the dangers of propaganda, further concretized the traditional report as the primary form of journalism and increased the perceived distance between journalism and literature.[71] Lippmann's own work for the government's war propaganda machine taught him how easily facts could be manipulated for the "manufacture of consent."[72] To combat what he perceived as the threat posed by subjectivity in news reporting, Lippmann advocated the education of journalists as professionals and the teaching of a scientific method of reporting that relied on the reporter's neutrality and detachment.[73]

For several decades the narrative report remained a subordinate strain of expression in the American press. But just as the cultural upheaval of the 1890s encouraged the use of narrative reporting, so did the Great Depression. As Hartsock notes: "In times of social transformation and crisis an objectified rhetoric proves even more inadequate. Instead, a greater need emerges for a rhetoric that attempts to help one understand other subjectivities, particularly subjectivities at the heart of such transformation and crisis: narrative literary journalism in short."[74] In the 1930s the literary report, or what was at the time called "literary reportage," emerged in magazines in reaction against what many perceived as the newspapers' failure to report adequately not just the facts of the depression but the possible meanings of these facts.[75] At the same time, a less political literary journalism flourished in the *New Yorker*, with Joseph Mitchell, A. J. Liebling, and Lillian Ross leading the way.[76]

The resurgence of the narrative report did not last, however. World War II, with its scientific, if catastrophic, advances, reenlivened newspaper reporting and the scientific values upholding the traditional report. Hartsock notes that this "triumph of science in World War II alone suggests that positivist assumptions had all but defeated subjectivity as a legitimate cognitive stance from which to interpret the world." [77] During the ensuing cold war, predicated as it was on a nearly monolithic anticommunist, pro-capitalist ideology, American political and cultural elites (and perhaps even a weary and fearful public) needed the authoritative, soothing voice of the traditional report. It was not until the cultural crises of the 1960s that the literary report resurfaced. This period saw the development of a critical culture that questioned received truths and institutional authority—including the supposedly objective stance of the traditional report. One result was the birth of the so-called New Journalism, the latest iteration of the literary report, which found its primary voice in non-fiction books and glossy magazines. [78] "Whatever else 'new journalists' wrote about," Schudson observes, "they were always implicitly writing about reporting itself." [79] In doing so they exposed the traditional report's "ideology of technique and neutrality," which tended to obfuscate institutional assumptions and values. [80] In rejecting objectivity for subjectivity, they were revealing the limitations of mere facts in explaining an increasingly puzzling world to the reader. The New Journalism meant instead to interpret the facts, as filtered through the journalists' own subjectivities, and in this way to uncover meaning.

The heyday of the New Journalism was a fascinating moment in the history of literary journalism. Although the genre was nothing new in the American press, the New Journalism by its very name at least claimed a unique historical status. The origin of the term is unclear, but it is most closely associated with, and was most often used by, Tom Wolfe, the form's self-appointed apologist. [81] It burst onto the scene in 1965, the year Wolfe published his collection of journalistic stories *Kandy-Kolored Tangerine-Flake Streamline Baby* and Truman Capote published *In Cold Blood* as a four-part series in the *New Yorker*. [82] Wolfe's stories examined in a startlingly fresh prose style the subcultures and countercultures popping up across America in the sixties. His characteristic style included repeated epithets, phonetic imitation of speech and sounds, and rapid shifts in viewpoint, a style hinted at in the title essay of the book: "There Goes (Varoom! Varoom!) That Kandy-Kolored (Thphhhhhh!) Tangerine-Flake Streamline Baby (Rahghhh!) around the Bend (Brummmmmmmmmm-mmmmmm)." [83] Capote's book-length story of two wayward young men's brutal murder of the Clutter family in Kansas—which he researched painstakingly for five years—achieves its glacial chill through the use of techniques such as the rendering of the killers' psyches through interior monologues. Other

New Journalists published their work in magazines friendly to the new voices and approaches, including *Esquire, New York, Harper's,* and *Rolling Stone.*[84]

The innovations of the New Journalism rubbed entirely against the grain of traditional journalism and, to some degree, previous literary journalism. "It is no wonder mainstream journalists set apart and castigated what they identified as New Journalism," writes Frus, "for in contrast to the illusion of neutrality . . . many of these pieces show how 'the way things are' has been naturalized by conventions of realism and objectivity, and they offer an alternative in their own self-accounting forms."[85] New Journalism was different from the literary reportage that had lived for years in the pages of the *New Yorker,* particularly in its experimentation with language and storytelling techniques and its explicit disavowal of neutrality and objectivity. Despite Mitchell's and Liebling's use of certain narrative conventions in their writing, including the first-person voice, they generally pretended to a kind of objectivity, or perhaps more accurately William Shawn pretended for them. In discussing the New Journalism, he once asserted that the *New Yorker's* literary reportage had always been unique in its use of the first person. "Subjective journalism may have had its American beginnings at the *New Yorker,*" he said, since writers there were using the first person. But "that is not New Journalism, because our pieces are as objective as is genuinely possible. The I in our first person reporting is still an observer—objective and impartial."[86] Shawn seemed to be drawing a distinction between the reporter as observer and the reporter as participant in the events being reported, but still, his claims about the *New Yorker's* literary reportage do not hold water, as Yagoda proves in his review of the magazine's Vietnam-era advocacy reporting.[87] Janet Malcolm herself, in writing about the Masson suit, suggested the degree to which her subjectivity colored her understanding of Masson:

> Being sued by a person who inhabits the pages of a book you have written is not, after all, the same as being sued by someone who exists only in life. You know your adversary more intimately than you know most merely real people—not only because you have had occasion to study him more closely than one studies the people one does not write about, but because you have put a great deal of yourself into him. "*Madame Bovary, c'est moi,*" Flaubert said of his famous character. The characters of nonfiction, no less than those of fiction, derive from the writer's most idiosyncratic desires and deepest anxieties; they are what the writer wishes he was and worries that he is. *Masson, c'est moi.*[88]

The tension between traditional journalism and the New Journalism exploded in a heated cultural debate in 1965—the fortieth anniversary of the *New Yorker*—when Wolfe published a parody of the *New Yorker* in the *New York Herald Tribune*'s Sunday magazine, which was titled simply *New York*.[89] Wolfe lampooned not only the magazine and its classic profile form but also its revered editor, William Shawn. "Rather than mimicking the *New Yorker*," Wolfe later explained, "I was going to give them a voice they couldn't stand. In the anti-parody, as I thought of it, the wilder and crazier the hyperbole, the better. It was a challenge—to use the most lurid colors imaginable to paint a room full of very proper people who had gone to sleep standing up, talking to themselves."[90]

Jim Bellows, editor of the *Herald Tribune*, sent an advance copy of the first of Wolfe's two articles, titled "Tiny Mummies! The True Story of the Ruler of 43rd Street's Land of the Walking Dead," to Shawn. "I was innocent enough to think that the old spirit of *The New Yorker* still flourished," Bellows wrote, recalling the incident. "After all, who had engaged in satire more than the good old *New Yorker*?"[91] Shawn apparently did not view the article as good-natured or even straightforward satire. In a letter to John Hay Whitney, publisher of the *Herald Tribune*, Shawn called Wolfe's articles "false and libelous" and "a vicious, murderous attack on me and on the magazine I work for." He asked Whitney not to distribute the issue of the magazine already in press and to drop publication of the second article. His plea went nowhere.[92] Bellows even sent Shawn's letter to both *Time* and *Newsweek*, which, the day after the first Wolfe article came out, published reports about the *New Yorker*'s attempt to halt publication of the magazine.[93] As Gardner Botsford, a longtime editor at the *New Yorker* and Janet Malcolm's husband, wrote in his memoirs, Shawn's letter was "a dumb move."[94]

Wolfe's article got many facts about the magazine's history and editorial practices wrong (although these factual inaccuracies could be understood as part and parcel of the anti-parody form), and was rather mean-spirited in its roasting of Shawn, a painfully private and even shy person.[95] But the parody effectively skewered the *New Yorker*'s culture and characteristic prose style.[96] Most famously, perhaps, Wolfe attacked the seemingly endless *New Yorker* sentence, calling it a "whichy thicket" with "all those clauses, appositions, amplifications, qualifications, asides, God knows what else, hanging inside the poor old skeleton of one sentence like some kind of Spanish moss."[97] After citing an example of a particularly egregious "whichy" sentence from a *New Yorker* article, filled with dependent clauses beginning with words such as "who," "which," "when," and so on, Wolfe launched into what would become known as his characteristic style: "*Wh-wh-wh-wh-wh-whoooaaaaaaugh!*—piles of whichy whuh words—*which, when, where, who, whether, whuggheeee,* the living whichy thickets."[98]

The *New Yorker* staff reacted with outrage, peppering the *Herald Tribune*'s editorial page with letters of protest, focused in large part on what E. B. White called the "violent attack" on Shawn.[99] Writers for the magazine published protests against Wolfe's "anti-parody" in other venues as well, most notably Dwight Macdonald's essay in the *New York Review of Books* which blasted Wolfe's reportage as "parajournalism," more entertainment than information. "It is a bastard form," he wrote, "having it both ways, exploiting the factual authority of journalism and the atmospheric license of fiction."[100] Shawn himself, in a 1978 interview, called it "a debased form of journalism."[101] The critical furor surrounding Wolfe's anti-parody, as well as the practice of the New Journalism in general, was widespread. According to Wolfe, both the journalism community and the literary establishment attacked the form, the former because it violated traditional news values and the latter because it "caused a status panic in the literary community."[102]

Ironically, the *New Yorker*, one of the significant incubators of American literary journalism in the twentieth century, largely dissociated itself from the New Journalism after Wolfe's articles, although it did publish Capote's "In Cold Blood," which it had commissioned years before. At the time, of course, Capote was not associated with the movement; it was not until after his 1965 publication of "In Cold Blood" in the *New Yorker* and the following year as a book that he became firmly established as one of the New Journalists. Yagoda notes that despite William Shawn's misgivings about some of Capote's techniques—such as the re-creation of a person's thoughts and private conversations—the *New Yorker* did not append an explanatory note to the account. It was the first and last time, Yagoda observes, that the *New Yorker* published "an extended piece of re-created narrative."[103]

Although the New Journalism as a self-conscious movement began to decline in the 1970s as investigative reporting reinvigorated American newspapers in the wake of the Vietnam War and Watergate, and as the cultural revolution sputtered out, literary journalism survived—and has even found its way into the newspaper. Its presence can be detected in the Pulitzer Prize Board's creation of the feature category in 1976 as well as the explanatory journalism category in 1985, both of which have historically depended on narrative reporting.[104] In 2001 the Nieman Foundation for Journalism at Harvard University initiated its successful Program on Narrative Journalism, which has concentrated its efforts on encouraging a narrative approach to newswriting in newsrooms across the country.[105] Its annual conference on narrative journalism is well attended by journalists, editors, and scholars alike. In 1999, in a large-scale study of the state of the American newspaper sponsored by the *American Journalism Review,* newspaper content from the mid-1960s was compared with that from the late 1990s.[106] Among many findings, researchers saw a marked growth in the use of feature stories on front pages and, in the newspaper at large, "soft" (that is, subjective, descriptive) leads, lengthy articles, and "bright" writing. Although the study did not specifically explore the use of the narrative report in the newspapers surveyed, its findings suggest that there has been an increased use of key elements of narrative reporting. Although no historical study exists on narrative journalism from the decline of the New Journalism to the present, there is ample evidence that the form is alive and well in the American press.

In 1989, when the Ninth Circuit majority affirmed the lower court's grant of summary judgment to the defendants in the *Masson* case, Judge Alex Kozinski wrote a strong dissent that was covered vigorously in the press.[107] In arguing that the case presented enough factual evidence to determine whether there was actual malice in the publication of the Masson profiles, and that the case should go to trial, Judge Kozinski undertook a multipage history of professional standards and practices in journalism, focusing on what he found to be general agreement in the profession that quotation marks indicate verbatim speech and that the techniques and conventions of the New Journalism generally ran counter to standard journalistic practice. "A school of thought known as the New Journalism advances the view that an author has the right to vary or rearrange the facts of a story in order to advance a literary purpose," he wrote. "This is a highly controversial view among journalists, one not shared by many who have spoken on the subject."[108] Several pages later he asserted that "the blurring of fact and fiction," a hallmark, he implied, of both the New Journalism and Janet Malcolm's Masson profiles, was a "practice widely condemned" in the world of journalism.[109]

What Kozinski failed to do was engage Malcolm's argument about the problems of stenographic quotation in reporting, particularly the in-depth reporting she practiced. Neither did he consider that there may be more than one legitimate tradition of journalism in America, with standards, practices, and conventions somewhat different from those of daily newspapers. To his way of thinking, Malcolm "deliberately twists the words of real, named individuals she purports to be quoting." [110] It is not that Kozinski's perspective was not legitimate, but it lacked a full-bodied theoretical grounding, neglecting to account for Malcolm's argument about the problems of quotation and the usefulness of translation and compression in conveying a speaker's meaning. In the end, Kozinksi's perspective stood on the solid foundation of the journalistic profession's commitment to objectivity.

Just a few years before Malcolm wrote about Jeffrey Masson, Dan Schiller argued that the news value of objectivity has worked throughout American press history as a disguise for social conflicts. It is "a framework legitimating the exercise of social power over the interpretation of reality. Those without institutional resources have, time and again, found themselves pilloried and marginalized in the press," he observed, "while crucial issues have been amplified in such a way as to lead the general public to accept institutional control." [111] Even a brief review of press coverage of the Masson-Malcolm case shows that Malcolm suffered this kind of public pillorying for what was, by the standards of daily journalism, her unconventional use of quotations. Although the *New Yorker*'s resources, both financial and cultural, were substantial, when the magazine and Malcolm found themselves in the middle of a voluble public controversy over press ethics and law, the press fed the controversy. The crucial issue involved the legitimacy of various professionally acceptable methods available to the press in representing reality. In a press married to the ideal of objectivity—an ideal underpinning the notion that verbatim quotation is both possible and necessary in the accurate and truthful portrayal of the world as it is—Janet Malcolm's understanding of quotation was ethically suspect. According to the received terms and norms of objectivity, to believe that some kind of translation must occur between speech and the written word was to disbelieve the journalistic premise that a report could correspond objectively and naturally to reality. The press on the whole criticized Malcolm and the *New Yorker* for this view, as did Judge Kozinski in his dissent. Both the press and the courts exercised their social power to uphold and reify the professional standards and ethics of traditional journalism. Janet Malcolm claimed that her quotations were accurate and truthful. She presented evidence at trial to support her argument that she had represented Masson largely by using his own words, or words very much like his own words, even though she "translated" these words from speech to prose and compressed quotations from different points in time into one monologue. In the end, though, whether one understood her quotations as true or false hinged on one's conception of truth and the attendant possibilities and limits of objectivity and language (as well as whether one believed that the typed notes from a breakfast conversation were authentic).

Bill Kovach and Tom Rosenstiel have suggested that truthful reporting relies on a kind of social contract with the reader in which the reporter is as "transparent as possible about . . . methods and motives." [112] The Supreme Court in its *Masson* decision suggested that, had Malcolm and the *New Yorker* explained her technique of rendering Masson's speech to the reader, the audience would have known that the quoted words were not verbatim—and thus there might have been little basis for Masson's libel suit. [113] But media ethics scholars Michael Killenberg and Rob Anderson have suggested, using *Masson v. New Yorker* as a springboard, that "few words published in news stories as direct quotations are verbatim accounts. Nevertheless, the profession's official stance, reflected in reporting textbooks, style books, and other public pronouncements, reinforces a mythology of quoting." [114] Can ethical journalists compress quotations from different time periods into one long quotation? Perhaps, but it is best to explain to their readers what they are doing, these scholars argue. Of the many who have written about the *Masson* case, Killenberg and Anderson are among the few who are willing to acknowledge and to confront what they call the "mythology of quoting." They note that the definition of verbatim quotation ranges widely "among interviewers, interviewees, editors, and readers" and suggest that ethical guidelines for quotation use are possible only when journalists acknowledge that they are not "mere conduits of information" but rather "intentional communicators, or *rhetors*." [115] The simple selection of a quotation from a longer interview is a rhetorical, or interpretive, act. "Each quote," the authors write, "no matter how literally accurate in a self-contained sense, is necessarily inaccurate in a contextual sense." [116] Subjectivity, then, permeates even the traditional report. In exploring the issues of the Masson-Malcolm dispute, Michael Hoyt, associate editor in 1991 of the *Columbia Journalism Review*, surveyed several empirical studies of quotation practices that found achieving verbatim quotation almost humanly impossible, even with transcriptions of tape-recorded conversations. Nevertheless, he implied, quotations have a place in reporting. "It appears that in the dangerous journey from someone's mouth through a reporter's mind and into print," Hoyt argued, "exact wording often falls by the wayside, while meaning tends to survive." [117]

The years when the Masson-Malcolm case occupied the public stage of the courtroom and news reports were also the years when deep academic and public anxiety surfaced about postmodern conceptions of the constructed nature of reality and the contingent nature of truth claims. The Masson-Malcolm dispute directly engaged the cultural conflict between the long-standing scientific belief in objective knowledge and objective reality and the newer postmodern notion of the subjective nature of all knowledge. Masson, his lawyers, and their supporters suggested that the journalistic value of objectivity, expressed in the Associated Press stylebook's admonition against any journalistic use of quotation that is not verbatim, honored the reality of human experience and the direct correspondence between language and the representation of an objective world. Malcolm, her lawyers, and their supporters challenged such notions of truth in their defense of her compression technique in the crafting of quotations—a technique that had long been used in American journalism and nonfiction writing but had not been explicitly recognized in any official professional publication. That the Masson-Malcolm dispute was an expression of the cultural conflict of its time was rarely, if ever, mentioned in the vast discourse surrounding the case. Such an observation is perhaps easier to make from a historical distance. [118]

The intertwined histories of the traditional report and the narrative report—and the *New Yorker*'s conflicted relationship with both kinds— suggest a long-standing, if often submerged, tension in American journalism between these two conceptions of the report and the role of the social contract in each. Of course, the traditional report is the dominant form, and its claim of accurately representing reality through facts, verbatim quotations, and an objective stance is commonly accepted among readers. To question these claims is to question the truth claims—and the basis of the social contract—of the traditional report. To question these claims is also to consider Janet Malcolm's reasoned, if controversial, challenge to the stenographic quotation.

Phyllis Frus has suggested that American culture and democracy would benefit from discarding formalist notions of what constitutes literature and journalism. Doing so, she claims, would result in a more complex, robust public discourse necessary in democratic society. [119] Is there room, and a need, for both the traditional and the narrative report in the public sphere? Can both maintain working, if somewhat different, social contracts with readers? If so, what should be the nature of these contracts? Can the techniques of translation and compression be used ethically in narrative reporting—and without running afoul of libel law? Does truthful journalism inhere mainly in the accurate reporting of facts and verbatim quotations? How do the selection and salience of these facts and quotations construct truth? How can courts properly balance, in the context of libel law and altered quotations, the social interest in free expression and a journalistic source's interest in speaking for himself or herself with as little mediation as possible? The answers to these questions, as contingent and historically conditioned as they may be, are important to American journalism and the public sphere, for the answers at any given moment set the boundaries for what journalism can do and be in American public life—and what we can imagine it will become.

CHAPTER THREE

The Historical Origins of the
Masson-Malcolm Dispute

To a historian looking for meaning in the interaction between events and texts and their cultural and social contexts, *Masson v. New Yorker*[1] began long before Masson and Malcolm even met. As we have seen, its roots can be found in the early twentieth century, when contemporary structures and ideologies of the American press, democracy, and First Amendment law were initially cast in their modern forms. Like many significant public controversies, the Masson-Malcolm dispute was less a matter of historical accident and more the product of a reactive compound produced by historical action. Of the many elements in this compound, the birth of modern First Amendment law in the early part of the century, and the later constitutionalization of libel law, are among the most important in explaining not only the shape of the dispute but also its implications for the practice and theory of free expression in the United States.

Given the particular sensational facts of *Masson*—the writer's seeming flouting of standard journalistic practice regarding quotation, the subject's uncontested claim of having slept with a thousand women, the *New Yorker*'s questionable decision to let a husband edit his wife's work—it is easy to forget the First Amendment dimensions of the case. But *Masson v. New Yorker* is the progeny of *New York Times v. Sullivan*,[2] one of the most significant First Amendment cases the U.S. Supreme Court has ever decided. In *Sullivan*, the Court offered its fullest articulation of the meaning of the First Amendment, inextricably linking the American press to the proper operation of American democracy. In *Masson*, the Court further interpreted the constitutional standard established in *Sullivan*—the actual malice standard—to protect the press from the chilling effects of the common law of libel. The alteration of a speaker's words will not constitute actual malice, the Court held, unless the quoted words are materially different in meaning from the speaker's actual words.[3] While the *Sullivan* decision suggested that only statements of fact were actionable in libel suits—that is, only facts were susceptible to a finding of falsity—in *Masson* the justices implied that some language, such as quotation, was neither actionable as fact nor protected as opinion. The meaning of quotation existed in some uncharted borderland between fact and opinion, but like statements of fact, it was susceptible to a determination of truth and would not receive blanket First Amendment protection. The most visible contribution of the ruling to First Amendment jurisprudence is what it suggests about legal liability in the instance of defamatory misquotations. Its most important contribution, however, is the easiest to overlook: *Masson* reimagined the role of truth in the judicial determination of liability in actual malice libel cases and the nature of the truth that must emerge from the public debate if it is to be protected as free expression by the First Amendment. In doing so, *Masson* shied away from *Sullivan*'s spirited protection of public discourse as a key instrument in democracy and instead suggested that protection might degrade the nature and quality of that discourse.[4] This rationale is hard to reconcile with the First Amendment theory expressed in *Sullivan*.

Exactly how *Masson v. New Yorker* reconceptualized the judicial notion of truth first articulated in *New York Times v. Sullivan*'s constitutionalization of libel law will be discussed later in this book. To understand the *Masson* ruling and its implications for freedom of expression, we must first understand its historical underpinnings.

A Brief History of American Libel Law

Modern American libel law, with its companion theory of First Amendment press protection and the necessary role of the press in democratic governance, predates the birth of *Masson v. New Yorker* by only twenty years. In 1964 the landmark Supreme Court ruling of *New York Times v. Sullivan* upended centuries of American libel doctrine that had originated in the common law tradition of England. This doctrine included the law of seditious libel, which made the criticism of government or government officials a crime.[5] True defamation, precisely because it was true, was considered even more damaging to the public peace and stable government than false defamation.[6]

That truthful statements could be considered libelous and thus criminal throughout much of American history often comes as a shock to those steeped in contemporary First Amendment press freedoms and untutored in the history of U.S. libel law. It must be remembered, however, that politics and religion were closely intertwined in England prior to and during the colonial era, and the English crown, perennially fearing social unrest and upheaval, did not tolerate political and religious dissent.[7] The same governmental fear that underlay the system of prior restraints on the press led to the later development of the doctrine of seditious libel in England's common law. The arrival of the printing press in 1476, and the easy distribution of dissenting views that resulted, only heightened the English monarchy's anxiety about public expression as potentially seditious. To censor public speech and possible dissent, Henry VIII and then Elizabeth developed a complex system of licensing, which forced publishers to submit for the censor's review any manuscript intended for publication. Any work published without a license was thus criminal. In the late seventeenth century, licensing died out in England, but the law of seditious libel remained.[8] By that time, both had already found their way to the American colonies.

New York Times v. Sullivan

When the Supreme Court decided *Sullivan* in 1964, licensing in the United States was an antique relic, all but forgotten. But the concept of seditious libel lived on in the common law under which American citizens could be prosecuted or, more likely, sued for damages for false and defamatory political statements.[9] Although the Court had turned its back on the federal law of seditious libel in 1812,[10] seditious libel persisted in state statutes and common law. When the Supreme Court noted in *Sullivan* that the federal law of seditious libel, in particular the Sedition Act of 1798, had been repudiated in the court of public opinion, it was suggesting not only that seditious libel was unconstitutional but also that the United States had since developed "a national awareness of the central meaning of the First Amendment."[11] This awareness was simple: the First Amendment protected a citizen's right to free expression on public issues, including criticism of government.

This right to free expression was the animating principle in what was other-wise a civil rights case. In March 1960 the Committee to Defend Martin Luther King placed a full-page fundraising advertisement in the *New York Times* detailing a series of state-sanctioned civil rights abuses in the South and call-ing for "material help" for those fighting for "the re-affirmation of our Con-stitution and its Bill of Rights." [12] This advertisement, headlined "Heed Their Rising Voices," led to a landmark Supreme Court case which has become America's defining judicial articulation of the First Amendment's promise of press freedom. [13]

Montgomery, Alabama, police commissioner L. B. Sullivan filed a libel suit against the *New York Times* and four black Alabama ministers whose names appeared in the advertisement, claiming that he had been libeled by its men-tion of police action against student protests and the attempted intimidation of King through trumped-up arrests. Although Sullivan himself was not men-tioned in the advertisement, he claimed that he was implicated and that the ad falsely claimed that he and the Montgomery police were responsible for bomb-ing King's home. It was the most unreasonable of readings. Although the sub-stance of the advertisement's charges was true, several minor inaccuracies existed in its account of police action. Finding against the *New York Times* and the other defendants, who had claimed truth as a defense, as well as lack of identification of and injury to Sullivan, a jury awarded the police commis-sioner $500,000 in damages. The Alabama Supreme Court upheld the judg-ment and the award. [14]

Alabama state government had found a powerful tool to silence press criti-cism of Jim Crow: libel law and the court systems. Libel at this point was en-tirely a matter of state law, and in a libel suit the burden of proof was on the defendant—that is, to avoid liability, the defendant had to prove the truth of the contested publication. What is more, in Alabama a judge could declare a publication to be "libelous per se," in other words, self-evidently defamatory and injurious to the person described, which is exactly what happened in the *Sullivan* case. As Anthony Lewis explained in his book on the case, the Alabama judicial system's use of libel law "made it forbiddingly difficult for news media to write anything about the realities of Southern racism without risking heavy damages for libel." [15]

In 1964 the Supreme Court of the United States heard and decided *New York Times v. Sullivan* and radically transformed the American law of libel. The Court ruled that public officials wishing to prevail in a libel action concerning the publication of statements about their official conduct have the burden of proving that defamatory material was published with "actual malice," a term of art the Court appropriated from the common law and transformed into a constitutional standard: knowledge of falsity or reckless disregard for the truth.[16] The case was landmark in addressing a serious free speech issue: the fact that, as in Alabama, some state governments were using libel law to silence criticism of government—and thus trampling on the long-established First Amendment principle of free public debate.[17] With its decision in *New York Times v. Sullivan*, the Supreme Court substantially extended First Amendment protection for those writing, publishing, and speaking about public officials.[18]

In constitutionalizing libel law with the creation of the actual malice standard, the Court articulated what has become a socially dominant First Amendment theory of the freedom of expression. "We consider this case," Justice William Brennan wrote, "against the background of a profound national commitment to the principle that debate on public issues should be uninhibited, robust, and wide-open."[19] The First Amendment's fundamental role, the Court suggested, is to further and protect that "robust" debate necessary in a well-functioning democracy, where the citizens are responsible for holding the government to high standards of behavior. Not surprisingly, *Sullivan* has been American journalism's sweetheart since 1964. It provided a constitutional rationale for the existence, operation, and protection of the American press: the press, as the primary vehicle for public discourse in the United States, was indispensable to the operation and sustenance of American democracy. While the press had trumpeted this role for itself long before *Sullivan*, it was now sanctioned and sanctified as constitutional doctrine.

A Brief History of the First Amendment

The First Amendment theory that emerged in *Sullivan* did not spring Athena-like, fully formed, from Justice Brennan's pen. Rather, it had been brewing both in the exercise of public life and among the intellectual elite for more than a century. According to the libel historian Norman Rosenberg, libertarian free expression theory and practice emerged in the early nineteenth century, representing "a democratization of political communication."[20] Of course, many groups were disenfranchised from this communication—slaves in the South, African Americans in the North, women, and employees in the workplace—but given the limited cultural terms of democratic participation available in this historical moment, it was a much more expansive conception than had existed before.[21] A new political culture, encouraged by the growth of the penny press and party newspapers, did in fact produce robust political debate. During the mid- to late nineteenth century, political libel law was vigorously debated, perhaps most profitably by Thomas Cooley, a professor at the University of Michigan Law School and member of the Michigan Supreme Court. Cooley argued against neo-Blackstonian defamation doctrines that insisted on strict liability for false political statements and for conditional privilege for public discussions of issues of public interest. More precisely, Cooley, along with other nineteenth-century theorists, believed "that a qualified privilege for false statements would encourage political debate without unduly sacrificing individual reputations or driving honest men from public life."[22] In this new political culture, criminal and civil libel suits largely disappeared.[23]

By the late nineteenth century, however, libel cases were again finding their way into the courts. What had changed? According to Rosenberg, the Pulitzer and Scripps style of popular journalism caused the courts to reformulate libel doctrine yet again. The party system fragmented, producing more fluid political alignments, and the party press disappeared. The prevailing social conflict, brought on by rapid industrialization in the antebellum period, was not between political parties but between the emerging populist movement and "a new political-corporate elite" who wanted to control and narrow political debate as a means of protecting the new economic order.[24] Rosenberg writes: "When relations between the new political and the new informational institutions could not be managed successfully or smoothed over in other forms, the legal system, including suits for political defamation, offered another means of continuing the political battle over what kinds of information could be disseminated and over how certain issues and personalities were to be discussed."[25] Instead of embracing Cooley's notions of qualified privilege, the courts turned to neo-Blackstonian doctrines insisting on "strict liability for political falsehoods."[26]

As Nancy Cohen demonstrates in her study of American liberalism in the Gilded Age, the political intellectuals of the era feared democratic majoritarianism in the new economic and social landscape and "invented a new liberalism that posited an active role for the state in society and economy, even as it justified constraints on democracy and the ascendancy of corporate capitalism."[27] The democratization of political speech that marked the early nineteenth century gave way before a more cramped notion of democracy. It was the birth of the administrative state which, until the middle of the twentieth century, increasingly displaced the participatory democracy of an earlier American liberalism.[28]

During this long, slow transformation of American political life, public intellectuals such as John Dewey and Walter Lippmann continued to debate the kind of democracy that the country needed.[29] And the idea of a more expansive right of free expression for the individual remained in the intellectual air, however suppressed it was in practice from the late nineteenth century through World War I. Legal scholars continued to discuss the meanings of free speech and the First Amendment in the American tradition.[30] Zechariah Chafee Jr., a professor at the Harvard Law School, wrote one of the most influential commentaries; titled "Freedom of Speech in War Time," it was published in 1919 in the *Harvard Law Review*.[31] As Anthony Lewis observes, "It may have been the best-timed law review article ever published."[32] In it, Chafee claimed that the framers of the First Amendment had meant "to wipe out the common law of sedition, and make further prosecutions for criticism of the government, without any incitement to law-breaking, forever impossible in the United States."[33] In his groundbreaking 1960 work *Legacy of Suppression*, revised and republished in 1985 as *Emergence of a Free Press*, Leonard Levy effectively challenged Chafee's claim, establishing that the historical record shows that the framers held essentially Blackstonian views about the First Amendment's meanings.[34] But Chafee's argument was persuasive, coming as it did just months after the Supreme Court had heard three Espionage Act cases in one month,[35] all unanimous opinions written by Justice Holmes upholding the various defendants' convictions under the act. Justice Holmes may have been even further influenced in the direction of Chafee's claim by his association and correspondence with federal trial judge Learned Hand, who had himself written an Espionage Act decision in 1917 in which he rejected the then-popular idea that hostile political attacks against the war were akin to treason.[36] Free speech, in Hand's formulation, is essential to democratic government. Speech with a "bad tendency" could not be punished, he asserted, only speech that directly invoked illegal action.[37] Because the people are sovereign in a democracy, a democratic government cannot punish the criticism of those to whom it is subordinate.[38]

In November 1919, the same year that saw the three notorious March Espionage Act cases and Chafee's law review article, the Supreme Court decided yet another Espionage Act case. But this time Justice Holmes wrote the dissent and in the process reformulated the meaning of the "clear and present danger" test he had articulated earlier that year in *Schenck v. United States*, which ironically produced the same judicial results as the "bad tendency" test it was meant to replace. In *Abrams v. United States*, Jacob Abrams, a Russian Jewish immigrant, and six others were charged with obstructing the American war with Germany.[39] They had printed leaflets criticizing U.S. policy in Russia and urging workers to strike in protest. The distribution of material the Court found to be seditious consisted largely of throwing the leaflets into the street from the window of a New York City building.[40] In *Abrams*, Holmes adopted a position very much like Hand's and Chafee's.[41] He argued that the government could not punish political criticism or the expression of beliefs unless the expression was likely to produce "immediate interference with the lawful and pressing purposes of the law [so] that an immediate check is required to save the country."[42] And the leaflets in the *Abrams* case, he believed, simply did not threaten such interference.

In *Abrams*, Holmes articulated a powerful theory of free expression in what has become one of the most oft-quoted passages in First Amendment scholarship. It is a theory inspired by the ideals of pragmatism that permeated Holmes's era, and it is a theory resurrected in *New York Times v. Sullivan*. Here one finds not only John Milton's concept of the marketplace of ideas but also the belief of John Dewey, Holmes's contemporary, that a fully robust democracy is the great American ideal. In his dissent Holmes declared:

> When men have realized that time has upset many fighting faiths, they may come to believe even more than they believe the very foundations of their own conduct that the ultimate good desired is better reached by free trade in ideas—that the best test of truth is the power of that thought to get itself accepted in the competition of the market, and that truth is the only ground upon which their wishes safely can be carried out. That at any rate is the theory of our Constitution. It is an experiment, as all life is an experiment. Every year if not every day we have to wager our salvation upon some prophecy based upon imperfect knowledge. While that experiment is part of our system I think that we should be eternally vigilant against attempts to check the expression of opinions that we loathe and believe to be fraught with death.[43]

Dewey, Holmes, and other pragmatists believed in the cultural contingency of knowledge and truth. For them, knowledge was never complete and truth never absolute—an insight that would find expression, though in somewhat different terms, in postmodernist thought some years later. Democracy was the solution to such contingency. As Louis Menand explains so well in *The Metaphysical Club*: "We do not (on Holmes's reasoning) permit the free expression of ideas because some individual may have the right one. We permit free expression because we need the resources of the whole group to get us the ideas we need. Thinking is a social activity. I tolerate your thought because it is a part of my thought—even when my thought defines itself in opposition to yours."[44] It is, then, in this moment of the early twentieth century—in the chambers of the U.S. Supreme Court, in the pragmatist philosophy of public intellectuals, in the ever-diminishing terrain for public participation in American democracy—that we find the seeds of *Sullivan* and its progeny.

The development of First Amendment doctrine in the early to mid-twentieth century did not stop with the *Abrams* decision. In 1925 the Supreme Court incorporated the First Amendment into the due process clause of the Fourteenth Amendment, thereby applying the free expression clause to the states, in *Gitlow v. New York*.[45] Six years later, in *Near v. Minnesota*,[46] the Court found that prior restraints on publication are presumed unconstitutional under the free expression provision of the First Amendment. And there were other important decisions. One of these was *Whitney v. California*, in which a woman named Anita Whitney, a member of a prominent California family, was convicted for violating the California Criminal Syndicalism Act for her involvement in the founding of the Communist Labor Party of California.[47] It took a number of years for the case to make its way to the Supreme Court, and when it did the Court ruled unanimously in 1927 to uphold Whitney's conviction. But Justice Louis D. Brandeis wrote a concurrence in the case, joined by Justice Holmes, in which he expressed a constitutional rationale for free expression that animates the *Sullivan* decision at least as much as did Holmes's dissent in *Abrams*.[48] Had Whitney's lawyers actually raised a First Amendment claim, the two justices may well have joined in dissent. But Brandeis took the opportunity in his *Whitney* concurrence to discuss, as legal scholar Bradley Bobertz has put it, "Whitney's free speech claim—a claim she had never herself asserted."[49]

The central point Brandeis made in asserting Whitney's right to free expression, Anthony Lewis has noted, was the indispensible role of "civic courage" in American democracy and the concomitant need to reject "fear as the basis for political action."[50] He also underscored the importance of free expression in the American people's exercise of their democratic duties:

Those who won our independence believed that the final end of the State was to make men free to develop their faculties; and that in its government the deliberative forces should prevail over the arbitrary. . . . They believed that freedom to think as you will and to speak as you think are means indispensable to the discovery and spread of political truth; that without free speech and assembly discussion would be futile; that with them, discussion affords ordinarily adequate protection against the dissemination of noxious doctrine; that the greatest menace to freedom is an inert people; that public discussion is a political duty; and that this should be a fundamental principle of the American government. . . . Believing in the power of reason as applied through public discussion, they eschewed silence coerced by law—the argument of force in its worst form. Recognizing the occasional tyrannies of governing majorities, they amended the Constitution so that free speech and assembly should be guaranteed.[51]

As the First Amendment scholar Vincent Blasi noted, Justice Brennan introduced his own famous articulation of the meaning of the First Amendment in the *Sullivan* decision with the Brandesian statement quoted above.[52]

The spirit and theory of Holmes's *Abrams* dissent and of Brandeis's *Whitney* concurrence set the tone and provided the language for *Sullivan*'s last-word repudiation of seditious libel, extension of First Amendment protection even to false political criticism, and articulation of a modern theory of the role of the press and free expression in democracy. In these compelling arguments for the First Amendment protection of political expression, Holmes and Brandeis staked their claim to the soil of American liberalism on which Dewey stood. It was a liberalism that spoke for the central role of free expression in a robust, public-centered democracy, and even though its implications for the development of American government were neglected as the nation increasingly grew into an administered democracy under the guidance of a different sort of liberalism, it managed to bequeath, as Menand has suggested, a lasting gift to the country: the First Amendment law of free expression.[53]

For Holmes and the other pragmatists of his day, Menand writes, "ideas are not 'out there' waiting to be discovered, but are tools—like forks and knives and microchips—that people devise to cope with the world in which they find themselves."[54] Holmes's reasoning in *Abrams* rests on this basic pragmatist assumption. Ideas are tools and are thus constantly changing to suit the work that needs to be done in any cultural moment. Sometimes a hoe is all that is needed, other times a pickaxe. When Police Commissioner Sullivan sued the *New York Times* for libel in an attempt to silence criticism of racial injustice in the South, the Supreme Court needed a new tool to stop the invidious use of state libel law to protect Jim Crow. The new tool was an idea about the meaning of the First Amendment and American democracy that liberal pragmatist philosophers and legal scholars had developed in the early decades of the century.

The Lippmann-Dewey Debate:
Democracy and Its Discontents

America's halting journey toward fulfilling the First Amendment's promise follows the rugged contours of the developing liberal state. During the course of this journey, liberal intellectuals and politicians hammered out the meaning of American democracy, trying to reconcile the relationship between the country's commitment to liberal values—freedom, self-government, due process—with the new economic order born in the late nineteenth century. Clashes between labor and producers on one side and corporatists on the other, as well as the attendant liberal loss of faith in the rational capacities of immigrants and of African Americans, many of whom were newly freed slaves, to govern well pointed to a basic conflict between the values of democracy and capitalism. In negotiating this conflict, liberals of the era compromised what had previously been liberalism's bedrock commitment to expanding participatory democracy through the political franchise and suffrage. As Cohen demonstrates in her revisionist history of liberalism in the Gilded Age, the liberal solution to the conflict lay in administrative government, which removed political power from the masses and insulated the growth and power of capitalism.[55] It was the death knell for a more participatory, a more liberal democracy in the United States—and the death went unmourned except by a notable few.

The twentieth century thus inherited a constricted liberalism, and in few arenas of public life were its constrictions more visible, at least to the present-day historian, than in law. In the terms of this liberalism, personal freedoms amounted primarily to the right to contract and to own personal property—the rights most at risk in the conciliation of liberal democracy with capitalism. The Fourteenth Amendment, added to the Bill of Rights in 1868, was an attempt to remove power from the states and place it in the hands of the federal government, particularly the power to safeguard individual liberties as articulated in the due process clause: no state had the right to deprive an individual of life, liberty, or property without due process of law.[56] But a fundamental question remained for the nation to answer: What is the nature of liberty? In 1905 the Supreme Court and the government found the primary liberty safeguarded in the Fourteenth Amendment to be liberty of contract, which was constitutionalized in *Lochner v. New York*.[57] This primacy of the idea of property in conceptions of liberty, traceable to John Locke's seventeenth-century writings, considered along with the string of Supreme Court cases upholding convictions for seditious libel in the post–World War I years, illuminates a nation that had not yet discovered the meanings of liberty understood today to be protected by the First Amendment. It was also a nation still crafting the content of its democratic political system and ideology, and in the years following *Lochner*, public intellectuals and social critics actively debated the form American democracy was to take. The outcome of this debate would have profound consequences for the development of a modern First Amendment theory and jurisprudence as well as an accompanying theory as to the role of the press.

Although the conversation about the proper shape of American liberalism was widespread, one can look to the dialogue between Walter Lippmann and John Dewey, which took place primarily in the 1920s, as representative of two dominant and competing strains of thought in the conversation. Lippmann's way of thinking proved to be either the more prophetic or the more persuasive, depending on the weight one wishes to ascribe to the influence of social theory on the development of political and social systems. Either way, Lippmann's notion of an administered democracy as a solution to the problem of a public ill educated for the demands of self-government ultimately came to define twentieth-century liberalism in America, although not easily or inevitably. Dewey's notion of a fully participatory democracy, with the public educated in the ways of social science, rational thought, and civic engagement, eventually fell by the wayside of history.

Lippmann began his career as a social and political theorist in earnest when he became an editor in 1913 for the *New Republic*, a newly founded magazine under the intellectual leadership of Herbert Croly. In his early work for the magazine, and in his book *Drift and Mastery*, Lippmann espoused a pragmatist faith in socialized democracy, a political system wedded to faith in the scientific method and public educability, a Deweyan vision of the rightful inheritance of American liberalism.[58] It was during these years that Lippmann first espoused objectivity as a workable quasi-scientific method for journalists to follow in gathering information and compiling it in news reports. Objectivity would provide, he suggested, a much-needed antidote to the misinformation of government and institutional propaganda that had been plaguing the press.[59] But by the early 1920s Lippmann's wartime experience working as a propagandist for the U.S. government caused him to doubt seriously the ability of the masses to act rationally. Massive U.S. government propaganda campaigns on the domestic front, aimed at snuffing out antiwar sentiment and controlling activities of presumably radical groups, had been largely successful in quashing dissent. This success suggested to postwar observers, including Lippmann, that the masses were alarmingly susceptible to propaganda's power.[60] Although this was a problem that could be remedied in part by the creation of a more responsible press dedicated to using a scientific, objective method to produce the news, it was a problem that also implicated the reader of the news, as Lippmann biographer Ronald Steel has suggested.[61] For Lippmann, there could never be a rational public because there exists "between man and his environment . . . a pseudo-environment." And man acts in accordance not with the reality of his environment but with the fictions of his pseudo-environment.[62] Democracy is thus threatened by the wholly modern "problem which arises because the pictures inside people's heads do not automatically correspond with the world outside."[63] Lippmann's solution was to have political scientists organize "public opinions . . . for the press."[64]

Lippmann expressed these deep misgivings about the capacity of the public to act rationally and meaningfully in democratic concert in *Public Opinion*, his 1922 landmark critique of American democracy. In a *New Republic* review, Dewey called *Public Opinion* "perhaps the most effective indictment of democracy as currently conceived ever penned."[65] In it Lippmann repudiated his previous pragmatist faith in a broad and deep conception of American democracy.[66] His critique centered on what he found to be a profound misconception about the role of the press in the governance of the country and the ability of the masses to participate rationally, and thus effectively, in self-government. The machinery of information that constituted the press and produced public knowledge could not adequately capture and explain the problems and circumstances of modern American society. For Lippmann, the very idea that "a mystical force called Public Opinion" existed and possessed knowledge capable of monitoring and leading governmental institutions was a shibboleth.[67] The problem was that the press simply could not provide the kind of expert knowledge necessary for the creation of a public opinion sufficiently well informed to guide the governance of a large country with complex social and political problems. "[The press] has, at great moral cost to itself," Lippmann wrote, "encouraged a democracy, still bound to its original premises, to expect newspapers to supply spontaneously for every organ of government, for every social problem, the machinery of information which these do not normally supply themselves."[68]

Lippmann was particularly concerned with distinguishing between news and truth and suggested how rarely the two actually coincide:

> The hypothesis, which seems to me most fertile, is that news and truth are not the same thing, and must be clearly distinguished. The function of news is to signalize an event, the function of truth is to bring to light the hidden facts, to set them into relation with each other, and make a picture of reality on which men can act. Only at those points, where social conditions take recognizable and measurable shape, do the body of truth and the body of news coincide. That is a comparatively small part of the whole field of human interest.[69]

Most news, Lippmann argued, was simply a record of events, sometimes not even an accurate record, and not the sense-making expression necessary for the illumination of truth. The press was the carrier of news, not necessarily the carrier of the truth, and the problem with the news was the partial nature of the knowledge it provided. Lippmann's conception of the role the news could play in informing the public was made even bleaker by his deep anxieties about the human capacity for intelligible communication. As the communication historian John Durham Peters has put it, "Lippmann's conception of language is motivated by a horror of its imperfections and a desire for the exact transmission of meaning."[70] This desire led him to trust more in the rule of experts, who could presumably be counted on to use language objectively and communicate meaning clearly, than in the rule of the masses, who presumably could not be.

Lippmann directly challenged what was then and has remained the self-assumed role of the American press as the nation's guardian and vehicle of self-governance. The press, he argued, "has come to be regarded as an organ of direct democracy, charged on a much wider scale, and from day to day, with the function often attributed to the initiative, referendum, and recall. The Court of Public Opinion, open day and night, is to lay down the law for everything all the time. It is not workable."[71] Wise and workable government required not the public-centered democracy envisioned by the founders and First Amendment theory and press theory, Lippmann suggested, but rather the rule of experts and politicians. Institutions peopled with experts who record and analyze the complex workings of the modern polity (through social science methods) were the means to the knowledge necessary for good government. These experts would illuminate the world of knowledge for the press while at the same time acting as a check on press abuse.[72]

Lippmann's understanding of the role of the press in democracy is at odds with the First Amendment theory later articulated in *Sullivan*. The press was not capable, according to Lippmann, of providing the kind of knowledge necessary for a robust, public-centered democracy, and he had little faith in the intellectual ability of the masses to govern well. Instead he advocated democratic realism—government by the elite, not the masses.[73] Lippmann is well known not just for his social responsibility theory of the press but for placing the value of social responsibility above that of the First Amendment.[74] What Lippmann seems not to have considered is that his experts might be no more capable of making sense of the world than the public he so disparaged.

Lippmann's vision of an administrative government and limited democracy nevertheless carried the day in modern U.S. history. The story of American government since the 1920s has been largely that of an ever-expanding state and an ever-diminishing democracy. But this story might have had a substantially different plot had another path been taken in the early years of the century, when it was still visible and viable. As one of America's most influential twentieth-century philosophers, John Dewey believed that democracy and freedom are synonymous, that self-realization resides in the individual's full participation, through intelligent judgment and action, in society and its governance. He believed that democracy is America's great experiment and that all citizens must actively participate in guiding public affairs. He believed, in short, that if America was to be a free society, its government must be a fully participatory democracy. And he believed, as Peters suggests, that "communication is the problem of getting people to be full, participatory members in the public life of a community."[75] Dewey's was the road not taken. In *John Dewey and American Democracy*, Robert B. Westbrook defines contemporary liberalism as both a repudiation of Deweyan ideals and a complete capitulation to democratic realism, a politics that narrowly defines democracy as "little more than an ex post facto check on the power of elites, an act of occasional political consumption affording a choice among a limited range of well-packaged aspirants to office."[76]

Dewey engaged, critiqued, and rebutted many of Lippman's arguments, although it is important to note that in many respects he agreed with Lippmann's current assessment of the irrationality of the public, the attendant problems for self-government, and the value of social science and government experts in the creation of knowledge. As noted earlier, Lippmann's early thinking owed much to Dewey, and both published in the pages of the *New Republic*. The primary difference between them lay in their wholly divergent solutions to the problem of democracy, communication, and the people: while Lippmann turned away from the public to elites and experts, Dewey turned toward the public. As the communication scholar Carl Bybee puts it, in the uncertain years following the First World War, when democracy seemed threatened from every corner, "Lippmann's blend of liberalism and elitism became more pronounced and Dewey's commitment to participatory democracy deepened."[77]

In *The Public and Its Problems*, his 1927 response to Lippmann's *Public Opinion*, Dewey argued that the public community which Lippmann so disparaged was still in the process of developing and that then-current vehicles for delivering information were inadequate in educating the public for its necessary role in democratic self-governance.[78] What is more, he wrote, the elites and experts whom Lippmann would have govern were no less prone to irrationality, self-interest, and corruption than the public at large: "No government by experts in which the masses do not have the chance to inform the experts as to their needs can be anything but an oligarchy managed in the interests of the few. . . . The world has suffered more from leaders and authorities than from the masses."[79]

The problem with the public, Dewey suggested, was the insufficient "methods and conditions of debate, discussion and persuasion," which in large part stemmed from the inability of the press to present compellingly the knowledge being produced by the new social sciences.[80] An informed public opinion could not be achieved without general access to this powerful knowledge, which was too often relegated to "secluded library alcoves," where it was "studied and understood only by a few intellectuals."[81] The knowledge generated by social science research—the knowledge needed to address the social and political issues of the day—must be presented not in the "technical high-brow" prose of academic journals but in a form that would have "a direct popular appeal," said Dewey.[82] Newspapers must allow for art, "so that an organized, articulate Public comes into being."[83]

Dewey was basically arguing for a kind of journalism other than the objectivist style of factual presentation that dominated the news of his day:

> The freeing of the artist in literary presentation . . . is as much a precondition of the desirable creation of adequate opinion on public matters as is the freeing of social inquiry. Men's conscious life of opinion and judgment often proceeds on a superficial and trivial plane. But their lives reach a deeper level. The function of art has always been to break through the crust of conventionalized and routine consciousness. Common things, a flower, a gleam of moonlight, the song of a bird, not things rare and remote, are means with which the deeper levels of life are touched so that they spring up as desire and thought. This process is art.[84]

He was suggesting that news must be interpretive if it is to convey real, usable knowledge and that it must reach beyond society's conventional values and understandings if it is to encourage new insights and solutions. News should do more than record the occurrence of events. It must make meaning of them. "The highest and most difficult kind of inquiry and a subtle, delicate, vivid and responsive art of communication must take possession of the physical machinery of transmission and circulation and breathe life into it," he wrote. "When the machine age has thus perfected its machinery it will be a means of life and not its despotic master. Democracy will come into its own, for democracy is a name for a life of free and enriching communion."[85] For Dewey, the objective journalism espoused by Lippmann, and informed by Lippmann's experts, was simply not capable by itself of making adequate sense of the world and bringing about a full-bodied democracy and the freedom such a democracy promised. What was needed was a kind of artistic journalism, interpretive and subjective in nature, to help bring into being "an organized, articulate Public."[86] As John Durham Peters suggests, "The fundamental dividing line between Dewey and Lippmann was their attitude toward democracy: Dewey thought that education, art, and science—the creation of intelligence—could make it possible; Lippmann thought that democracy at best could be improved by providing the public with objective facts about the outside world. Dewey wanted to improve people's lives and discourse; Lippmann wanted to improve their data-base."[87]

What underlay Lippmann's and Dewey's differing conceptions of American

democracy, and the role of the press in helping democracy reach its full potential as a political and social system, were fundamentally incompatible conceptions of human freedom, particularly in the realm of public expression.
Lippmann understood freedom to inhere in the public's access to accurate information—to facts as opposed to fallible opinion often disconnected from
the reality of actual human events and conditions. "Liberty is the name we give
to measures by which we protect and increase the veracity of the information
upon which we act," he wrote.[88] He even went so far as to suggest that all news
articles "should be documented, and false documentation should be illegal." [89]
For Lippmann, then, freedom was contingent on the availability of accurate information about the world, an information consisting not of opinions but of
facts about "objective reality." For liberty, he argued, "is not so much permission as it is the construction of a system of information increasingly independent of opinion." [90]

Dewey shared Lippmann's concern about the problem of misinformation
and its deleterious effect on the shaping of public opinion and thus public affairs. He also shared Lippmann's conviction that a more scientific method of
social inquiry was necessary to uncover more trustworthy information on
which to base social and political decision making. But he did not share Lippmann's somewhat facile categorization of expression as either opinion or fact
or his conception of human freedom as primarily contingent on factual
knowledge of the world. He did not, in other words, entirely agree with Lippmann's solution to the problem of misrepresentation that characterized too
much of the news of their day. Rather than emphasizing merely the role of accurate factual information in freeing people from the distortions of "publicity"
in public communication, Dewey stressed the role of conversation, of open
and unfettered public discussion of the concerns of the day. For Dewey, the answer to the problem had less to do with the uncovering of "facts" than with en-
suring that expression was free. "Without freedom of expression," he wrote,
"not even methods of social inquiry can be developed. For tools can be evolved
and perfected only in operation; in application to observing, reporting and organizing actual subject-matter; and this application cannot occur save through
free and systematic communication." [91] When freedom of expression was realized, then, the public could form experimental beliefs and ideas based on
knowledge produced by social inquiry, and could act on those beliefs. Such a
communal process was, for Dewey, the very meaning of democracy. Central to
Dewey's understanding of freedom of expression was the realization that social

beliefs and ideas are always contingent, created in response to present conditions and knowledge. For Dewey the pragmatist, there were no such things as "absolute standards" and "eternal truths."[92] Truth was what was discovered and agreed upon through the process of free social discussion—and was necessarily changeable. In Dewey's view, each generation must necessarily arrive at its own truths, and the only means by which such truths could be had was through free expression.

First Amendment Theory in *Sullivan*: A Vision of Democracy and the Press

Of the two theories of democracy articulated in the Lippmann-Dewey debate, Dewey's idea of a fully participatory democracy has most fully animated modern First Amendment theory and jurisprudence. Several decades before Justice William Brennan wrote in the *Sullivan* decision the Court's fullest theoretical justification yet of press freedom, the philosopher Alexander Meiklejohn was formulating and articulating his groundbreaking theory of the First Amendment in law review articles and books.[93] Although his interpretation of the First Amendment's meaning is sometimes deemed absolutist,[94] Meiklejohn meant to offer constitutional protection not to all speech but to any speech relating to a citizen's responsibility and capacity for self-governance. What Meiklejohn understood as absolute and inviolate was not so much an individual's right to speak but rather, as Norman Rosenberg has suggested, "the system of democratic self-government to which the First Amendment was inextricably tied."[95] Free speech was simply a necessary corollary to self-government.

Meiklejohn did not believe in judicial neutrality; indeed, he believed that judges were fallible and thus should not be trusted with regulating the political speech necessary in a well-functioning democracy.[96] But Meiklejohn *did* believe in the hierarchical ordering of speech in law, and this ordering was foundational to the exclusive value he placed on the role of self-governance in the protection of free speech. Meiklejohn argued that, under the First Amendment, political speech could never be regulated or abridged by government.[97] In other words, the First Amendment absolutely protected political speech. But nonpolitical speech, Meiklejohn suggested, was protected not by the First Amendment but rather by the due process clause of the Fifth Amendment, which permits the restriction of nonpolitical speech as long as due process is met.[98] This assumption that a bright line can be drawn between political and nonpolitical speech was roundly attacked by other scholars, and Meiklejohn, apparently deciding that his critics had a point, later expanded his notion of speech qualifying as political (and thus deserving of protection) to include most forms of public expression.[99]

Meiklejohn was an idealist, and he wrote his First Amendment theory as a response to what he understood to be the peril of Oliver Wendell Holmes's clear and present danger test to free expression in America.[100] Meiklejohn hated the clear and present danger test, and it is easy to see why. As applied in *Schenck v. United States*, the first of the infamous Espionage and Sedition Act cases before the Supreme Court in 1919, the clear and present danger test did little more than the previous bad tendency test to protect speech. The Supreme Court upheld the anarchist Charles Schenck's conviction for conspiracy to obstruct military recruitment and cause insubordination in military forces. Despite his formulation of the clear and present danger test, Holmes had yet to discover the meaning of the First Amendment for which he became famous. In a matter of months, however, Holmes wrote his first opinion that was truly protective of free speech, in *Abrams v. United States*. But this time he was writing the dissenting opinion and attempting to guide the Court in its application of the clear and present danger test. Many scholars have located the birth of modern First Amendment theory and jurisprudence in Holmes's *Abrams* dissent.[101] Meiklejohn viewed things differently.

In *Free Speech and Its Relation to Self-Government*, Meiklejohn excoriated Holmes for what he saw as the dangerous individualism and skepticism of his thinking in his *Abrams* dissent. Meiklejohn read the dissent as emphasizing an individualist concept of free speech that overvalued the individual's contribution to the marketplace of ideas and the fierce competition in the market among individual contributions. Meiklejohn argued that Holmes's conception of truth-finding "had made intellectual freedom indistinguishable from intellectual license."[102] He suggested, too, that Holmes placed too much importance on the value of truth to the project of self-governance. More important than discovering truth, he claimed, is the First Amendment's role in "the sharing of whatever truth has been won."[103] And for Meiklejohn, it was not important that everyone be allowed to speak. "What is essential," he wrote, "is . . . that everything worth saying shall be said."[104] Meiklejohn thus was finally concerned with protecting the quality of public discourse (which perhaps encouraged subsequent First Amendment theorists to identify, order, and prioritize the worth of different kinds of speech, even the worth of different kinds of political statements).[105] And he took a decidedly collectivist approach in his theory.[106] The role of the First Amendment, based in the value of self-government, was to discover through rational public discourse of high quality the general, collective good.

Although historical orthodoxy follows Meiklejohn in finding the marketplace of ideas theory to be the foundation of Holmes's *Abrams* dissent, history may well have been distorted through Meiklejohn's influential work. Although Meiklejohn and Holmes were contemporaries, they stood on either side of a philosophical divide common in the early twentieth century. Meiklejohn was an idealist who believed in absolute principles, whereas Holmes was a pragmatist (although he did not classify himself in this way), skeptical that foundational principles and absolutes existed. Truth and principle were, Holmes believed along with the formal philosophers of pragmatism, socially constructed and always in flux in the great experiment of living.[107] Through his book *The Common Law* and his influential essay "The Path of the Law,"[108] Holmes anticipated legal realism, which called into question the traditional understanding that principle is the foundation of law, that law is a kind of science, and that there is a neutral hierarchy and order in law.[109] So what Meiklejohn saw in Holmes's *Abrams* dissent was a mind philosophically at odds with his own. Even though Holmes had come around in *Abrams* to protecting free expression and to setting the outer boundaries of free speech at the moment before it actually incites violence against the government or disruption of the peace, Meiklejohn still found in Holmes's dissent a dangerous upholding of individual expression over an emphasis on the collective good which Meiklejohn believed the self-governance value of the First Amendment demanded. To read the *Abrams* dissent in this way, however, is to read it ahistorically. As Louis Menand has carefully argued, Holmes and his fellow pragmatists (including John Dewey) believed that "coercion is natural" in human affairs and that "freedoms are socially engineered spaces" that give room to individual expression and liberty.[110] When Holmes wrote in his dissent that it was natural for men who believed in the correctness of their premises and their power to sweep away all opposition through law, he was acknowledging a conception of freedom that departed from Meiklejohn's natural rights philosophy. And when he wrote that "when men have realized that time has upset many fighting faiths, they may come to believe even more than they believe the very foundations of their own conduct that the ultimate good desired is better reached by free trade in ideas," he was suggesting that immutable principle could not be counted on to be the foundation for law or to guide the affairs of men.[111] (As Menand suggests, Holmes's Civil War experience taught him to be skeptical of principle as a justification for the use of violence and force.)[112] Meiklejohn found this rejection of principle offensive.

And contrary to what Meiklejohn and other legal scholars have seen as an individualistic bent to Holmes's notion of the marketplace of ideas, Holmes suggested in his dissent that law and human action should be based on a collective notion of what truth is, however partial and contingent a discovered truth may be. "The best test of truth," he wrote, "is the power of that thought to get itself accepted in the competition of the market."[113] He did not imply that one person's truth was somehow going to emerge victorious in the competition; in fact, pragmatic philosophy, which permeated the intellectual air he breathed, opposed this notion. Rather, the more people who contributed their ideas to the marketplace, the more likely some amalgam approximating truth was to emerge. Legal scholar Robert Post makes a similar point: "In *Abrams* Holmes explicitly oriented his theory of the First Amendment toward the value of truth, which he linked to the concept of 'experiment.' This strongly suggests that the *Abrams* dissent is best understood as an expression of American pragmatic epistemology, with which Holmes was very familiar."[114] From a contemporary perspective, it is unfortunate that Holmes chose the metaphor of the market when the more precise word may have been "democracy." For it is democracy about which he seems to be writing rather than a literal market. "That at any rate is the theory of our Constitution," Holmes wrote. "It is an experiment, as all life is an experiment. . . . While that experiment is part of our system I think that we should be eternally vigilant against attempts to check the expression of opinions that we loathe and believe to be fraught with death."[115] This theory Holmes invokes is not a theory of the marketplace, although that is apparently what most legal historians have chosen to take from his *Abrams* dissent. It is the theory of democratic experiment, the theory of self-governance that so consumed Meiklejohn's thought on the meaning of the First Amendment. The distance between Meiklejohn and Holmes was not so great as subsequent scholars, and Meiklejohn himself, have imagined.

Although *Sullivan* did not offer the full protection for political speech that Meiklejohn advocated, his theory of the central meaning of the First Amendment animates Justice Brennan's *Sullivan* opinion and its justification of press protections. At the heart of the theory is a conception of democracy and freedom animated by a faith in civic participation that Meiklejohn shared with Oliver Wendell Holmes, despite Meiklejohn's protests to the contrary. The main difference between the two thinkers was their differing conceptions of truth in public discourse. Meiklejohn assumed that immutable, noncontingent truth exists in the world of human affairs and is ascertainable through public debate. But it was Holmes's conception of truth, not Meiklejohn's, that animated *Sullivan*: truth is contingent, constructed, multiple, and always in the process of being reborn. To whatever extent press expression could access and deliver truth about events and issues deemed politically and socially relevant, *Sullivan* suggested that that expression should be protected.

If there is any widely agreed upon principle in modern American political philosophy, it is that democratic government is the political ideal. John Dewey's pragmatism, which viewed democracy as the only ethical ideal, begins and ends with this notion.[116] The thinking of Dewey and Meiklejohn and Holmes and Brandeis permeated the *Sullivan* decision, which inextricably linked First Amendment theory and democratic theory in viewing press freedom as necessary to a robust democracy. It must be acknowledged, however, that the modern American experience of democracy is not the participatory democracy that Dewey in particular advocated. This disconnect between the vision of democracy articulated in *New York Times v. Sullivan* and the realist democracy at work in America—a democracy in which citizens participate in democratic decision making merely by voting government officials into and out of power—may have contributed to what some view as the Supreme Court's diminishing enthusiasm for press freedom in libel doctrine. It is exactly this diminishment that legal scholar Lee C. Bollinger has identified as the essential problem of the Supreme Court's decision in *Masson v. New Yorker.*[117]

In *Masson*, the Supreme Court rejected the lower federal courts' use of the "rational interpretation test" in determining whether allegedly defamatory altered quotations are actionable in a libel claim or whether they receive constitutional protection. The "rational interpretation test" offered protection to altered quotations as long as they were *rational* interpretations of what the plaintiff actually said.[118] In rejecting this test, the Court said that constitutional protection for the rational interpretation of a speaker's actual words would "diminish to a great degree the trustworthiness of the printed word, and eliminate the real meaning of quotations."[119] The problem, as the Court saw it, was that such protection "would give journalists the freedom to place statements in their subjects' mouths without fear of liability." [120] As Bollinger has argued, the *Masson* Court was articulating an idea about the meaning of free expression at odds with *Sullivan*'s vision. In *Masson*, "the Court refuses to extend First Amendment protection to speech because in its view to do so would undermine the *character and quality of public discourse*." [121] This constitutional concern with protecting the quality of public discourse was not expressed in the *Sullivan* decision. [122]

What, then, counts as public discourse in the realm of expression protected by the First Amendment? Does speech about a public figure involved in intellectual and social intrigues in the psychoanalytic community count? The answer provided by First Amendment jurisprudence, as it has developed from *Sullivan* to *Masson*, is a resounding yes. The *Sullivan* decision was concerned, of course, with allegedly defamatory speech about a public official, not a public figure. The *Sullivan* Court even declined to define who would qualify as a public official. [123] But as the *Sullivan* case line developed, and as the Court extended constitutional protection to speech about public officials and public figures, it became clear that constitutional protections covered any speech about "public" people. In *Sullivan* the Court famously wrote, "We consider this case against the background of a profound national commitment to the principle that debate on public issues should be uninhibited, robust, and wide-open." [124] This constitutionally protected "debate on public issues"—what Bollinger called "public discourse"—has come to encompass a very wide range of speech indeed. The *Sullivan* idea is that truth—whatever truth is to be had in human affairs—can be discovered only in the give-and-take of public discussion and community conversation. Self-governing citizens must have knowledge of this truth, as contingent as it may be, so they can act accordingly in all areas of public and private life.

The *Sullivan* notion of what constitutes truth in public discourse is much more complicated than is commonly recognized. Not only did the Court in *Sullivan* distinguish between factual statements, which are susceptible to a determination of truth or falsity, and ideas and beliefs and opinions, which are not, but it also determined that in many cases factual error should receive constitutional protection. "Erroneous statement is inevitable in free debate," Justice Brennan wrote, "and . . . it must be protected if the freedoms of expression are to have the 'breathing space' that they 'need . . . to survive.'" [125] In its articulation of the actual malice standard—that false and defamatory factual statements receive constitutional protection unless they are published with knowledge of falsity or reckless disregard for the truth—the Court established that not all falsehoods are created constitutionally equal.[126] Only those defamatory falsehoods published with a certain degree of intentionality or awareness may be considered libelous. In determining that only false and defamatory *factual* statements are actionable in libel suits, the Court acknowledged that in many arenas of human endeavor, truth is so closely tied to perspective or ambiguous contexts that it is not even discoverable. "The tenets of one man may seem the rankest error to his neighbor," the Court wrote in making the point.[127] In such instances, the notion of judicial truth could have no meaning. In making such a bright-line distinction between factual expression that was in certain cases beyond constitutional protection and nonfactual expression (such as ideas, beliefs, and opinions) that received constitutional protection, the *Sullivan* Court was engaging, if only implicitly, in a debate about the nature of truth that in the coming years became *the* central concern in the oftentimes heated intellectual dispute between objectivist and postmodern scholars. Was it always possible to distinguish between factual and nonfactual expression? And how could one determine the truth of a statement that was not clearly factual? In the years ahead, the Supreme Court would find itself wrangling, again and again, with such difficult problems.

This tension between objectivist and postmodern knowledge claims and related conceptions of truth permeated the Masson-Malcolm dispute over the alleged falsity of altered quotations. In *Masson*, the Court was forced to determine how the First Amendment should deal with speech that takes the form of defamatory quotations altered in some fashion by a journalist and attributed to a public figure. Was this a kind of public discourse deserving of constitutional protection? Yes, the Court determined, but only if the alteration did not effect a material change in the speaker's meaning.[128] Masson's was the voice of the objectivist, an inheritor of a Lippmannian notion of objective journalism and a Lippmannian belief that to protect the quality of public discourse was to safeguard human liberty. Although it would be going too far to suggest that Malcolm and the *New Yorker* were postmodernists, their position on the permissibility of altering a speaker's actual utterances so as to render better the truth of the speaker's meaning is a position dependent on postmodern conceptions of truth and language. Their understanding of what journalism needed to be—artful communication that relays the meaning, not simply the facts, of human events—was an inheritance from Dewey, as was their sense of the sometimes constructed nature of truth. While Lippmann (and Masson) suggested that one should protect the quality of public discourse so as to enable human freedom, Dewey (and Malcolm and the *New Yorker*) suggested that one should protect the freedom of public discourse so as to enable communities to arrive at truths (even contingent truths) on which to base their decisions and beliefs. In the end, the Supreme Court found Masson's position more persuasive.

CHAPTER FOUR

———— ✣ ————

Libel at the *New Yorker*

IN THE HISTORY OF AMERICAN JOURNALISM, THE POWER OF LIBEL LAW TO chill press expression has been a notable constant in a sea of change. In the late nineteenth century, at the very moment the press began to professionalize, libel suits against the press began to proliferate. Appellate courts, in turn, increasingly supported plaintiffs. As a result, newspapers came to see libel law as a substantive threat to their freedom and financial stability.[1] As early as the 1890s, large newspapers in the United States began hiring their own lawyers to review copy for possible defamation and to consult on various legal issues, particularly libel threats and claims.[2] These newspapers had begun to self-censor, and no wonder. Before the landmark 1964 U.S. Supreme Court decision in *New York Times v. Sullivan*,[3] which pulled libel law into the constitutional penumbra, the law often operated in a strict-liability regime. Libel law was the province of the separate states, and in many courts, defendants bore the burden of proving the truth of their contested statements.[4] There was no First Amendment protection for defamation. To escape liability, defendants in libel suits generally had to prove the truth of the allegedly defamatory and false publication—an often difficult enterprise.[5] In other words, falsity and fault were presumed. (After *Sullivan* and several key cases extending its ruling, public and private plaintiffs had to prove both falsity and fault to prevail—a high constitutional barrier to a successful libel suit.)[6]

As libel historian Norman Rosenberg has demonstrated, libel law from 1920 to the late 1950s, though draconian in form and theoretically threatening to press freedom, "rarely loomed as a major threat to most publishers."[7] With the advent of World War I, Rosenberg argues, a national surveillance state emerged, and with it new tools for controlling press expression, such as government censorship, the Espionage and Sedition Acts, and prior restraints.[8] Libel law was no longer the weapon of choice, at least in cases involving political speech. Until the *Sullivan* case in the early 1960s, for example, the *New York Times* did not encounter a serious libel threat.[9] Nevertheless, the experiences of the late nineteenth century had taught the press to be vigilant against the potential dangers posed by libel law. By the 1920s, more newspapers than ever before were hiring in-house counsel to read for libel; some even purchased libel insurance.[10] Libel law did not again emerge as a major threat until the late 1950s and early 1960s, when television and print news began to cover social problems aggressively and southern politicians and courts began to wield the law as a blunt weapon against civil rights activists' use of the mass media. (The *Sullivan* case was the ultimate resolution of this appropriation of libel law to silence the press.)[11] But the press of the 1920s and 1930s did not have the clarity of historical hindsight. It had already learned that libel law was a sleeping dragon—and it took that dragon seriously.

Legal and historical scholars have thoroughly documented and analyzed the development of American libel law in the twentieth century.[12] Few if any studies, however, explore how particular publications responded to it across time. Libel threats, real and perceived, influenced editorial decision making and processes, press content, the use of a publication's resources, and finally the financial well-being of newspapers and magazines throughout the modern age. Libel law is thus one of many social forces that have historically exerted pressure on American journalism and shaped press expression and the institution of the press itself. The nature and effects of this force deserve further study.

The discussion in this chapter offers a partial understanding of the shaping force of libel law on the *New Yorker*, a magazine with a long-established presence in both American culture and American journalism. It examines libel complaints the *New Yorker* received in its first forty years of existence, from its inception in 1925 to the era of *Sullivan*, focusing on those most revealing of the editorial and legal strategies the magazine developed, in tandem with the respected law firm of Greenbaum, Wolff & Ernst, to manage libel threats. A small New York City law firm from 1915 to 1982, Greenbaum, Wolf & Ernst became known for handling famous literary and free expression cases, including the *Ulysses* censorship case and the Kinsey obscenity case.[13] The firm also served clients in the arts such as the actor Dustin Hoffman, the novelist Edna Ferber, and the Dramatists Guild, as well as media and publishing organizations such as the *New York Times,* the *New Yorker,* Harper & Row, and Random House.[14] Alexander Lindey, a lawyer at the firm who wrote several important legal books, including *Entertainment, Publishing, and the Arts,*[15] worked closely with *New Yorker* editors and in-house counsel to protect the magazine against libel claims.[16]

The editorial and legal strategies that the *New Yorker* and Lindey developed to handle libel threats evolved through the years in response to particular threats the magazine faced as well as the changing terrain of libel law in American society. These strategies thus developed piecemeal, in fits and starts, and while it is inappropriate to think of them as formal policies, they can be framed as general practices. In addition, some editorial processes served the dual purposes of protecting the *New Yorker* against libel threats and building its reputation as an icon of accurate journalism, although the latter was the primary goal. I do not mean to suggest that the magazine's editorial and legal strategies for warding off libel challenges were unique to the *New Yorker.* In fact, given Lindey's role in helping devise them, it is likely that these and similar strategies were used by other publications he and his partners counseled. How those other publications responded to libel law is a subject for future exploration, but this discussion begins to fill the knowledge gap.

In 1932, not many years after the *New Yorker* began publication, Alexander Lindey, along with his law partner Morris Ernst, published a book reviewing the then-current state of libel law in America, titled *Hold Your Tongue! Adventures in Libel and Slander.* This was also the year Greenbaum, Wolff & Ernst began representing the *New Yorker.* Unlike many scholars and legal experts of the day who were more sanguine about the power of libel law to regulate journalistic responsibility and accuracy, Lindey and Ernst perceived it as anathema to freedom of the press. "If, then, the hope of clean government and nonpredatory business lies in free speech, in speech without danger of legal reprisal, in the utterance of new ideas, the entire body of our law of libel awaits revision," they wrote. "For in the last analysis the mandate of that law is almost always, 'Hold your tongue,' or at least 'Mince your words.'"[17] Lindey would do all he could over the years to prevent the *New Yorker* from having to hold its tongue or mince its words. Substantive revision of the law did not come until *New York Times v. Sullivan* some thirty-two years later, but in those intervening decades the *New Yorker* held its own against libel law's threat to free expression.

The libel complaints and related sources cited in this book—memoranda, legal documents, and magazine copy—can be found in the *New Yorker* records housed in the New York Public Library.[18] The legal files provide little information about complaints and cases after *Sullivan*, so while this discussion takes into account libel suits against the magazine in the post-*Sullivan* era, including *Masson v. New Yorker*, it necessarily focuses on those complaints and cases documented in the magazine's official records.

The Delmonico Building

Within a decade of its founding the *New Yorker* had become an American icon of literary sophistication, publishing both fiction and fact for a national readership.[19] Almost from the beginning, it was forced to confront the vagaries of libel doctrine—and in short order developed clear and remarkably effective editorial and legal strategies for dealing with the law of libel and its threats.

An unhappy confrontation with New York's common law of libel taught the *New Yorker* in only its second year of publication an early lesson about the dangers of libel complaints. In the October 16, 1926, issue of the magazine, George S. Chappell wrote an article under the pseudonym "T-Square" briefly criticizing the architecture of the Delmonico Building on Fifth Avenue.[20] One of the magazine's early editorial interests was architectural criticism, a genre much more popular then than now in mainstream publications.[21] It was also a genre that was apparently less protected in the New York of the day from defamation suits. The architect of the building sued the *New Yorker* for libel, claiming that Chappell had characterized the building as having "faulty design" and being "without proper proportions," and that the characterization was false and damaging to his professional reputation.[22] In fact, Chappell's brief description was even less precise, and much more figurative, than the architect suggested: "Every proportion appears to be unfortunate. The central tower, curiously set on no particular axis, has the grace of an overgrown grain elevator. Of the detail one of the profession said, 'Isn't it curious how a simple element like a band-course or a molding can produce a feeling of nausea?'"[23] In overblown language that stretched Chappell's criticism beyond the outer boundaries of any reasonable construction—and the sentence beyond any reasonable length—the architect charged in his complaint that the article had led readers

> to believe that the plaintiff had designed and constructed the said Delmonico Building in an incompetent manner and without proper proportions or grace,

and so as to call forth unfavorable criticism from other architects, and further to imply general unskillfulness, carelessness, and ignorance by the plaintiff in his profession as architect and impute to him general professional ignorance and want of skill and lack of knowledge of the design and proportion of large office buildings and of the details thereof, and to impute that the plaintiff was personally guilty of bad taste, sensationalism and incompetency, and of egotism.[24]

Today, of course, such a libel complaint would never survive summary judgment, if a plaintiff could even find a lawyer to take the case. Chappell's criticism fell squarely within what is now, and was even then, the opinion privilege of the common law of libel.[25]

A New York state court, entirely neglecting the privilege, denied the *New Yorker's* motion to dismiss the case.[26] The magazine decided to settle before trial. While the *New Yorker's* records of the case are incomplete, James Thurber's memoir of his days working at the magazine suggests why the publication took that course. Thurber, who was the managing editor at the time, consulted with the *New Yorker's* counsel about the dispute after the motion to dismiss the case failed. The lawyer who represented the magazine before it began its long relationship with Greenbaum, Wolff & Ernst advised that a jury could very well decide that, in Thurber's words, "the plaintiff's reputation had been inexcusably injured by a young smart-aleck magazine."[27] The *New Yorker* took the advice and settled.[28]

A letter from the *New Yorker's* attorney to Thurber suggests the difficulty the magazine might have faced under the strict liability rules of libel and the court's obvious inclination to regard the article as conveying not simply opinion but facts.[29] "Whether the article could have such an application and meaning as charged by the plaintiff would ordinarily be a question of fact for the jury," the lawyer explained. "Therefore, we should be preparted [sic] to prove, by expert testimony, that the design of the building was without proper proportions and grace and that the facts stated with respect to the design were true."[30] The *New Yorker* realized that proving the truth of what was clearly an opinion was a nearly impossible task.

Soon after the Delmonico settlement, the *New Yorker* began reading all copy for libel. Editors and lawyers worked in concert, with editors sending any articles they perceived as containing potential defamation to the lawyers for review.

Murder, He Wrote

The early libel complaints against the *New Yorker* illustrate the many ways in which libel law could be and was abused by the unscrupulous, or at least those the magazine's editors and legal counsel considered to be unscrupulous. In 1932 the lawyer Madeline DeFina threatened to file a criminal libel complaint against the *New Yorker*. She claimed that Alexander Woollcott had defamed her client, Edward Lawrence Hall, by portraying him as a murderer in an article published in the magazine's "Shouts and Murmurs" department.[31]

Whether DeFina's client *was* a murderer had never been decided in a court of law because the district attorney, who strongly suspected Hall, could not even prove that a murder had taken place. As Woollcott himself wrote in the contested article, "The District Attorney had (and still has) no notion whatever as to where, when, or how this murder—if, indeed, there has been a murder—was accomplished."[32] The woman the district attorney believed Hall to have murdered—a woman Hall claimed to have married—was nowhere to be found, alive or dead. And Hall refused all judicial attempts to get him to reveal her whereabouts. Although Eugenie Cedarholm had not been seen by anyone for several years, Hall maintained that she was happy and healthy and had in fact borne him three children during the years she had been living incognito. To reveal her whereabouts, Hall claimed, would be to endanger her life. (Hall cited a disgruntled ex-suitor, but earlier in the case he had claimed that she was hiding from a narcotics ring that had threatened her life.)[33] An intensive investigation lasting several years never produced sufficient evidence to convict Hall of murder, but the district attorney did succeed in convicting Hall of forgery. Hall had signed Eugenie Cedarholm's name on a lease for property she owned, for which he had been collecting rent. The judge sentenced Hall to twenty years in prison. Woollcott's wry assessment of the conviction was that there are "more ways than one of skinning a cat."[34]

The *New Yorker*'s editors and lawyers treated DeFina's threat more like a civil than a criminal libel complaint. Katharine Angell White, a general editor of the magazine at the time, contacted a lawyer who had worked on the Hall case, Lyman Sessen, to get information about DeFina. "He laughed heartily," she wrote to the *New Yorker*'s counsel, "and said we could not possibly libel Hall by calling him a murderer and that he would be very happy to help us squelch the matter before it ever came to a case."[35] Sessen suggested that DeFina's claim was not actionable for the obvious reason that a suit must originate with the damaged party. There had not been enough time between the publication of the article and DeFina's letter of complaint for her to have gained her client's consent, Sessen claimed. (Hall was serving his prison sentence in Sing Sing.) Her motivation for making such a frivolous complaint, he theorized, was the possibility that her client might be released on appeal, inherit Cedarholm's money, and pay DeFina a hefty fee for defending him.[36]

The DeFina incident provides an early example of what would become the *New Yorker*'s standard editorial response to libel complaints. Engelhard, Pollak, Pitcher & Stern, the law firm representing the magazine at the time, wrote to DeFina just days after her initial letter of complaint. Theirs was a terse, two-sentence response, with the final sentence settling the matter: "Because the article you mentioned in your letter was improper in no respect, we have advised our client that there is nothing to do about it."[37] The same day the law firm informed the *New Yorker* of its correspondence with DeFina, adding: "We think there should be no retraction. It would be difficult, it seems to us, to injure Mr. Hall's reputation."[38] The lawyer's letter apparently served its purpose. The magazine did not hear from DeFina again.

Greenbaum, Wolff & Ernst and the *New Yorker*

Thus began the *New Yorker*'s practice of generally refusing to publish retractions. In the same year as the DeFina episode, Greenbaum, Wolff & Ernst started representing the magazine. Among the first correspondence in the *New Yorker* records documenting this new relationship is a letter from Katharine White to Morris Ernst thanking him for a copy of a book he had just published. "It should certainly be a textbook for all editors," she wrote. "We are reading it avidly around here and I am grateful to you for giving me a copy."[39] The book could only have been *Hold Your Tongue!*, the book on libel Ernst wrote with Alexander Lindey, the man who would emerge as one of the leading literary lawyers in the country. The *New Yorker* had secured as its primary counsel a good man for the job.

One year later, in 1933, on the advice of its lawyers, the magazine instituted a new libel protection process for profile authors and their editors to follow. Authors were to provide editors with a memorandum giving the sources of their information and the relevant dates. The purpose was twofold. On the one hand, such substantiation was a means of quality control, of holding writers to certain professional standards. On the other, it provided editors and lawyers with at least some protection in the face of potential libel suits.[40] By this time the magazine under editor Harold Ross had already established its fabled fact-checking department. In 1927 checkers were verifying all facts in pieces scheduled for publication. Within one decade, Ben Yagoda has written, the department had become "an institution, famous for its Canadian Mounty–like determination to hunt down any fact, no matter how obscure," in both fact and fiction pieces.[41] This rigorous fact-checking was merely one part of a much larger editorial apparatus that strove for accuracy as well as flawless prose. An editor went over every fact piece accepted for publication line by line with its author. Copyeditors, fact-checkers, and assigning editors then reviewed and marked page proofs; all edits and queries were transferred to a master proof, which the assigning editor used to complete the editing, usually consulting with the author every step of the way.[42] Though stemming largely from Ross's devotion to journalistic accuracy and lucid prose, which Yagoda pegs to Ross's earlier work as a newspaper reporter,[43] this editorial process appears to have served the magazine well in preventing possible libel claims.

While *New Yorker* editors actively screened manuscripts for possible libel, they were also doing their best to keep the magazine's tone edgy and its substance hard-hitting. In a 1936 letter to Lindey asking him to review a three-part profile, one of the magazine's editors, John O. Whedon, wrote: "We don't doubt that it is full of libel, but would like to publish as much of it as you think we can get away with. On the points that you consider dangerous we would be grateful for suggestions as to how we might cover ourselves without pulling our punches altogether—if you have any." In a witty postscript Whedon added, "If you happen to know of any libel concerning Hines [the subject of the profile] that we haven't got in here and that you think would add to the story, we'd welcome that too."[44] Despite the swagger in Whedon's approach, he took the threat of libel seriously. The magazine even asked its lawyers to review a three-part profile on Hitler. "Being uncertain as to whether it is possible to libel Hitler or not," Whedon wrote to Lindey, "we'd like to have you look it over and give us your opinion on it."[45] As might be expected, Lindey found nothing legally objectionable in the profile.

If some *New Yorker* editors considered the lawyers' libel review valuable, others chafed under it, including St. Clair McKelway during his three-year stint from 1936 to 1939 as managing editor. One of the magazine's most celebrated writers, McKelway joined the *New Yorker* staff in 1933 after leaving the *Herald Tribune*.[46] He thus brought a newspaper reporter's sensibility to the magazine, including the deeply held conviction that the constraints of libel law conflicted with the journalist's prerogative to report the world as he saw it. In a 1937 letter to Whedon, McKelway complained bitterly that the Greenbaum lawyers were too swift to excise potentially libelous material in the manuscripts they reviewed:

> I wish somehow it could be got into the heads of those lawyers that we are running a magazine and not publishing legal briefs. In my experience in this office they have continually objected to stories and we have continually overruled their objections not getting into any trouble at all. If it had been up to the lawyers, for instance, we should never have run the piece on Fanny Holtzman and yet after the thing had been published Miss Holtzman asked Mrs. Harriman [the author of the piece] to a cocktail party. It seems to me that the lawyers on the whole are taking the easy way out of this problem by always telling us that we can not publish such and such a piece, where if they worked a little harder at it they would be able to figure out how we could publish a piece and get away with it. We might even consider some day whether the firm Greenbaum, Wolff & Ernst is a good firm to have as libel lawyers. All newspapers have libel lawyers who are experienced in the publishing game and on the whole newspapers get away with a great deal more than we are allowed to get away with.[47]

That libel law was a problem in the publishing business was clearly the consensus at the *New Yorker*, although different editors approached the problem differently. Whedon, for example, was solicitous of the lawyers' advice while McKelway was contemptuous. As the magazine's early brushes with the law in the Delmonico and DeFina cases taught, libel law was ripe for judicial misapplication and for abuse by possible fortune-seekers. It was this threat to the magazine's right to publish what it wished that most concerned the editors. Both Whedon and McKelway showed little concern for a potential libel plaintiff's right to reputation in their desire "to get away with" more potentially defamatory reporting within the *New Yorker*'s pages.

Of Furs and Fans

In the post-depression years, businessmen and businesses were sensitive to even the semblance of criticism. Take, for example, what seems to have been the *New Yorker*'s innocuous observation in a November 1937 "Talk of the Town" story that Charles Brand of Charles Brand Furs was "a somewhat mousy man." Not amused, Brand threatened a libel suit unless the magazine published an apology.[48] "Do you think we ought to run a little note saying that on further acquaintance we find Mr. Brand to be a veritable lion, or can we safely tell him to crawl back into his hole?" Whedon queried Lindey the day he received Brand's complaint.[49] Although Lindey suggested that Brand would likely drop the matter, Whedon responded to Brand, "We do not see how the description of you in the story could conceivably hold you up to ridicule and we feel sure that on reconsideration you will agree with us."[50]

Such became the magazine's typical response to libel threats: reject the complaint, and then ask the complainant to agree with the New Yorker's assessment of things. It was the response the magazine used in 1938 when the Fan Company threatened a libel suit unless the magazine explained and retracted a witty barb about the business's name change. "The Japanese Fan Company at 225 Fifth Avenue has just changed its name to The Fan Company," the New Yorker noted, "which reminds us that we mustn't forget to send our pet leopard out and get him spot-cleaned."[51] Anti-Japanese sentiment was entrenched in the country, a boycott drive against Japanese goods was under way, and the Fan Company obviously thought it would be better for business if it dropped the word "Japanese" from its name.[52] The New Yorker skewered the move.

For its part, the Fan Company's complaint was an unsophisticated attempt to gain free publicity. "Your article carried the obvious and open insinuation that by the change of the name of this company . . . we were attempting to mislead the public," the president of the company complained. "Had you taken the trouble to investigate the facts you would have found that we are an entirely American owned concern." Such a reading of the New Yorker item was a transparent stretch. The Fan Company was wantonly hoping the New Yorker would publicize the company's status as an American-, not a Japanese-, owned business. The magazine refused the company's repeated requests for retraction and explanation in a series of variations on the standard libel response: "We do not see how any injurious implication can fairly be derived from what was stated. Certainly none was intended. We think that upon consideration you will agree with us."[53] In the face of such refutation, the Fan Company eventually gave up.

Although the New Yorker's retorts to these libel complaints do not seem especially calibrated to assuage hurt feelings—with their edge of condescension, they seem more likely to enrage—they almost always worked. In the 1942 annual summary of its work for the magazine, Greenbaum, Wolff & Ernst noted that in the ten years it had represented the New Yorker, "we have managed,

without cramping the style or dulling the barbs of your editors and contributors, to keep you out of trouble." [54] The previous year, during which most of the
firm's work for the magazine had centered on libel questions, had been as salu-
tary as the prior nine. Greenbaum, Wolff & Ernst had managed to avoid five
threatened suits by "explanation or persuasion"—four of which involved libel
threats lodged by complainants' attorneys. The magazine would use this approach against libel complaints to great effect throughout the years, although
in a few notable instances the technique failed entirely. Even before the 1942
summary, it had not averted all suits. In 1938 a complaint arose that would
keep Alexander Lindey busy that year and beyond.

William James Sidis v. The New Yorker

In August 1937 the *New Yorker* published a short profile on William James
Sidis, then thirty-nine, who had been a child prodigy. It appeared under the
title "Where Are They Now?" and the subtitle "April Fool!" When Sidis was still
a child, the newspapers had covered his amazing accomplishments with vigor,
including his lecture on four-dimensional bodies to math scholars at age
eleven and his graduation from Harvard at age sixteen. Since that time he had
actively avoided publicity and managed to live his life in obscurity. The *New
Yorker* profile reviewed Sidis's younger days and accomplishments, as well as
his notoriety, and told the story of his subsequent life, which included a major
breakdown, an unlikely job as a clerk, a withdrawal into obscurity, and a
passion for collecting streetcar transfers. It ended with a description of the
author's interview with Sidis at his rented room in Boston, including observations about the way he spoke and laughed and the disarray of his room. At the
end of the article, when the interviewer "was emboldened, at last, to bring up
the prediction, made by Professor Comstock of Massachusetts Institute of
Technology back in 1920, that the little boy who lectured that year on the
fourth dimension to a gathering of learned men would grow up to be a great
mathematician, a famous leader in the world of science," Sidis is quoted as saying, "with a grin," how strange it was that he was born on April Fool's Day.[55]

What was probably an interesting profile for *New Yorker* readers was, to
Sidis, a profound invasion of his private life. He filed suit in federal district
court against the *New Yorker*'s publisher, F-R Publishing Corporation, claiming three causes of action: two for invasion of privacy and one for malicious
libel.[56] The *New Yorker* filed a motion to dismiss the privacy causes of action,

claiming insufficient grounds. The magazine chose not to file a motion to dismiss on the malicious libel complaint until the disposition of the privacy motion for dismissal, claiming that its answer to the libel cause would depend on this disposition.[57] The federal district court granted the *New Yorker*'s motion. Sidis appealed, and the U.S. Court of Appeals for the Second Circuit affirmed the lower court's dismissal.[58] Sidis appealed again, this time to the United States Supreme Court, which declined to accept the case.[59] At this point the *Sidis* case was two years old, and all vital signs to the contrary, it lived on for four more years as Sidis pursued his complaints in novel ways.

He was likely encouraged in his pursuit by the interest his case generated in legal circles of the day. Privacy law was still somewhat unsettled terrain in New York and the other states that recognized it, and the case raised important concerns about basic conflicts between privacy law and press freedom. The key legal issue was whether Sidis was a public figure or a private person, a distinction important both in privacy law and, after *New York Times v. Sullivan*, in libel law. Sidis had clearly been a public figure in his youth, but did he continue to be a public figure after living for many years in much-sought-after obscurity? If he was a public figure, to what degree was the press allowed to delve into his private life? Both the federal district and appellate courts held that the press had a limited right to scrutinize the private life of a public figure. They further held that, even though Sidis had tried to shield himself from public attention since his childhood, "his subsequent history, containing as it did the answer to the question of whether or not he had fulfilled his early promise, was still a matter of public concern."[60] As law review articles analyzing and criticizing the *Sidis* rulings suggest, the legal climate of the day tended to favor privacy rights over press freedoms.[61] The rulings notwithstanding, the legal consensus in academic circles was that privacy law should protect Sidis's right to live without the press exposing personal details of his life. The appellate ruling, one law review argued, "testifies to the cold treatment which, after half a century of evolution, the right of privacy still suffers at the hands of unsympathetic courts, lending an indirect and untimely sanction to some abuses of the press."[62]

At the heart of the legal wrangling over the case, and probably Sidis's commitment in pursuing it over the course of six years, was what even the Court of Appeals identified as a certain mercilessness in the *New Yorker* article:

> It is not contended that any of the matter printed is untrue. Nor is the manner
> of the author unfriendly; Sidis today is described as having "a certain childlike

charm." But the article is merciless in its dissection of intimate details of its subject's personal life, and this in company with elaborate accounts of Sidis's passion for privacy and the pitiable lengths to which he has gone in order to avoid public scrutiny. The work possesses great reader interest, for it is both amusing and instructive; but it may be fairly described as a ruthless exposure of a once public character, who has since sought and has now been deprived of the seclusion of private life.[63]

In oral arguments before the Second Circuit, Alexander Lindey maintained, as he relayed in a letter to Harold Ross, "that the publication of the story of Sidis's career, and the attendant 'intrusion' upon his privacy were fully justified because Sidis's later life was a tragic illustration of the havoc caused by the ruthless parental exploitation of gifted children; and that the public had a legitimate interest in learning the facts about him." Judge Patterson apparently was having none of it. According to Lindey, he "brushed aside this argument rather angrily, and said that in his opinion the article was cruel and unjustified."[64]

Buoyed by the controversy surrounding the dispute, Sidis made it known after the Supreme Court refused to hear his case that he planned to file amended privacy complaints and to pursue the original malicious libel complaint against the *New Yorker*. "It is hard to believe," Lindey wrote Ik Shuman, the magazine's managing editor, in February 1941, "but the attorneys for Sidis still don't feel themselves licked. They not only want to go ahead on the libel count, but have stumbled on a new theory for a possible revival of the right-of-privacy count." As Lindey later explained it, the new theory went like this:

> The two original right-of-privacy counts were predicated on the assumption that though the facts related concerning Sidis were true, his privacy had been invaded. In the amended complaint the right-of-privacy counts contain a new element: allegations of falsity.
>
> The question of law thus raised is a novel one. What Sidis and his lawyers are probably trying to establish is a new cause of action grounded in the twilight region presently existing between breach of the right of privacy and libel. Thus far the issue of falsity has not been of any consequence in right-of-privacy cases; where falsity was established, together with legal injury, the cause of action automatically became one of libel.[65]

Sidis was now alleging, unlike in his earlier privacy complaints, that the *New Yorker* profile contained falsehoods about his life.

It took two years for Sidis to file his amended complaint. "The Boy Wonder

is riding again," Lindey wrote Shuman in February 1943, informing him
that the magazine had been served with a new complaint.[66] Back in federal district court, lawyers for the New Yorker argued that the original dismissal of
Sidis's right-of-privacy counts was a final disposition preventing him from
amending the same counts. In May 1943 the court found in the New Yorker's
favor, dismissing the amended complaints.[67] Undeterred, Sidis found new
counsel. "It looks like more fun ahead," Lindey informed Shuman.[68] "I'm sorry
Mr. Sidis is such a die-hard," Shuman responded. "If the government had a
subsidy program for lawyers without briefs we might have fewer foolish lawsuits, but on second thought that might develop more foolish lawyers. Vive la
democracie!"[69]

Despite such moments of humor, Sidis's constant legal pressure was beginning to wear on the magazine. When he filed yet another amended complaint
for "malicious libel" in early 1944, seeking $10,000 in damages, Lindey sug-
gested again to both the New Yorker and Sidis's lawyer the possibility of settlement.[70] Several years earlier, when Sidis filed his amended privacy complaints,
Lindey had tried to negotiate a settlement in which Sidis would write several
articles for the New Yorker for pay, to be published under his real name or a
pseudonym. These negotiations had fallen through.[71] But with a malicious
libel complaint to contend with, Lindey suggested the same proposal to Sidis's
new lawyer.

Such a proposal was the New Yorker's way to avoid making what it called a
"straight-money settlement." For the twelve years Greenbaum, Wolff & Ernst
had represented it, the New Yorker had refused to settle claims.[72] It was a prece-
dent Lindey and the editors did not want to break, at least not directly. As
Lindey had observed several years earlier in an annual summary of the firm's
services for the magazine, this practice had served the magazine well:

> We must confess that we feel a little proud over the record of our association
> with The New Yorker. During the past eight years your publication has dealt
> constantly and sometimes sharply with personalities and current topics, and
> we have taken special pains not to ask your authors or editors to pull their
> punches. Yet The New Yorker (unlike many another publication) has paid out
> not one penny either by way of settlement or judgment. From the publishing
> point of view this is something of a record. You have not only saved money
> which might otherwise have been paid out to claimants, but you have, by es-
> tablishing a reputation for not being a sucker, discouraged strike suits. Conse-
> quently you have been much less plagued than other periodicals.[73]

It appears that Sidis and his lawyers refused the magazine's offer of an article-writing settlement, for in 1944 the *New Yorker* broke down and paid $500 to settle the malicious libel suit.[74] Exactly why the magazine chose this route to resolution is unclear from the record, but it may well have been simply to get rid of a troublesome litigant. Just three months later Sidis died of a cerebral hemorrhage at the age of forty-six.[75] The *Sidis* case was the magazine's first major litigation.

The Cat Woman and the *New Yorker*

As interminable and troublesome as the *Sidis* case was to the *New Yorker* and Lindey, the Rita Ross case was a special instance. It began the same year as *Sidis* and ran just as long, but while Sidis had a legitimate complaint in the eyes of many law review authors and legal experts, Ross was the master of the nuisance suit. By the time she was finished with the *New Yorker*—filing one ridiculous claim after another, hauling the magazine into court, and bombarding its offices with bizarre correspondence and phone calls—the magazine had given in and settled. If the *New Yorker* editors and lawyers had known it would take only $25 to satisfy the antagonist they had taken to calling the "Cat Woman," they might have settled years earlier.

The *New Yorker*'s long affair with the Cat Woman began with a profile titled "Lady of the Cats" published in the May 14, 1938, issue. The author, Eugene Kinkead, had interviewed Ross on several occasions and chronicled her work with stray cats around the city.[76] The profile began:

> Since 1919, Miss Rita Ross has done her best to rid the city of half a million homeless cats which the S.P.C.A. estimates roam its streets. Almost single-handed, during that period she has turned over more than two hundred tons of cats to the Society for painless destruction. Like the Post Office ideal, Miss Ross is deterred neither by snow, nor rain, nor heat, nor gloom of night on her round of deadly mercy. On Sundays and holidays, blown along by the high March wind or baked by August, in buildings rotten and sagging, through streets that crawl and smell, almost always among people who are hostile or derisive, she has followed her incomprehensible star. It is a bad day when she gets only six cats; it is a good one when she gets sixteen. Once, when the S.P.C.A. recklessly provided her with one of its wagons and a driver, she bagged fifteen hundred. She has the peculiar reputation of being able to move off under her own weight in cats.[77]

Ross first complained about the article in June, and in a phone conversation with Lindey, which he related to Shuman, she "went on at great length about how deeply she had been disappointed in Kinkead, and how sorely humiliated she had been by the New Yorker piece and particularly by the revelation of her age." [78] In an undated letter to the *New Yorker*, likely written soon after the article was published, Ross expanded on her displeasure in a diatribe that almost seems a *New Yorker*–style parody of a complaint:

> None of this would have happened had he [Kinkead] been man enough to see me at the shelter and either apologize or explain. I am so angry at him I could scratch his eyes out. He came enough when he wanted that rotton [sic] story he wrote on me. I willingly gave him valuable time all free too. I helped him in every way I could. I wonder if he knows I am usually paid for my stories yet I never asked the New Yorker anything. I merely requested certain things be held in abeyance but they weren't. The idea of him saying I was so old. It's none of any ones [sic] business how old I am. And my real name, causing my mother who is very ill to faint! Causing me to be scolded. As I said before the reason I take this and my other objections so to heart is because it was supposed to be a friendly story. [79]

On August 17, 1938, Ross visited Lindey in his office, where she again complained that the article had hurt her feelings, in particular the revelation of her age, thirty-seven, and Kinkead's failure to continue to visit her after the article was published. At this point it appeared that she would sue for libel, and as Lindey wrote to Shuman: "Frankly, I can't guess the result. I may yet be able to drag the thing out to a point where the lady loses interest. But I doubt it. She freely admits that she is a vindictive person and that she never forgets what she deems to be an affront." [80] Lindey suggested that if Kinkead talked with and apologized to Ross, she might drop her threatened suit. [81] Kinkead politely refused. [82]

By the fall, what had at first appeared to be a libel suit had transmogrified into a suit for breach of contract. Noting her new grounds, Ross explained to Lindey that "a Supreme Court proceeding such as the libel" would be too expensive and take too long. [83] Despite her earlier letter stating that she had provided the *New Yorker* with her life story for free, Ross now claimed that she had made a verbal contract with Kinkead at the Avenue A Food Shop on Twenty-third Street. He had promised, she claimed, that the magazine would pay

$1,000 for her story.[84] Ross had her day in court before a municipal court judge in November 1938. Unable to produce witnesses to the verbal contract, she lost the case on dismissal. She predictably appealed and kept the *New Yorker* involved in the suit for another year.[85]

During the same span of time Ross began a second suit against the author of the profile for $500, alleging that the magazine had neglected to pay her for services rendered. Exactly what these alleged services were is unclear from the record, but what is clear is the *New Yorker*'s exasperation with Ross. The magazine's dealings with her were becoming increasingly uncomfortable. In January 1939 a postcard signed "Sincerely, Marian" arrived in Lindey's offices. "Please be informed," it read, "that Miss Ross is going to have a baby."[86]

"I think you should know that Rita Ross had a fight with her girlfriend, and that the latter has been sending in stool-pigeon information," Lindey informed Shuman. Kinkead stepped in with a warning. "I wouldn't believe this was necessarily 'Marian,'" he explained. "Miss Ross assumes numerous forms, both in person and script."[87] Marian, it turned out, was indeed probably Rita Ross herself. Lindey decided to confront Ross with both barrels blazing in an attempt to end her courtroom shenanigans. In late January, Lindey, Kinkead, and a young lawyer by the name of Harold Stern from Greenbaum gathered in a district attorney's office and met with Ross for an hour and a half. "She couldn't have enjoyed the conference," Lindey reported to Shuman, "and we hope it will have the effect of bringing her to her senses."[88]

Ross was a lost cause, as the *New Yorker* was to learn in the following years. While the second suit lingered on the court calendar, she bombarded Lindey's offices with correspondence and phone calls. He instituted a no-reply policy in the hope of discouraging her.[89] The letters and calls continued. "Rita dies hard," he wrote to Shuman six months later.[90] The second suit was dismissed late in 1939. Lindey informed Shuman:

> Another chapter has just been written in the chronicles of the Cat Woman. As Gene Kinkead no doubt reported to you, the case was tried in Brooklyn on Monday of this week. The judge apparently sized up Miss Ross at the outset, and treated her with the indulgence due a sick person. He permitted her to tell her rambling story and reserved decision. The decision has just come down, and it is judgment for the defendant. That means we have won.
>
> . . . Maybe Miss Ross will stay put; maybe she will think up another wrinkle to get you into court. She is bound to tire sooner or later.[91]

Whatever levity Lindey had mustered in his letter to Shuman evaporated when he learned that Ross had filed a complaint with the President Justice of the municipal court charging that Lindey and Stern had improperly and corruptly influenced the judge who had decided against Ross in her latest suit. The lawyers were summoned before the President Justice and examined in light of Ross's charges, an episode Lindey referred to in his annual summary of services to the *New Yorker* as "highly unpleasant." Ross had gone too far, and Lindey was, as he told Ik Shuman, "wracking my brains for an expedient to put an end to this travesty." He admitted that he had no viable solutions. "We can if we wish (a) get Rita down to the District Attorney's office again, or (b) start a suit to enjoin her from molesting you, or (c) take her into the Magistrate's Court on some charge or other, or (d) start proceedings to have her committed as a psychopathic case." [92] They decided that the best way to handle Ross was "to play along defensively," hoping that she would eventually tire of the game. [93]

Immediately after Lindey and Stern's unpleasant experience before the President Justice, the tireless Ross began a third suit to recover $60 for what she alleged to be damage to her clothing caused by Kinkead while attempting to help her rescue a kitten from a hole in a wall. "I don't know what in the hell we can do except beg the courts to protect us against this goddamn female," Shuman wrote to Lindey. "I hope that the law schools taught you what to do but I'm afraid they haven't." Lindey even asked the municipal judge to intervene in Ross's latest suit, which he refused to do. In January 1940, after persuading Ross to put the suit on the court's reserve calendar, Lindey floated the idea to Shuman of buying a release for $25 when she made her next move. In February he told Shuman the latest news: "Rita's poison pen is still scribbling away merrily. I have just received another note signed 'Francis S. M.' There can be no doubt, of course, as to the identity of the writer. The sum of the communication is that Rita proposes to get married to give Kinkead's child (!) a name." [94]

In September, when Ross began pressing her third case, Lindey decided to get serious about what had seemed before a last-resort measure. "You must be getting a little tired by this time of Miss Ross's monkeyshines," he wrote Shuman. "Let me know when you reach the end of your patience. We can then consider the advisability of going into the Magistrate's Court on a criminal charge, and asking that Miss Ross be committed to Bellevue for observation as a psychopathic person." [95]

It never came to that. Ross showed signs in 1941 of losing interest. In a February postcard sent to Lindey she asked: "What assurance have I that Mr. K. is sorry for hurting my feelings. If I could be sure I would take a *very nominal* amount and call everything square."[96] Why the *New Yorker* did not take the opportunity to settle is unclear, but for the next few years Ross continued to bombard their offices with letters, postcards, and telephone calls.[97] In December 1943, at about the same time Lindey was attempting to arrange an article-writing settlement in the *Sidis* case, Harold Stern finally settled the Rita Ross affair. In a witty letter to Ik Shuman, he told the story of the *New Yorker*'s final dealings with the Cat Woman of Kinkead's profile:

> I suppose Gene Kinkead told you about the event which, while not so epoch making as the "Moscow Pact" is quite an event in my young life. We settled all of Rita Ross's matters with her for the sum of $25 in hand paid. I am enclosing herewith for your files a duplicate original of the release signed by none other than Rita Ross herself together with her affidavit attesting to the fact that she knew what she did.
>
> . . . I don't know whether you are interested in the fact that it has taken me literally months of telephone conferences with Rita to get her to come to this office and she finally did on the now famous date, December 3rd.[98]

Yankee Schwartz v. The New Yorker

The *New Yorker* had amassed solid experience dealing with libel and other complaints arising from its profiles by the time the alleged mobster Yankee Schwartz filed his libel claim against the magazine. Although the *Sidis* and Cat Woman cases had been troublesome, they presented factual issues and legal questions that were easy enough for the magazine to answer. The Schwartz case was another story, dealing as it did with an alleged libel against an alleged underworld figure.

The case arose from a three-part profile by Richard Boyer about the jazz musician Duke Ellington. The article in question, published in the July 8, 1944, issue of the magazine, described Julius "Yankee" Schwartz as a hit man hired to persuade the owner of a Philadelphia theater to release Ellington one week early from a performing contract so his band could play at the opening of the Cotton Club in 1927: "The Cotton Club people acted with the forthrightness that was characteristic of the prohibition era. They called Boo Boo Hoff, a friend and an underworld power in Philadelphia, and Boo Boo sent an emissary known as Yankee Schwarz [sic] to the theatre man. 'Be big,' Yankee Schwarz pleaded. 'Be big or,' he mumbled embarrassedly, 'you'll be dead.' The choice presented no dilemma to the theatre man. Duke's band arrived at the Cotton Club a few minutes before the opening."[99]

Schwartz filed a libel complaint in the Supreme Court of the State of New York in January 1945, claiming the *New Yorker*'s portrayal of him in the Ellington profile was false and defamatory and had damaged his jewelry business in the amount of $100,000.[100] The *New Yorker* began investigating the matter. An independent investigator the magazine hired discovered that the source of the Schwartz anecdote was not a witness to the incident. The source believed in the story's truth but based his belief on conjecture, given other facts. He could not, in other words, provide persuasive testimony as to the truth of the contested anecdote. What is more, the *New Yorker*'s investigator learned that both Duke Ellington and the emissary of the Cotton Club claimed that the episode never happened and they, not Schwartz, had persuaded the theater manager to release Ellington from his contract. It was becoming clear that the *New Yorker* could not prove the truth of what it had published. The magazine's editors and lawyers realized that, if the case went to trial, the *New Yorker* would likely lose.[101]

The question then became how much the magazine would lose. The investigator believed that Yankee Schwartz was a person of questionable reputation and background. If he were questionable enough, and the *New Yorker* could prove it, a jury would be unlikely to award much in damages. But problems abounded in establishing proof. The investigator's report detailed a litany of suspected illegal activity. Both a Philadelphia detective and a bail bondsman who believed Schwartz to be a member of the Hoff gang refused to testify. The Philadelphia Police Department, according to the *New Yorker*'s investigator, was staffed with many who used to be on Hoff's payroll and would not provide information about Schwartz. People who had known about his alleged involvement in illegal diamond transactions had either died or disappeared. Both the Office of Price Administration (OPA) and the FBI had Schwartz under surveillance in connection with the suspected counterfeiting of gasoline ration coupons, but neither had sufficient evidence to arrest him.[102] And the OPA had shared information only after getting the *New Yorker*'s promise of confidentiality. According to Greenbaum, Wolff & Ernst, a jury might return either a nominal or a sizable verdict on the basis of the evidence. It was impossible to predict.[103] The law firm recommended settlement, and the *New Yorker* took its advice. In November 1945 the magazine paid Yankee Schwartz $1,250 to settle his libel claim.[104] Its long-standing practice of not settling cases had been undone, first by a former child prodigy and later by an alleged gangster.

Soapland

The *New Yorker* was reluctant to print corrections and retractions even when it became clear it had made an error in its reporting. One such error occurred in James Thurber's 1948 five-part series on radio soap opera, a hugely popular genre at the time. In the first article of the series called "Soapland," Thurber wrote that Emmons C. Carlson, promotion manager for the NBC affiliate in Chicago, had sued Irna Phillips, a star of the soap *The Guiding Light*, over rights to the radio program. A circuit court judge, Thurber wrote, "dismissed Carlson's claims as fantastic." Carlson's lawyer contacted the *New Yorker* only five days after the article ran, claiming the "statements made as quoted are wholly false and libelous. I am writing you in my own behalf as it is certainly not pleasing to me that you infer that Mr. Carlson's claim was 'fantastic.' I think that upon an investigation as to my professional standing you will determine that I do not represent clients with respect to fantastic (perjured) claims." [105] As it turned out, the lower court decision was reversed on appeal, with Carlson ultimately winning a substantial out-of-court settlement.[106] Furthermore, as the lawyer wrote to Thurber, it was unclear from the record whether the lower court judge meant to characterize Carlson's claim or a Special Master's report of the case as fantastic.[107]

Whether the error could be interpreted as legally libelous on the part of either Carlson or his lawyer was another question. As Lindey wrote to Hawley Truax, first treasurer of the magazine and then chairman of the board, "Although we have done a considerable amount of legal digging, we have not been able to find any authority bearing specifically on the question of whether Schiek [Carlson's lawyer] and Carlson are libeled in the Thurber article." He recommended waiting to see what Schiek would do next. "We have written to Schiek, and it may be that he will be satisfied to let the matter drop. If he is still full of fight, we may be able to persuade him to blow off steam in the Department of Correction and Amplification [a section of the magazine that appeared occasionally to correct errors]. If he is after money, that's another matter." [108] Lindey made frequent and very effective use of the waiting technique over his many years representing the *New Yorker*. He would draw things out as long as possible when litigation was threatened, hoping the complainant would tire of the conflict or lose interest and let the matter drop. It was a technique that clearly did not work with Sidis or Rita Ross but did in many other instances. In the "Soapland" case, the magazine waited until Thurber's final piece in the series to append at the very end of the article an "Apologia" that said the first article had given "an incomplete account of the law suit" Carlson brought against Phillips. After explaining the appellate court's reversal of the lower court's decision, Thurber's correction read: "The fact of that settlement eluded the well-intentioned researches of myself and of several assistants. My regrets and apologies." [109] The "Apologia" made no mention of the first article's claim that the lower court judge called Carlson's claim fantastic. (Lindey told Thurber he should excise this part of the article when he published "Soapland" as a book.) [110] Apparently the New Yorker was willing to go only so far in correcting its errors. Still, Schiek did not take his libel complaint to court.

The most interesting part of the incident is James Thurber's response to the error, which provides unique insight into the New Yorker's editorial culture and the perspective of one of its most acclaimed writers, editors, and cartoonists. Although Thurber began working on the New Yorker staff as managing editor, Harold Ross soon moved the administratively challenged Thurber to the editorship of the "Talk of the Town" department, which became under his editorial pen a classic humor feature of the magazine. [111] Thurber left the New Yorker in 1935 to freelance, but he never truly left, continuing to contribute his prolific work and sharing his opinions on the doings of the magazine in the years to come. His error in "Soapland" clearly galled Thurber, a painstakingly careful reporter. In a three-page, single-spaced typed letter to the magazine after Schiek submitted his complaint, Thurber detailed the many steps he had taken to research the Carlson litigation. From the moment he had been told the story, he wrote in his letter, "I realized this was touchy business and I set about checking it." After going to much trouble to uncover the facts, and using the research help of several assistants, Thurber had what he believed was the full story. After detailing these efforts in almost a page of text, he wrote: "I am interested only in pointing out that I did not hit this a glancing blow but did all in my power to get the thing right. I was neither for Mr. Carlson or Miss Phillips but cared only for the truth." [112]

Thurber's efforts to document his story accurately show that even the best-intentioned and most diligent journalists sometimes get things wrong. It is precisely for this reason that contemporary libel law protects, under the aegis of the Constitution, honest error in public discourse. "I still insist on taking the blame," Thurber wrote, "but the record as above shows that I ran into the kind of deadend and human fallibility that confound even the most careful man." Although the letter tends toward the defensive, Thurber had reason to be defensive. Apparently he had been after the *New Yorker* for years to employ experienced reporters to help writers research their in-depth stories. He complained that this was the kind of person he had needed—and had expressed the need for—to help him on the "Soapland" series:

> I say without passion or anger that this slip is of the kind that will occur and occur again if we do not have in addition to our checking department a high-class newspaper man who could work with an author and do further reporting on matters of this kind. The checkers, like the editors, and because of the standard the editors have set up, are inclined to overcheck the minute and unimportant facts, and in at least four instances in my first article the editors and checkers changed the truth in my statements and made them erroneous. I was able to catch these mistakes. The system of silly and ridiculous queries always will slow down the magazine but I would not mind this so much if it were offset by the careful research of the kind of journalist I am recommending.[113]

Thurber referred to the magazine's fact-checking department, well known by the 1940s for its scrupulousness in checking even the smallest details, and a complex editing process that included Ross's extensive (some thought excessive) queries on galley proofs.[114] Ross's queries came as the last passageway for a piece in a long and Byzantine editorial pipeline.[115] "From the early days of the magazine," Yagoda notes, "it was understood that contributions were subject to queries, changes, and sometimes wholesale rewriting."[116] Thurber's questioning of the *New Yorker*'s editorial processes may have surprised those outside the magazine's culture. As early as 1948 the magazine had earned a pristine reputation for its factual and stylistic accuracy. These processes and the reputation Thurber questioned in his letter about the "Soapland" error would become, more than forty years later, the object of a much more public questioning in *Masson v. New Yorker.*

Thurber's eyesight had been failing for a good many years, and by the time he wrote his "Soapland" series, he was almost completely blind. He ended his letter to the *New Yorker* this way:

In eight years on three different newspapers neither the papers nor myself were ever sued for libel or anything else as a result of my stories. In the series called "Where Are They Now" I had the help of a dozen different expert reporters and I wonder why this system was dropped. Surely someone could have joined with me in my long efforts to find a Chicago reporter who could have got the Phillips' story right.

It will now be said at the office that a blind man can't do journalistic work, and to this canard, if it is cast about, I reply that neither can a blind magazine.[117]

Despite Thurber's obvious irritation with the magazine over the incident, he wrote about it with humor in his memoir of his life at the *New Yorker* working with Ross. After briefly noting the error he had made in "Soapland," he explained that his "Apologia" smoothed over any hurt feelings with the aggrieved lawyer. "But Ross continued to have a lot of fun with me about these cases," he wrote. "Every now and then he would break in on me, grin, and say, 'How's the defendant?' or 'You haven't got a leg to stand on, Thurber.'"[118]

Fybish v. The New Yorker

As libel complaints continued throughout the 1950s at the *New Yorker*, the magazine's lawyers and editors honed the tactics they had learned in the preceding decades for fending them off. The Yankee Schwartz case had taught the magazine the usefulness of in-depth investigations into the character of those complaining of libel. Libel law is, after all, meant to protect one's right to reputation, and if a reputation was already tarnished, that information could be used to dissuade the unhappy subject of the *New Yorker*'s report from pursuing a defamation claim. Such was the magazine's approach to a complaint from a doctor mentioned in a "Reporter at Large" article on the phenomenon of dance-lectures which had been sweeping the city in the wake of World War II. Single people from across the city would gather to hear a lecturer discuss the then popular topic of personality change as a means of finding a mate. After the lecture they would dance and, if lucky, find their soul mate. In an article titled "Mingle!" Walter Bernstein reported that one of the lecturers, a Dr. Nathan Fybish, explained the phenomenon this way: "The lecture is an intellectual filter for raw, red passions."[119]

In a letter to the *New Yorker* dated November 1950, Fybish complained through his lawyers that the article libeled him. Fybish was mentioned only twice in the long piece, which focused mostly on a dance-lecturer named Dr. Murray Banks. In addition to including the Fybish quotation, Bernstein wrote, "Only the Village Forum, a splinter outfit, always hears the same speaker—Dr. Fybish, the passion-filterer." Apparently Fybish claimed that the *New Yorker* had given the false impression that he was a "quack." [120] He did not claim, notably, that he had not spoken the words the writer attributed to him.

Alexander Lindey responded to Fybish's complaint in typical fashion within the week: "We are unable to see how Dr. Fybish has been libeled." [121] The matter dragged on without resolution, and in July 1951 Lindey suggested to Truax that the magazine put a private investigator on the case, which Fybish had decided to pursue in the courts.[122] Truax advised holding off for the time being.[123] In October of that year Lindey was finally able to hire an investigator to look into Fybish's past. The investigator turned up nothing of interest.[124]

The case continued to languish in the courts, and it was not until a year later that the magazine again turned its attention to its defense when it appeared that the case would go to trial. The *New Yorker* planned to mount a "fair comment and criticism" defense. Recognizing a potential problem similar to the one the magazine had run into in the Delmonico Building case, Lindey wrote to Milton Greenstein, editorial counsel to the *New Yorker* who became vice president of the magazine in 1962, about the defense: "The trial judge may not be fully familiar with the current latitude of criticism, and we shall most likely have to enlighten him. I suggest that you get some of your researchers busy digging out instances of unsparing critical comment on public performers, published around the time of the Fybish piece." [125] As the magazine planned its defense, it continued to investigate Fybish, this time through the help of one of its employees who had attended a Fybish dance-lecture. The young woman wrote to the Village Forum, which sponsored Fybish's lectures, asking for information about any articles or books he had published. Lindey commissioned another investigative report on Fybish, which again turned up nothing the magazine could use against him. "It would seem that there are no skeletons in the doctor's closet," Lindey wrote Greenstein. "At any rate, we haven't uncovered any." [126]

As it turned out, Lindey's "fair comment and criticism" defense did all the work he hoped it would. The *New Yorker* did not need any dirt on Fybish after all. On May 18, 1955, almost five years after the disputed article was published, a New York trial judge dismissed the case because there was no question of fact to submit to the jury. "I am satisfied that there is no libel per se," the judge said.

"I am satisfied that by no stretch of the imagination can this language be interpreted as a libel against this plaintiff." [127] The *New Yorker* had not implied that Dr. Fybish was a "quack"—at least in the judge's estimation.

The CBS News Director

The *New Yorker* used these tactics even with the most powerful of complainants. In 1954 Wells Church, director of CBS News, complained that he had not made a derogatory statement about Edward R. Murrow attributed to him in Charles Wertenbaker's profile of Church. The statement read, "Ed Murrow has collected the Goddamnedest bunch of camp followers, and not one of them is worth a damn." Church also objected to the article's characterization of him as "'a Murrow boy' himself." In a prolonged back-and-forth between *New Yorker* executives (not the *New Yorker*'s main counsel, Alexander Lindey) and Church's lawyer, it eventually became clear that Church, for his part, wanted to discover Wertenbaker's source for the quotation, while the *New Yorker*, for its part, wanted to avoid printing a retraction. In a letter confronting the *New Yorker*'s stonewalling tactic, Church's lawyer demanded of Raoul Fleischmann, the president of the magazine, that it either justify the quotation or run a retraction: "It may reasonably be assumed that the attitude of The New Yorker Magazine in this instance is that although the statement might never have been made by Mr. Church and was in fact falsely attributed to him, you find in it nothing damaging to Mr. Church's reputation and that therefore he has no grievance. With this attitude Mr. Church is in serious disagreement as he feels that the article has violated his legal rights." [128] In another letter written the same day to Truax, Church's lawyer had complained that the *New Yorker*'s replies to Church's complaint were "equivocal, if not evasive." [129] The magazine's tactic was not going to work as well with the high-powered as it had with others.

Eventually, Wertenbaker himself came upon a solution to the conflict. Although he refused to reveal his source to Church (he did reveal it to the *New Yorker*), he realized that the quotation had gotten Church into trouble at CBS. He offered to write a private note of apology Church could use at CBS saying that although he believed his source to be reliable, he had to accept Church's denial that he had made the statement.[130] He wrote the letter, and after some back-and-forth between Lindey and Church's lawyer over what seemed to Church the impersonal form of the original letter and the mocking nature of

Wertenbaker's characteristic and idiosyncratic blue crayon signature, the matter was finally settled.[131]

Filler-Whittey v. The New Yorker

As the 1950s wore on, libel complaints against the magazine began to include demands for large damage awards.[132] In one case, two Nevada residents filed suit against the *New Yorker* over a 1954 article written by A. J. Liebling which told the story of a man named Joe who had been thrown off a freight train in front of a ranch house. The ranch house belonged to "Letty," referred to in the article as "an old coyote," who cared for the injured Joe and then married him. They remained married for twenty-two years. Both Harry Joe Filler and Lettie Virginia Whittey filed suit against the magazine for libel. Filler claimed the article falsely implied that he had been "illegally riding on a freight train as a tramp and that he had been forcibly thrown off." He demanded $50,000 in damages. Whittey charged that the epithet "old coyote" was defamatory.

The *New Yorker* claimed "non-libel, justification, common report, and publication in good faith in the ordinary course of business, with no intent to injure."[133] The case lingered in the court system for more than seven years, with the *New Yorker* taking offensive action in the fall of 1956 when it appeared that Filler and Whittey were going to press the case to trial. Alexander Lindey was not worried about the "old coyote" remark. He thought it would be easy enough to prove, through the testimony of residents of the Lake Pyramid area of Nevada, where Filler and Whittey lived, that "old coyote" was "no more defamatory than a colloquial 's.o.b.' would be here."[134] The Filler complaint, though, bothered him. "The gist of the allegedly defamatory charge . . . is that he was thrown off a freight train," Lindey explained to Milton Greenstein, editorial counsel for the *New Yorker*. "If we plead justification, we will have to allege that he was in fact so thrown off. I seriously question the advisability of making this allegation unless we have some basis for it."[135]

Lindey needed proof, and he went to Nevada to get it. There he talked at length with a Reno lawyer who agreed to help him research the case, including locating former or current residents who could testify at trial about the local meaning of "old coyote" in the Pyramid Lake area as well as someone who could testify that Joe Filler had in fact arrived at the Whittey ranch on a freight train.[136] Part of the problem was that Liebling could not remember exactly who had given him the information about Filler's arrival in Pyramid Lake. "Either Joe or Harry Drackert or Joan Drackert (Harry's wife) or maybe all of them told me about how Joe had been thrown from the train," he wrote by way of explanation. In the course of Lindey's investigation, the Drackerts both denied giving this information to Liebling. "It is quite possible," Lindey wrote to Greenstein, "that if Liebling searches his memory, he may remember a personal talk with Joe. Liebling would of course be our best witness if he could truthfully say that Joe himself was the source of the episode." [137]

Liebling obviously was not the careful reporter Lindey needed him to be in this instance. Whether the freight train episode was part of Liebling's tendency to embroider his stories is impossible to tell from the record. [138] In October 1962 the cases were discontinued without costs because the plaintiffs never pursued them all the way to trial. [139] All along, the *New Yorker* had refused to settle, and in the end, the magazine managed to outlast Filler and Whittey.

The Case of the Unhappy Philosopher

In an episode with many similarities to the Masson-Malcolm dispute, the well-known English philosopher Ernest Gellner threatened to file a libel suit against the *New Yorker* in both New York and London over an article by Ved Mehta on Oxford philosophy published in the December 9, 1961, issue of the magazine. Titled "A Battle against the Bewitchment of Our Intelligence," the long feature (it took up the greater part of the issue in which it was published) tells the story of Mehta's meeting with Gellner in London. [140] Like Masson in Malcolm's profile, Gellner comes off as something of an egomaniac from what he says about himself. Mehta quotes him as saying: "I am a prophet. . . . I am ahead of my times. . . . I am the Malcolm Muggeridge of philosophy." [141] In a letter to the editors of the *New Yorker* Gellner wrote, "Such humorless and megalomaniac rubbish was not uttered by me to Mr. Mehta, or anyone else, nor was anything resembling it." [142] Perhaps predictably, the *New Yorker* refused to print Gellner's letter and, in an extraordinary gesture, editor William Shawn himself wrote a three-page response rebutting point by point Gellner's interpretations of Mehta's article and claims of fabrication and libel. As to the allegedly fabricated quotation, Shawn wrote that he believed Mehta, who "claims that you did say it (and has careful notes to that effect)." [143] Gellner also claimed that he never read to Mehta, as described in the article, passages from a transcript of one of his BBC programs which he carried in his pocket. He also argued that the transcript would not be "crinkly" and "yellow" as Mehta described it. The implicit issue here was the fact of Mehta's blindness. Shawn replied: "If he [Mehta] doesn't *know* a visual detail, he doesn't use it. He didn't know at that moment that the sheets were yellow, since he was unaccompanied and since he did not ask you the color. However, he later obtained a B.B.C. transcript, and he has, in fact, shown it to me. The sheets are crinkly and yellow." Shawn continued: "I do not feel that it's necessary to discuss Mehta's blindness with you; I think you do him many injustices in your remarks, and I will let it go at that." [144]

Shawn's letter was never sent to Gellner. It appears in the *New Yorker* records as an unsigned draft. In a letter to Greenstein about the case, Lindey recommended against sending it: "I doubt whether a letter from Shawn to Gellner, however temperate and sensible, will do much good. The letter as drawn merely asserts that, with respect to everything in the article objected to by Gellner, Mehta was right and Gellner was wrong. This is hardly the kind of communication calculated to pacify a man. I have nevertheless made some slight changes in the draft, which I am returning herewith. My present view is not to send it." [145] In his memoirs of working at William Shawn's *New Yorker*, Mehta wrote that Greenstein indeed counseled Shawn not to mail the letter "on the ground that it could only serve to complicate the legal situation." [146] The *New Yorker* refused to print as written a second letter to the editor that Gellner submitted but did suggest to Gellner's New York lawyer that the magazine would print its own revision of the letter if Gellner agreed not to pursue a libel claim against the *New Yorker* "anywhere in the world, arising out of the Mehta article," and with the understanding that the magazine would publish a reply from Mehta if he chose to respond. Further, the *New Yorker* would not pay Gellner's legal fees or costs. [147] Not surprisingly, Gellner turned down the offer.

Gellner apparently was not the only significant English philosopher who felt that Mehta had misrepresented his remarks. Bertrand Russell and A. J. (Freddie) Ayer, both eminent philosophers in England, also suggested that Mehta had misquoted them or, worse, fabricated quotes. In a letter to Gellner, Russell wrote: "I did not make the remark [Mehta] attributed to me for I admire your book immensely. I have written to him mentioning that this is the case. I might mention that I had an indignant letter from Freddie Ayer in which he assures me that many remarks attributed to him by Mehta were not his, and represent in fact the opposite of what he felt." Russell then goes on to give Gellner some advice, which perhaps he eventually took to heart in deciding not to pursue his libel claim further: "I hope you will have not been too troubled by this experience. In a long life I have come to expect approval only when it no longer matters and hatred when I am saying something of value and importance." [148] Ayer apparently also wrote to Gellner about the issue, for Gellner replied, giving Ayer the name of his lawyer in New York. He noted that "suing in America is out of the question, given the laxity of U.S. libel laws and the expense and unpredictability of litigation," but he thought that the *New Yorker*, which kept a London office, would be more susceptible in England. [149]

Both Mehta and Shawn claimed that the quotations were accurate; Gellner, Russell, and Ayer claimed that they were not (although Gellner was the only one of the three philosophers who threatened a libel suit). Whether Gellner made the self-aggrandizing statements Mehta attributed to him is impossible to determine from the record. Perhaps he simply wished that he had not said them. Perhaps he said them and did not remember. Or perhaps Mehta made them up as Gellner claimed. (For his part, Mehta maintains in his memoir that his account of his conversation with Gellner was true.) [150] Whatever the case, Gellner seemed to struggle with the decision of whether to pursue his libel claim. In his letter to Ayer he wrote:

> There may be something to be said in favour of discouraging the Mendacious-Mehta kind of journalism, of the smear technique which in this case does not even have a political motive. I am not an advocate of excessive restraint in print, and saw no ground for complaint when certain reviewers credited me with contemptible motives—but they did this as their own opinion, over their own signatures. But the Mehtod is quite different—to invent statements and credit them to the victim as his own words. [151]

When the London office asked Greenstein in April 1962 what had happened with "the case of the unhappy philosopher," Milton Greenstein replied that the consensus in New York was "that the matter is dead." [152] Gellner had apparently decided to drop the matter, perhaps following Bertrand Russell's advice. When Mehta was preparing a manuscript of his article for book publication, Greenstein sent him a tear sheet of the article marked with suggested deletions of passages containing factual details that Gellner had protested. He suggested that Mehta should, as he apparently had suggested to Greenstein, tell his book publisher about the Gellner incident. [153] When Mehta's book of essays appeared the following year, the essay on the philosophers no longer contained what Gellner claimed was "megalomaniac rubbish" falsely attributed to him. [154]

Libel at the *New Yorker* from 1925 to *Sullivan*: Piecing It All Together

Of all the libel complaints the *New Yorker* fielded from its inception in 1925 to the early 1960s, only a handful were litigated—and of these, no judgments were made against the magazine. During this time the *New Yorker* settled only a few cases, as we have seen. In the first, involving the article criticizing the Delmonico Building's architecture, the criticism was mild, even for the day, and the judge who refused to dismiss the case did not understand the established protections of the "fair comment and criticism" doctrine. In the William James Sidis malicious libel complaint and the Yankee Schwartz complaint involving the alleged libel of an alleged gangster, the magazine agreed to reach a settlement only after concerted efforts to avoid doing so appeared futile.[155] In addition, the magazine essentially paid off Rita Ross with a nominal sum to get her off its back. In cases that were litigated, such as the early 1940s Jessie Costello case, in which the defendant in a notorious murder trial in Massachusetts sued the magazine for libel over an article telling her story, the magazine would attempt "to tie up the litigation." [156] In this case the *New Yorker's* tactic of drawing things out in hopes that complainants would tire of the dispute worked. The Costello case died what Lindey called "a natural death." [157]

During these years *New Yorker* editors and Alexander Lindey developed other ways to protect the magazine against libel complaints. In addition to establishing early in its existence a rigorous editorial and authorial review process including documentation of sources, fact-checking, and libel review, the *New Yorker* generally refused to publish retractions (even in a few cases when an error had been made) and to settle claims. Instead the magazine's lawyers used what they called "explanation" and "persuasion" to fend off those who complained of defamation. Lindey, with the *New Yorker's* approval, also employed investigators to discover information about libel complainants which proved critical in fending off the complaints. In ways both large and small, the *New Yorker* used its considerable financial, legal, and editorial resources to discourage libel suits and protect its editorial and business interests.

From 1932 to at least the late 1960s the magazine maintained a close relationship with Greenbaum, Wolff & Ernst, with Lindey working as chief retained counsel. This relationship undoubtedly helped the *New Yorker* achieve a strong libel defense record during the forty years reflected in the magazine's records. From the beginning, Lindey and the editors understood libel suits as a significant threat to the magazine's editorial independence and financial well-being, but as the years wore on, they saw the threat increase. In 1946, after the child prodigy and Cat Woman cases had taxed the resources and patience of the staff for years, and after the magazine came to the bitter realization that it would need to settle the Yankee Schwartz case, Harold Ross hired in-house counsel Milton Greenstein to help, among other things, read for libel. (Greenstein was replacing previous in-house counsel.) In one of the final circuits of the maze-like editorial path all articles and fiction traveled, Ross had Greenstein, like his predecessor, read all pieces in what was called "the bank"—the manuscripts stored and ready to be run. One May evening, when libel queries showed up on a story about to go to press, a frustrated Ross demanded that a new system be devised for Greenstein to show that he had indeed read each banked manu-script. "It is preposterous," he fumed. "It is always inexcusable (in theory, at least) for a libel query to be brought up on press days on a piece that has been around a long time. . . . I have been living in a fool's paradise on this libel busi-ness. I don't want to be doing so any more."[158] Several weeks later Ross wrote a note to Greenstein expressing concern about invasion of privacy suits. He had read about such a suit against Marjorie Kinnan Rawlings in the *New York Times* that morning (a jury found in her favor), and William James Sidis's privacy claim had come to mind, "a litigation that dragged on for years." "I have always worried about these grounds for suits," Ross wrote. "Theoretically, all publica-tions would be put out of business, especially such publications as ours."[159]

From the mid-1950s forward, as American news publishing changed to in-clude pointed coverage and critiques of social problems, Lindey began sending Milton Greenstein libel memos discussing important cases and developments in the law in both state and federal courts, including issues such as the increas-ing size of punitive damage awards, the "fair comment and criticism" defense, the seeming fusion of libel and privacy claims, the moribund state of criminal libel law, and the use of libel law to silence or harass the press. The climate for media libel suits in the United States was heating up, and the *New Yorker* was responding. Lindey's most important and historic libel memo, at least for the purposes of this book, was written on the heels of the Supreme Court's 1964 decision in *New York Times v. Sullivan*. "In April of this year," he noted, "not less than seventeen libel actions brought by public officials in three Southern states against newspapers, magazines and a television network were pending in the state and Federal courts."[160] After detailing some of these cases, he outlined the *Sullivan* case, noting its importance but hesitant about its ultimate ability to protect the press. "Although the decision was a substantial forward step in safe-guarding the freedom of criticism in the political arena," Lindey wrote, "it did not quite justify the hosannas with which it was greeted, nor the extravagant claims that were made for it." [161] For Lindey, the Court had not gone far enough in protecting the press, for "a publication would still be liable for libel if it acted with malice." Whether Lindey had made the important and necessary distinction between common law malice and actual malice—the constitutional standard erected in *Sullivan* requiring that a publisher act with knowledge of falsity or reckless disregard for the truth in order for a public official plaintiff to prevail in a libel suit—is unclear, but his argument works in either case, at least as the law stood immediately in the aftermath of *Sullivan*:

> Here is the rub, and it's a rub indeed. Malice is neither an absolute term nor a palpable one: it must be inferred from the acts of the defendant. Whether or not it is present in a given case is a question for the jury. And so if a jury is hell-bent on whacking the defendant with a verdict, all it has to do is find malice; and if it finds malice, the judgment may well be permitted to stand, because the existence of malice is an issue of fact, and on such issues the appellate courts are traditionally reluctant to overturn verdicts.[162]

Lindey perceived a number of fault lines in the *Sullivan* protections; as we will see, these fault lines would emerge as the actual malice standard and constitutionalized libel law continued to evolve. He concluded with this observation: "In the publishing business, libel has always been a hazard. It is impossible to write contemporary history or to comment courageously on matters of public interest without hurting reputations. The moral of this summary of recent cases is not that publishers should yield to timidity and run for cover when sued, but that they should be vigilant and scrupulous, and take no unnecessary chances." [163] Even now, his 1964 advice to the *New Yorker* stands as solid counsel.

From the *New Yorker*'s first year of publication in 1925 to the *Sullivan* era of the 1960s, libel law buffeted the magazine and led editors and lawyers to devise editorial and legal strategies to protect against the threats and nuisances of potential libel suits. Although the law of defamation during this period was generally not life-threatening to major press publications, the *New Yorker* understood the potential of libel law to do major damage to press freedoms.

During its first forty years, the *New Yorker* resisted the encroachment of libel law on its freedoms of expression. Both the magazine and its lawyers took pride in publishing factual statements they believed were important in reporting the world around them, even if those statements were injurious to a subject's reputation. In its zeal to protect its freedoms, or perhaps simply its reputation, the *New Yorker* usually resisted printing retractions or corrections. This is a fact that, for better or worse, must be acknowledged. But it is also important to recognize that the libel readers at the magazine were not censors so much as they were standard-bearers for truth, or what editors and writers at the magazine took to be truth, within the magazine's pages. In this most fundamental of ways, the *New Yorker* carved an important place for itself in the American marketplace of ideas on which democracy depends.

The revision in libel law that Alexander Lindey and his partner and co--author Morris Ernst hoped for came with the Supreme Court's constitutionalization of libel law in *New York Times v. Sullivan* in 1964. But as Lindey recognized in his *New Yorker* libel memo written almost thirty years after the publication of *Hold Your Tongue!*, *Sullivan*'s actual malice standard would prove less protective of the press than the press, at least, would have wished.

Other libel cases were filed against the *New Yorker* in the years following *Sullivan*, and a number were litigated in the federal courts. Of all the cases that reached judicial resolution, not one judgment was entered against the magazine.[164] Of these, *Masson v. New Yorker* is the most important, both for its status as the only case in the magazine's history to be heard by the Supreme Court and for its further articulation of the constitutional actual malice standard in *New York Times v. Sullivan*. Although a jury ultimately found in favor of the magazine and Malcolm, the financial cost to the *New Yorker* of defending the case, upwards of $2.5 million, was substantial.[165] The injury to its reputation may have been even more costly as the institutional press aggressively questioned both the ethics and fact-checking procedures of the magazine.[166] The press-protective spirit of *Sullivan* notwithstanding, libel law during the years of the Masson-Malcolm dispute was a greater threat to the magazine than it was in the *New Yorker*'s first forty years.

Cross-currents in editorial policy worked against the *New Yorker* as the Masson-Malcolm case played out in both the federal courts and the court of public (and press) opinion. On the one hand, the magazine had long before established a reputation for scrupulously maintaining factual accuracy. On the other, it had not followed the strict dictates of professional standards as they

developed in the world of daily journalism, allowing the use at times of composite characters, translated speech, and compressed quotations. In *Masson v.
New Yorker*, the Supreme Court suggested that the magazine's "reputation for
scrupulous factual accuracy" could (and likely would) "lead a reader to take the
[disputed] quotations at face value." [167] When Judge Alex Kozinski of the Ninth
Circuit ruled that Malcolm's publisher, Knopf, should be dismissed from the
case before it went to trial, he reasoned that the publishing house had good
cause to rely on the *New Yorker*'s own investigation of Masson's claims and thus
was legally protected in the libel suit. "The magazine's sterling reputation for
accuracy and the existence of its fabled fact-checking department gave Knopf
sufficient reason for dismissing Masson's claims that he was misquoted,"
Kozinski wrote.[168] In the end, the *New Yorker* was a literary magazine that had
historically paid a certain amount of deference to its writers. While the *New
Yorker* understood its fact writers as journalists, at the same time it also understood them as artists. And while the magazine upheld strict standards of
factual accuracy, what it perceived as fact was at times different from what
traditional journalism would understand to be factual. As it turned out, the
utterances of a person were not necessarily, in the *New Yorker*'s editorial opinion, matters of fact. This disconnect between the professional standards of
the literary journalism of the *New Yorker* and the traditional journalism of
the daily press—and between the magazine's reverence for factual accuracy
and allowances for a certain creative license—created conditions ripe for the
Masson-Malcolm dispute.

CHAPTER FIVE

~~~

Masson v. New Yorker
in the Early Years

WHEN JEFFREY MASSON FILED HIS FIRST COMPLAINT AGAINST JANET
Malcolm in 1984, it was simply one in what many scholars have characterized
as an unusual explosion of libel cases in the 1970s and 1980s.[1] A number of social and cultural forces produced this marked shift in the arena of libel law.

According to defamation scholar Rodney Smolla, the proliferation of libel
suits was in part a reaction to "a new legal and cultural seriousness about the
inner self." Historically, libel law was meant to redress wrongful damage to
what Smolla terms a plaintiff's "relational interest" in maintaining a good
reputation in society.[2] It was not meant to provide compensation for psychological or emotional injury. But by the time Masson filed his suit, such compensation had become the larger part of the purpose, even if implicit and
unspoken. As Smolla notes, the huge damage awards in libel trials of the era
suggested that juries were compensating psychological injury rather than verifiable damage to reputation.[3]

Another cultural force at play was the public libel plaintiff's sense of being
hamstrung by the high constitutional barrier to recovery set by the actual malice standard. An Iowa Libel Research Project study of media libel cases involving public plaintiffs from 1974 to 1984 found that these plaintiffs prevailed in
their suits only 10 percent of the time.[4] The study highlighted the actual malice
privilege as a key explanation for this low public plaintiff success rate. Marc
Franklin's study of libel cases decided between 1977 and 1980 found that plaintiffs, both public and private, prevailed only 5 percent of the time.[5] Two studies
conducted by the Libel Defense Resource Center, one on media libel cases de-

cided between 1979 and 1982 and the other for 1982 to 1984, found that a substantial majority of plaintiffs' verdicts continued to be overturned in the appeals process.[6] For the most part, such plaintiffs knew they had little chance of prevailing, yet many sued nonetheless. The reason they did, according to data gathered by the Iowa Libel Research Project, was less to win a large damage award than to prove the falsity of the allegedly defamatory statement.[7] These plaintiffs largely believed that their lawsuits, even when unsuccessful, not only vindicated their damaged reputations but also penalized the press by forcing media outlets to pay the cost of defending the case.[8] Libel cases of the era provide clear proof of the punishing costs associated with defending against a libel suit: ABC spent about $7 million in one libel case; CBS News spent several million defending against a libel suit brought by General William C. Westmoreland;[9] and the *Washington Post* spent well over $1 million in a libel suit filed by the president of Mobil Corporation.[10] Even beyond the fear of excessive damage awards, the possibility of facing such high defense costs is enough to chill press expression, especially for publications with small pocketbooks. As Norman Rosenberg has noted, "The fact that defamation law now apparently favored defendants erased some of the stigma traditionally associated with filing a libel suit."[11]

Yet another factor contributed to the rise in libel suits: an increasing public disdain for what was widely perceived as the media's unprecedented corporate power and arrogance. Popular discontent with the press has always existed in America, but in the early 1970s, in the wake of the *Washington Post*'s muckraking exposés of the Watergate scandal, it became a defining sentiment in the public sphere.[12] As the media historian and sociologist Michael Schudson has noted, the Nixon administration actively demonized what it perceived as a liberal press biased against it long before the Watergate scandal broke. The administration promoted the use of the term "the media" to refer to the press because, Schudson suggests, it sounded unpleasant and manipulative. "The administration insisted that the media were not, as they often claimed to be, the voice of the people," Schudson writes. "Nor were they, as many had traditionally understood them, the voice of wealthy publishers, on the one hand, or organs of political parties, on the other. Instead, they were an independent and dangerously irresponsible source of power."[13] Bob Woodward and Carl Bernstein's investigation into Watergate, heralded by some as excellent journalism and decried by others as irresponsible, simply fed a negative perception of the press that had already worked its way into public opinion. As Smolla observes, "In the aftermath of Vietnam and Watergate, the American press grew in glamour, power, and profitability, but not in heartfelt esteem." [14] Joining the Nixon White House's conservative critique of the media, a host of critics decried what they saw as the press's hostile attitude toward government. [15]

Even before Watergate, though, during the cultural upheaval of the 1960s, the public sphere was roiling with discontent. The post–World War II expansion of higher education, coupled with a cooling off of cold war ardor after the Cuban missile crisis, prepared the public for intellectual engagement with the significant issues of the day. Add the public recognition of government news management during the Vietnam War, the horrors of that conflict, and the assassinations of John F. Kennedy, Martin Luther King Jr., and Robert Kennedy, and the result was a widespread and potent skepticism. It was what Schudson has called "the rise of a critical culture." [16] As the relationship between press and government turned adversarial during the Vietnam era, the press began writing not just about the war but about the government's attempts to manipulate information about the conflict in order to shape more positive, or at least less negative, news coverage. [17] By the time the libel suit explosion of the late 1970s and early 1980s arrived, the public had long since learned the need for critical judgment.

The difference in this later era, though, was that the public had turned the skepticism previously trained almost exclusively on government toward the press, the vehicle of public discourse itself. The government's management of news in the Vietnam era, and the discourse about this management in the press, had taught people to think about the construction of news, and not just the government's construction. With the newfound role of Americans as critics of public institutions, the press found itself in the middle of a credibility crisis. And the same critics whose attitudes toward the press had soured sat on juries in media libel trials. An October 1984 *Newsweek* poll revealed that an overwhelming majority of Americans had little faith in the press; television news garnered a mere 26 percent confidence rating, with newspaper reporting only slightly higher at 34 percent. [18]

The press, sensing the crisis well before *Newsweek* verified its existence with such stunning numbers, responded with the creation of ethics codes and ombudsman posts, as well as the short-lived National News Council. In 1973 Sigma Chi Delta (now the Society of Professional Journalists) unanimously approved a code of ethics that quickly became an exemplar in the field. [19] It spoke directly to public concerns about the contemporary role of media in society, urging journalists and press institutions to avoid political involvement that might compromise their credibility or objectivity; to act responsibly and with self-restraint in reporting; to report as representatives of the public, not as a special class somehow removed; to respect the privacy and dignity of subjects of reports; and to reject any gifts or special privileges offered in the course of their work.[20] In 1975 the American Society of Newspaper Editors revised its canons, calling the new document a statement of principles, and the Associated Press Managing Editors Association devised its own standards.[21] By the early 1980s many newspapers had adopted their own ethical codes (with the notable exceptions of the *New York Times* and the *Los Angeles Times*), as had the major network news departments.[22] The National News Council was created in 1973 as a watchdog organization, an attempt by the press to police itself. Lacking the support of the *New York Times* and the teeth and will to enforce its regulations, the Council folded in 1984.[23] To conservative critics, the failure of the council was yet one more sign of press arrogance and unregulated power.

Burnett and *Tavoulareas*

As press organizations scrambled to clean up the sullied public image of news organizations, high-profile libel cases kept stirring the public's interest and discontent. One of the most sensational occurred in 1976, when Carol Burnett sued the *National Enquirer* for libel, claiming that the tabloid had wrongly reported that she had drunkenly confronted Henry Kissinger in a Washington, D.C., restaurant.[24] In 1981 a jury found that the *Enquirer* had published false and defamatory statements about Burnett with actual malice. In a deposition presented at trial, the ostensible writer of the disputed article said that he did not trust his source for the information and that the article had actually been written by a senior editor at the paper. The tabloid's fact-checking procedures were also revealed to be careless and deficient. In what was a ringing indictment of the *Enquirer*'s news practices, the jury awarded Burnett $1.6 million in damages.[25] Although a California state court of appeals ultimately reduced the punitive damages award to $150,000 and upheld the compensatory damages award of $50,000, the panel of judges chastised the *Enquirer* in its opinion, writing: "We have no doubt the [paper's] conduct was reprehensible and undertaken with the kind of improper motive which supports the imposition of punitive damages."[26]

On the one hand, the jury's stunning award of punitive damages in the

Burnett suit, which accounted for $1.3 of the total $1.6 million awarded, can be understood as the public judicial chastening of a tabloid that had willfully reported sensational falsehoods about a well-liked celebrity.[27] It was the kind of journalism no one in the mainstream press wanted to defend. On the other hand, the notably large damage award operated as a chilling influence on the speech of other, more reputable publications. As press lawyer James Goodale noted at the time, although juries did not generally punish responsible journalism with disproportionate awards, "that doesn't mean they wouldn't."[28] He went on to cite the excessive award an Alabama jury had initially given the Montgomery police commissioner in what became the landmark libel case *New York Times v. Sullivan.*[29] His warning proved prescient.

The press reported avidly on the Burnett litigation. A small sample of the mainstream coverage suggests widespread public and industry interest: *Time* magazine carried several articles on the dispute; the *Nation* published a cover story and other commentary; and the *New York Times* carried more than twenty-five articles during the life of the case.[30] As a *Times* news analysis observed, "the Burnett case has aroused enormous public sympathy" as well as a surprising indifference among editors, publishers, and journalists to the the judicial encroachment upon press freedoms.[31] "According to journalists and lawyers specializing in First Amendment cases," Jonathan Friendly wrote, "the lack of outrage stems primarily from a deep ambivalence about The Enquirer and its methods."[32] The press had taken the measure of public, legal, and industry sentiment about the specific standards and practices embodied in the *National Enquirer,* and across the board, social sentiment was against this particular strain of press expression. But as a subsequent high-profile libel case made clear, public discontent was spreading to the mainstream press.

Not long after the jury verdict in the *Enquirer* case, another federal jury in Washington, D.C., awarded Peter W. Tavoulareas, the president of Mobil Oil Corporation, $2 million in damages in his libel suit against the *Washington Post.*[33] In 1979 the *Post* published two articles claiming that Tavoulareas had set up his son as partner in a shipping management company that handled no-bid contracts from Mobil worth millions of dollars. Tavoulareas sued the newspaper in 1980 for $50 million, claiming the *Post's* charges of nepotism and wrongful acts were defamatory and untrue.[34] That the president of Mobil would seek such a large damage award was in itself somewhat shocking. That the jury found for him and awarded more than $2 million was even more shocking to press lawyers and the profession of journalism.[35] Although the trial judge set aside the jury verdict and award, holding that there was "no evidence in the record" that the *Post* had published the story with actual malice, the U.S. Court of Appeals for the District of Columbia reinstated the verdict and damages, ruling that the article did contain false statements published with reckless disregard for the truth.[36] If the original jury verdict had been shocking, this latest ruling set off near-panic in journalistic circles. The opinion, written by Judge George E. MacKinnon joined by then-judge Antonin Scalia, stated that the *Post*'s editorial policy of publishing "hard-hitting investigative stories" was relevant to the inquiry as to whether the newspaper had acted with reckless disregard for the truth.[37] It was a major reinterpretation, largely unsupported by precedent, of the actual malice standard established in the *New York Times* case.

It is hard to imagine the opinion being penned without the 1979 Supreme Court ruling in *Herbert v. Lando*,[38] in which the justices refused to offer First Amendment protection to the editorial process in a libel suit. Although the *Tavoulareas* majority in the appellate court curiously did not cite the *Lando* decision, the Court's refusal in that case to protect the editorial process from a libel plaintiff's inquiry seems a necessary precursor to the *Tavoulareas* claim that an editorial policy encouraging aggressive investigative reporting can be circumstantial evidence of actual malice.

In a sharply worded dissent in *Tavoulareas*, Judge Skelly Wright criticized the majority's ruling as a constitutionally impermissible intrusion into the newsroom: "In my judgment, we do not sit, even in reviewing a libel verdict, as some kind of journalism review seminar, offering our observations on contemporary journalism and journalists. Our mission is to see that the First Amendment is vigorously protected and that libel verdicts not supported by clear and convincing evidence do not stand."[39] Judge Wright claimed that the majority's ruling sprang from its antipathy to the muckraking propensities of the *Washington Post* and other press organizations. "This deep hostility to an aggressive press," he wrote, "is directly contrary to the mandates of the Supreme Court and the spirit of a free press. . . . In my judgment, neither a newspaper's muckraking policy nor its hard-hitting investigative journalism should *ever* be considered probative of actual malice."[40] He also lambasted as constitutionally impermissible what he saw as an excessive award of damages on the basis of scant evidence: "If this excessive jury verdict on these mundane, flimsy facts is upheld, the effect on freedom of expression will be incalculable. The message to the media will be unmistakable—steer clear of unpleasant news stories and comments about interests like Mobil or pay the price."[41]

The press celebrated Judge Wright's dissent while it decried the majority's ruling. In an op-ed piece published in the *New York Times*, Anthony Lewis observed: "I think the hateful comments on investigative journalism give it [the majority ruling] away. It is a reaction against Watergate."[42] Major newspapers across the country, including the *New York Times, Washington Post, Denver Post*, and *St. Petersburg Times*, protested the ruling's heavy-handed review of editorial decisions made regarding the articles. For A. M. Rosenthal, executive editor of the *Times*, the majority opinion essentially described the workings of a good newspaper. The decision was, he said, "garbage."[43] Three years later, in 1987, the same federal court of appeals, in an *en banc* rehearing of the Tavoulareas case, reversed the earlier ruling of the three-judge panel, holding that the gist of the *Post* articles was substantially true.[44] The court further ruled that the adversarial posture of investigative reporting did not, as the earlier court of appeals opinion asserted, imply an inclination to publish with reckless disregard for the truth.[45] The record in the case showed, the court wrote, overwhelming evidence that the *Washington Post* "published the article in good faith. The contention that the *Post* engaged . . . in a pattern of 'slanted reporting' indicative of actual malice is utterly without merit."[46] But the damage had been done to the *Washington Post*'s reputation and credibility. From 1982, when the jury found for Tavoulareas, until 1987, when the D.C. Circuit reversed *en banc* its earlier three-judge panel reinstatement of the jury verdict, the jury's indictment of the newspaper's conduct in reporting on the Mobil incident colored public perceptions of the *Post* and likely of the press at large.[47] The September 15, 1983, issue of the *New York Times* actually ran an editorial-style advertisement on the editorial pages in which the Mobil Corporation, in a fascinating public relations move, claimed that, contrary to what the press was saying, large jury verdicts against the media did not threaten the First Amendment.[48] Rather, the Mobil ad claimed, the First Amendment protection "awarded the press" in *Sullivan* was "an extraordinary insulation from libel responsibility" that, if misused, threatened not only press credibility but also the public interest.[49]

The *Tavoulareas* case highlights the cultural and political complexity of free expression issues. The original appellate court ruling was in part the intellectual product of Antonin Scalia, who later became a U.S. Supreme Court justice known for his staunch conservatism. The *en banc* opinion was written by another conservative judge, the same Kenneth Starr later made famous as the special prosecutor in the Bill Clinton–Monica Lewinsky affair. That two well-known conservative judges should come to such different legal conclusions regarding the same facts in a First Amendment libel case suggests the ideological complexity of free press issues. Although support for the press's First Amendment rights is often understood as a key tenet of American liberalism, such support is clearly not the sole province of liberal thought.

Westmoreland and *Sharon*

As highly publicized as *Burnett* and *Tavoulareas* were, they merely set the stage for two intense and intensely covered libel cases in the early 1980s. Couched in the profound political problems and events of the era and involving the wartime actions of high-profile public officials, both *Westmoreland v. CBS* and *Sharon v. Time* galvanized public attention on libel law and the conduct of major American news media.[50] Fueled by growing discontent with the press in the preceding decade, the trials in these cases contributed to an unprecedented cultural moment in which the American public and press together took stock of the role of the media in public life and weighed the social value of press freedom against that of press responsibility.

In January 1982 CBS broadcast a documentary titled *The Uncounted Enemy: A Vietnam Deception*, in which it characterized General William C. Westmoreland, then retired from the army, as the lead conspirator in suppressing and altering crucial intelligence information regarding "the enemy" during the Vietnam War. This conspiracy, according to the documentary, was part of a military effort to deceive the government and public about the size of enemy forces in order to persuade them that the United States was winning the war.[51] Soon after the broadcast, Westmoreland held a press conference in which he denied the allegations and demanded an apology. CBS refused.[52] Later, when CBS offered to broadcast a follow-up program and allow Westmoreland fifteen minutes to tell his side of the story, Westmoreland refused.[53] From September 13, 1982, when General Westmoreland filed suit against CBS, to February 19, 1985, when he and CBS in a joint statement announced his dropping of the $120 million libel action after eighteen weeks of trial testimony in a federal district court in Manhattan, the *New York Times* published more than 150 stories about the trial.[54] The *Washington Post* published almost one hundred stories.

Such intense news coverage documented not only the complexities and at times the manipulation involved in the military's handling of the Vietnam War but also CBS's failure to follow its own professional standards in putting together the contested report. News coverage of the Westmoreland case became a means for the press to investigate in broad terms the professional standards of journalism and, more narrowly, the degree to which CBS adhered to or veered from them.

Four months after *The Uncounted Enemy* aired, *TV Guide* published charges that the report did not follow CBS News standards for accuracy and fairness. These charges prompted CBS to launch an internal investigation, which produced a sixty-eight-page report detailing the reporting and editorial procedures used in the program.[55] In particular, the president of CBS News, Van Gordon Sauter, acknowledged that the report did not fairly balance interviews representing the program's thesis and Westmoreland's views. He also suggested that "deception" was a more appropriate description of the military misreporting of enemy troop strength than "conspiracy." Mike Wallace, the CBS correspondent who narrated the disputed program, himself admitted that he should have been more involved in the fifteen months of reporting and editing the program (he spent a mere three weeks on the project). Sauter changed CBS News procedures so as to require correspondents to be more involved in complex reporting projects.[56] Months later, a national public television broadcast of *Inside Story*, a weekly program critiquing the press, reported that the producers and staff of *The Uncounted Enemy* either had not interviewed, or had not included interviews with, high-ranking military officials involved in Vietnam-era intelligence. "If you're going to make a case that there was a conspiracy at the highest levels of American intelligence," said *Inside Story* correspondent Hodding Carter, "then you have to go to the highest levels and allow the chief conspirators to talk."[57]

This very public exposé of the failure of CBS News to follow its own standards in reporting serious charges against retired U.S. military officials further shook the public's dwindling faith in the press. This was not the high-minded, hard-hitting investigative reporting that had brought the Pentagon Papers and Watergate to the attention of the American public. Rather, this was the work of a press willing and able to do mighty damage to a public official's reputation on the basis of incomplete and at times unfair reporting—or so it seemed to many. Floyd Abrams, one of the most prominent libel lawyers in

the United States, suggested that the cost of the case, financial and reputational, had been extraordinarily high, not only for Westmoreland but also for
CBS.[58] In 1984, even before the Westmoreland suit was settled, press lawyers at
a Practising Law Institute conference marking the twentieth anniversary of
New York Times v. Sullivan noted the "growing public antagonism" toward the
press. As the keynote speaker, Judge Irving R. Kaufman, then chief judge of the
United States Court of Appeals for the Second Circuit, remarked, jurors in libel
suits, like their fellow citizens, generally saw news organizations as "aloof and
arrogant, insensitive to human needs and concerned only with the profits
reaped from sensational coverage."[59] Public trust in and esteem for the press
were at an all-time low, at least for the post–World War II era.

At the very moment the Westmoreland trial was under way on the third
floor of the federal district court, Ariel Sharon, then a former general and defense minister of Israel, and soon to be prime minister, was engaged in his own
$50 million libel trial against *Time* magazine only six floors up.[60] In a February
1983 issue, *Time* published an article about the massacre in Beirut of hundreds
of Palestinians the previous year. Titled "The Verdict Is Guilty," the article suggested that Sharon was responsible for the massacre because he encouraged the
Christian Phalangists who carried it out. The key factual issue involved the
truth of the report's claim that Sharon had urged the Gemayel family to re-
venge the murder of Lebanon's president-elect Bashir Gemayel.[61] Claiming the
allegation to be false and defamatory, Sharon filed libel suits against *Time* in
both Tel Aviv and New York. "I'm struggling to remove the mark of Cain from
myself, from the State of Israel and from the Jewish people," he is reported to
have said. *Time*'s lawyers characterized the suit as a savvy political maneuver.
Sharon had recently announced his plans to run for prime minister of Israel,
and the trial, they argued, was an attempt to salvage his political future.[62]
Time's own tactic was to suggest that the disputed article could be read in a
non-defamatory way and the case should thus be dismissed. A federal judge
denied *Time*'s motion for dismissal, holding that a reasonable reader of the article could easily infer that Sharon had condoned the massacre.[63]

Unlike the Westmoreland case, which was dismissed before trial testimony
was concluded, the Sharon case led to a jury decision. In January 1985, after a
two-month-long trial, jurors found that the disputed article in *Time*, though
containing false and defamatory information, was not published with actual
malice. *Time* was not liable. Although Sharon did not win his case, both he and

the magazine claimed victory. The contested publication did not rise to actual malice, according to the jury's findings, because *Time* did not publish the article with either knowledge of or reckless disregard as to its falsity. But in an unusual courtroom event, the verdict strayed beyond the bounds of the legal issues in the case. After delivering the verdict, the foreman read a statement from the jurors criticizing *Time*'s reporters and editors for being negligent and careless in their work on the article.[64] In discussing the jury statement, a *New York Times* editorial observed, "It seemed to give voice to widespread discontent with influential media that are quick to dish out criticism but unwilling or reluctant to present a contrary judgment or to confess error."[65] The *Washington Post* ombudsman acknowledged that the magazine should have admitted its error in judgment early in the dispute. Its unwillingness to do so, he suggested, would leave "doubts about the magazine's reporting and editing, and reinforc[e] those who think the media have become a wielder of the arrogance of power."[66] Although the legal verdict was in favor of the news magazine, the moral verdict was against it.

The highly public examination of what some considered sloppy and careless reporting on the part of two major American press institutions—CBS News and *Time* magazine—placed media practices front and center on the public agenda. After the *Sharon* verdict and before the *Westmoreland* settlement, *Newsweek* published a cover story detailing the crisis of public confidence in the press. Given the news media's vulnerability to error, increasing public and industry scrutiny, and America's critical and skeptical culture, the article observed, "the news media face a greater challenge than ever in maintaining the public's trust."[67] The profession of journalism had gauged the American public's sentiment toward the press and found it hostile. First Amendment experts worried that the potential financial burden of defending libel suits like Westmoreland's and Sharon's might chill press expression in the future. The combined legal costs for the Westmoreland case were estimated to be at least $7 million.[68] Abrams noted that small press organizations could not afford to defend themselves against deep-pocket libel plaintiffs and thus might be hesitant to publish aggressive investigative reports in the future. Henry Kaufman, general counsel for the Libel Defense Resource Center, suggested that the Westmoreland matter should never even have been brought to trial. Noting the funding Westmoreland received from conservative legal groups, Kaufman considered the case largely a means for these groups to attack what they perceived as the liberal media.[69]

Credibility Crisis

If the spate of high-profile media libel suits—from *Burnett* to *Tavoulareas* to *Westmoreland* and *Sharon*—damaged public opinion about the press in the post-Watergate era, the Janet Cooke episode, arriving as it did in the midst of the suits, did its share of damage, too. In 1980 the *Washington Post* published a front-page story about an eight-year-old heroin addict living in a Washington, D.C., ghetto.[70] "Jimmy's World," written by reporter Janet Cooke, set the city in turmoil. Readers reacted with alarm, and the city government assumed a defensive posture over what it took to be an attack on its social policies.[71] The *Post* defended the article in editorials, even noting that city officials had discovered the identity of the child, which Cooke had ostensibly cloaked with a promise of confidentiality.[72] The article won the Pulitzer Prize for feature writing in 1981, as the *Post* reported in a front-page story on April 14, 1981.[73] Just two days later the *Post* reported, again on the front page, that the Pulitzer Prize committee had withdrawn the award after Cooke admitted to fabricating the story.[74] The scandal ignited a firestorm of censure from both the public and the press, and in the weeks that followed, the latter compulsively dissected and analyzed what most saw as Cooke's profound betrayal of journalism and the resulting loss of credibility.[75]

Although Jeffrey Masson filed suit against Janet Malcolm and the *New Yorker* the year before the Westmoreland and Sharon libel trials came to a close, the greater part of the Masson-Malcolm dispute took place in the aftermath of the spate of high-profile libel cases and the Janet Cooke scandal. It was a time when the news media had been widely derided in the public sphere as overly powerful, arrogant, and socially irresponsible—in short, as abusive of their First Amendment–derived rights to publish freely. The press itself felt acutely the chill of public opinion. A brief review of major journalism trade conferences and seminars in 1985 alone highlights the news media's profound concern over what they believed to be a credibility crisis. The Poynter Institute for Media Studies held a conference for representatives of both the newspaper and television press to discuss this pressing issue.[76] At the American Society of Newspaper Editors' annual convention, poll results were presented showing that only 50 percent of the public gave newspapers high marks for reporting facts accurately. Although the poll found that only 32 percent considered newspapers highly credible, 84 percent had either some or great respect for newspapers.[77] The Associated Press Managing Editors' annual convention released and discussed the results of a poll showing that 85 percent of news-paper journalists believed that improving credibility was a "high priority" for their newspapers.[78] And finally, the American Newspaper Publishers Association put the issue front and center on the agenda at its annual convention, prompted by a poll showing that 54 percent of the public believed that press reports were biased.[79] News organizations were in the grip of a deep anxiety about their credibility, and as the public exposure of sloppy and even fabricated reporting in the libel trials and the Janet Cooke exposure made clear, their credibility problems were not entirely undeserved. It was in the context of this troubled relationship between the public and the press that the Masson-Malcolm dispute erupted.

Masson Sues

The first article in Janet Malcolm's two-part profile of Jeffrey Masson was published in the December 3, 1983, issue of the *New Yorker*, which she mailed to him by overnight express several days before the issue hit the newsstands. She also included galleys of the second article. "I think you're going to love it," she told him.[80] He didn't. The profile was, he told me in an interview, a "tremendous shock." He elaborated: "From the moment I read it until the trial was over was not a happy period and was something deeply distressing. All of us wish there were certain things we could erase from our life. I would like to have erased that article, those two articles."[81]

Masson contacted his lawyer, James Brosnahan, almost immediately, hoping he could do something to stop the publication or at least change the content of the second article. Brosnahan, who had brokered a $150,000 settlement for Masson from the Freud Archives in a wrongful discharge suit, called the *New Yorker* to see what could be done about the second piece, asking for several alterations. A multimillion-dollar libel suit was at stake, he informed the magazine.[82] He even spoke with Janet Malcolm, who had no interest, he said, in making changes.[83] In the end, the *New Yorker* declined to make any alterations in the forthcoming article.[84]

Brosnahan detailed his consultation with Masson, as well as his assessment of the viability of a possible libel suit, in a memo for his firm's files. Masson "confirmed that the quotes were by-in-large [sic] accurate," the memo read. "I told him that people might indeed get a negative view of him from the article, but it would come primarily from things he had actually said." (Masson has disagreed with this assessment of their meeting. He remembers telling Brosnahan that he believed Malcolm had misquoted him.)[85] Brosnahan told Masson that he did not advise a lawsuit. Masson replied, said Brosnahan, that "he certainly had no interest in bringing a libel suit unless I thought it was a 'very good one' and that we would be pretty well assured of winning. This I told him was clearly not the case and we agreed that no action would be brought."[86]

If Brosnahan's memory of the meeting is correct, Masson changed his mind quickly about the matter of misquotation. In a letter he subsequently gave to Brosnahan to help him prepare a list of complaints about the article for the *New Yorker*, Masson wrote, "There is no doubt in my mind: every quotation from me is either false (I simply never said it), distorted, twisted, taken out of context, misquoted or tendentious."[87] He ultimately changed his mind about filing a lawsuit, too, but not before looking for an alternative. "I did ask the *New Yorker* would they give me some space to respond, would they themselves appoint something like a special master, somebody who would look into this, would they even give me some pages to respond," Masson explained. "And the answer was 'no.' And, I mean, it was not even a dialogue. It's just, the attitude was 'We're the *New Yorker* and you have to live with this.'"[88]

Brosnahan decided he could not represent Masson because he had previously appeared as counsel for the *New Yorker*.[89] After spending quite a while looking for a lawyer who would represent him on a contingency basis, Masson finally found one, Michael Brooks Carroll, who handled the case in the early stages. It was Carroll who ushered a series of five libel complaints through U.S. district court until the last was finally accepted as actionable in court in late 1984.[90] Unable to obtain access to Malcolm's interview tapes until 1986, Masson had identified in his early complaints a number of what he claimed were misquotations that he later found were recorded on tape.[91] These memory lapses turned out to be an important part of Gary Bostwick's defense of Malcolm at trial. In the *Village Voice*, Robert Boynton described Bostwick's tactic as demonstrating to the jury "that Masson had essentially reverse-engineered his suit by comparing the 250,000 words he had uttered on tape to his 12,000 words of quotes in Malcolm's article until he finally found a few passages that appeared not to have documentation."[92]

If Masson reverse-engineered his suit, then the defense was actively helping him along in his endeavor. James Wagstaffe, then an associate at Cooper, White & Cooper and part of the team representing Malcolm and the *New Yorker*, told me that when Masson filed his first suit claiming misquotation, the Cooper-

White team "would leak out by way of request for judicial notice to the court the various tapes that showed a high percentage of the things that he said he'd never said, he actually did say word for word." The process continued, Wagstaffe said, as Masson amended complaint after complaint until "the case eventually winnowed itself down to those quotations that weren't on tapes." According to Wagstaffe, at trial the defense used the results of this cat-and-mouse technique to argue that Masson's memory of what he had or had not said simply was not reliable.[93] Boynton has argued that Bostwick's tactic at trial "was disingenuous because Masson did not have access to the tapes until February 1986, when he revised his last complaint. Before that he couldn't possibly have 'known' what he had actually said."[94] In assessing this series of events, it is important to ask whether it was reasonable to expect Masson to remember every word he had spoken in over forty hours of interviews which had taken place a year or two in the past.

In the final complaint, Masson identified nine quotations that he claimed were false and defamatory and asked for at least $100,000 in general damages, $100,000 in special damages, and $10 million in punitive damages. In addition to the defamation claim, he asserted invasion of privacy, saying that he had been "shocked and offended" by the *New Yorker* profiles' revelations of personal details. Malcolm had told him her article would concern his psychoanalytical theories, he claimed, not expose details of his private life.[95] With this complaint, Masson's lawsuit began its official twelve-year journey through the federal judicial system and the public sphere.

Masson v. New Yorker in Federal District Court, 1986–1987

The district court for the Northern District of California first considered Masson's libel complaint in 1986, when it granted partial summary judgment for Janet Malcolm, the *New Yorker*, and Knopf, ruling that four of the twelve allegedly libelous passages were substantially true and thus non-actionable.[96] In 1987 the district court considered the remaining eight contested statements in deciding the defendants' second motion for summary judgment.[97] Interestingly, in this early iteration of *Masson* the court made no statements about established journalistic practices in its consideration of the issues or its interpretation of the actual malice standard. Journalistic ethics, however, became key points of judicial consideration in later stages of the case and underlay the legal conception and role of truth articulated in the Supreme Court's further interpretation of the actual malice standard.

In considering a motion for summary judgment, a court must review disputed facts in the light most favorable to the non-moving party, in this case the plaintiff. The district court in *Masson* thus had to assume that the contested statements were deliberately or recklessly altered or fabricated, as Masson claimed, although Malcolm maintained throughout the life of the case that they were not. Because Masson disputed the authenticity of Malcolm's "hand-written and typed notes," the court could not consider the notes in its analysis of the disputed statements' accuracy.[98] In the summary judgment phase of a libel case involving a public figure in which the defendant is the moving party, the judge must determine whether "a genuine factual issue as to actual malice exists."[99] In making this determination, the district court "carefully analyzed each disputed passage separately, comparing the alleged defamatory material with relevant portions of the tape-recorded interviews to determine whether rational jurors could find by clear and convincing evidence that defendants entertained serious doubts about the accuracy of the printed material."[100]

In choosing the word "accuracy" instead of "truth" or "falsity" to describe the constitutionally prescribed judicial standard, the district court characterized its conception of truth in the reporting of quotations—an important element of the actual malice standard. Scholarship on ethical journalism, however, often makes a clear distinction between accuracy and truth, conceiving accuracy as "getting the facts straight" and truth as the more complicated project of "making sense of the facts."[101] In 1947 the Hutchins Commission chided the press for favoring accuracy over truth, pointing out that reports could be "factually correct but substantially untrue."[102] More recently, the Committee of Concerned Journalists, in its 2004 discussion of its core journalism principles, described "journalistic truth" as dependent on, rather than synonymous with, "reliable, accurate facts."[103] The journalistic concept of accuracy is thus largely fact-based, and if one takes this conception as the district court's meaning in "assessing the accuracy of the printed material," then one expects the court's assessment to treat quotations as facts. Put more clearly, one expects the court, using a correspondence theory of truth, to determine whether the disputed statements reflect the actual words Masson used, as recorded on tape.

But that is not the direction the court pursued. In fact, the summary judgment posture of the case, which forced the court to assume that Malcolm had deliberately or recklessly altered or fabricated the statements, prevented such a course—if, that is, the court were to clear Malcolm and the other defendants. Instead, the court adopted the rational interpretation standard as the proper test for determining whether Malcolm's alteration of quotations constituted actual malice.[104] In adopting this standard, the district court interpreted the Supreme Court's rulings in *Bose Corporation v. Consumers Union*[105] and *Time, Inc. v. Pape*[106] as rejecting the simple inference of actual malice on the basis of literal inaccuracies in the contested statements or the failure to use verbatim quotations.[107] "The fact that an author selected 'one of a number of possible rational interpretations' of a conversation or event that 'bristled with ambiguities,'" Judge Eugene Lynch wrote, was "not enough to create a jury issue of 'malice.'"[108] The court thus focused its inquiry "on whether the author's choice of words in each disputed passage was a rational interpretation of Mr. Masson's tape-recorded statements"[109]—thereby apparently abandoning a search for mere accuracy.

To understand how the rational interpretation test might work, consider the court's discussion of what it deemed the "most problematic, disputed passage" in Malcolm's article.[110] She wrote: "A few days after my return to New York, Masson, in a state of elation, telephoned me to say that Farrar, Straus & Giroux had taken *The Assault on Truth* [Masson's book]. 'Wait till it reaches the best-seller list, and watch how the analysts will crawl. They move whichever way the wind blows. They will want me back, they will say that Masson is a great scholar, a major analyst—after Freud, he's the greatest analyst who ever lived.'"[111] Although Malcolm claimed that she took handwritten notes of this conversation, the court could not consider these in its deliberations because Masson claimed that the conversation never took place. Identifying the sting of the passage as portraying Masson "as a grandiose egotist and full of braggadocio," the court then proceeded to examine the tape-recorded interviews for statements Masson made that were "similar[ly] egotistical."[112] The court's opinion lists a near-avalanche of boastful statements, including "For better or for worse, analysis stands or falls with me now" (a phrase Malcolm actually attributed to Masson later in the quoted passage) and "When this book comes out . . . I really feel it spells the beginning of the end of psychoanalysis."[113] Whether these similar statements are as "egotistical," and thus as defamatory, as the disputed statement—"the greatest analyst who ever lived"—the court did not consider. Rather, assuming that portraying a person as egotistical is defamatory, the court claimed that the similar statements, taken together, would prevent a reasonable jury from concluding "that Malcolm entertained serious doubts about the *accuracy* of the [contested] passage."[114] In other words, the district court used the troublesome concept of accuracy to gauge whether Malcolm had truthfully represented Masson's character.

In the end, the district court found that each disputed statement was protected for one or more of three reasons: (1) it was non-defamatory; (2) it was substantially true; or (3) it was "a rational interpretation of ambiguous conversations."[115] The court thus extended journalism's traditional understanding of accuracy by equating it with truth and then equating truth with rational interpretation of ambiguous words. The legal conception of truth in this early stage of the *Masson* case's life, then, hinged on the author's interpretation of the speaker's meaning. If the interpretation was rational to a reasonable reader, the disputed statement would be true (and not knowingly or recklessly false); if it was not rational, the disputed statement would presumably be false (knowingly or recklessly), thus losing constitutional protection.

The district court took what was already the subjective determination of actual malice and made it even more subjective through the conceptual haze of the rational interpretation standard. For the court to issue a factual finding of actual malice, it would have to discover clear and convincing evidence that the author *knowingly* or *recklessly* interpreted the speaker's meaning *irrationally*. To state the matter this way is to see exactly how broad the district court's conception of legal truth actually was—and how difficult it would be for a plaintiff to survive a summary judgment motion.

The Journalist and the Murderer

In 1989, fairly early in what would become long and intense coverage of the *Masson* case, Janet Malcolm instigated, perhaps inadvertently, a lively and at times hostile public debate about press practices and ethics with her publication in the *New Yorker* of a two-part article titled "The Journalist and the Murderer."[116] The opening paragraph of the first article quickly became known throughout the world of journalism: "Every journalist who is not too stupid or too full of himself to notice what is going on knows that what he does is morally indefensible. He is a kind of confidence man, preying on people's vanity, ignorance or loneliness, gaining their trust and betraying them without remorse."[117] The series told the story of a convicted killer's lawsuit against the journalist and nonfiction writer Joe McGinniss. Although the content of the articles, later published as a book, garnered its share of attention, the primary focus of the near-frenzied press coverage that ensued was what one *New York Times* editorial called "Miss Malcolm's sweeping indictment of all journalists."[118]

The news media covered not only the publication of the articles but also the uproar they precipitated in the press itself. In covering Malcolm's articles, the press was, in effect, covering itself—defending itself against what it perceived to be Malcolm's attack on the industry's ethics and methods, and in turn attacking those of Malcolm. For example, both *New York Times* articles devoted to the subject turned Malcolm's words against her, anointing her a con artist for not acknowledging the *Masson* suit in the article—that is, for neglecting to own that she "had been accused of the same kind of behavior" of which she was accusing McGinniss and, indeed, all journalists.[119] One article mistakenly reported that in court "Miss Malcolm [had] conceded the fabrications [of quotations and dialogue], but said she acted only in an effort to get behind the facts to the truth. She, too, she seemed to be saying, was one of the confidence men."[120] Although the *Times* later acknowledged in a printed correction that Malcolm had not admitted to any fabrication—a misperception that was likely the result of the journalist's confusion about the summary judgment posture of the case, in which the court could not consider Malcolm's handwritten notes because Masson contested them as fabrications—much of the *Times*'s later coverage consistently if implicitly presented Malcolm as a fabricator. One *Times* editorial drew a distinction between daily journalism and nonfiction writing, the latter, it implied, being much more susceptible to the practitioner as con artist: "The difference [between daily journalists and nonfiction writers] is time. People who write for newspapers and news magazines have varying probity, intelligence, and style. What none of them have is time—time to work on what Miss Malcolm calls her 'Japanese technique,' to ask questions 'as if I were passing the time of day,' time to develop, in short, a con."[121] The *Times* was suggesting, of course, that Malcolm belonged to the nonfiction, or literary journalism, camp. The newspaper also implicated literary journalism's characteristic immersion technique, in which the writer immerses herself in the life and world of her subject, as easily leading to deception. Thus the *Times* represented the traditional report as the ethical foundation of journalism—and challenged the ethical foundation of nonfiction and literary journalism.

Why Malcolm chose to publish such an incendiary article in March 1989— several months before the Ninth Circuit affirmed the district court's grant of summary judgment and many months after Masson's appeal had been argued before the circuit court—is a question best answered by Malcolm herself. Although she refused to be interviewed for this book, she did tell Gwen Davis, who wrote an article on the second *Masson* trial for the *Nation* in 1994, that when she wrote the articles in 1987 the case had been summarily dismissed.[122] In 1989 she likely could not imagine that the *Masson* case might—or even *could*—wend its way to the Supreme Court. Perhaps she believed that the district court's grant of summary judgment was, in effect, the final word on the case, a dismissal of a bothersome suit brought by a bothersome subject, a decision so logical and right that the Ninth Circuit would of course affirm it. Perhaps she completely misjudged the power and the terms of the social contract created by the dominance of the traditional report in American culture—a contract that presumed the reporting of quotations to be largely stenographic in nature, at least according to the Supreme Court's *Masson* opinion and much of the commentary in the daily press. What is clear now, from the vantage of historical perspective, is exactly how damaging these articles became, if not to Malcolm's defense in the case then at least to her reputation in the press and among the public, and ultimately, perhaps, to the perception of the literary report.

The articles may even have contributed to the continuation of Masson's lawsuit. Judge Alex Kozinski's dissent in the Ninth Circuit, understood by many involved in the case to have placed it on the Supreme Court's radar screen, refers to "The Journalist and the Murderer" in a footnote describing Malcolm as "an exceptionally talented writer."[123] The dissent thus suggests that Kozinski had read the articles and, as I discuss shortly, that he took great exception to Malcolm's argument, presented in other writings, that any altering of quotations beyond the cosmetic should be protected in libel suits by the First Amendment. Whether he was influenced by Malcolm's portrayal of journalists as betrayers of their subjects is unclear, but Masson thought so. "I think it was that that incensed Kozinski and that also gave him some material," Masson told me.[124]

When Alfred A. Knopf published the book version of *The Journalist and the Murderer* in 1990, Malcolm was again impugned in the pages of the *New York Times*, this time in a book review. Written by Fred Friendly, former CBS News president and then a professor at the Columbia University Graduate School of Journalism, this review was even more critical than the previous coverage of the articles and the controversy they engendered. In particular, Friendly focused on Malcolm's discussion of the journalistic quotation in her afterword to the book. There, Malcolm responded to the vociferous criticism she had sustained after the publication of "The Journalist and the Murderer" articles and directly addressed the idea of the social contract between writer and reader and its grounding in what she called "actuality." Malcolm states, "The writer of nonfiction is under contract to the reader to limit himself to the events that actually occurred and to characters who have counterparts in real life, and he may not embellish the truth about these events or these characters." [125] Yet representing the actuality and truth of a subject's speech is inherently problematic, she argues. Speech is always filled with incomplete thoughts, circumlocutions, and odd syntax, and the writer must somehow render this speech readable. Stenographic representation of speech shows "how the literally true may actually be a kind of falsification of reality." [126]

Friendly cast Malcolm's methods as fabrication and, like the reviewers of the earlier articles, made a distinction between daily journalists and nonfiction writers (or narrative journalists), writing: "Ms. Malcolm's belief that authors of nonfiction books have more license than a stenographer is likewise shunned by serious journalists. Cleaning up a subject's syntax is one thing, but rearranging sentences from one interview to another and paraphrasing quotations and inserting inflammatory phrases are the stuff of which theater is born. It is embellishment." [127] Like Malcolm, Friendly addressed the issue of the social contract in journalism. But in implying that Malcolm had fabricated the quotations Masson contested, Friendly was effectively criticizing a social contract that would allow for anything other than stenographic quotation: "Are the guidelines for quotations something the author need not reveal? Must we know whether the provocative quotes are verbatim or merely manufactured out of bits of various conversations?" [128]

Likely sensing the damage Friendly's criticism might cause to her reputation, Malcolm responded with a letter to the editor in what turned out to be a rare public statement about her collective work and the issues in the case, including her use of direct quotation: "I would like to categorically say that in the three books and two long articles of nonfiction I have published I have never mixed fact and fiction. In fact, I have never been in the slightest bit tempted to do so, since what my subjects do and say is far more interesting than anything I could imagine for them." [129] Malcolm and Friendly understood in profoundly different ways the role of quotation in the representation of truth in a journalistic report—as well as the terms of the social contract between reader and journalist. The source of their differing views may very well have been, as

Friendly's distinction between "serious journalists" and nonfiction writers suggests, the inherent conflict between the objectivity of the traditional report and the subjectivity of the literary report. A mere six months after Malcolm replied to the *Times*, the Supreme Court agreed to hear *Masson v. New Yorker*, and Malcolm made few public statements thereafter about her work or the case. Her indictment of journalists as con men in *The Journalist and the Murderer* became a common theme—and a point for attack by Masson's lawyers and the press at large—in the coverage of the case spanning the next five years.

Masson v. New Yorker in the Ninth Circuit, 1989

Before the U.S. Supreme Court granted *certiorari* in the Masson case, of course, the Ninth Circuit had its turn with the dispute. When the district court granted summary judgment for Janet Malcolm and her co-defendants, Masson appealed the decision. The Ninth Circuit, adopting the same evidentiary standards and much of the same reasoning used in the district court, then affirmed the district court's order.[130] Key to the Ninth Circuit's decision making, as in the district court's, was the rational interpretation standard, again supported through reference to *Bose* and *Pape*.[131] If the "fabricated quotations are . . . 'rational interpretations of ambiguous remarks made by the public figure,'"[132] the court found, actual malice cannot be inferred. But the court clarified a key legal principle: actual malice can be inferred if the fabricated quotations "'alter the substantive content' of *unambiguous* remarks actually made by the public figure."[133] The Ninth Circuit, in limiting the use of the rational interpretation standard to *ambiguous* remarks, thus implicitly addressed the lower court's conflation of the separate falsity and fault elements in a libel case, at least in instances in which quotations represent unambiguous remarks. If falsity were found in such an instance, knowing falsity, or the actual malice level of fault, could be inferred.

   In considering the disputed quotations on a motion for summary judgment, the court again assumed, this time forthrightly, that the quotations were fabricated or altered.[134] Adopting the same procedure used by the lower court, the Ninth Circuit compared each contested statement against the tape-recorded interviews. When the court deemed Masson's remarks to be ambiguous, it used the rational interpretation standard to protect the statement; when the court deemed Masson's remarks to be unambiguous, it repeatedly found that the contested statement did not alter the "substantive content" of Masson's

tape-recorded statements. In determining whether Malcolm's attribution of
the words "intellectual gigolo" to Masson's description of himself constituted
actual malice, the court wrote, "While it may be true that Masson did not use
the words 'intellectual gigolo,' Malcolm's *interpretation* did not alter the substantive content of Masson's description of himself as a 'private asset but a
public liability' to Eissler and Anna Freud." [135]

Perhaps in response to the district court's problematic adoption of the term
"accuracy" (associated in journalism largely with the reporting of facts) as a
synonym for legal truth, the Ninth Circuit seemed to be studiously avoiding
using the word. The court also seemed to avoid using the terms "truth" or
"meaning," choosing instead the lack of alteration of "substantive content" as
the operative definition of legal truth in the context of altered quotations (or,
conversely, the alteration of "substantive content" as the operative definition of
legal falsity). Deciding whether the substantive content of a quotation has been
altered clearly involves a determination of meaning. And determining meaning is exactly what the lower court and the Ninth Circuit did when they compared the contested statements against the tape-recorded interviews in their
search for "a genuine factual issue as to actual malice." [136]

What makes libel cases so conceptually difficult—especially ones involving
allegedly false and defamatory quotations—is this understanding of *meaning*
as a "factual issue." There is no alternative, of course, given that libel suits by
their very nature demand the consideration of meaning, and determining the
meaning of a disputed factual statement is clearly not an issue of law but, in
legal parlance, an issue of fact. Still, meaning and fact, certainly in journalism,
and seemingly in popular discourse, appear to be distinct concepts. For example, the Committee of Concerned Journalists sees the reporting of accurate
facts as merely the first stage in truthful reporting; the next is to convey "a fair
and reliable account of their [the facts'] meaning." [137] What does it mean to
find that the *meaning* (or the "substantive content") of actual spoken words
has been changed through misquotation in such a way as to create a factual
issue regarding the author's knowing falsity or reckless disregard for truth? It
first requires the reported words to be different in some way from the spoken
words, and it then requires a judgment about the magnitude of discrepancy
between the meaning of the actual utterance and the meaning of the disputed
statement. As the legal scholar David Anderson puts the matter: "Was the difference between the truth and the defamatory allegation substantial enough to
justify a judgment that the latter harmed the plaintiff in some way that the for-

mer did not." [138] This difference in meaning is the factual issue. In the 1989 Ninth Circuit iteration of *Masson*, as in many libel disputes, determining whether a factual issue existed, and thus whether the case should go to trial, was a matter of judging the truthful (or false) meaning of words. No useful distinction was made between fact and meaning; rather both terms were elided under the greater—and remarkably cloudy—legal conception of truth.

Like the district court opinion, the majority opinion in the Ninth Circuit did not take journalistic standards into account in determining whether actual malice existed in the alleged misquotations. Judge Kozinkski's ringing dissent, however, did. To determine whether "the right to doctor quotations [is] important to the operation of a free and robust press" [139]—what Kozinski called the "real question" [140] of the case—the dissent delved deeply into professional standards guiding "whether, and under what circumstances, journalists may alter or invent quotations." [141] His dissent ranged widely in the literature of journalism to establish the following claim: "The authorities are adamant and uniform in condemning the use of altered quotes that are not faithful to the meaning intended by the speaker." [142] Although the dissent acknowledged that absolute verbatim quotations are rarely achieved in journalism, it claimed, by way of citing the literature, that "it is a firmly-rooted journalistic convention that the central meaning, the spirit, of a speaker's words must be truly conveyed." [143]

Although Kozinski's emphasis on a "central meaning" standard at first seems similar to the "substantive content" element in the majority's rational interpretation test, it is not. In fact, Kozinski understood truth and meaning in the context of altered quotations in a radically different way from the majority, and the difference appears to hinge on the concept of ambiguity in speech. He explained this essential difference in a footnote: "Under the central meaning standard, where the words uttered are ambiguous, they may not be altered to remove the ambiguity because that would change the spirit of what the speaker said; under the reasonable interpretation standard adopted by the majority, the author is given precisely that privilege." [144] To understand Kozinski's distinction, consider his analysis of the disputed statement "he had the wrong man." In the passage as reported by Malcolm, Masson was describing a conversation he had with Kurt Eissler after Eissler had fired him as director of the Freud Archives. [145] When Eissler requested that Masson leave his post quietly, Masson reportedly asked: "Why should I do that? Why? You know, why should one do that?" Eissler responded, "Because it's the honorable thing to do," about which Masson commented, "Well, he had the wrong man." [146] The tape-recorded interview, however, shows that Malcolm cut a significant part of this purported exchange and thus, in Kozinski's view, radically changed Masson's central meaning:

> Masson's actual answer . . . was quite a bit more elaborate: "'Because it's the honorable thing to do, and you will save face, and who knows, if you never speak about it and quietly and humbly accept our judgment, who knows in a few years if we don't bring you back?' Well, he had the wrong man." Masson was clearly saying that he is the wrong man to be bribed into silence by the hope that they would bring him back a few years later.
>
> The contrast between the two statements could not be sharper. As reported by Malcolm, Masson portrays himself as a swine, boasting that he would never be swayed to do the right and honorable thing. Masson's unedited statement makes him sound more like a hero, someone willing to speak the unpleasant truth even if it damages his career. . . . The majority's willingness to approve Malcolm's alteration on the ground that she could reasonably have understood Masson to be calling himself a swine demonstrates that the majority's rationale has no meaningful bounds.[147]

For Kozinski, then, the ambiguity in the actual spoken words was an essential part of the quotation's meaning; to edit out the ambiguity was to alter that meaning radically and to create a factual issue with regard to actual malice for jury consideration.

As Kozinski wrote in the opening sentences of his opinion, the essential difference between his position and the majority's rested on the meaning of quotations: "The majority and I part company on a simple but fundamental point: the meaning of quotations. As I see it, when a writer uses quotation marks in reporting what someone else has said, she is representing that those are the speaker's own words or something very close to them."[148] Later in the opinion, Kozinski supported his view of the meaning of quotations and quotation marks through his review of professional standards. While acknowledging that these standards were not "dispositive of the legal question before us,"[149] he rejected the First Amendment protection of a practice—altering or fabricating quotations—that the profession itself disavowed as unethical. "Unlike my colleagues," he wrote, "I am unable to construe the first amendment as granting journalists a privilege to engage in practices they themselves frown upon."[150]

For Kozinski, professional standards must guide the court's identification of those journalistic principles and values that are deserving of constitutional protection.[151] "Unlike the majority," he wrote, "I would start with the proposition that what somebody says is a fact, and that doctoring a quotation is no more protected by the first amendment than is any other falsification."[152] While the majority opinion tended to treat meaning as a kind of fact, Kozinski rejected this broad rationale and treated the reporting of a speaker's actual words, not their meaning, as fact. If there is a material inaccuracy that is also defamatory, he asserted, actual malice may exist.[153] Cosmetic changes are not materially inaccurate, but complete rephrasing and invention are.[154] In effect, any alteration beyond the cosmetic in a purportedly verbatim quotation most likely would satisfy Kozinski's understanding of material inaccuracy.

In the lower court and Ninth Circuit majority opinions, no mention is made of the technical meaning of quotation mark and quoted expression. The courts apparently saw no necessary relationship between the journalistic conception of truth in quotation and the legal determination of truth in quotation—or between established journalistic standards and the courts' interpretation of press protections. Kozinksi's dissent, however, lighted the way for the Supreme Court to consider just these issues.[155]

The Objectivity Question in the Masson-Malcolm Dispute

The court documents and press discourse surrounding the Masson-Malcolm dispute were shot through with questions that lay at the heart of the then-current culture wars about the role of language in public life. Was there such a thing as objective knowledge about an external reality that could be communicated through language? That is perhaps an overly academic articulation of the problem that animated public concerns over "politically correct" language, the explosion of the literary canon, and the history profession's broadening of the American historical narrative to consider the roles of groups and individuals who had been omitted from previous historiography. But it is an apt description of the essential problem that first occupied intellectuals and then became the purview of the public at large. Social and cultural norms were changing, and some of the change involved new ways of thinking about the nature of knowledge and language and truth.

Part of this cultural and intellectual change involved attacks on objectivity, both in academia and in the public sphere. In the academy, these attacks targeted the foundations of knowledge, including, as the historian Peter Novick explains in *That Noble Dream*, "the determinacy of meaning; distinctions between fact and value, and between knower and known; traditional canons of what it meant to be 'rational'; perhaps above all—a proposition too banal to articulate and too sacred to question—that the meaning, and the justification, of science and scholarly work was 'progress toward the truth.'" [156] Those who were doing the attacking believed that knowledge is largely constituted of indeterminate meanings, that language and its meanings are unstable, and that truth is not unitary but multiple, contingent, a matter of perspective.

This critique of objectivity, differing mainly in degree from Dewey's pragmatist notion of the contingent nature of truth in human affairs, informed the broad cultural and social transformations of the late 1960s and 1970s. When Jeffrey Masson filed his libel claim in the early 1980s, he did so in an atmosphere that was only becoming more charged with strife over the question of objectivity. During the era of the Masson-Malcolm dispute—which comprised the years 1984 to 1996—"postmodernist" became a kind of dirty epithet lobbed at challengers of objectivity by those standing guard over the objectivist way. Masson and Malcolm occupied opposing sides of this debate, at least as far as their differing conceptions of truth in quotation went. Masson understood a quotation to represent the "objective" reality of the words a speaker uttered by representing those words nearly verbatim (he did allow for minor cleanup of quotations). Malcolm understood a quotation to represent the *meaning* of a speaker's utterance, not a strict stenographic transcription of speech into the written word. (Of course, neither Malcolm nor the *New Yorker* presented themselves as postmodernist—a certain kiss of death in that cultural milieu.) The postmodernist critique of objectivity in the academic disciplines had its counterpart in the newsroom, where some journalists were increasingly chafing under the constraints of the objectivity standard of the traditional report. The New Journalism movement of the 1960s and early 1970s was one such journalistic expression of discontent with the objectivity paradigm—and this discontent never entirely evaporated. But the New Journalism also raised the ire of many traditional journalists for being, in their view, irresponsible, nonstandard, and unethical. The Masson-Malcolm dispute was in many ways a working out of this journalistic tension as well as the larger gestalt shift in both the academic and popular understandings of the nature of knowledge and truth.

From the government's efforts to manage news in the Vietnam era to the explosion of libel cases in the late 1970s and early 1980s, when Jeffrey Masson filed his libel suit against Janet Malcolm, to the Janet Cooke debacle, the press increasingly discussed the profession of newsgathering and reporting in its news products. While during the Vietnam conflict the press focused on the government, in the following years the press turned its attention on itself as it reported libel suits filed against the news media, press scandals, and what the chairman of the National News Council called in 1981 "the permissiveness and arrogance of the 'New Journalism.'" [157] With the rise of the critical culture in the United States came a widespread skeptical attitude among the public toward both the government and the press. Add to that the advent of an aggressive investigative journalism and the growth of news corporations, and conditions were ripe for increased public scrutiny of the profession of journalism. As media libel and invasion of privacy suits popped up across the nation, in part as a reaction to the reemergence of personal reputation as a valuable social commodity, the press found itself in the position of reporting on its own professional practices and ethical standards.

During the period leading up to the Masson-Malcolm dispute, then, the press was teaching itself and the public how the press worked, in both actuality and the ideal. It was also teaching itself and the public how to talk about the press—its legal rights, its social responsibilities, and its role as watchdog and guardian of American democracy. The press became not simply a vehicle for discussing political and social affairs in the public sphere but the actual subject of such discussion. In covering the libel cases that went before the courts, the press invariably provided the public with a primer on the meaning of the First Amendment as articulated in *Times v. Sullivan*. The degree to which the public learned the lessons the press had to teach is uncertain, but it is clear the press was attempting to fashion public discourse about the conflict between an individual's right to his or her reputation and the press's First Amendment right to freedom of expression. In the metanarrative constructed by the press, the First Amendment trumped reputation. The extent to which the press learned the lesson that libel plaintiffs had to teach—that the press should on the whole be more responsible and careful about reporting defamatory facts—is also uncertain. But the very existence of a full-bodied discourse in the public sphere on such issues is a sign that both sides were at least hearing each other.

Masson launched his lawsuit against Malcolm in this atmosphere of public distrust of the press. It was an attitude reflected in the stunningly large punitive damages that juries had been awarding media libel plaintiffs since the late 1970s. In the Libel Defense Resource Center's study of media libel cases decided between 1979 and 1982, 30 percent of punitive damage awards were in excess of $1 million. In a follow-up study of cases decided between 1982 and 1984, 41 percent were.[158] The average damage award for 1980s media libel cases was slightly over $2 million. Contrast this figure with the average pre-*Sullivan* award of $49,513.[159] Masson himself sought a staggering $10 million in punitive damages.

The libel suits and exposures of press fabrications at the time put the American public, or at least those members of the public who showed up on the jury bench in libel suits, in a punishing mood. Large damage awards levied against the press are not just punishing, though. They are also chilling, even if later overturned on appeal. In his dissent in *Time, Inc. v. Hill*, a "false light" invasion of privacy suit, Justice John M. Harlan noted: "In many areas which are at the center of public debate, 'truth' is not a readily identifiable concept, and putting to the preexisting prejudices of a jury the determination of what is 'true' may effectively institute a system of censorship. Any nation which counts the *Scopes* trial as part of its heritage cannot so readily expose ideas to sanctions on a jury finding of falsity. . . . 'The marketplace of ideas' where it functions still remains the best testing ground for truth." [160] Anthony Lewis, the former *New York Times* columnist who has written so well on the *Sullivan* case, put it another way: "One man's truth is not another's. That is the central meaning of the first amendment: the right to differ about political truth, the right to criticize those who govern us without being held to a standard of temperateness or truth." [161] Although Lewis was addressing the idea of political truth and the subject matter of government decisions, which he believed should be beyond the reach of libel actions under the protective umbrella of the First Amendment, his point about the contingent nature of truth is one that must be considered in any assessment of the Masson-Malcolm dispute and its journey through the courts.

As *Masson v. New Yorker* made its way toward the Supreme Court during the 1980s, the lower federal courts struggled to conceptualize what constituted truth and falsity in libel cases involving alleged misquotation and actual malice as established in *New York Times v. Sullivan*. If the quotation was a rational interpretation of a speaker's words, then it was considered truthful and protected under the First Amendment, the courts ruled. As the record shows, the Supreme Court rejected this test of falsity in misquotation, opting instead for the material alteration test, which found falsity to exist when a quotation was altered so as to change materially its original meaning.[162] In the chapters that follow I return to the Supreme Court's conception of truth in language as articulated in *Masson* and its role in constitutional libel law, providing a full accounting of just how far it is from what Harlan and Lewis identified as the *Sullivan* ideal. For the time being it is sufficient to note that the interpretation of meaning in an altered quotation, the comparison of that interpretation with an interpretation of the meaning of the actual spoken words, and the measurement of the material difference between the two interpretations—all of which is required in the Supreme Court's *Masson* test for falsity and actual malice in altered quotations—are complex and imprecise elements of a complex and imprecise test. Justice Harlan noted that truth in public discourse is often "not a readily identifiable concept."[163] Finding truth by way of the *Masson* test would be a hard project indeed.

CHAPTER SIX

⟨∾⟩

Libel Law and the Postmodern Dilemma

The Search for Truth

IN 1964 THE UNITED STATES SUPREME COURT ARTICULATED A FIRST Amendment theory famously protective of free expression: "We consider this case," Justice William Brennan wrote in the landmark libel case *New York Times v. Sullivan*, "against the background of a profound national commitment to the principle that debate on public issues should be uninhibited, robust, and wide-open."[1] This theory guided both constitutional jurisprudence and the operation of the press in the American public sphere for decades. But the Court eventually lost some of its passion for *Sullivan*'s protective spirit, first with its decision in *Milkovich v. Lorain Journal* in 1990,[2] and again one year later with its decision in *Masson v. New Yorker*.[3] Central to this significant judicial shift in attitude was the Court's struggle with a fundamental postmodern dilemma: how to determine what constitutes truth in language.

In *Sullivan*, the Court tipped the constitutional balance in favor of free expression and against the competing social interest of reputation. The new weight in the social scale was the actual malice standard, which the Court defined as publication with knowledge of falsity or reckless disregard for the truth.[4] Furthermore, *Sullivan* established that an allegedly false and defamatory statement must be factual in nature to be actionable.[5] The implied logic was that only factual statements were open to a determination of falsity. But in the line of cases that followed *Sullivan*, it became clear that the Supreme Court could not maintain a bright-line distinction between language that was purely factual and language that was not, such as opinion, rhetorical hyperbole, epithets, parody, the rational interpretation of ambiguous sources and events, implication, and altered quotations. As the Court continued to accept actual malice cases, more and more of the cases involved not the further interpretation of the standard, or not merely that interpretation, but the determination of whether the *kind* of language being disputed was protected under the First Amendment. If the Court found that the language was not protected, it determined how the actual malice standard should be applied to determine falsity and fault. In this judicial work, the Court increasingly analyzed the truth or falsity not only of factual assertions but also of expression that was not clearly factual. As a result, it sometimes expanded and sometimes restricted the kinds of speech the First Amendment protected. As the last cases in the *Sullivan* line—*Milkovich* and *Masson*—make clear, the Court ultimately moved toward restriction.

In the process, the Supreme Court moved away from the First Amendment theory and animating spirit of *Sullivan*. In *Masson*, the Court did not consider forthrightly the meaning of the First Amendment articulated in *Sullivan*: the protection of "debate on public issues [that is] uninhibited, robust, and wide-open, and . . . may well include vehement, caustic, and sometimes unpleasantly sharp attacks on government and public officials."[6] Rather, as the legal scholar Lee Bollinger has observed, the *Masson* Court refused to extend "First Amendment protection to speech because in its view to do so would undermine the *character and quality of public discourse*."[7] This protection of the quality of public discourse was not a new value in First Amendment jurisprudence (consider, for example, the Court's justifications for refusing to extend First Amendment protections to obscenity).[8] It was not exactly a new value in the *Sullivan-Masson* line of actual malice cases either.[9] In *Garrison v. Louisiana*, decided just seven months after *Sullivan*, the Court asserted in *dicta* that "the known lie" receives no constitutional protection because its utterance is "at odds with the premises of democratic government."[10] Even so, Bollinger's point—that *Masson* was the first U.S. Supreme Court decision to refuse to offer First Amendment protection to speech in order to protect the quality of public discourse—is important. The *Masson* decision and rationale were decidedly in contrast with the insistence in *Sullivan* that public discourse, regardless of its quality, receives First Amendment protection because it is a defining element of a democratic society.[11]

With the *New York Times v. Sullivan* actual malice rule, the Court transformed the role of truth and falsity in libel law. Prior to *Sullivan*, libel law in many states was predicated on the assumption that truth inhered in the strict correspondence between language and reality, that there was, in other words, an always knowable reality.[12] The defendant in such a libel suit was usually faced with the difficult burden of proving the truth of an allegedly defamatory, false statement, a requirement of the strict liability posture in the common law of libel.[13] This approach assumed that a universal, static truth was knowable not only to the defendant but also to everyone else in the courtroom—and that this truth was the same truth for everyone. This is exactly the concept of truth that the majority opinion in *Sullivan* theoretically rejected. It must be noted, however, that this rejection was subtextual and not at all articulated in the Court's formulation of the actual malice standard. In other words, the *Sullivan* Court was not focused on dealing with the problem of indeterminacy in language (although the majority opinion did make the point, repeatedly, that determining the truth of beliefs, ideas, and opinions was an impossible task).[14] It was not until much later in the *Sullivan* line of actual malice libel cases that the Court clearly recognized and confronted an essential linguistic problem plaguing defamation law: that unitary truth, if such a truth existed, was not always discoverable in expression.[15]

In *Sullivan* the judicial emphasis shifted from the role of truth in libel law to that of falsity and the related issue of fault as articulated in the actual malice standard. In a libel suit, a public official plaintiff now carried the First Amendment–derived burden of proving the falsity of the contested statement—and not only its falsity but also the defendant's knowledge of its falsity or reckless disregard for truth. Beyond compensating plaintiffs for injury to their reputations, the primary function of libel law was not, as it was prior to *Sullivan*, to punish a person for failing to tell the truth. Rather it was to identify and punish defamatory and knowing or reckless falsehoods. By shifting the judicial emphasis from truth to falsity and fault, the *Sullivan* actual malice standard protected all speech about public officials and government, even defamatory falsehoods, as long as the publisher *believed in* the truth of the contested statements.[16]

In *Sullivan* and its immediate progeny, the Supreme Court did not question explicitly the concept of ascertainable truth. Although the new judicial emphasis on falsity and fault rather than truth in allegedly libelous expression theoretically allowed for the existence of multiple versions of truth, the *Sullivan* Court did not consider this implication of its decision. After all, the expression at issue in the case was a newspaper advertisement of political and social import that, although containing several factual inaccuracies, was substantially true. Contrary to statements made in the ad, black student leaders had not been expelled for singing "My Country 'Tis of Thee" on the steps of the Alabama state capitol but rather were expelled for their sit-in protest at the lunch counter in the Montgomery courthouse. Martin Luther King Jr. had been arrested four, not seven, times.[17] But these errors of fact did not negate the substantial truth of the civil rights group's advertisement: that government in Alabama and across the South was attempting to intimidate and even terrorize black citizens fighting for their rights. Accuracy and truth are not the same thing, the *Sullivan* Court suggested. In creating the actual malice standard and shifting the judicial emphasis from truth to falsity in libel cases involving public officials—that is, in transforming the fault element from a strict liability standard predicated on the defendant's establishment of truth to the actual malice standard predicated on the defendant's *belief* in the truth—the *Sullivan* Court meant to protect honest factual error in public expression.

The point was to erect a protective wall around the robust, uninhibited debate on which democratic government depends and to prevent the use of libel law to punish criticism of government and its officials. *Sullivan* required the plaintiff to prove that the disputed expression was false as well as that the publisher did not believe in the truth of the expression. After *Sullivan*, then, the determination of liability emphasized the state of mind and conduct of the speaker. In emphasizing the publisher's honest *belief* in the truth of allegedly libelous expression as protection against liability—this is, after all, the meaning of the actual malice standard—the *Sullivan* Court established that truth itself would no longer be the sine qua non of libel. This fundamental change in libel law eventually led the Court to consider that truth might to some extent depend on perspective, and that, in some instances, it simply was not discoverable.

Like all major constitutional revolutions, the *Sullivan* decision opened the door to a range of unintended, unforeseen consequences. In the related libel cases immediately following *Sullivan*, the Court was faced with the need to interpret further the meaning of the actual malice standard and the kinds of speakers to whom it should apply. In time the Court pulled speech about public figures under the First Amendment umbrella and staked out the various meanings of knowing falsity and reckless disregard for the truth, the two independent prongs of the actual malice standard.[18] In this particular strain of cases in the post-*Sullivan* line, the Supreme Court focused on protecting honest factual inaccuracies to avoid the chilling effect on public debate that Sullivan and other plaintiffs were hoping to effect.

There was another strain of cases, though, in which the Supreme Court increasingly grappled with the nature of truth itself in expression. The inevitable—and unforeseen—implications and extensions of *Sullivan* forced the Court into the muddy waters of distinguishing factual expression from expression that simply was not factual in nature. Just as one unforeseen effect of *Sullivan* was to open up the editorial process to judicial supervision,[19] another was to force courts to determine what was fact and what was not—both activities that carry heavy First Amendment dangers. How could courts determine the truth or falsity of expression that was not factual or existed in some hazy borderland between fact and pure opinion? This was the question the Supreme Court increasingly encountered in the post-*Sullivan* line. As cases of this nature emerged and were decided, in the realm of both libel and privacy law, the Court came to recognize that one single, indisputable truth simply was not always identifiable in contested expression. Although the actual malice standard had always theoretically encompassed *this* reality, it took a while for the Supreme Court to realize, or at least to come to jurisprudential terms with, the consequences of the actual malice standard in practice. Ultimately, *Milkovich* and *Masson* retrenched on the First Amendment protections promised in the early stages of the recognition.

The following discussion outlines two strains of cases in the *Sullivan-Masson* line, those that further interpreted the meaning of the actual malice standard and those in which the Court distinguished between *factual* expression and *nonfactual* expression. In this second strain of cases, the Court established how far First Amendment protections would reach beyond pure opinion and honest factual inaccuracies and determined how truth tests would operate in unprivileged contested statements that were not purely factual. The first line of cases is examined in chronological order. In the second line, *Gertz v. Welch*[20] is examined first because of its importance in suggesting to lower courts that the First Amendment protected all opinion. The discussion then backtracks to an earlier case that paved the way for the distinction *Gertz* made between factual expression and opinion before resuming its chronological progression.

To consider the ways in which constitutional jurisprudence has grappled with postmodern language problems is to try to reconcile two systems of thought based on radically different assumptions about knowledge. Yet as my analysis demonstrates, the issues of language and truth implicated in the *Sullivan* line require such a conciliation. Postmodern theory—with its rejection of foundations and first principles and its insistence that texts are polysemous and their interpretations indeterminate—is skeptical about fixed meanings and truth claims.[21] Constitutional law, like all law, is predicated on the notion that truth is stable and discoverable. Indeed, how could a legal system with justice as its goal assume otherwise? When postmodern assumptions about the indeterminacy of truth in language find their way into constitutional libel rules (even if it is through the back door), how can the rule of law continue to function in anything but an ad hoc and chaotic way? Can or should these postmodern assumptions be expunged from libel law, or at least ignored? What impact do the answers to these questions have on a First Amendment theory that envisions robust, unfettered public discourse as essential to American democracy?

Defining the Actual Malice Standard

I look first at the U.S. Supreme Court cases in the *Sullivan* line in which the Court focused on protecting honest error in factual expression. These cases illuminate the meaning of the actual malice standard.

Garrison v. Louisiana: The "Known Lie"

Just seven months after the Court introduced the actual malice standard in *Sullivan*, it began to define actual malice further in *Garrison v. Louisiana* (1964). In *Garrison*, the Court reversed the Louisiana Supreme Court's criminal libel conviction of Jim Garrison, a New Orleans prosecutor who had accused eight judges of incompetence, taking too many vacations, and being influenced by organized crime. In effect, the Court found that criminal prosecution for criticism of public officials and their public conduct is unconstitutional unless the disputed expression reaches actual malice: "Only those false statements made with the high degree of awareness of their probable falsity demanded by *New York Times* may be the subject of either civil or criminal sanctions."[22] The ruling did not overturn Louisiana's criminal libel law under which Garrison had been charged. This is an important point. Even though the Supreme Court overturned his conviction, it did not wipe out the concept of criminal libel for calculated falsehoods about public persons (as distinct from criticism of government at large, which *was* repudiated in *Sullivan*). Some criminal libel statutes continue to exist in state law, although they are rarely used and are often overturned by state and lower federal courts.[23]

The question in *Garrison* was whether Jim Garrison's accusations pertained merely to the judges' official conduct or also to their private lives—that is, the Supreme Court was called to determine what qualifies as "official conduct." A wide purview was granted to the meaning of the term as introduced in *Sullivan* several months earlier. In this manner the Court found a broad range of speech to fall under the protection of the First Amendment and expanded *Sullivan's* meanings. In *dicta*, however, the *Garrison* Court also considered the damaging power of the knowing falsehood in communication about political affairs, noting that such lies are capable even of bringing down governments: "Although honest utterance, even if inaccurate, may further the fruitful exercise of the right of free speech, it does not follow that the lie, knowingly and deliberately published about a public official, should enjoy a like immunity. At the time the First Amendment was adopted, as today, there were those unscrupulous enough and skillful enough to use the deliberate or reckless falsehood as an effective political tool to unseat the public servant or even topple an administration."[24]

The "known lie," the Court reasoned, can wrongly interfere not only with a public servant's reputation but also with democratic governance and its social and political goals. *Garrison* is thus important for emphasizing, as *Sullivan* implied but did not directly address, that the *calculated* falsehood receives no constitutional protection because it plays no useful role in public discourse and citizens' surveillance of government. In *Garrison*, the Court acknowledged the importance of the role of falsity in the First Amendment area of libel law and also reaffirmed the central meaning of the First Amendment articulated in *Sullivan*. Inaccuracies would be protected if expressed in good faith, but the calculated lie would not. The proper functioning of democracy, the Court implied, depended on it.

St. Amant v. Thompson: Belief in Truth and Serious Doubts

In 1968 *St. Amant v. Thompson*[25] provided a further conceptual definition of the reckless disregard prong of the actual malice standard: a plaintiff must show that the defendant held serious doubts regarding the truth of the publication in question.[26] In *St. Amant* the Supreme Court overturned a Louisiana libel ruling against a candidate running for sheriff. In a televised speech the candidate had accused his opponent of taking a union bribe. He had received this information from an affidavit but did not verify it through other channels. He believed, however, that the defamatory information was accurate. Although the candidate's accusation was later proved to be false, his *belief in the truth* was enough to protect him, the Court ruled, from a finding of actual malice.[27]

In *St. Amant* the truth or falsity of the disputed expression was readily discernible in the judicial inquiry, but it was not determinative. The speaker's belief about the expression's truth or falsity was what mattered. The *St. Amant* Court, then, clarified that the actual malice test was a subjective test, an inquiry into the state of mind of the person who published a contested statement:

> "Reckless disregard," it is true, cannot be fully encompassed in one infallible definition. Inevitably its outer limits will be marked out through case-by-case adjudication. . . . [But the] cases are clear that reckless conduct is not measured by whether a reasonably prudent man would have published, or would have investigated before publishing. There must be sufficient evidence to permit the conclusion that the defendant in fact entertained serious doubts as to the truth of his publication. Publishing with such doubts shows reckless disregard for the truth or falsity and demonstrates actual malice.[28]

To prove reckless disregard, a plaintiff must show that the defendant held serious doubts regarding the truth of the publication in question. If the defendant believed in the truth of the publication, the defendant would be protected. This distinction between *truth* and *belief in truth* is a critical element in the Court's interpretation of the meaning of actual malice, for it firmly establishes the theoretical foundation for the Court's eventual confrontation with the problem of correspondence notions of truth in the area of libel law—that is, the notion that truthful expession inheres in the simple, direct correspondence between words and reality. *St. Amant* is also important for establishing instances in which professions of belief in truth will not be protective, such as in the case of a fabricated story or the use of unverified, unreliable sources.[29] Again, the Court was establishing the outer boundaries of *Sullivan*'s protection of expression as well as the broad outlines of the role of truth in libel law. Libelous falsehoods were protected so long as they were not calculated or reckless.

Gertz v. Welch: Protecting More Speech

Through the years, the Supreme Court decided several important cases that, step by step, extended the actual malice standard not only to public officials but also to public figures.[30] The most significant is *Gertz v. Welch*, decided in 1974 and recognized for defining two kinds of public figures who, like public officials, must prove actual malice in order to prevail in libel suits: (1) all-purpose public figures; and (2) limited, or "vortex," public figures. *Gertz* is also known for its holding that private persons, when libeled, do not, under the First Amendment, have to prove actual malice in order to prevail in libel suits but rather must show at least negligence. In justifying the different fault standard for public and private persons, Justice Lewis Powell discussed the marked difference between public and private plaintiffs' ability to reply to defamatory charges:

> The first remedy of any victim of defamation is self-help—using available opportunities to contradict the lie or correct the error and thereby to minimize its adverse impact on reputation. Public officials and public figures usually enjoy significantly greater access to the channels of effective communication and hence have a more realistic opportunity to counteract false statements than private individuals normally enjoy. Private individuals are therefore more vulnerable to injury, and the state interest in protecting them is correspondingly greater.[31]

Public persons not only have greater access to the media but also, as Powell noted elsewhere in the opinion, have exposed themselves to greater risk of defamation by working in the public sphere. The First Amendment demands that their burden in libel suits be greater than that of private persons, who have little chance of effectively countering a false charge.

In this case a Chicago attorney by the name of Elmer Gertz sued *American Opinion*, a publication of the conservative John Birch Society, for defamation. The magazine had falsely accused Gertz of being a communist and of engineering the "frame-up" of a police officer convicted of killing a child.[32] Overturning lower court decisions, the Supreme Court ruled that Gertz was a private person, not a public figure, and was thus responsible for proving a lesser fault standard than actual malice but at least that of negligence.[33] As Norman Rosenberg notes, "*Gertz* . . . finally abandoned all applications of the traditional common law principle of strict liability for libelous falsehoods."[34] Although in *Gertz* the Court widened the scope of *Sullivan*'s purview as it pulled even more speech into the protective penumbra of the Constitution, *Gertz* was in fact a drawing back from the even more speech-protective plurality opinion issued three years earlier in *Rosenbloom v. Metromedia, Inc.*, which held that anyone libeled in the discussion of a public issue, even a private person, must prove actual malice.[35]

Harte-Hanks Communications, Inc. v. Connaughton:
Avoiding the Truth

Definitional issues regarding the actual malice standard continued to concern the Supreme Court even twenty-five years after *Sullivan*. In *Harte-Hanks Communications, Inc. v. Connaughton* (1989),[36] Daniel Connaughton, a candidate for a municipal judgeship, sued the publisher of the *Hamilton Journal News*, an Ohio newspaper, for defamation. He claimed the newspaper had published a grand jury member's false accusation that he had tried to bribe her in the criminal investigation of one of his opponent's colleagues.[37] The Court affirmed lower court rulings in favor of Connaughton, holding that while "failure to investigate will not alone support a finding of actual malice," evidence of the press's "purposeful avoidance of the truth" would.[38] The *Journal News* had, the Court affirmed, neglected evidence in its possession suggesting Connaughton's innocence, including a tape recording of the conversation in which his accuser, Alice Thompson, claimed Connaughton tried to bribe her, as well as Connaughton's and others' denials of the charges.[39] This purposeful avoidance of the truth of the bribery claims constituted the reckless disregard for the truth prong of the actual malice standard.

Although *Garrison*, *St. Amant*, and *Harte-Hanks* are certainly not the only Supreme Court cases staking out the meanings of actual malice and the role of truth in libel cases involving First Amendment privileges, they make the most important contributions to the definitional evolution, at least for the purposes of this book. Belief in truth, these cases assert, does not exist when the publisher of a defamatory statement was aware of its likely falsity, had serious doubts as to its truth, or purposefully avoided the truth. The existence of fabrications and unverified, suspect sources also showed that the publisher did not believe in the truth of the publication. These negative definitions of the meaning of actual malice in libel law suggested the Court's growing awareness that, in the rough and tumble of political debate and public discourse, truth is not always easily recognizable.

Truth, Fact, Opinion, and Ambiguous Language

We turn now to that strain of cases in the *Sullivan* line in which the Court distinguished between factual and nonfactual expression. In these cases, the Court confronted the language dilemmas that have most concerned postmodern thinkers: whether and how to determine the truth of language falling along the entire range of expression from fact to opinion.

Gertz v. Welch: Opinion versus Fact

Gertz v. Welch (1974), discussed earlier, also addressed the different protections offered to factual statements and opinions in First Amendment libel jurisprudence, and it is this contribution to the landscape of libel law that most concerns us here. For seventeen years following *Gertz*, an observation made in the opinion's *dicta* seemed to extend *Sullivan's* First Amendment protection for political speech to all opinion. "Under the First Amendment there is no such thing as a false idea," wrote Justice Powell. "However pernicious an opinion may seem, we depend for its correction not on the conscience of judges and juries but on the competition of other ideas. But there is no constitutional value in false statements of fact."[40] The Court in *Gertz* apparently understood opinion as outside the realm of factual expression and thus not susceptible to a determination of falsity. As libel reform scholar David Anderson has observed, *Gertz* suggested to some lower courts that the First Amendment protected opinions wholesale: "They [the lower courts] read *Gertz* as creating an absolute protection for opinion, so that the defendant's motive and the honesty with which the belief was held were irrelevant."[41] This protection of opinion was in sharp contrast to the concept of liability for factual statements, in which motive and honesty of belief in the truth of a statement had become the central considerations.

Until the Supreme Court decided *Milkovich v. Lorain Journal* in 1990, the opinion doctrine was, according to Anderson, "the fastest growing body of defamation law. . . . Of all the constitutional defamation rules . . . the opinion rule best served as an early screening device by which judges could dispose of cases they considered unmeritorious. Perhaps for that reason, it was used to resolve many cases that at common law would not have been thought to involve opinion."[42] *Gertz* drew a bright-line distinction between opinion and fact, and *Sullivan* and its progeny to this point had concentrated all actual malice analyses on statements of *fact*, not opinion or ideas. It made sense, then, for the lower courts to read *Gertz* as offering First Amendment protection to opinion.

Gertz clarified the position of false statements of fact in the First Amendment libel privilege: they have no place unless they are honest errors, that is, unless the publisher believed in their truth. But despite this foundational principle of the privilege, several other Supreme Court cases decided in the *Gertz* era presaged the trouble the Court would have in maintaining any kind of bright-line distinction between fact and opinion, between actionable language requiring a truth test and non-actionable language.

Greenbelt Cooperative Publishing Association v. Bresler: Rhetorical Hyperbole

The first such case is *Greenbelt Cooperative Publishing Association v. Bresler* (1970),[43] decided several years before *Gertz*, in which a Maryland real estate developer sued a local newsweekly for characterizing his negotiations at city council meetings as "blackmail."[44] As a state legislator and private developer deeply involved in the city of Greenbelt's development, Bresler conceded his public figure status and thus had to prove actual malice in order to prevail in his suit. The newsweekly had published several reports on the public debates, detailing Bresler's attempt to exchange his rezoning request for land he wished to develop as a high-density residential neighborhood and then sell to the city as the site for a proposed school. In both reports, citizens attending the meetings were reported as having called Bresler's negotiations "blackmail."[45]

The Court found the newsweekly's use of the term "blackmail" in its reports to be constitutionally protected speech, asserting that the plaintiff's charge that the paper had accused him of committing a crime was not actionable. "The Greenbelt News Review," the Court wrote, "was performing its wholly legitimate function as a community newspaper when it published full reports of . . . public debates in its news columns."[46] What is more, the Court found that the use of the word "blackmail" was rhetorical hyperbole, which even "the most careless reader" would have recognized.[47] Rhetorical hyperbole was a way of expressing opinion, not fact, the Court asserted. In *Greenbelt*, just six years after the *Sullivan* decision, the Supreme Court encountered its first post-*Sullivan* libel case in which the determination of the facticity of speech was crucial to the determination of constitutional protection for that speech. The Court recognized that interpretation plays a role in deciphering the meanings of words and deciding whether the question of truth is even relevant—and in the process continued to uphold the animating principle of the First Amendment articulated in *Sullivan*: the protection of speech, even speech containing honest errors of fact, to further the value of self-government.

Time, Inc. v. Pape: Rational Interpretation
of Ambiguous Language

After *Greenbelt* and before *Gertz*, the Supreme Court encountered another case suggesting the deep problematic in language raised by the actual malice standard: expression is often difficult to categorize as either fact or something other than fact. In *Time, Inc. v. Pape*,[48] the Court protected press freedoms when a journalist uses ambiguous sources. A *Time* magazine article about police civil rights abuses was the object of the dispute. It summarized an official government report on the abuses, and in depicting an episode of police brutality, presented allegations as facts. The Court ruled that the news report was a protected rational interpretation of the police report, which did not draw clear distinctions between allegations and facts.[49] In finding the rational interpretation standard to be comprehended by the actual malice standard, the Court recognized the limitations of ambiguous language in representing a stable, determinate truth—and the difficulty of interpreting such ambiguous language in the search for truth. Facts in ambiguous expression are difficult, if not impossible, to locate. Again, the Court upheld the publisher's *belief in the truth* as the point of inquiry in a libel determination.

National Association of Letter Carriers, AFL-CIO v. Austin:
Figurative Epithets

Just three years later, in 1974, the Court again was faced with determining whether allegedly false and defamatory statements were sufficiently factual so as to lose constitutional privilege. In an opinion issued the very same day as the *Gertz* opinion, the Court decided *National Association of Letter Carriers, AFL-CIO v. Austin*,[50] a case in which non-union letter carriers sued several letter carriers' unions for libel under a Virginia insulting words statute. (The courts treated the case as a libel case.) The *Carrier's Corner*, a union newsletter, had published the names of several non-union letter carriers under the heading "List of Scabs" as part of the unions' organizing initiatives.[51] The three plaintiffs, all listed as scabs in the newsletter, filed libel complaints against the local and national union; the defendants filed demurrers;[52] and the trial court dismissed the demurrers, finding that state libel laws are applicable to statements uttered in the context of labor disputes.[53] The jury found for the plaintiffs, awarding both compensatory and punitive damages. Even though the trial judge erroneously instructed the jury to apply the common law malice standard rather than the actual malice standard required under federal labor policy (which adopted the First Amendment standards of *Sullivan*),[54] the Supreme Court of Virginia affirmed the jury's finding.[55] While the Supreme Court granted *certiorari* in this case to settle several issues of law, the finding of most significance to this discussion involves the Court's analysis of the epithets "scab" and "traitor" used in the union newsletter. Identifying the non-union letter carriers as scabs "was literally and factually true," the Court wrote, and such speech is protected under federal labor laws. (Interestingly, the majority did not invoke First Amendment protections, although Justice William Douglas did in his concurrence.)[56] Noting that "there must be a false statement of fact" before the actual malice standard can be met, the Court found that the epithet "traitor" was not a factual statement because it was used "in a loose, figurative sense to demonstrate the union's strong disagreement with the views of those workers who oppose unionization."[57] The Supreme Court reversed the judgments of the lower courts.

As both *Greenbelt* and *National Association of Letter Carriers* illustrate, in the decade following *Sullivan* the Supreme Court was engaged in the difficult conceptual work of defining what constituted an actionable factual statement in a libel suit involving constitutional privilege. As so often happens in the judicial articulation of definitions, it was easier for the Court to say what a factual statement was *not* than what it *was*. It was not rhetorical hyperbole, and it was not an epithet used as a loose figure of speech. As the years passed, the Court continued to face libel cases challenging the status of a contested statement's factual nature, including *Milkovich* and *Masson*. The distinction between fact and opinion erected in *Gertz* proved a difficult one to sustain.

Cantrell v. Forest City Publishing: Implications of Fact

In a false-light invasion of privacy suit against a newspaper publisher in Ohio, the central issue was whether a false implication in a news report could constitute actual malice.[58] Margaret Cantrell's husband had been killed when a bridge collapsed into the Ohio River. In reporting on the bridge disaster for the *Cleveland Plain Dealer*, Joseph Eszterhas wrote: "Margaret Cantrell will talk neither about what happened nor about how they [the family] are doing. She wears the same mask of non-expression she wore at the funeral."[59] He had neither seen nor interviewed Cantrell during a visit to her house, but, the Court noted, his story "plainly implied" that he had.[60] In considering whether the report portrayed Cantrell in a false light with actual malice, the Supreme Court ruled that the implications that Eszterhas had interviewed and observed Cantrell were "calculated falsehoods" and thus constituted knowing falsity.[61]

When translated to libel law, the *Cantrell* Court's finding suggested that the implication of defamatory false facts could easily reach the "knowing false-hood" prong of actual malice. Although defamatory fabrication self-evidently constitutes actual malice, the idea that *implications* can be false and defamatory considerably complicated the First Amendment landscape of libel law. Because an implication in this sense is not a *statement* but rather a *suggestion* of fact, it is a somewhat ambiguous representational convention of language. An implication is an *indirect* expression, and *Cantrell* raised the difficult question of how to determine whether contested language has *indirectly* expressed a false fact. The Supreme Court would not answer this question in the context of a libel suit for another sixteen years. And when it did in the case of *Milkovich v. Lorain Journal*, it charted a whole new course for First Amendment libel law.

Bose v. Consumers Union: Rational Interpretation of Ambiguous Events

In *Bose Corp. v. Consumers Union of United States, Inc.* (1984)[62] the Supreme Court protected the rational interpretation of ambiguous events rather than sources, as it had done in *Time, Inc. v. Pape*. In reviewing a new Bose audio speaker system, a *Consumers Report* article described its sound with a striking metaphor: "Individual instruments heard through the *Bose* system seemed to grow to gigantic proportions and tended to wander about the room. For instance, a violin appeared to be 10 feet wide and a piano stretched from wall to wall."[63] Employing descriptive language that suggested "a misconception" of an ambiguous event, the metaphor did not, according to the Court, "place the speech beyond the outer limits of the First Amendment's broad protective umbrella."[64] The statements at issue walked "the line between fact and opinion."[65] Even so, the Court acknowledged the limitations of language in representing ambiguous events and gave constitutional protection to what it considered an unflattering and technically inaccurate description "of an event 'that bristled with ambiguities' and descriptive challenges for the writer."[66] As in *Pape*, the Court upheld the publisher's *belief in the truth* as the point of inquiry in a libel determination. Although the disputed statement may have been inaccurate, the Court said, that inaccuracy did not negate the substantial truth of the description. Exactly what that truth was, however, was impossible to say. In both *Pape* and *Bose* the "rational interpretation" of ambiguous sources and events led to expression in which an unambiguous, unitary truth was simply not discoverable.

Philadelphia Newspapers, Inc. v. Hepps:
When Truth Is Unknowable

Philadelphia Newspapers, Inc. v. Hepps (1986) involved the media libel of private persons. The *Philadelphia Inquirer* published a series of articles claiming that a corporation was linked to organized crime. Under Pennsylvania common law, the private person plaintiffs were not required to prove falsity; rather falsity was presumed. The newspaper was thus faced with proving the truth of its publication. Finding this strict liability offensive to First Amendment protections, the Supreme Court ruled that when the defamatory publication involves matters of public concern, a private libel plaintiff must prove falsity even when the fault level is negligence rather than actual malice.[67] The Court thus once again pulled matters of public concern into the First Amendment penumbra.

In *Hepps* the Court finally explicitly acknowledged what it had only hinted at in earlier cases such as *Pape* and *Bose*: that truth and falsity are not always indisputable and readily discernible. The burden of proof for truth or falsity (whether on the defendant or on the plaintiff) becomes important, the Court said, only when "the evidence is ambiguous," that is, only when the truth or falsity of the allegation is unknowable:

> The allocation of the burden of proof will determine liability for some speech that is true and some that is false, but *all* of such speech is *unknowably* true or false. Because the burden of proof is the deciding factor only when the evidence is ambiguous, we cannot know how much of the speech affected by the allocation of the burden of proof is true and how much is false. In a case presenting a configuration of speech and plaintiff like the one we face here, and where the scales are in such an uncertain balance, we believe that the Constitution requires us to tip them in favor of protecting true speech.[68]

Although such a rule certainly protects some false and defamatory publications, the Court asserted, First Amendment theory demands such press protection. Again, the idea of ambiguity, so important in the rational interpretation standard as articulated in both *Pape* and *Bose*, complicates the First Amendment arena of libel law. In *Hepps*, the Court clearly acknowledged that truth and falsity are sometimes impossible to locate in expression.

Hustler Magazine, Inc. v. Falwell: Parody

In *Hustler v. Falwell* (1988) the Reverend Jerry Falwell brought a libel, invasion of privacy, and infliction of emotional distress suit against *Hustler* magazine. The contested language appeared in a parody of an advertising campaign for Campari liqueur that featured celebrities discussing their "first times"—drinking Campari, that is. The *Hustler* parody depicted Falwell admitting his "first time" was "during a drunken incestuous rendezvous with his mother in an outhouse."[69] By the time the case reached the Supreme Court, the only surviving claim was that of emotional distress, for which the Fourth Circuit had ruled in favor of Falwell.[70] The Supreme Court reversed, ruling that the parody, though "offensive" to Falwell and "gross and repugnant in the eyes of most," expressed a constitutionally protected opinion or idea.[71] The "outrageous" language used in the parody "could not reasonably have been interpreted as stating actual facts about the public figure involved," the Court wrote.[72] And if false, defamatory facts did not exist, neither did actual malice. In other words, the First Amendment precluded an infliction of emotional distress claim—and, by extension, a libel claim—based on "caricature," which is by its very nature "often not reasoned or evenhanded, but slashing and one-sided."[73]

The *Hustler* case is important here for three reasons. First, it underscores the Court's historic preoccupation with and insistence on drawing lines between actionable false and defamatory facts and non-actionable opinion or expression of ideas. In the later case of *Milkovich*, the Court retreated from this practice, asserting that existing First Amendment doctrine adequately protected free expression without the "creation of an artificial dichotomy between 'opinion' and fact."[74] Later in this chapter I examine the *Milkovich* holding and its reasoning in depth, but for now it is sufficient to note that the *Milkovich* Court was working against previous constitutional rationales. Second, *Hustler* continued the Supreme Court's negative definitions of factual language. Like rhetorical hyperbole and epithets, parody did not constitute factual language, the Court determined. Finally, in its finding that the parody in question was part of a long tradition of social and political cartoons and satire in public discourse, the *Hustler* Court continued to cleave to *Sullivan*'s animating First Amendment theory.[75]

Milkovich v. Lorain Journal: Connotations of False Facts

Almost two decades after *Gertz*, *Milkovich v. Lorain Journal* (1990) established that the Supreme Court would not offer wholesale First Amendment protection to opinion, or at least all expression that claimed to be opinion, despite the suggestion in *Gertz* that it might. In *Milkovich*, the Court swept the *Gertz* opinion dictum under the rug—where it also attempted to put the existing fact and opinion distinction tests developed in the lower courts over the years. The *Gertz* dictum was not intended to erect constitutional protection for opinion, the *Milkovich* Court asserted. Rather it "was merely a reiteration of Justice Holmes' classic 'marketplace of ideas' concept."[76] Thus the contextual factors applied by the lower courts to determine whether a contested statement was factual and actionable—or opinion and not actionable—were developed with "a mistaken reliance on the *Gertz* dictum."[77]

In addition to rejecting what it deemed "an artificial dichotomy between 'opinion' and fact" in constitutional doctrine,[78] *Milkovich* focused on the problematic issue of the implication of false facts—first raised in the *Cantrell* privacy case and now the explosive centerpiece of a libel suit. In an Ohio newspaper column a journalist implied, according to the Court, that a high school wrestling coach had lied under oath in a judicial proceeding about his role in a brawl following a match. Milkovich, the coach, had testified that he had nothing to do with instigating the brawl, but the columnist, in commenting on the coach's testimony, wrote that anyone who had attended the wrestling match "knows in his heart" that Milkovich lied[79] and that his lies served as a lesson to his athletes and students: "If you get in a jam, lie your way out."[80]

According to the Court, the columnist's implication that Milkovich lied was not "loose, figurative or hyperbolic language" that clearly constitutes opinion.[81] Instead the columnist *connoted* the *fact* that Milkovich had lied and committed perjury—and this fact was susceptible to being proved false. Thus the contested statements were not protected opinions, even though they occurred in an opinion column in the sports section. In *Milkovich* the Court held that the First Amendment protects expression as opinion except when it contains "a provably false factual connotation."[82] Even though the Court refused to accept the publisher's contention that every First Amendment defamation case requires "an inquiry into whether a statement is 'opinion' or 'fact,'" its ruling nonetheless mandated the judicial search for actionable facts in contested statements.[83]

As the legal scholar Martin Hansen has argued, "*Milkovich* casts light not only on the Court's broader theory of First Amendment defamation doctrine but also, and more significantly, on its underlying view of how language operates in everyday communication."[84] *Milkovich* put forward a view that departed markedly from the Court's previous acknowledgments of the interpretive challenges of language. *Milkovich* assumed "that language . . . is stable and unequivocal," Hansen suggests.[85] In refusing to adopt a multifactor test for determining when defamatory language is sufficiently factual to be actionable, the Court turned its back on the "totality of circumstances" or contextual test articulated in *Ollman v. Evans* by the D.C. Circuit in 1984.[86] For more than sixteen years the lower courts had relied on various tests to distinguish fact from opinion, the *Ollman* four-part test being one of the most widely used.[87] This contextual test, articulated by then-judge Kenneth Starr, included the threshold determination of whether a contested statement had "a precise core of meaning for which a consensus of understanding exists or, conversely, whether the statement [was] indefinite and ambiguous."[88] If a consensus meaning was found to exist, a court would determine whether the statement was verifiable and the linguistic and social context of the statement suggested expression of opinion or facts.[89] "The richness and diversity of language, as evidenced by the capacity of the same words to convey different meanings in different contexts," required something more, the *Ollman* majority asserted, than "a bright-line or mechanical distinction" between factual expression and opinion.[90]

Justice William Brennan's dissent in *Milkovich* suggested that the majority had in fact used a test very much like the *Ollman* test to determine whether the column implied defamatory false facts:

> Among the circumstances to be scrutinized by a court in ascertaining whether a statement purports to state or imply "actual facts about an individual," as shown by the Court's analysis of the statements at issue here, . . . are the same indicia that lower courts have been relying on for the past decade or so to distinguish between statements of fact and statements of opinion: the type of language used, the meaning of the statement in context, whether the statement is verifiable, and the broader social circumstances in which the statement was made.[91]

It was the correct method, Brennan asserted, but the majority misapplied it. The column at issue in *Milkovich* did not imply the false fact that Milkovich committed perjury. Rather, Brennan argued, the columnist "reveals the facts upon which he is relying" and "makes it clear at which point he runs out of facts and is simply guessing."[92] The columnist was writing in an editorial, which is a journalistic form known for containing opinion. "Furthermore, the tone and format of the piece notify readers to expect speculation and personal judgment," Brennan continued. "The tone is pointed, exaggerated, and heavily laden with emotional rhetoric and moral outrage."[93] When the columnist wrote that "anyone who attended the meet . . . knows in his heart" that Milkovich lied, he was operating in the realm of First Amendment protected rhetorical hyperbole.[94]

This fundamental disagreement between the majority and the dissent over the kind of language at issue—Was it opinion, rhetorical hyperbole, or a connotation of false, defamatory facts? Was it actionable or protected language?—highlights the deep problem in locating a unitary, stable meaning in certain kinds of language. The majority viewed the language problem presented in *Milkovich* from what Hansen calls "a rigid, acontextual approach."[95] The dissent, by contrast, took into account the context of the disputed statements to determine that the columnist "not only reveals the facts upon which he is relying but he makes it clear at which point he runs out of facts and is simply guessing."[96] How to reconcile such fundamentally different interpretations of the language at hand and its meanings? The conflict underscores the power of the postmodern argument that language often contains indeterminate meanings and thus does not always yield to verifiability analyses. In choosing to view the meaning of language as stable and determinate, the *Milkovich* Court implicitly rejected such a view of language and privileged the protection of reputation over *Sullivan*'s "vital guarantee of free and uninhibited discussion of public issues."[97]

Masson v. New Yorker:
The Material Alteration of Quotations

By the time *Masson v. New Yorker* was decided by the Supreme Court in 1991, it had become clear that determining when contested language was sufficiently factual so as to be actionable was highly problematic. Determining the truth of a self-evidently factual statement was one thing, but determining the truth of ambiguous, not purely factual expression was another. *Masson v. New Yorker*, which attempted to apply the actual malice standard to altered and allegedly false and defamatory quotations, also ran into the problem of ambiguous language: How to establish the truth or falsity of the *meaning* of an allegedly altered and defamatory quotation?

To reiterate, the well-known psychoanalyst Jeffrey Masson had filed a libel suit against Janet Malcolm and the *New Yorker* in 1984 claiming that he had been libeled by altered, misleading quotations attributed to him.[98] The Court acknowledged early in its opinion the need to confront the meaning of quotations, and more particularly quotation marks, in its consideration of the facticity of the disputed language.[99] "In general," Justice Anthony Kennedy wrote for the majority, "quotation marks around a passage indicate to the reader that the passage reproduces the speaker's words verbatim. They inform the reader that he or she is reading the statement of the speaker, not a paraphrase or other indirect interpretation by an author."[100] The Court made this assertion without any reference to established authority—grammatical, journalistic, or otherwise. Following the lead of Judge Alex Kozinski's dissent in the Ninth Circuit *Masson* opinion, the Supreme Court emphasized that fabricated quotations, especially ones that defame the speaker, may be even more damaging than another person's criticism, because "it is against self-interest" to malign oneself.[101]

The Court did not end its consideration of the meaning of quotation marks here. In continuing to explore the issue, it embarked on a fascinating rumination on the degree of constitutional protection afforded to altered quotations in different genres of publication. Despite the conventional meaning of quotation marks, the Court pointed out, there are instances when quotation marks are used, "yet no reasonable reader would assume that such punctuation automatically implies the truth of the quoted material."[102] When a work claims status as docudrama or historical fiction or admits to re-creating conversations from memory, for example, quotation marks may not be expected to indicate verbatim speech.[103] In these genres and instances, the Court implied, altered or fabricated quotations would not be held to the standard of truth generally prescribed in libel law and more specifically in the actual malice standard. The contested work in *Masson*, however, "as with much journalistic writing," did not claim special status and in fact "purports to be nonfiction, the result of numerous interviews."[104] A reasonable reader could thus be expected to understand the quotations to represent the actual words spoken.

In discussing the meaning of quotations in different genres, the Court reasoned that the nature of an author's social contract with the reader—sometimes implicit as in docudrama, historical fiction, and journalism, sometimes explicit as in works that admittedly re-create conversations from memory—is an important element controlling the level of First Amendment protection afforded defamatory and fabricated quotations. If readers know that what they are reading is not fact, there can be no actual malice. This idea of the social contract is absent from most professional codes of journalistic ethics, at least in explicit terms.[105] Although the Court was not quite equating legal standards with ethical standards—what ethics scholar Jay Black has called "a false equation"[106]—its emphasis on the social contract as a controlling element in determining First Amendment protections for disputed quotations seems to mandate the creation of a corresponding journalistic principle. Judge Kozinski's dissent in the earlier Ninth Circuit ruling looked to existing journalistic standards in formulating what he called the central meaning test, a test affording First Amendment protection only to those quotations that do not make alterations beyond the cosmetic. The Supreme Court also considered existing journalistic standards—and more—in its discussion of the social contract. The Court articulated not only a legal test for determining in which genres altered quotations are actionable but also an ethical principle for journalists: the journalist should establish clear social contracts with the reader regarding the meaning of quotations when departing from traditional journalistic forms such as the news report.

In approaching the constitutional question in the *Masson* case—"whether, in the framework of a summary judgment motion, the evidence suffices to show that respondents acted with the requisite knowledge of falsity or reckless disregard as to truth or falsity"[107]—the Supreme Court turned its attention to the meaning of falsity in altered or fabricated quotations. First, the Court rejected the idea that any alteration, such as the correction of grammar or syntax, would constitute falsity: "If every alteration constituted the falsity required to prove actual malice, the practice of journalism, which the First Amendment standard is designed to protect, would require a radical change, one inconsistent with our precedents and First Amendment principles."[108] By acknowledging that journalists often do alter quotations, at least for the purposes of eliminating "grammatical and syntactical infelicities,"[109] the Court saw its role as protecting both the First Amendment *and* what it considered to be standard journalistic practices. Second, the Court rejected Masson's contention that knowing or reckless falsity inhered in the alteration of any quotation beyond the correction of grammar or syntax—what Masson saw as "deliberate falsehood[s]."[110] In supporting this rejection, the Court considered the reconstruction from interview notes of a speaker's statement to be common journalistic practice: "That author would, we may assume, act with knowledge that at times she has attributed to her subject words other than those actually used. Under petitioner's proposed standard, an author in this situation would lack First Amendment protection if she reported as quotations the substance of a speaker's derogatory statements about himself."[111] The Court assumed, then, that the reporting of quotations is an essential element of a news report, for earlier in its opinion it admitted that "paraphrase or other indirect interpretation by an author" could replace direct quotations but lacked the authority of quotations.[112] The Court did not even consider that a proper legal standard of falsity might equate with what a *New York Times* editor claimed at the time was the paper's ethical standard of falsity: the placing within quotation marks of anything *besides* the speaker's exact words.[113] The *Times*'s editorial standard did not even allow for the correction of grammar, syntax, or verbal tics, while the Supreme Court's standard would clearly allow for much more. But the same *Times* article that explained the newspaper's policy about the use of quotations—and assured readers that the *Times* traveled the ethical high road— went on to provide the policies of other prestigious print news publications, each of which departed to some degree from the *Times*'s strict rules. *Time*, the *Nation*, *Newsweek*, and *Harper's*, according to editors at the respective magazines, allowed minor changes to quotations, depending on the circumstance. The *Atlantic* checked all quotations with the speakers, and if there was an objection, the speaker and writer would work out a solution.[114] As much as Masson's lawyers, and the press at large, may have wanted the use of verbatim quotations to be a settled ethical principle in journalism, the principle clearly changed with circumstance—perhaps even as it moved from the genre of daily newspapers, the birthplace of the traditional report, to that of magazines, where the narrative report (like Malcolm's profile of Masson) has long flourished. The Supreme Court recognized this much in its ruling.

Rejecting "any special test of falsity for quotations,"[115] the Court then emphasized the actual malice standard's historical basis in the "substantial truth" doctrine of common law, which "overlooks minor inaccuracies and concentrates upon substantial truth."[116] It is this doctrine—"minor inaccuracies do not amount to falsity so long as 'the substance, the gist, the sting, of the libelous change be justified'"[117]—that underpins the concept of falsity in the actual malice standard. Applying the substantial truth doctrine to the issue in *Masson*, the Court concluded "that a deliberate alteration of the words uttered by a plaintiff does not equate with knowledge of falsity . . . unless the alteration results in a material change in meaning conveyed by the statement."[118]

The Court thus rejected the Ninth Circuit's use of the rational interpretation standard in the context of altered quotations, claiming that it would eliminate not only "any method of distinguishing between the statements of the subject and the interpretation of the author" but also "the real meaning of quotations."[119] Such a standard would, the Court observed, "ill serve the values of the First Amendment" by diminishing "to a great degree the trustworthiness of the printed word.[120] But neither did the Court adopt Judge Kozinksi's proposed central meaning test. Although both the district court and the Ninth Circuit majority focused *implicitly* on the meaning of the disputed quotations, the Supreme Court's material alteration test, like Kozinski's test, forthrightly identified the speaker's meaning and the disputed quotation's meaning as the points of inquiry. But the Supreme Court's understanding of meaning was more limited than the lower courts' and broader than Kozinski's. At heart is the idea, articulated previously by Kozinski, that ambiguity should not be edited out of a speaker's statement: "The quotation marks indicate that the author is not involved in an interpretation of the speaker's ambiguous statement, but attempting to convey what the speaker said. This orthodox use of the quotation is the quintessential 'direct account of events that speak for themselves.'"[121] At the same time, the Court recognized that the exigencies of reporting often interfere with journalists' sincere attempts to capture quotations verbatim, and so minor errors in quotation are unavoidable. The Court thus focused its determination of falsity on a quotation's *meaning* and whether that meaning is *materially different* from the speaker's meaning, refusing to focus simply on a quotation's deviation from the actual words spoken, excepting cosmetic edits, an approach Kozinski advocated in his labeling of a speaker's utterance as a *fact*.

The Supreme Court's ruling therefore seems to strike a balance between the Ninth Circuit's majority opinion and its dissent. In its rationale for the material alteration test, the Court continually turned to what it understood as standard journalistic practice in the crafting of quotations. In other words, the Court turned to the journalism profession for guidance in its own formulation of the concept of falsity in the context of misquotations. In this sense, established journalistic standards and their presumed underlying conceptions of truthful quotation guided the Court in its conceptualization of legal truth underpinning the actual malice standard. The substantial truth doctrine in *Masson* thus encapsulates, at least in part, the journalistic conception of truthful quotation.

When the Supreme Court applied its newly articulated material alteration test to each of the six disputed passages that survived into this iteration of the case, it found that all but one differed materially in meaning from the tape-recorded statements and thus created "issue[s] of fact for a jury as to falsity."[122]

The Court therefore reversed the judgment of the court of appeals and re-manded the case "for further proceedings consistent with this opinion." [123] The same problems that plagued the lower courts, however, remained in the Supreme Court's formulation and application of the material alteration test. First, the separate elements of falsity and fault were conflated in the test's em-phasis on "knowledge of falsity." Second, the inquiry into knowing falsity re-quired an interpretation of meaning, which, according to Lee Bollinger, "is highly uncertain and ambiguous." [124] In the summary judgment posture of *Masson*, the courts were determining whether factual issues existed in the al-tered quotations by determining the meanings of both Masson's tape-recorded utterances and Malcolm's quotations as well as the differential between these meanings. This conflation of fact with meaning makes the inquiry into whether an altered quotation reaches actual malice "far less certain of yielding a correct answer as to whether it [does]." [125]

Of course, as established in *Sullivan*, only statements of fact are actionable in libel claims. The "degree of 'factualness'" of an altered quotation, the Court noted, is "far less" than a clear statement of fact, such as saying "that someone 'used cocaine.'" [126] However, *Masson*'s legal conception of truth locates truth in a single utterance rather than a collection of utterances made over time and confusingly treats interpretation of meaning as somehow fact-based.

From *Sullivan* to *Masson*: Libel Law and the Postmodern Dilemma

The actual malice standard established in *Sullivan* shifted the judicial inquiry in libel cases from truth to belief in truth, a shift that not only theoretically al-lowed for the existence of multiple versions of truth but also offered a wider scope of press protection than the common law of libel by attempting to mea-sure belief rather than truth. The standard was predicated on *Sullivan*'s First Amendment theory espousing the necessary role of the press in a participatory democracy. But as the standard developed, establishing belief in the truth of contested expression increasingly proved to be a muddy determination. The problem lay in the ambiguity that often colors human affairs and the language used to represent those affairs. Many uses of language, it appeared, lay some-where between libel law's classic division of speech into factual expression (which is potentially actionable in a libel suit) and expression that is not factual (which is not actionable in a libel suit). This realization, of course, was not unique to First Amendment jurisprudence in the area of libel law. The common law had long before developed the defense of fair comment to protect opinion, commentary, and criticism on matters of public concern, but prior to the constitutionalization of libel law, its limits varied widely among state and federal jurisdictions.[127] And distinguishing between unprotected false statements of fact and protected opinion or comment was as problematic under the common law of libel as it was after *Sullivan*. As a World War II–era media law textbook noted: "Drawing the line in the specific case is sometimes very difficult, and is fraught with uncertainty. This is because, in the very nature of things, the line between fact and opinion is shadowy. Some statements are readily recognized as statements of fact; others as statements of opinion. In between lie many cases where the interpretation is doubtful."[128]

Tracing the trajectory of Supreme Court actual malice cases shows the Court dealing more and more with the problems of determining truth or falsity in allegedly defamatory language as well as determining whether allegedly defamatory and false language was actionable (that is, factual) and susceptible to verification in the first place. The Court reemphasized the importance of *belief* in truth—not truth itself—in the First Amendment protection of speech (*St. Amant*). Such a regime privileged the coherence notion of truth over the correspondence notion, for protection required simply that the version of "truth" the defendant professed be believable. Unitary truth was not required. Of course, not every contested statement would pass this coherence test of truth. The known calculated lie (*Garrison*), the fabricated story (*St. Amant*), the use of unverified, unreliable sources (*St. Amant*), and the purposeful avoidance of the truth (*Harte-Hanks*) all belied belief in truth and were not protected speech under the actual malice standard. Some speech was more unitary in its meanings than others.

Beyond these delimitations, the Supreme Court expanded the protective mantle of the actual malice standard for contested speech on the basis of the rational interpretation of ambiguous sources and events (*Pape* and *Bose*)—instances of language that were neither clearly fact nor opinion. If the publisher believed in the truth of such an interpretation, the speech was protected. The Court also recognized that the truth of contested expression cannot always be determined, in which case the constitutional balance should tip toward protection (*Hepps*). And throughout the 1970s and 1980s the Court repeatedly found certain instances of language not sufficiently factual to be actionable in a defamation suit: rhetorical hyperbole; loose figurative language such as epithets; and parody (*Greenbelt, Letter Carriers,* and *Hustler*). In these cases, the notion of truth was simply irrelevant. Through these largely negative definitions, what constituted factual expression was delimited and inscribed within fairly narrow boundaries. It seemed that the First Amendment protections of *Sullivan* were progressively expanding.

In this same time period, though, there was one type of language that suggested a significant fissure in the protections: the implication of false facts. In *Cantrell v. Forest Hill Publishing,*[129] a 1974 false-light invasion of privacy case, the implication of false facts was found to be unprotected speech, existing beyond the protective umbrella of opinion, presumed by many lower courts to have been established in *Gertz.* The fissure widened in 1990 when the Supreme Court ruled in *Milkovich* that the First Amendment did not protect statements connoting false facts, even when uttered in the context of an editorial shot through with opinion. The implication of false facts, yet another instance of ambiguous language, was deemed sufficiently factual to be constitutionally suspect. While expression that rationally interprets ambiguous sources and events is protected, expression *using* ambiguous language may or may not be. But how to determine whether an interpretation is "rational"? And how to determine whether ambiguous language connotes a false fact? The *Milkovich* fissure widened considerably when the Court, treating quotations as facts, ruled in *Masson* that an allegedly defamatory altered quotation was libelous if it differed materially in meaning from the original words spoken. The *Masson* material alteration test required the court or fact-finder to determine whether to treat the contested quotation as factual utterance, to determine whether the words in the printed quotation were different from the words actually spoken, and to measure the difference in defamatory meaning between the words printed and the words spoken. It was a language situation illustrating the point that postmodernists were wont to make: language can have indeterminate meanings, and in such situations truth claims are suspect. In *Milkovich* and *Masson* the Court was analyzing not the truth or falsity of factual assertions but rather the truth or falsity of the meanings of language not clearly factual in nature. With this shift in First Amendment jurisprudence, the purview of protected speech in libel law constricted.

In both *Milkovich* and *Masson* the Court seemingly rejected its earlier recognition that a direct correspondence between language and reality did not always exist, that a unitary truth was not always discoverable. Both decisions retrenched on the principled insistence of the *Sullivan* line of cases that only certain kinds of language—those that were firmly factual—were susceptible to a libel charge. The logic was that truth or falsity, or belief in truth, could be reasonably determined in factual language situations—but could not in the case of language existing closer to the opposite end of the fact-opinion continuum. While some postmodernists would insist that the truth of all language is disputable—that all facts are cultural constructions—such a view of language is untenable in law, journalism, and social institutions at large. The *Sullivan* line (with the notable exceptions of *Milkovich* and *Masson*) engages postmodern conceptions of truth—but only up to a point. An appropriately press-protective First Amendment jurisprudence requires the coherence notion of truth that is theoretically and implicitly embodied in the actual malice standard and was eventually developed in the *Sullivan* line. But all versions of truth are not equal. In other words, in the practical world of law and everyday life, we must decide whether truth can be found or whether we are dealing with what the philosopher Judith Lichtenberg has called "indestructible ambiguity or indeterminacy." [130] When such indeterminacy exists, the search for truth becomes purposeless—and First Amendment protection for such speech must ensue.

As my case analysis has demonstrated, constitutional libel law can operate in a principled way even as it acknowledges that truth is not discoverable in all instances of language. Postmodern assumptions about the nature of truth and knowledge in language are built into the actual malice standard itself and have been usefully incorporated into the standard's development. Libel law thus proceeds, as Lichtenberg suggests all practical activity must, "on the assumption that there is objective truth, even if sometimes in the end we conclude that within a particular realm the concept of truth does not apply, or that in any case we will never discover it." [131] A positive jurisprudence demands that we acknowledge certain foundations—the distinction, for example, between fact and opinion in language—even as we acknowledge their limits. When these limits stymie efforts to discover truth, we must turn away from the search for foundations as the predicate for our actions toward what the philosopher Douglas Litowitz terms "the contingent beliefs of the members of our community." [132] The problem for free speech occurs, as in *Milkovich* and *Masson*, when the Court refuses, in contravention of the *Sullivan* case line, to acknowledge this possible eventuality in the search for truth.

The circumstantial and contextual methods for determining when language is factual and when it is not is, on its face, the only reasonable method to use in an age when the pre-*Sullivan* presumption that a common, knowable, uncontested truth exists has been largely discarded. But as the deep disagreement about how to apply such a method between the *Milkovich* majority and the dissent illustrates, the determination in instances of ambiguous language—including *Masson*'s altered quotations—can be fraught with irresolvable conflicts of interpretation. Libel law, at least as transformed in *Sullivan*, allows for the existence of multiple, contingent, constructed truths, and later cases in the *Sullivan* line even express a postmodern conception of truth—that is, a skepticism about the notion of a fixed, immutable truth.[133] In the logic of this understanding of truth, then, it is possible that ambiguous uses of language can be understood by some reasonable readers to convey facts and by other reasonable readers to convey opinion or some other form of protected figurative expression.

In tipping the constitutional balance toward those readers who would have understood the ambiguous language as factual, and thus toward the protection of reputation over press freedoms, both *Milkovich* and *Masson* retrench on *Sullivan*'s promise. The *Masson* Court downplayed the *Sullivan* self-government rationale almost entirely, suggesting instead that a central purpose of the First Amendment is to safeguard the quality of the "debate on public issues" even as it provides breathing space for error in that same debate. Alexander Meiklejohn argued that the point of the First Amendment was not that everyone speaks but that everything worth saying is said.[134] For Meiklejohn, then, safeguarding the quality of public debate was an integral part of the rationale for self-government. The *Masson* Court was simply articulating a long-standing conception of the First Amendment's meaning. But the instrumental value of libel law has never been, historically, to protect the quality of public discourse. It has been, rather, a device that allows someone whose reputation has been wrongly damaged to gain restitution through peaceful means. Law in the United States provides very limited means for punishing the press (or anyone else, for that matter) for publishing false statements of fact that are not defamatory. In other words, there are great swaths of public communication for which no legal recourse exists to combat the publication of false information. To expect libel law under the First Amendment to protect the quality of public discourse is to expect libel law to do something it is not designed to do. Such a rationale for the role of freedom of expression in public life had not been an explicit element of First Amendment actual malice jurisprudence until *Masson*. Its appearance marks a worrying turn in the *Sullivan* line.

Perhaps it was difficult for the Supreme Court to maintain *Sullivan*'s vision of the role of the press in furthering America's participatory democracy when such a democracy simply does not exist in American public life. Perhaps this fissure between First Amendment theory and political and social reality weakened over time the judicial supports of the central meaning of the First Amendment as expressed in *Sullivan*. With the press becoming ever more a corporate conglomerate and seeming to become less the guardian of the public interest, such a judicial shift toward concern over the quality of public discourse as expressed in *Masson* is easily explainable and understandable. But it is worth considering what has been lost in the shift and what stands to be lost if the shift continues away from the broad freedom of expression articulated in *Sullivan*.

CHAPTER SEVEN

—⤜⤛—

The End of the Line
for *Masson*

MASSON V. MALCOLM IS, IN THE END, A STORY ABOUT TRUTH. WHO WAS telling the truth about whether Masson uttered the self-incriminating remarks that were the subject of the case—Masson or Malcolm? How can we determine whether a speaker's words are truthfully represented in press expression? At what point does the alteration of a quotation materially change the speaker's meaning and thus become something other than the truth? What constitutes truth in First Amendment libel jurisprudence, and what *should* constitute such truth? Is it possible, given the vicissitudes of memory and utterance, that sometimes the truth is simply not discoverable? If so, how should courts handle such instances in libel cases implicating the First Amendment? These are questions *Masson v. New Yorker* raised during its twelve years in the federal courts and in the news. And these are questions this book explores in telling the story of the judicial and cultural life of the dispute.

Janet Malcolm answered a few of these questions (from her perspective, of course) explicitly in her several published comments about the case. Since the U.S. Supreme Court ruling in *Masson*, however, she has been largely silent about the dispute and its specifics, except during trial testimony. Even so, her writing after *In the Freud Archives* has relentlessly pursued the general theme of truth—how we construct its meaning in different cultural settings, how we adjudge its presence or absence, how language works to approximate reality. It is as if the questions raised in Masson's lawsuit got under her skin and never left, asking themselves again and again with every new subject she undertook. As the critic and journalist Craig Seligman observed in a long review of Malcolm's collective work, her major themes are "the elusiveness of truth; the paucity of the means (therapeutic, journalistic, etc.) we pursue it with; and the unreliability of narrative." [1]

In *The Journalist and the Murderer*, Malcolm famously shone a bright light on the moral ambiguity of the journalist-subject relationship. More to the point, she highlighted how the journalist and the subject approach reality from different perspectives, each seeing a different story, each perceiving a different truth or set of truths in the same events, facts, and utterances. "On reading the article or book in question," she wrote, "he [the subject] has to face the fact that the journalist—who seemed so friendly and sympathetic, so keen to understand him fully, so remarkably attuned to his vision of things—never had the slightest intention of collaborating with him on his story but always intended to write a story of his own." [2] Story is the vehicle by which truth is delivered, yet a story always has a point of view, Malcolm suggested. And that point of view may see a different truth than another point of view would.

Truth in storytelling is a theme Malcolm explored in the context not only of journalism but also of biography and criminal law. In *The Silent Woman*, her biography of Sylvia Plath and Ted Hughes, Malcolm considered the "voyeurism and busybodyism" at the heart of biography. [3] If the "journalist is a kind of confidence man," the biographer is "like the professional burglar, breaking into a house, rifling through certain drawers that he has good reason to think contain the jewelry and money, and triumphantly bearing his loot away." [4] What is more, this burglar has an attitude. "The pose of fairmindedness," Malcolm wrote, "the charade of evenhandedness, the striking of an attitude of detachment can never be more than rhetorical ruses; if they were genuine, if the writer *actually* didn't care one way or the other how things came out, he would not bestir himself to represent them." [5] Objectivity is a standard shared in both journalism and biography (and in history in general), one that is widely believed to be an indispensable part of truth-seeking and truth-telling. Malcolm's insistence that both professions are less than objective—that objectivity is merely a rhetorical device—has alienated her from the society of traditionalists.

In *The Crime of Sheila McGough*, Malcolm went even further in her suggestion that truth and storytelling are always at odds with each other. This conflict, of course, implicates the discovery of truth that trials and legal cases demand. Speaking nothing but the truth, as the court commands of witnesses, Malcolm wrote, "runs counter to the law of language, which proscribes unregulated truth-telling and requires that our utterances tell coherent, and thus never merely true, stories."[6] Law thereby places all who testify in a double bind. They must tell the whole truth, but the language they must use to do so leads them toward meaningful narrative, toward stories that require that not all the truth be told. But "law stories are empty stories," Malcolm contends. "They take the reader to a world entirely constructed of tendentious argument, and utterly devoid of the truth of the real world, where things are allowed to fall as they may. . . . The method of adversarial law is to pit two trained palterers against each other. The jury is asked to guess not which side is telling the truth—it knows that neither is—but which side is being untruthful in aid of the truth."[7]

In the first trial of *Masson v. New Yorker*, the jury decided that Jeffrey Masson's story "aided" the truth more than Janet Malcolm's did. In the second trial, the jury thought Malcolm's story did a better job. Such contradictory results lend support for Malcolm's theory about the roles of truth and narrative in law. They do little, though, to resolve the central problem the case presented after the Supreme Court's ruling: How can a jury or judge measure the difference in meaning between a speaker's actual words and a quotation? How can one determine when a change in meaning becomes material in terms of truthful representation and defamatory meaning?

Masson on Remand to the Ninth Circuit, 1992

The Supreme Court ruled on *Masson* in 1991, reversing the Ninth Circuit's affirmation of summary judgment for the defendants and remanding the case for further proceedings.[8] The case thus began its descent of the federal judicial hierarchy, following the same path it had ascended, and landed again in the Ninth Circuit for the following determinations: (1) whether, under California law, the so-called incremental harm doctrine protected the defendants; and (2) whether Masson had presented enough evidence to establish a case against not only Janet Malcolm but also the publishers of the disputed quotations, the *New Yorker* and Alfred A. Knopf.[9] Writing for the Ninth Circuit again, but this time not in dissent, Judge Kozinski found that the incremental harm doctrine—which protects a defendant against a libel judgment when the false, defamatory passage is deemed to inflict no reputational injury beyond that caused by other defamatory but truthful passages of the publication—"is not an element of

California libel law." [10] The case against Janet Malcolm would definitely go to trial.

In addition, the Ninth Circuit found that Masson had presented sufficient evidence that the *New Yorker* had reason to doubt the accuracy of the quotations, first because the *New Yorker* initiated the fact-checking process with Masson before the articles went to press, and second because Masson raised questions about the accuracy of quotations that might not have been adequately investigated.[11] Again the court looked to what it considered to be established journalistic standards to guide its decision making. "To the extent they were actually aware that Malcolm was changing quotations during the editing process," Judge Kozinski wrote, "The New Yorker's editors had a responsibility to ask her to explain a practice that, on its face, is so inconsistent with responsible journalism." [12] Of course, the actual malice standard, with its emphasis on showing the author's and publisher's knowing falsity or reckless disregard for truth, demands that courts review the writing, editorial, and publishing processes. But what is noteworthy about this instance is the court's judgment that the editing of quotations is irresponsible journalism and thus inherently suggestive of actual malice. In effect, the Ninth Circuit prescribed both legal and ethical journalistic behavior.

In affirming the district court's 1987 grant of summary judgment to Knopf, the Ninth Circuit again prescribed acceptable journalistic behavior. Knopf was "entitled to rely on" the *New Yorker's* investigation of Masson's allegations because the "magazine's sterling reputation for accuracy and the existence of its fabled fact-checking department gave Knopf sufficient reason for dismissing Masson's claims." [13] Not only did the court find that the *New Yorker's* history of accuracy and fact-checking held it to a higher standard of truth in quotation than might apply for "even daily newspapers," [14] but it also found that a later publisher could be held to a lesser standard of care because of the first publisher's reputation. As previously discussed, many of the disputed quotations in the *Masson* case appeared in a monologue Masson purportedly delivered over lunch [15]—fourteen pages of well-crafted, fluid quotation without a single verbal tic or "grammatical or syntactical" infelicity.[16] One might assume that no reasonable reader would expect this exceptionally long monologue to be quoted verbatim because practically no speaker is capable of such sustained perfect utterance. The Ninth Circuit, however, assumed the opposite. "Readers of reputable magazines such as The New Yorker," Kozinski wrote in a footnote, "are far more likely to trust the verbatim accuracy of the stories they read than are the readers of supermarket tabloids or even daily newspapers, where they understand the inherent limitations in the fact-finding process." [17]

Judge Kozinski sent the case to trial with both Janet Malcolm and the *New Yorker* as defendants. In discussing the First Amendment implications of the case, he did not refer to the conflict between the competing social values of press freedom and the right to reputation. Rather he suggested that the essential conflict in the case involved press freedom and the public trust. "The First Amendment," he wrote, "protects the right to debate vigorously the issues of the day. . . . Yet the freedom of the press, like all other rights, carries with it a responsibility. One of these is not to abuse the public trust by knowingly or recklessly publishing falsehoods. Janet Malcolm and the New Yorker may have fallen short of this standard." [18] The Supreme Court had charted this philosophical course. In its *Masson* opinion the Court did not concern itself with its *Sullivan v. New York Times* theory of the First Amendment—that free, robust debate sustains democracy and requires the protection of the First Amendment. Instead the Court refused to protect public discourse under the First Amendment because to do so might compromise the quality of that discourse. [19] The landscape of First Amendment jurisprudence and theory was changing.

The First Trial, 1993

Because no records are kept of jury deliberations, it is difficult to gauge exactly how the juries in the two ensuing federal trials used the Supreme Court's material alteration test in coming to their respective decisions, or to what degree the jury decisions reflected the test's prescription of journalistic behavior. The press covered both trials, however, and interviewed jurors after each, so there is a record of what some of the jurors said soon after their deliberations about the decision-making process. In chapter 1 I documented the first trial and, at least in part, the jury reasoning that led to a finding against Malcolm and a declaration of mistrial on the damages award. (Press interviews with jurors after the trial provide some access to the rationale behind their partial verdict.) The jury found that all five quotations in dispute were materially different in meaning from Masson's actual spoken words—that is, they all met the Supreme Court's test for falsity in the instance of altered quotations. All of the contested quotations, the jury believed, were defamatory. But only two, the jury found, were published with actual malice: "sex, women, fun" and "he had the wrong man." The trial record showed that Malcolm had discussed both passages with her editor. This editorial review, the jurors apparently reasoned, gave her an opportunity to realize that she had mistakenly attributed her own words in her notes to Masson in the "sex, women, fun" passage and that she had edited the "wrong man" quotation so as to change Masson's original, non-defamatory meaning. Jurors in the first trial seemed to conclude that Malcolm had acted not with knowing falsity, the first prong of the actual malice standard, but rather with reckless disregard for the truth, the second prong.[20] Although the actual malice standard by its very nature encapsulates the falsity element of libel within the fault element, the two elements are usually treated separately in judicial determinations. That is, courts generally determine first whether falsity exists and second whether fault can be proven. The *Masson* Court's articulation of the meaning of the actual malice standard in the context of altered quotations confused the issue of the falsity and fault determinations considerably. The jury was of course applying the Supreme Court's material alteration test in *Masson*, which said that altering a quotation does not constitute actual malice unless it materially changes the meaning of the speaker's own words. But in the Supreme Court's *Masson* opinion, in describing the legal rule of the material alteration test, Justice Anthony Kennedy used the term "knowing falsity" rather than "actual malice," isolating that prong of the standard as key in altered quotation libel cases involving the First Amendment. "A deliberate alteration of the words uttered by a plaintiff," he noted, "does not equate with knowledge of falsity . . . unless the alteration results in a material change in meaning conveyed by the statement."[21] The problem here is that the Court seemed to say something other than it meant. Later in the opinion the Court asserted that the evidence in the case created "a jury question [as to] whether Malcolm published the [disputed] statements with knowledge or reckless disregard of the alterations."[22] It does not seem, then, that the Supreme Court meant only to implicate the knowing falsity prong of the actual malice standard in the determination of fault in altered quotation libel cases. It seems, rather, that the Court meant that knowing *or* reckless falsity existed when a quotation had been deliberately altered and had a materially different meaning from the words spoken. The Court had wrapped into one the falsity and fault determinations required in a libel suit.

As the responses on the special verdict form in the first trial indicate, the jury concluded that two of the quotations were false ("sex, women, fun" and "wrong man") and that Malcolm had published them with either knowing falsity or reckless disregard for truth.[23] From interviews with jurors we know they determined that Malcolm had acted with reckless disregard for the truth in misreading her notes, failing to catch the changed meaning of the "wrong man" edit, and mistaking her own words in her notes (or what the jury took to be her own words, "sex, women, fun") for Masson's. The jury instructions in the first trial clarified the Supreme Court's material alteration test, providing that in order for Masson to prove a quotation false, he must show that his words "were deliberately or recklessly altered in a way so as to effect a material change in meaning."[24] The falsity determination required not only a material change in meaning but also *deliberate* or *reckless* alteration—both words implicating a fault inquiry. The jury instructions further provided that Masson had to prove Malcolm "was aware at the time of publication of the false, defamatory meaning"[25] and that "at the time of publication" she "published the challenged quotations with knowledge that they were false or reckless disregard for whether they were false."[26] This latter instruction seems superfluous, given the earlier fault instruction combining the actual malice with the fault inquiry. Its one contribution to the libel inquiry was to establish that actual malice must occur at publication. The jury had its work cut out in finding its way through the somewhat confusing terms of the inquiry.

Given news reports of the jury's reasoning in reaching its verdict, as discussed in chapter 1 and revisited briefly in this chapter, it appears that the jury may have confused the reckless disregard prong of actual malice with the lesser fault standard of negligence. Just two years before the Supreme Court decided *Masson v. New Yorker*, it clarified the difference between these two fault standards in *Harte-Hankes Communications, Inc. v. Connaughton*, finding that actual malice is more flagrant than "an extreme departure from the standards of investigation and reporting ordinarily adhered to by responsible publishers."[27] While such a departure might constitute negligence, it was not enough, standing alone, to constitute actual malice. "Purposeful avoidance of the truth," however, was enough.[28] In essence, the jury in the first *Masson* trial appeared to conclude that Malcolm *should have known* that two of the quotations were false had she taken the time during the editing process to think more carefully about her editing. In other words, the jury may have simply concluded that she acted with negligence, not with purposeful avoidance of the truth, which would have constituted actual malice.

That the jury in the first trial of *Masson v. New Yorker* appeared to have such a hard time applying the actual malice standard to altered quotations is easy to understand, especially in light of the forty-five pages of jury instructions accompanying the special verdict form. In addition, in their assessment of whether the quotations they identified as false and defamatory had injured Masson's reputation, the jurors may have applied the incremental harm doctrine—despite the Supreme Court *Masson* ruling placing it outside the scope of the First Amendment and the Ninth Circuit *Masson* ruling that it was not part of California law. The jurors' use of the incremental harm doctrine is one way to explain why they deadlocked on how much money to award Masson for damages, with some suggesting a mere dollar and others a million. An alternative explanation for the damage impasse exists, however. James Wagstaffe, who helped argue the *New Yorker*'s case at trial and was responsible for handling the damages aspect of the case, believes that *Masson v. New Yorker* was "a case that had no damages." The notion of the libel-proof plaintiff and the incremental harm doctrine "were all legal concepts that percolated into liability and damage concepts in the trial," he told me. Many defense lawyers in libel trials are afraid to bring up the topic of damages, Wagstaffe said, because they don't want the jury even to consider the possibility that damages could be awarded. "They argue these cases by saying, 'It's not false, not false, not false,' rather than saying, 'It's not false and, by the way, he suffered no damages.'" So Wagstaffe set out to show at trial that Masson had not suffered damage as a result of Malcolm's profile. In the closing argument he wrote with Charles Kenady, lead counsel for the *New Yorker*, he made the point that "Jeff Masson was going to come out of this with flying colors; in other words, he'd made himself a public figure at the highest level, and he was parlaying that into money."[29] Masson had, in the time that passed between filing his complaint in the case and the first trial, published four books, some of which had done quite well.[30] Either Wagstaffe's strategy worked, or the jury applied the discredited incremental harm doctrine. Or perhaps what happened lies somewhere in between.

That the jurors could deadlock on the issue of the monetary award, and with such a stark range of figures in consideration, suggests that some did not believe that the false defamatory quotations had hurt Masson's reputation any more than his own truthful defamatory quotations had, or they simply believed that he had not suffered harm. Gwen Davis noted in the *Nation* that it was hard to see how Malcolm's profile had damaged Masson. He had, after all, gone on to publish many books and had become a kind of "international literary celebrity."[31] Masson himself acknowledged to me that although he believed he had been damaged by the disputed quotations, "there was no proof that I'd been damaged." He was not teaching, he noted, but it was hard to prove that this was a result of the quotations.[32]

Press Coverage of the First Trial

In May 1993 the *New York Times* published a front-page story about the case even before jury selection began.[33] The article was meant to prepare the newspaper's readership for the day-by-day intensive trial coverage the *Times* would deliver over the next three weeks. Both the story's headline, "On Libel and the Literati: *The New Yorker* on Trial," and its subheads—"40 Hours of Tapes," "Lost Breakfast Notes," "Checks and Balances" (referring to the fact that Malcolm's editor at the *New Yorker* who worked on the *Masson* articles was also her husband), "Journalism and Betrayal," "Cast of Characters"—suggested the paper's perceptions of the trial's concerns, issues, and ultimate meanings.[34] The headline set Janet Malcolm and the *New Yorker* apart from the world of serious journalism: they were instead the "literati," the glamorous class of the publishing world. Before the trial had officially begun, it was declared to be "part libel case, part journalism seminar, part high-brow soap opera"[35]—which is exactly how the ensuing coverage portrayed the trial. And, perhaps predictably, the introductory article returned to Malcolm's "sweeping attack" in *The Journalist and the Murderer* "on the 'morally indefensible' behavior of journalists, who betray their subjects 'without remorse,'" framing Malcolm both as a pariah among her peers and as the con artist she had accused Joe McGinniss of being.[36] The article implied that Malcolm was not a real journalist, that her methods ran counter to those taught in journalism schools, and that her work was deceptive. It implied, in short, that her kind of narrative reporting was not real, or ethical, reporting. In attempting to distance itself from Malcolm, the *Times* had reified the traditional report and, in the process, passed judgment on Malcolm and the *New Yorker*.

The *New York Times* reported the trial with day-by-day front-section coverage. In regard to Malcolm's methods, the issues addressed most damningly in the trial—and covered most negatively in the *Times*—were her compression and translation techniques, the first involving the joining of quotations from different interviews and the second the rendering of spoken speech into the written word. Almost invariably Malcolm's compression technique involved translation, although the technique of translation could stand alone. In an article covering Masson's lawyer's cross-examination of Malcolm, the *Times* reported at length the dialogue about compression and translation that en-sued.[37] At the beginning of his questioning, Masson's lawyer read from Malcolm's afterword to *The Journalist and the Murderer*: "The idea of a reporter inventing rather than reporting speech is a repugnant, even a sinister one." His point, of course, was to suggest that Malcolm did not practice what she preached. He then used phrases such as "rearranging events" and "creating a conversation" to portray her techniques as "sinister" fabrication. Malcolm re-sisted such a characterization: "'This thing called speech is sloppy, redundant, repetitious, full of uhs and ahs,' she said at another point in her testimony. 'Sometimes we say the opposite of what we mean. Something has to be done to render a readable quotation.'"[38] Malcolm's testimony as well as her writing about the case challenged traditional journalism's standard that to report speech is to transcribe quotations verbatim. Malcolm also argued in the after-word Morgan quoted that stenographic or verbatim quotation often demon-strates "how the literally true may actually be a kind of falsification of reality."[39] Spoken and written speech are not the same, Malcolm contended. In putting speech on the page, the writer must filter it just as the ear does in verbal trans-actions. "Only the most uncharitable (or inept) journalist will hold a subject to his literal utterances and fail to perform the sort of editing and rewriting that, in life, our ear automatically and instantaneously performs," she wrote.[40] Malcolm's challenge to the truth claims of the verbatim quotation received lit-tle play in press coverage of the trial and the case at large.

This was not the first time Malcolm's techniques were mentioned in the *New York Times*'s coverage of the trial, and it was not the last. Anna Quindlen wrote an op-ed column condemning the technique of compression along with any altering of quotations: "There are a dozen reasons not to tidy up a quote, from the danger of ironing out the quirky syntax of the individual to putting an ever-so-slight bend in the meaning. But at base it's because this thing called life is sloppy, and slice-of-life is what a reporter is meant to reflect, not some tidier or more dramatic composite version."[41] The *Times* later reported on the 1986 deposition of William Shawn, who had since died, which was read in court.[42] In the deposition Shawn defended Malcolm's use of the compression tech-nique, noting that she was a responsible practitioner. But such coverage did not counterbalance the *Times*'s unadulterated disapproval of Janet Malcolm's methods, which it had expressed through previous trial reports and edito-rial statements. The *Times* solidified this disapproval with a Sunday feature, published after closing arguments the preceding Friday, reexamining Malcolm's journalistic practices questioned at trial: "In interviews, writers and editors associated with over 20 magazines said most credible publications would frown on such practices as Ms. Malcolm's." [43] This was, in essence, the *Times*'s final commentary on Malcolm's narrative techniques.

The Second Trial, 1994

After Judge Eugene Lynch declared a mistrial in *Masson v. New Yorker* in 1993, the case was in disarray for several months as the litigants and Lynch discussed the next step. In August 1993 Judge Lynch held a one-hour hearing in which he reportedly tried to talk Masson and Malcolm into negotiating a settlement in the case. He had a reputation for urging settlements and thus lightening the judicial workload and expense. Charles Morgan, Masson's lawyer, wanted a damages-only trial that would consider all the disputed quotations, not just the ones the jury had found libelous. Gary Bostwick, Malcolm's lawyer, wanted the entire case retried. The *New Yorker*'s lawyers wanted the magazine severed from the case on the basis of the jury's findings. If there was no settlement, Lynch suggested, a retrial would likely be necessary.[44] Although negotiation apparently took place, the parties did not find a way to settle their differences outside the courtroom.[45] According to Morgan, Malcolm refused to settle. "She takes the position that she was not wrong and will fight it to the end despite what the jury [in the first trial] told her," he said to a *New York Times* reporter.[46] According to a *Village Voice* article, Malcolm suggested in settlement talks that Masson should write her a letter of apology.[47] It is easy to see why negotiations stalled.

On Friday, September 10, 1993, Judge Lynch ordered a new trial and severed the *New Yorker* from the case. In his ruling he wrote that the issues of liability and damages were too intertwined to be separated. "While plaintiff argues in favor of retaining the jury's [defamation findings]," he wrote, "the court sees no intellectually honest way of parsing the case in this manner." [48] He also ruled that Masson had to pay the magazine's court costs, estimated at $20,000. Charles Kenady, a lawyer for the *New Yorker*, made a public statement that the magazine continued to support Malcolm and to publish her work.[49]

Jury selection for the second trial was completed by the end of September 1994, and the trial proper began in early October. Judge Lynch again assigned jurors the entire Masson profile to read over the weekend. Even before opening arguments took place, the *Times* commented on the change in Janet Malcolm's appearance since the first trial. "In place of the dour defendant with the down-cast eyes," the *Times* reported of Malcolm's presence in the courtroom on the last day of jury selection, "she was vivid in a green tailored suit with a short skirt and white stockings and with aviator glasses perched on her head."[50] It was an observation repeated in other press coverage of the trial itself. Writing for the legal newspaper the *Recorder*, Howard Mintz observed that Malcolm "clearly worked on the stand to do something about her cold and taciturn public persona, which smacked of arrogance to the first jury. Malcolm took great pains to smile and address jurors directly during the retrial, seeming more sure of her facts."[51] Gary Bostwick, Malcolm's lawyer, acknowledged after the trial that he had hired a speech consultant to help prepare her to testify. According to Bostwick, Malcolm read the transcripts of her interviews with Masson five times so they would be fresh in her memory. "She was much more persuasive, more convincing, more on top of her facts," Bostwick reportedly said of her testimony in the second trial.[52] Part of the preparation appeared to involve a kind of makeover. Press coverage of the first trial had described Malcolm variously as "dowdy,"[53] "proper," "morose,"[54] and "timid"[55] with "owlish glasses,"[56] a "severe bearing,"[57] and a "prickly" demeanor.[58] Coverage of the second trial often noted Malcolm's more colorful appearance—tailored dresses in soft pinks and greens, white stockings, brown suede pumps, and the absence of gray hair. The large glasses remained, but this time, according to press coverage, she looked more like Jackie O. and less like an owl.[59]

Many involved in the trial attributed Malcolm's ultimate win in the second trial at least in part to her rehabilitated look and demeanor. After the trial Bostwick told a reporter for the *New York Times* that Malcolm's victory was due to his increased emphasis on the meaning of actual malice and Malcolm's being better prepared.[60] Charles Morgan, Masson's lawyer, told me that he was not able to convince the second jury, as he had the first, that Malcolm deliberately changed Masson's language to make him look bad—primarily because Malcolm presented herself so much better in the second trial. "I think that Gary did a great job," he said, "and I think they really worked on her and sanitized her. And that probably was the difference."[61] Paul Kleven, who assisted Morgan, said that Malcolm "tended to just be a little more glib about some things" in the first trial but was better prepared to answer questions in the second.[62] According to James Wagstaffe, one of the lawyers for the *New Yorker* who was assistant counsel in the first trial and observed the second, the change in appearance was Malcolm's idea. "Between trials, Janet came to the conclusion that you've got to be a little more Californian, your hair color, the color of your clothes."[63]

In the second trial's opening arguments, Bostwick used children's blocks lined up on the jury box to illustrate how Malcolm ordered and rearranged Masson's words spoken across many months of interviews. After playing a segment of a tape-recorded interview in which Masson's speech was particularly disjointed and hard to follow, he arranged the letters on the blocks to spell the word "story," as if to show how Malcolm went about ordering Masson's sometimes chaotic utterances. Malcolm testified: "It took me months to get this story and write this speech. I was following here a technique that the New Yorker is known for about ordering people's speech."[64] In testifying about Masson's long monologue over lunch at Chez Panisse as recounted in her profile, Malcolm said: "It tells it in this completely fluid and complete and dramatic way. This is not the way people talk. This speech is the result of months of work, bit by bit, to get the whole story and to get the speech. At the lunch it was full of interruptions, full of digressions. The monologue was the result of my talking to him 50 or 60 times."[65] At one point during testimony she asserted, "I didn't make up anything in this piece; if it's there, he said it."[66]

The first trial was conducted in a packed courtroom to heavy media coverage. The second trial was not nearly so well attended and the coverage was, in comparison, light. Several interesting moments in the second trial were reported, including Bostwick's reading a passage from Malcolm's profile quoting Masson as saying that he had learned to speak fluent German during a six-month visit to Munich (also mentioned during the first trial; see chapter 1). The *Nation* reported this incident, including Masson's response to Bostwick: "I never said that," he testified. "Anyone who said that would be a braggart and a liar." Bostwick then played an interview tape in which Masson said he had learned to speak fluent German in six months. "So would you say you were a braggart and a liar?" Bostwick asked.[67]

Perhaps the most important moment in the trial, though not the most dramatic, occurred when Masson testified under Bostwick's cross-examination that of several statements he made about learning fluent German in a short time, Malcolm had chosen the most damning to use in her profile. In subsequent conversations, after he boasted about learning German in six months, he admitted to Malcolm that he actually could not speak fluent German. On the stand, as Bostwick continued to ask questions about Masson's exaggerated claim, Masson testified that Malcolm had a choice as to which statement to use—one in which he exaggerated or one in which he set the record straight. "She wanted to show me at my worst," he said. "Whenever she had a choice she always took the worst one." As soon as Masson said these words suggesting that Malcolm had acted with malice, Bostwick asked Judge Lynch to allow into evidence eight interview passages the court had previously blocked as too defamatory for the jurors to hear. Bostwick wanted the jury to hear that Malcolm had not always used the most damaging quotations and information available to her in her characterization of Masson.[68] And so for the first time in the history of the case, defamatory passages from the interviews that Malcolm did not use in her profile were made public. "For the next two days Bostwick laced his withering cross-examination with some of the more lurid information Masson had shared with Malcolm," Boynton wrote. "After reading the passage in question and then forcing Masson to elaborate on it in great detail (thereby drawing out the experience as long as possible), Bostwick would curtly scold him in his most pious preacher's voice: 'And she didn't use any of *that*, did she now?' "[69]

It was a painful moment in the trial for Masson. In referring to the episode in an interview with me he said, "I made one terrible error that opened things up in a way that made sure I was going to lose." His lawyers had told him not to say anything on the stand beyond answering the question. "And that's very hard for somebody like me," Masson said, "or anybody steeped in university culture to do because you have a tendency to answer with side comments and looking at other issues and exaggeration and dramatic flair and so on. And that's just not what you do in a trial." He continued: "You know, I didn't mean literally 'every single time.' I meant if you look at the piece and you look at the transcript [of the taped interviews] you can see there were many times when [Malcolm] could have put a nice quotation in, and didn't. That's all I meant, and that clearly she was after me. Which was clearly true. But what they did then was look at every single thing in there that I had said that could be seen as making me look bad that Malcolm did not put in. So the jurors got to hear that. And that was very embarrassing and painful."[70]

The jury deliberated for almost four days before finding in Malcolm's favor on Wednesday, November 2, 1994. It had been another month-long trial covering much the same territory as the first, but this jury came to a markedly different conclusion. "In contrast to the previous verdict, when the room was crowded and the atmosphere electric," David Margolick wrote for the *New York Times*, "the room today was largely empty and the mood subdued—a

reflection, perhaps of collective public exhaustion with a seemingly interminable case."[71] According to the special verdict form, the jury found that only
two of the disputed quotations were materially changed in meaning from
Masson's actual words, that is, only two met the Supreme Court's test for falsity
in altered quotations: the "wrong man" and "I don't know why I put it in" quotations. (In the first trial, the jury had found that all five contested quotations
met the legal test of falsity.) Of these, Masson was able to prove that only one
was defamatory: the "wrong man" quotation. (In the first trial, the jury had
found that all five were defamatory.) Most important, the jury found that Malcolm had not acted with actual malice, that is, with knowledge of falsity or reckless disregard for truth. (In the first trial, the jury found that Malcolm had acted
with actual malice in regard to the "sex, women, fun" and "wrong man" quotations.) In the second go-round, Masson had not been able to prove his case.[72]

When the verdict was read, Malcolm wept and hugged her husband and her
lawyer. In talking to the press afterward she said: "I guess I think it's over and I
hope it's over. Enough already." This time around "no one accepted [Masson's]
sinister reading," Malcolm said. "They realized that my notes were authentic."
Masson was, of course, deeply disappointed. "We really lost, no question about
that," he told a reporter. "It's very different from last time, much worse."[73] The
juries in the two trials came to very different conclusions, and their opposing
verdicts point to the inherently ambiguous nature of interpreting meaning as
called for by the Supreme Court's material alteration test. Interestingly, one
juror in the second trial said that the jury did not find Malcolm's methods to
be unethical: "'The entire jury felt that a journalist should be able to make
an article presentable,' Levya [a juror in the second trial] said, as long as the
writer does not distort the truth."[74] The New York Times did not deem the second trial worthy of daily coverage and devoted a total of five articles to it.
The New Yorker had been dismissed from the case as a result of the first trial,
and Janet Malcolm was the sole defendant. Although the Times proclaimed
the jury's verdict—this time in favor of Malcolm—on the front page, total
news coverage of the second trial was much more subdued.[75] The Times noted
that the verdict was not a full vindication of Malcolm or her methods, and
although the jury cleared Malcolm of libel, it did find that she had falsified two
of the quotations—just not knowingly. Despite rather evenhanded discourse
about these methods during the two trials and in the New York Times's coverage of the second trial, the paper's coverage of the first trial had vigorously in-
dicted them.

In the Aftermath of the Trial

Several weeks after the verdict in the second trial was announced in November 1994, Tom Goldstein, the dean of the graduate school of journalism at the University of California, Berkeley, announced the hiring of Jeffrey Masson to co-teach with him a course on journalism ethics titled "Ethical Issues in Journalism." It would cover matters such as how to write about reluctant subjects and those with whom one disagrees, the problems of blending psychology with biography, and the use of documents as sources. The announcement precipitated widespread protest among the student body. An editorial in *Rosebud*, a student newsletter published by the school's chapter of the Society of Professional Journalists (SPJ), attributed the appointment to "a disease known as star-fucking." It was apparently Goldstein who the editorial suggested had the disease. "What's next?" the unsigned editorial asked. "Ollie North teaching political reporting? Ivan Boesky teaching business reporting? Janet Wood . . . teaching sources and methods?" The last was apparently an erroneous reference to Janet Cooke, the *Washington Post* reporter who was forced to return the Pulitzer Prize after her feature on a heroin-addicted child was shown to be fabricated. Goldstein responded in a letter to students censuring the editorial's "ugly journalism" and reminding the newsletter's editors and journalists of the need to follow the SPJ Code of Ethics. In a subsequent meeting with students, he read a statement saying that he had disapproved of Masson's lawsuit for a long time and had made efforts to help settle the case. Even so, it was Goldstein who told a *Washington Post* reporter after the second trial that he hoped the verdict would not be seen as "a vindication of the practice [Malcolm] conceded." Although journalistic ethics "should be decided by journalists and not the courts anyway," he continued, "I think journalists pretty much agree it's not good practice to rearrange quotes and events." Goldstein refused to tell the students how much he would pay Masson.[76] Despite the brouhaha, Goldstein apparently stuck to his guns. Masson taught the course.[77]

Meanwhile, Masson appealed the second jury verdict to the Ninth Circuit. In 1996, the appellate court affirmed. The case was officially ended after twelve years in the federal court system.[78] In a fascinating reversal of its years-long criticism of Malcolm, the *New York Times* published in 1995, the year before the Ninth Circuit put the case to bed, an op-ed defending Malcolm under the well-known byline of Anthony Lewis.[79] Lewis, author of the acclaimed history of *New York Times v. Sullivan*, the libel case that was the progenitor of *Masson v.*

New Yorker, reported that Malcolm's granddaughter, Sophy Malcolm Tuck, had pulled a shiny red notebook from her grandmother's bookshelves in her summer home the evening of August 11, 1995. Therein Malcolm reportedly found her missing penciled notes from a conversation with Masson she said took place in her New York City home in 1983. The notes contained three of the quotations contested at trial: "intellectual gigolo," "sex, women, fun," and "the greatest analyst who ever lived." (Masson had testified that the conversation never took place.) These were probably the most defamatory of the five quotations Masson disputed, but ironically they did not include the two the jury in the second trial found to be false. "I immediately knew what it was," Malcolm said in a phone interview with a reporter for the *Washington Post*. "I guess I sort of felt weak in the knees." She elaborated on the story for a *New York Times* reporter, saying: "I went into the kitchen, where my husband was finishing the dishes, and said, 'Gardner, I have found the notes.' They are in this little red book. . . . I theorized that Sophy had pulled the notebook out of the bookcase, where it had been sitting all these years, perhaps attracted by its bright red color." Masson challenged the notebook's authenticity. "I am convinced these are fabricated, just like the quotes," he told the *Post* reporter. "This is the adult version of 'the dog ate my homework,' or, in this case, 'the dog just spat up my homework after 12 years.'" Malcolm asserted in an affidavit that the notes were genuine and her account of their discovery true.[80]

In his *New York Times* column Anthony Lewis reported that he himself had reviewed the notes and believed them to be authentic, and that this new evidence suggested that Masson's denial that Malcolm had taken these notes was likely "as false as his denials of having said things that turned out to be on tape." Lewis noted that among these things were Masson's comments that "'the analytic mafia' might put out 'a contract on me' and that he ran around the Freud home in London 'with hundred of Freud's letters sticking out of [my] pockets.'" Although Lewis did not address Malcolm's challenged methods, he did proclaim the judicial system's long countenancing of the case a miscarriage of justice, particularly in light of Masson's demonstrated poor memory of what he had said during interviews with Malcolm. "A sensible legal system," he wrote, "would not put a writer under a debilitating burden for 10 years because she had a wealth of evidence but could not locate some handwritten notes."[81]

Almost a month after Lewis's column appeared, Masson responded in a letter to the editor of the *New York Times* on September 23, 1995. He challenged a number of Lewis's assertions: "I never said Freud twisted his findings for personal gain. I said he denied the actual extent of child sexual abuse because of a failure of moral courage. A board member of the Sigmund Freud Archives did not pay me off: my lawsuit was settled out of court." He also noted that Malcolm had testified that the notes were on loose sheets of white paper, not in a notebook, and that William Shawn said Malcolm had told him that all quotations in the profile were on tape.[82]

In a way, Anthony Lewis cleared Malcolm even more fully than the judicial system did (if not of ethical violations then at least of any legal breach). It is ironic that this vindication appeared in the *New York Times*, which had previously largely condemned Malcolm's journalistic methods and standards, particularly her technique of compression and its related narrative devices, in its news and editorial coverage of the case and trials. Lewis's editorial column, however, was unlikely to reverse the damage done to Malcolm's reputation by the case's collective history and press coverage. Craig Seligman's long article on Janet Malcolm and her work in a 2000 issue of *Salon* begins by passing judgment on this phenomenon: "The public pillorying of Janet Malcolm is one of the scandals of American letters." In discussing press coverage of Masson's libel suit and its effect on Malcolm's reputation, he noted: "The public spectacle had been huge and humiliating, her reporting widely criticized and mocked. The lawsuit gained her more notoriety than any of her books ever had; thenceforward everything she wrote would be a target."[83]

In writing about Janet Malcolm's work and the second trial for the English newspaper the *Guardian* in 1994, James Wood noted that Malcolm was reluctant to talk with him about the case, which was at trial at the time. He undertook his own defense of her. "Perhaps Malcolm's best defence," he wrote, "is the admission that has provoked such self-righteousness from other journalists: that she compresses, compacts, and otherwise soothes quotations into artistic shapes. But if one were truly guilty of fabricating quotes, would one admit to a habit guaranteed to be called fabrication by one's enemies? It is not the manoeuvre of a guilty person." Wood also quoted Robert Gottlieb, former editor of the *New Yorker* and a friend of Malcolm's: "She is not like other journalists," he told Wood. "She's an intellectual, with a kind of East European Puritanism; she would never commit the kind of sloppiness, idleness and stupidity that is alleged. She is the most rigorous person I know. They are preposterous allegations."[84]

There is, of course, another side to the story, and it belongs to Masson and his lawyers. Masson still maintains, many years after the case was finally resolved in the courts, that Malcolm invented the quotations he disputed. In discussing the case, Masson suggested that some of the disputed quotations simply did not make sense—that is, they were statements he simply would not have made, given his beliefs and actions:

> Almost everywhere throughout the piece there are little inventions. But some of them were hurtful. And, you know, people often say, "Why would she do that? What are her motives?" And partly I think it's just that she didn't think about it deeply enough. I mean, take one [an invention]. 'What will people say when your book comes out?" And then she has me say, "Oh, they'll say I'm the greatest analyst who ever lived." Now, it doesn't make any sense! You know, why would I be telling her that I've had nothing but trouble from analysts and they don't like who I am and they don't approve of me and they can't stand this material about child sexual abuse and they don't want to hear about it. Why would I then suddenly change and say, "Oh, they'll have to admit I'm the greatest analyst who ever lived?" when I wasn't an analyst anymore, didn't want to be . . . I mean it's one of those phrases that I could not have said. It should be impossible. Why would I say that? It doesn't make any sense from any point of view. It's not logical. It doesn't follow the narrative. It's not historical. I couldn't have said it.[85]

He acknowledged that some of the quotations he disputed in early complaints turned out to be on tape: "Oh, how could I be so stupid, but there they are [the quotations on tape] and you have to live with it. But there were other things that were definitely not on tape and that I had not said and that I couldn't have said." He attributes this error to the fallibility of memory and said he told Malcolm that if she could produce evidence that he had made the disputed statements—in particular, her written notes of the conversations she said contained the quotations—he would give up the case. The notes Malcolm claimed to find in the red notebook in 1995 do not exist, Masson asserted. In his letter to the editor of the *New York Times* about the lost-and-found notebook, he suggested that Malcolm and her lawyers should make the notes public. "There was no more word about it," he said. "She never showed them to me nor to the public. So, there are no notes like that."[86]

The truth of the Masson-Malcolm dispute rests in part on whether Malcolm's interview notes—either the typed version entered as evidence at trial or the handwritten version Malcolm claimed to find in the red notebook—

are accurate renderings of Masson's own words. Janet Malcolm has claimed they are (with the exception of the "wrong man" quotation that was on tape and was judged to be contextually false owing to faulty editing). Jeffrey Masson has claimed they are not. Both seem utterly convinced of the truth of their respective positions. Masson himself has said that the jury in the second trial seemed to believe they were both telling the truth.[87] The history of *Masson v. New Yorker* suggests that it was one of those libel cases Justice Sandra Day O'Connor had in mind when she wrote in *Philadelphia Newspapers v. Hepps* that it is sometimes impossible to determine whether speech is true or false.[88] In *Hepps*, the evidence in the case was ambiguous—the allegations against the defendant were unverifiable—and thus the disputed statements resisted determinative falsity and fault tests.

In *Masson*, Malcolm's interview notes were fundamental in establishing whether she had altered quotations so as to make them false and whether she acted with actual malice. Three of the disputed quotations were contained in these notes, two of which were commonly understood to be among the more defamatory of the five ("sex, women, fun" and "the greatest analyst who ever lived"). Masson claimed the notes were invented; Malcolm claimed they were authentic. The first jury seemed to believe Masson's story, the second jury Malcolm's story. In the early iterations of the case, the federal district court and the Ninth Circuit were forced to assume, under the summary judgment posture of the case, that the interview notes were not authentic, as Masson asserted. The Supreme Court, too, could not consider the notes in its review of the lower courts' grant and affirmation of summary judgment for Malcolm and her co-defendants. In the judicial search for truth in *Masson v. New Yorker*, the authenticity of the interview notes was a key issue, and their authenticity came down to the classic "he said, she said" conundrum.

Even if one assumed that the interview notes were authentic, there still remained the problem of comparing Masson's actual spoken words as recorded on tape and in the interview notes with the disputed quotations. Malcolm did not reproduce stenographic quotations in her profile, so in applying the Supreme Court's so-called material alteration test, judges and jurors in the case were forced to compare the meaning of Masson's actual spoken words (contained in the interview transcripts and notes) with the quoted words in the profile and to determine whether the differential in meaning was "material" or substantial. As the Court explained, the determination rested on whether the quotation "would have a different effect on the mind of the reader from that which the pleaded truth would have produced." [89] In discussing this judicial determination, Lee Bollinger insightfully observed that discovering the truth or fairness of an altered quotation is an uncertain business:

> A fundamental problem raised by *Masson* . . . is that of articulating the latitude we think the Constitution should guarantee to citizens, and the press, to report on the statements of public officials and public figures. Framed in this way, we understand immediately that the inquiry into "falsity" in this context, which is essentially one of interpretation of meaning, is highly uncertain and ambiguous. For the First Amendment that means, not that an "interpretation" can never be "unfair" or cause injury to reputation, but that a legal inquiry is far less certain of yielding a correct answer as to whether it is. [90]

In *Masson v. New Yorker*, as in *Philadelphia Newspapers v. Hepps*, the truth was simply not discoverable given the facts of the case. The determination of the truth or falsity in *Masson* was made even more difficult because of the ambiguity not only of the meanings of certain disputed quotations (such as "sex, women, fun" and "intellectual gigolo") but also of the process demanded by the Supreme Court's material alteration test. It is important to acknowledge that, in one way, the *Masson* test leans toward protecting expression, since the Supreme Court refused to accept the proposition that any alteration of quotations is a falsification of reality—a position largely supported by the professional standards of journalism. Even so, the interpretation of meaning called for in the *Masson* test, given its inherent uncertainty and imprecision, is less protective of expression than the spirit of *Sullivan* might have it.

Conclusion:

The Meanings of the
Masson–Malcolm Dispute

IN ITS SIMPLEST TERMS, *MASSON V. NEW YORKER* IS A STORY ABOUT TWO competing conceptions of what makes a truthful report of the world. It is the story of two forms of reporting in American journalism—the traditional and the literary—and the continuities and ruptures in their respective development across the twentieth century. At its most complex, it is the story of the continued decline of *New York Times v. Sullivan*'s First Amendment promise of robust protection for public discourse, a diminishing judicial vision of the role the press should play in sustaining democracy and a vibrant public sphere.

In this book I have approached the *Masson* case in part through the method of microhistory, but I believe the highly particularized Masson-Malcolm legal dispute reflects the broader social, cultural, and intellectual patterns in twentieth-century thinking about the American press, the First Amendment, and democracy. These are lofty ideas and meanings to be found in one libel case, to be sure, but *Masson v. New Yorker* is not simply "one libel case." It is part of a long line of constitutional libel cases dating back to 1964, when the Court first articulated in its landmark *Sullivan* decision what the American public and the American press have come to perceive as the central meaning of the First Amendment: that the great American experiment in democracy demands that "debate on public issues . . . be uninhibited, robust, and wide-open."[1] As one of the U.S. Supreme Court's more recent articulations of the role of the First Amendment in press expression, *Masson v. New Yorker* carries with it the weight of all that came before in the *Sullivan* line—including the attendant free expression and democratic theories that found voice in this jurisprudence and its scholarly and legal debates. The meanings of *Masson v. New Yorker* and its related controversies extend beyond the legal rulings in the case to the values and norms expressed in the triangular relationships among American democracy, First Amendment theory, and the press.

In telling the story of *Masson v. New Yorker* I have made three interrelated historical arguments throughout this book. First, the deep divisions that developed between traditional and literary journalism across the twentieth century led to seemingly irreconcilable debates about how best to represent "reality" and "truth" in journalistic expression. The Masson-Malcolm dispute was a product of these divisions and an expression of these debates. Second, the dispute was a public manifestation of a larger shift in American intellectual history: the philosophical project that became the postmodern critique of objectivity. Hostile reactions against this critique arose in all areas of American social, cultural, and intellectual life; in journalism the backlash widened the perceived divide between traditional and literary approaches and inflamed the related debates. Third, the *Masson* case forced the courts to address the problem of representing "truth" in expression—a problem at the heart of the postmodern critique of objectivity—both in the practice of journalism and in the constitutional arena of libel law. In choosing to use daily journalism's understanding of an objective, fact-based truth in developing a judicial test of truth for altered, defamatory quotations, the Supreme Court ignored other journalistic traditions in which a consensus or holistic truth was often the goal. The result was a judicial retrenchment on the press-protective First Amendment theory and jurisprudence established in *New York Times v. Sullivan*.

This book has provided a descriptive and analytical history of the Masson-Malcolm dispute. In addition to these historical arguments, I have implicitly put forward several normative claims about the appropriate role of press discourse in American democracy, as well as the appropriate constitutional protections for press discourse. I wish to make these claims more explicit here, while acknowledging that I am on somewhat fragile ground in doing so. Normative claims invite debate because they often venture beyond the realm of the actual into the realm of the possible, the speculative, the unknowable. The gap between "is" and "ought" is significant, and I thus make such claims with humility—and with the firm and edifying belief that robust public discussion furthers our collective knowledge and understanding. Scholarly and professional discussion of the issues my claims raise may push us all toward better thinking about, and perhaps solutions for, the problems at hand.

My first claim is that when constitutional libel cases involve ambiguous language situations in which truth is highly contingent and unknowable, and the discovery of truth is highly unlikely, First Amendment imperatives demand that courts protect freedom of expression over individual reputational interests. Courts should not, of course, arrive at such conclusions lightly. Next, *Sullivan's* First Amendment principle that unfettered public discourse plays a vital role in democracy, and the foundational role this principle plays in press theory, suggest that both the American judiciary and the American press believe democracy is predicated on an active public sphere where citizens engage in political decision-making beyond simply voting. I suggest that this aspirational ideal of participatory democracy that undergirds contemporary First Amendment and press theory is an ideal worth working toward—even as we acknowledge that existing political and social structures in the United States limit such attempts. Finally, this ideal, which embraces personal liberty and democratic striving, requires the American press to pursue multi-perspectival news, to recognize more fully the uses and limitations of the traditional objective report, to refine the methods and standards that structure American journalism, and to embrace a broader range of press expression, including the literary, or narrative, report.

In this chapter I review and extend the historical arguments and normative claims I have made in telling the story of *Masson v. New Yorker*. I also suggest a way out of the language dilemma embodied in the postmodern objectivist critique and expressed in the Masson-Malcolm dispute: the *via media* of the American pragmatist tradition. This middle passage embraces a pragmatic conception of truth, that is, a consensus truth arrived at through the sense-making work of communities that share languages, experiences, and traditions. The bases for discovering such a pragmatic truth are, then, the community practices and institutions of those who share a common culture. It is neither a universalizing nor an unchanging truth, but a contingent and consensual truth born of "the democratic practice of truth-seeking."[2] To my way of thinking, the American profession of journalism would better serve democratic ends by giving up its quixotic claim of representing "objective truth" in news reports and working instead toward the discovery and presentation of pragmatic truth (or truths). Such truth would always be open to change and reinterpretation as the community conversation, carried on in part through the medium of journalism, continues. The democratic nature of such truth-seeking demands that this community conversation be broadened to include as many voices as possible speaking in a broad range of forms, from the traditional report to the literary report and beyond.[3]

"Truth" in Traditional and Literary Journalism

As both traditional and literary journalism developed across the twentieth century in the United States, each producing its own professional norms, standards, and values, a point of contention in both the professional practice and disciplinary study of these traditions was how journalistic methods and expression could best represent the "reality" and "truth" of human experience. The standard of objectivity profoundly shaped the social practice and intellectual environment of traditional journalism. As Michael Schudson writes in *Discovering the News*, objectivity is "the belief that one can and should separate facts from values."[4] In the arena of traditional journalism, this belief produced a form of press expression that valued the gathering and relaying of facts above all else. In traditional journalism, the expression of values—which Schudson defines as "an individual's conscious or unconscious preferences for what the world should be"—has usually been viewed with suspicion. The result has often been a kind of news report laden with decontextualized facts, a report in which the possible range of meanings of the facts provided is left for the reader to divine with little help from the journalist. As Schudson has noted, by the 1920s or so the objectivity standard was firmly entrenched in American journalism: "Far more than a set of craft rules to fend off libel suits or a set of constraints to help editors keep tabs on their underlings, objectivity was finally a moral code. It was asserted in textbooks used in journalism schools and in codes of ethics of professional associations. It was a code of professional honor and a set of rules to give professionals both guidance and cover."[5] In challenging the code of objectivity, literary journalism was challenging what had become a foundational moral code of professional journalism. Although the code was certainly valued in the narrative tradition, it was not embraced as monolithic. Literary journalism made use of objectivity as it saw fit, variously adopting, adapting, and rejecting its rules.

Literary journalism, with its reliance on narrative to contextualize the facts, is characterized less by objectivity and more by subjectivity, that is, by the understanding that all reports of the world are colored by the perceptions of their authors. In the traditional report, "truth" and "reality" have traditionally been thought to be best expressed through the concatenation of facts, often through the inverted pyramid form. In such journalism, facts are understood to correspond to the world "out there" and "truth" is understood to reside in this correspondence. In the literary report, "truth" and "reality" have generally been thought to inhere in the interpretation of facts, often through narrative. Literary journalism's notion of truth is often holistic and its understanding of the journalist's professional code catholic. The whole literary report, some of its historical practitioners would aver, is true, even if some facts are not, at least as they might be assessed by an "objective" journalist.

These two different visions of what constitutes "truth" and "reality" in press expression and of how best to represent the events and phenomena of the world through language have long produced debates and divisions within American journalism. *Masson v. New Yorker* was the product of these debates and divisions—and brought them into both public discourse and the constitutional regime of libel law, with its attendant free expression and democratic theories. In telling the story of *Masson v. New Yorker*, I have attempted to map the history of the changing fortunes of the traditional and literary traditions in American journalism. Given the *New Yorker*'s status as the first named defendant in the case and the key role the magazine has played in the development of a distinctively literary American journalism, the *New Yorker* was the natural focus for exploring the history of literary journalism, its similarities with and differences from traditional journalism as embodied in the daily newspaper, and the threat of libel law to the press in the years prior to and following *Sullivan*.

As the editorial history of the *New Yorker* attests, the traditional report's focus on facts and its dependence on the standard of objectivity were also part of the literary tradition of journalism, at least as practiced at one of America's most culturally significant magazines. And narrative technique has arguably always found its way into the reports of traditional journalism. The main difference between the two traditions, then, is one of emphasis and perspective. Each stresses certain conventions. The traditional report emphasizes the relaying of factual information through the use of the inverted pyramid style, neutrality, detachment, balance, and objectivity. The literary emphasizes the conventions of storytelling: character, dialogue, emplotment, and point of view, to name a few. It is not that the literary tradition in American journalism does not value facts, as has often been assumed by the opponents of the New Journalism, including Judge Alex Kozinski of the Ninth Circuit in his 1989 *Masson* dissent. If the long-standing editorial policies at the *New Yorker* are any indication, accuracy and facts are indeed central to the narrative enterprise.

That said, in pursuing the story form, some journalists in the literary tradition, including a number who wrote for the *New Yorker*, seem to have relied implicitly on a hierarchy of facts. That is, some facts appeared to be more important to them than others. It did not matter to Janet Malcolm or her husband and editor, Gardner Botsford, for example, that bits of the Masson monologue she reported as being delivered over lunch at Chez Panisse were actually uttered on a pier. Facts that did matter, apparently, included what Masson ate at lunch: baked goat cheese and striped bass with fennel. (Malcolm claimed in trial testimony that what she reported as Masson's meal constituted truthful facts. Masson claimed he ate neither the cheese nor the fish.) Malcolm suggested that the fact that Masson actually spoke some of the lunch monologue at different locations and at different times was unimportant. What was important, she said, was that he said what she reported. She compressed quotations and translated Masson's speech to the written page, but these narrative techniques did not, she insisted, constitute invention, fictionalization, or fabrication. She believed that her portrait of Masson and her portrayal of events in his life were truthful.

Masson as well as many practitioners of and apologists for traditional journalism did not accept Malcolm's particular hierarchy of facts. To them, facts were facts: words uttered at one point in time constituted facts, and to graft them onto temporally removed quotations was to tamper with, to falsify, reality. They simply did not buy Malcolm's argument that compression and translation were necessary if she was to represent truthfully Masson's speech across time. Part of the disconnect between Malcolm's and Masson's positions surely rests on the natural and powerful human desire to speak for oneself, to represent the self through words of one's choosing without a third party's intervention as "translator." It is a compelling position. "It's not the journalist's job to shape what a person should have said to make it either look better or worse or different," Masson told me. "You know, you're not writing fiction here. . . . That somehow never got through to [Malcolm]. And I think that's a concept that's hard for the New Yorker to take. I don't know to what extent they've changed it in subsequent years. But if you're going to write something about somebody and it's controversial, that somebody has got to be able to look at it and say, 'Look, this is what I really said,' or 'Hey, look, we've got the tapes. Let's go back and see what I've said.'"[6]

In Masson v. New Yorker, Jeffrey Masson and Janet Malcolm disagreed about what truth in quotation means. Masson argued that it inheres in the reporting of nearly verbatim speech, a position based on a correspondence theory of truth. Malcolm argued that it inheres in the translation (and compression) of speech into fluid, cogent prose that represents the speaker's meaning, a position based on a coherence theory of truth. Their disagreement was in part philosophical. In articulating the material alteration test as the method prescribed by the First Amendment for determining falsity and fault in allegedly altered, defamatory quotations, the Supreme Court sidestepped this essential philosophical difference. In his 1989 dissent in the Ninth Circuit Court, Judge Alex Kozinski forthrightly proclaimed a quotation to be a fact. "Unlike the majority," he wrote, "I would start with the proposition that what somebody says is a fact, and that doctoring a quotation is no more protected by the first amendment than is any other falsification."[7] The Supreme Court was not so forthright, although it implicitly came to the same conclusion in finding that a reasonable reader of the Masson profiles "would understand the quotations to be nearly verbatim."[8] The problem with the Court's material alteration test is precisely this assumption that a quotation in a journalistic work is a factual statement always susceptible to a test of truth or falsity. It is not that fabricated, defamatory quotations should receive First Amendment protection. Such protection would, of course, be reprehensible. The point is that the material alteration test does not acknowledge that quotations cannot always be viewed as factual statements. The test demands interpretation, comparison, and weighing of the actual spoken words and the written quotation. But what happens when the actual spoken words are not recoverable? What happens when the words spoken are ambiguous in meaning and rambling to boot, as is so often the case in speech? In these instances, the speaker's actual utterance can hardly be treated as a fact. Yet the material alteration test assumes that it can.

It is important to note that the apparently irresolvable problem in the Masson-Malcolm dispute went beyond whether the techniques of compression and translation falsified Masson's words. Simply put, Masson claimed that he did not make several of the defamatory statements Malcolm attributed to him in her profile. "I may have said many things about myself that you wouldn't want printed," Masson has acknowledged. "But they were all true. I mean, there's a big difference between that and something that comes up that's not true even if it's not as bad as what you say about yourself."[9] For her part, Malcolm claimed that Masson did utter these disputed quotations, even if the exact words had been altered somewhat (though not materially, from Malcolm's perspective) through translation and compression. It is entirely possible that, given these opposing claims, neither of which could ultimately be proved, the "truth" of the disputed language was and always would be impossible to locate.

Historically, traditional journalism has been loath to allow speakers to review their quotations before publication. The reasons are obvious to anyone acquainted with traditional norms. The presumptions are, first, that what a speaker says in an initial interview is likely to be the most candid and honest response, and second, that given the chance to review a controversial or damaging statement, the speaker is likely to revise away its content to avoid damage to self or others. Janet Malcolm did not allow Masson to review the quotations she attributed to him in her profile, perhaps for these reasons. Traditional journalism generally plays by these rules and expects interview subjects to understand them. Narrative journalism, particularly the kind that results from the writer's immersion in the world and life of the interview subject, may well require a different social contract with the subject than traditional journalism would. Malcolm's relationship with Masson, built across months of interviews and in the context of a kind of friendship that developed in their long conversations, was different from the rather formal relationships that often form between reporters and subjects in the world of daily journalism, although even in that world the reporter-subject relationship frequently exists on ambiguous terrain. In daily journalism, vetting quotations generally serves little purpose. In a literary journalism that uses techniques like compression and translation, reviewing the resulting quotations or monologues seems an important ethical duty the author owes the subject, given the primacy of such quotations in self-presentation. Reviewing such quotations seems doubly important when the content is potentially damaging to the speaker's reputation. Given the advantage of historical perspective, it is easy to suggest that Malcolm may have owed Masson at least this much.

Several of the court opinions in the twelve-year judicial life of *Masson v. New Yorker* considered, and even prescribed, journalistic standards in their assessments of the Masson-Malcolm dispute. The U.S. Supreme Court and the 1992 Ninth Circuit opinions collectively observed that different genres of publication inherently lay claim to different levels of credibility on the part of readers. Different kinds of publications could thus be legally held to different standards of truth in quotation: magazines like the *New Yorker* should be held to the highest standard, followed by, in order, daily newspapers and supermarket tabloids. Docudramas, historical fiction, and works claiming to re-create conversations from memory might not be held to even the lowest standard of truth in quotation.[10] The courts repeatedly discussed the role of the social contract between journalists and readers in press expression (not a Rousseauean notion of social contract but rather a simple, depoliticized notion that journalists should be clear with readers about the nature of the information they are providing). And in these discussions, the courts implicitly suggested the possibility of a new legal test for determining in which publications altered and defamatory quotations are actionable, as well as a new ethical journalistic standard: in any form of reporting besides traditional news reports, journalists should make explicit contracts with the reader regarding the meaning of quotation marks.[11]

Masson is one more case in the *Sullivan* line in which the Supreme Court passed judgment on the social propriety of journalistic standards and, in doing so, pulled ethical concerns into the legal arena. In the process, the Court largely ignored the existence of a literary tradition and its related conventions in American journalism. It assumed that the traditional report's conventions of nearly verbatim quotation and ostensibly objective presentation of information were those on which the *New Yorker's* reading public relied. Janet Malcolm's profile of Jeffrey Masson, the Court asserted, provided "the reader with no clue that the quotations are being used as a rhetorical device or to paraphrase the speaker's actual statements. To the contrary, the work purports to be nonfiction, the result of numerous interviews."[12] The Court seemed to be referring to Malcolm's techniques of compression and speech translation and implied that they existed outside the realm of nonfiction in the sphere of fiction or invention. Such an assumption ignored what had been the *New Yorker's* long-established convention of crafting lengthy passages of speech in its reportage—a convention that many readers of the magazine would likely have understood as producing something other than stenographic, verbatim quotation. While most readers of the *New Yorker* would understand the context of the truth claims, the Supreme Court ignored the context and relied solely on the text itself.

The Supreme Court suggested in *Masson* the legal and ethical importance of a social contract between journalist and reader when a work of journalism uses quotations differently than a traditional report would. This social contract would presumably explain how quotations were gathered and presented, the context in which they were spoken, and the degree to which they departed from a verbatim rendering. Such a social contract generally seems workable

and useful, but the sticking point in the Supreme Court's version is the elevation of traditional journalism's norms regarding the use of quotation. The necessary selection of quotations and the problems of capturing context in news
reporting mean that even verbatim quotations can be used misleadingly. Even
verbatim quotations can, in essence, be false. For social contracts to be broadly
useful in press expression, all forms of journalism must make use of them and
for all manner of conventions and newsgathering techniques.

Of course, each and every article in a newspaper or magazine does not need
to begin with an explicit statement explaining the techniques of its creation.
Each publication has its own general principles, conventions, and characteristic forms, and these are often spelled out in statements of principles or codes.
Readers, media critics, and the courts need to recognize more forthrightly that
there are other journalistic traditions in the American press than that of the
daily newspaper, that each tradition has its own norms and conventions, and
that each publication within a tradition has its own particularized norms and
conventions. When a report departs from a publication's governing norms, an
explicit social contract is needed. In the case of Janet Malcolm's profile of Jeffrey Masson, many readers of the New Yorker and of the book version of the
profile may well have understood, contrary to the Supreme Court's assertion in
the Masson ruling, that Malcolm's rendering of Masson's speech was not verbatim. A critical reader would likely assume that a long, perfectly spoken monologue had been translated from speech into prose. Malcolm's compression
technique presents a more difficult problem because readers cannot necessarily determine through critical assessment when the technique has been used—
that is, when words spoken at one moment in time have been grafted onto
words spoken at another moment. As editor William Shawn stated in his deposition, compression had long been "acceptable literary practice" at the New
Yorker "if it is done . . . to make something coherent . . . or for literary reasons
and not to in any way violate the truth of the situation or of what the person is
saying or distorting anything."[13] But did this longtime practice constitute a
tradition that the New Yorker did not need to explain to its readers? The practice of daily objective journalism has rarely assumed that a publication needs
to explain conventions and norms to readers, even ones that involve the context and meaning of a speaker's words, such as the use of quotations from multiple sources to inject "balanced" opinion into a report, and the reporting of
quotations without providing the context in which a reporter's question
was asked and answered or the content of the question that elicited the quota-

tion. Such omissions in traditional reports seem no more acceptable than Janet Malcolm's failure to acknowledge the use of compression in the Masson profiles.

Forthright social contracts between publications and readers, as well as journalists and subjects, would be extraordinarily useful in this postmodern age, when what constitutes fact and truth is such contested terrain. Expose the nails and glue of newswriting structures in both traditional and literary reporting, and let the readers join more fully and consciously in the construction of the world contained in a report. Such transparency also provides readers with more robust means for evaluating the credibility and authority of news reports.

The Critique of Objectivity

The journalistic debate about the objectivity ideal which emerged in the 1960s and later found expression in the legal and press discourses of *Masson v. New Yorker* was one manifestation of a gestalt shift in Western epistemology. The profound social and political dislocations of the 1960s affected journalism in various ways, one of the most powerful being a growing discontent among some journalists with the ideal of objectivity. At issue was the extent to which a theory of press expression tied to objectivity could represent a reality that seemed fractured and contentious. It had never before been more clear that groups of Americans defined along racial, ethnic, class, and gender lines found different sets of facts to be important in representing the world—and that these disparate groups could interpret the same set of facts quite differently. In the 1960s there arose a powerful, if transitory, challenge to the dominance of the traditional report and its related ideal of objectivity. The so-called New Journalists rejected objectivity and embraced instead the subjectivity of narrative in their attempts at representing the "reality" and "truth" of human experience. Their reports read like short stories, and while the literary form in which they wrote was rooted in a long tradition of American literary journalism dating at least to the late nineteenth century, their experimentation with language and representation—and the voluble attack they launched against traditional journalism—made the New Journalism seem like something new indeed.

It was during this crucial decade that what we have come to call "the postmodern critique of objectivity" emerged not only in the profession of journalism but also in the broader academic world of knowledge creation. The ideas that language is unstable, knowledge is always incomplete, and "truth" is necessarily indeterminate arose across the academic disciplines, and while voiced in different terms and in different knowledge paradigms, the net result was the fracturing of a prior objectivist consensus about the nature of knowledge. These ideas were often met with hostility in the profession of journalism and in the academy at large.

In the 1970s the tensions between a traditional journalism tied to the institutional processes, norms, and standards of the daily newspaper and a literary journalism attuned to the craft concerns of narrative came to a boiling point in press reaction to the Janet Cooke debacle. I have explored this history. Still, it seems useful here to offer Jeremy Iggers's interpretation of the Cooke affair, for it presents a powerful explanation of press reaction to *Masson v. New Yorker* in the decades that followed:

> The new journalism was a threat to the old, but a very difficult threat to attack head-on. If the old order was to defend its traditions and territory, a less formidable enemy would have to be discovered—or created. Cooke and her misdeeds were propelled to prominence because it served powerful interests in journalism to make an example of her case. Her transgressions became the pretext for a counter-revolution in American journalism, a reassertion of authority by an old guard whose authority had been steadily eroded for decades. What followed in the wake of Cooke's error was a reassertion of the traditional newsroom hierarchy, a banishing of the "new journalism," a "tightening up in editing," and a new fundamentalism of facts.[14]

In the years leading up to the Masson-Malcolm dispute, public confidence in the press had been waning. With the rise of the critical culture in the 1960s, the rebirth of muckraking journalism in the investigative reporting of the latter years of the Vietnam War and Watergate, and the resurgence of literary reporting in the form of the New Journalism, traditional journalism found its authority threatened. The explosion of libel suits in the 1970s and 1980s was one artifact of the public's increasing distrust of and discomfort with the press, which included anxiety about the increasing corporate power of the media. To protect itself, the press turned toward what Iggers has so aptly termed "a new fundamentalism of facts" in its creation of ethical codes and public discussion of its own practices and standards.

In this way the objectivity critique in the profession of journalism lost power, although as the Masson-Malcolm dispute demonstrates, it never entirely faded away. In academia, however, the objectivity critique gained ground. Disciplines as diverse as philosophy, history, political science, anthropology, and mathematics realigned in the wake of the critique. In all cases, David Harvey argues in *The Condition of Postmodernity*, the result was a general repudiation of "meta-narratives," that is, of "large-scale theoretical interpretations purportedly of universal application."[15] Historian Peter Novick explains the result somewhat differently. "In virtually every disciplinary realm, very much including the historical," he writes, "one found either factional polarization, or fragmented chaos."[16] Some scholars continued to defend the "sacred" foundations of disciplinary communities: the primacy of facts and theory in the discovery of knowledge and the traditional understanding that "the meaning, and the justification, of scientific and scholarly work was 'progress toward the truth.'"[17] Some thoroughgoing postmodernists embraced the objectivity critique with revolutionary zeal, indulging in unmitigated relativism. Others sought a middle ground between the two positions in the American tradition of pragmatism, which placed faith in the shared languages and experiences of communities as the only foundation for the search for contingent, but meaningful, truths.[18]

Like most paradigm shifts, the postmodern critique of objectivity had its antecedents. In the early part of the twentieth century, a band of public philosophers introduced a new way of thinking to the American landscape of ideas. This way of thinking became known as pragmatism, and as one of its most prominent proponents, John Dewey did more than any other pragmatist to insist on the primacy of democracy and experience in any philosophical system. For Dewey, the only absolute in human affairs was the democratic method embedded in social experience. It was the means to truth, or whatever truth could be ascertained, and thus the means to knowledge, however contingent. Viewing all human action and reality as embedded within social and cultural contexts and thus always open to interpretation, Dewey's pragmatism rejected determinate truth as a chimera. At the same time, however, it did not espouse the relativism and nihilism of what became certain postmodern propositions, such as the contingency of *all* truth claims. Dewey placed his faith in shared experience and the contingent truths that were to be found through decision making and knowledge-seeking in democratic communities. For Dewey, the kind of journalism that best served this vision was a journalism of art—what I have argued is another name for literary journalism. And for Dewey, the primary means by which any truth could be discovered was through free expression. My suggestion for how courts should handle the problem of allegedly false, defamatory quotations in constitutional libel cases (discussed in the next section of this chapter) is offered in this pragmatic spirit—in the belief that America's democratic experiment demands that the First Amendment protect as much expression as possible, even some expression that is erroneous or misguided, in the search for truth.

Journalists can learn a good deal about meaningful ways to address the problems of objectivity in professional news practice and expression from the longstanding conversation among professional historians about similar problems in the practice and writing of professional history. For example, James T. Kloppenberg has suggested that pragmatism offers a solution to contemporary historians caught between the old positivism of history conceived as social science and what some see as the interpretive relativism of the linguistic turn in historical scholarship. A "pragmatic hermeneutics" that admits "that interpretation is important" but does not claim "that everything is interpretation" is Kloppenberg's answer to the problems of historical scholarship.[19] As Joyce Appleby and her co-authors suggest in *Telling the Truth about History*, the "material remains" of the past impose "definite limits to the factual assertions" that a historian can make about the past, even as they create "boundaries around the range of interpretations that can be offered about an event or development."[20] That said, the incontrovertible claim of postmodernity in the realm of history is that "there can be a multiplicity of accurate histories."[21] The pragmatic historian, then, looks for historical truth in the democratic consensus of a disciplinary community. Such truth is contingent and always open to reinterpretation. And the finding of such truth is always dependent on the proper functioning of democratic institutions. Still, the truths of the pragmatic historian, even though neither universal nor founded on first principles, are truths that can construct meaningful shared knowledge and instruct principled action. They are, in the end, the only kind of historical truths we have.

If pragmatism is a useful answer to the problems of history in a postmodern age, it may be a good answer to the problems of journalism, too. After all, journalism often conceives of itself as the first draft of history. Journalism historians as well as journalists would do well to take the linguistic turn in their work, albeit a turn toward a pragmatic conception of historical and public discourse and the kinds of truth such discourse can discover. Cultural historian Hayden White has done much to open historical inquiry to such linguistic concerns. In *Tropics of Discourse*, White reminds historians that prior to the French Revolution, historians in the West made a distinction between truth and error rather than fact and fiction, "with it being understood that many kinds of truth, even in history, could be presented to the reader only by means of fictional techniques of representation." Historians dealt with "real, rather than imagined events," but theorists "recognized the inevitability of a recourse to fictive techniques in the *representation* of real events in the historical discourse." It was an era when "the imagination no less than the reason had to be engaged in any adequate representation of the truth; and this meant that the techniques of fiction-making were as necessary to the composition of a historical discourse as erudition might be." In the nineteenth century, with the elevation of science and reason, truth was identified with fact, which was in turn identified as the opposite of fiction.[22] These nineteenth-century historians "did not realize that the facts do not speak for themselves, but that the historian speaks for them, speaks on their behalf, and fashions the fragments of the past into a whole whose integrity is—in its *re*presentation—a purely discursive one."[23] Until history took the cultural or linguistic turn in the 1970s, this nineteenth-century notion of the representation of the known world through language survived and flourished. It is still, over a century later, the notion that defines traditional journalism in America.

For journalism to take the linguistic or cultural turn, at least in the terms of pragmatism, would simply be for journalists and their readers to become more aware of the rhetorical strategies at work in journalism's representation of the world—and for journalists to acknowledge them more forthrightly. Literary journalism, because it works in many ways against the established conventions and values of traditional journalism, is already largely self-conscious about its own rhetorical strategies—but as the Masson-Malcolm dispute has taught us, the literary tradition in American journalism needs to continue developing clearer standards for articulating the newsgathering and newswriting methods used in constructing its reports.[24] Traditional journalism also needs to develop this kind of self-awareness, as does the reading public for contemporary journalism. All forms of journalism must acknowledge that news reports are social and cultural constructions, that "facts" are not the same as "truth," that the ultimate arbiter of truth is not the press but rather the public in its vital work in America's democratic experiment. These acknowledgments should be reflected in professional codes of ethics and conduct and in the mission statements of news outlets. They should also be reflected in social contracts between publications and readers and journalists and sources, as well as more self-reflexive forms of news reports—that is, reports that offer accounts of how and why information was gathered and the assumptions that underlie inter- pretation and analysis of information. Transparency, not objectivity, may well be the news value that we most need in our postmodern age.

Libel Law and Truth in the Masson-Malcolm Dispute

Masson v. New Yorker forced these broad intellectual and cultural debates about the objectivity of knowledge and the nature of "truth" in American press expression into the courts. The dispute not only dramatized the competing conceptions of truth at stake in the objectivity critique but also required the courts to confront the claims of the critique in the constitutional arena of libel law. When the Supreme Court adjudicated these issues in *Masson v. New Yorker*, it embraced traditional journalism's valuing of fact and objectivity and rejected a broader conception of truth implicit in the practice of literary jour- nalism. In choosing this path, the Court turned away from the First Amend- ment theory animating *New York Times v. Sullivan*, opting to value less the free, uninhibited exchange of ideas necessary to democracy and more the "trust- worthiness" of public expression.[25]

Prior to *Sullivan*, libel law was entirely a matter of state law, and in the so- cial conflict between the right to reputation and freedom of expression, the legal scales were tipped in favor of the former. The common law of libel placed the burden of proof on the defendant; that is, to prevail in a libel suit, the defendant generally had to prove the truth of a disputed defamatory statement or to assert an affirmative defense such as the fair report privilege. It was a strict liability standard that carried with it substantial threats to press freedom. As the history of the *New Yorker*'s handling of libel threats illustrates, the common law of libel was a real threat to the press in the pre-*Sullivan* years. Even though the *New Yorker* ultimately suffered few direct losses from libel claims—it pre- vailed in the cases that actually went to trial and paid largely nominal settle- ments to only a handful of libel claimants—it spent a good deal of financial and editorial resources combating the libel threat. Editors and counsel read *New Yorker* copy for libel, writers were asked to keep scrupulous records of in- terviews and newsgathering activities, and the magazine's fabled fact-checking department was brought into being. All of these events and phenomena were part of a system intended not just to promote high standards of accuracy and truth in the magazine's pages but to defend against the chilling power of libel law as well.

In the 1920s and 1930s, when the magazine was developing and honing its legal and editorial strategies for dealing with libel threats, large newspapers were increasingly hiring in-house counsel to be what Norman Rosenberg called "libel censors." He noted that a New York newspaper settled more than $100,000 in libel claims in 1924 before instituting a financially effective "system of prepublication censorship."[26] Exactly what effect this system had on editorial freedom is unclear, but, as we have seen, the *New Yorker* did resist the encroachment of libel law on its freedom of expression.

In the 1950s, libel complaints against the magazine became more explicit in asking for what were at the time large awards for damages. This phenomenon was likely the result of the magazine's tremendous growth in the years during and immediately after World War II, a time when the *New Yorker* became a national institution, and with that iconic status and financial success it also became an attractive target for libel suits. Even so, the magazine was highly effective in shutting down libel complaints and suits through various legal strategies. By the 1980s, when the Masson-Malcolm dispute arose, the climate for libel litigation had grown heated in the United States, despite the increased press protections of the landmark 1964 decision *New York Times v. Sullivan*.

Sullivan transformed the common law of libel under which the *New Yorker* operated for the first forty years of its existence. In *Sullivan*, the Supreme Court erected a high constitutional barrier against recovery in libel suits filed by public officials. This barrier was the actual malice standard, which asserted under the imprimatur of the First Amendment that public officials must prove that an allegedly defamatory and false statement was published with knowing falsity or reckless disregard for the truth. As *Sullivan*'s progeny grew in number, the Court extended the reach of the actual malice standard to a broader array of plaintiffs and continued to interpret the meaning of the standard. The strict liability standard of the common law of libel was largely an artifact of the past. In *Sullivan*, the Supreme Court for the first time recognized in the law of libel a significant threat to freedom of the press, something the *New Yorker* and its lawyers had discovered forty year before. And as *Masson v. New Yorker* itself demonstrated, the promise of *Sullivan* could not withstand the cultural and social pressures that would materialize in the years ahead.

When *Sullivan* was first decided, the First Amendment theorist Alexander

Meiklejohn declared it to be "an occasion for dancing in the streets."[27] That *Sullivan*'s promise would never be fully realized—and that Meiklejohn's hope for the eventual First Amendment protection of *all* political and social speech has not come to pass—should not surprise us. In the end, *Sullivan* was simply too revolutionary for the cultural and political context of its moment. The dominance of the traditional report in press expression and the professional standards that supported it precluded a more sophisticated press discourse from gaining prominence in the public sphere. The presentation of facts has long been the prime goal of news reporting. Readers have largely been left to construct meaning, to arrive at the greater truth or truths conveyed in the facts, on their own. It is thus meaningful, and perhaps even expected, that *Sullivan*'s legal breakthrough in the expansion of First Amendment protections for ex-pression came not from a news report but from a political advertisement paid for by a group with its own conception of truth.

Since *Sullivan* was decided in 1964, a long line of Supreme Court cases elab-orating on and refining its rulings has ensued. By the time the Court decided *Masson v. New Yorker* in 1991, the expression-protective spirit of *Sullivan* had receded. This diminishing emphasis on the central purpose of the First Amendment in public life may well be, at least in part, a judicial response to the increasing skepticism about unitary truth and its discoverability in the post-modern age. In *Sullivan*, the Court transformed the legal role of truth in libel law. The defendant no longer had to prove truth to prevail; after *Sullivan*, the public official (and later many other kinds of plaintiffs) had to prove the falsity of a disputed statement, and not just falsity but the defendant's knowledge of or reckless disregard for falsity. The judicial emphasis was less on the truth or falsity determination required in a libel suit and more on the fault determina-tion. This emphasis was an artifact of *Sullivan*'s actual malice standard. Al-though by concentrating more on the defendant's belief in truth or falsity than on actual truth or falsity the *Sullivan* decision theoretically allowed for the ex-istence of multiple versions of truth in expression, the point of the decision was to protect honest error in substantially true expression. In *Sullivan* and its immediate progeny, the Court did not consider the nature of truth—whether it is unitary and ascertainable or multiple, contingent, and difficult to locate. But as the *Sullivan* case line developed, the Court began to confront the nature of truth itself in expression as it attempted to distinguish between factual ex-pression subject to tests of falsity and nonfactual expression receiving First Amendment protection. In extending that protection to opinion, rhetorical hyperbole, and rational interpretation of ambiguous sources and events, the Court recognized that truth is not always discoverable in expression, that truth often is not unitary but multiple, not absolute but contingent.

First in *Milkovich v. Lorain Journal* (1990) and then in *Masson v. New Yorker* (1991), cases decided in consecutive years, the Supreme Court pulled back from its previous expansionist approach to First Amendment protection for expression not purely factual in nature and its recognition that truth can be multiple and provisional. In *Milkovich* the Court refused constitutional protection to speech that conveys "a provably false factual connotation."[28] In *Masson*, the Court refused constitutional protection to altered quotations materially changed in meaning from the speaker's actual words. In both cases, then, the Court refused to protect ambiguous uses of language capable of being understood as conveying false facts. The problem with this approach is the difficulty in interpreting ambiguous language and determining whether it indeed conveys false facts.

The problem of interpretation is at the heart of the conflict between the Supreme Court's majority and dissenting opinions in *Milkovich*. It is also the problem highlighted in the conflict between the first jury's libel judgment against Janet Malcolm in *Masson v. New Yorker* and the second jury's judgment in her favor. The circumstantial and contextual method articulated in *Ollman v. Evans* for determining whether language is factual is likely the best method to use, especially if we acknowledge that truth is contingent and constructed. If, after applying this method, reasonable readers cannot agree whether the disputed language is factual or nonfactual in nature, the language should be protected under the First Amendment. If the nature of the language is undiscoverable, then its truth is not discoverable either.

Such an approach would surely have protected the expression at issue in *Milkovich*, where the majority and dissent did not agree that the disputed expression was factual. The approach is more problematic in the instance of allegedly false quotations, the legal issue in *Masson*, but it is still valuable. It would require determining whether a disputed quotation had "a precise core of meaning for which a consensus of understanding exists" or whether it was "indefinite and ambiguous."[29] (Is the meaning of "intellectual gigolo" indefinite or precise, for example? If indefinite, the quotation should not be treated as a factual statement.) The approach would also consider whether the quotation was verifiable (is it susceptible to proof or disproof?) as well as its cultural, social, and linguistic contexts. In the case of *Masson*, several of the disputed quotations ("intellectual gigolo," "sex, women, fun," and "the greatest analyst that ever lived") simply were not verifiable given the dispute over the authenticity of Malcolm's typewritten notes. (It must be pointed out that this dispute involved a matter of fact for the jury, not a question of law for a judge, to decide.) What is more, the social context of many of the quotations—their occurrence in an improbably long monologue delivered over lunch in perfectly cadenced and syntactical speech—suggests that the quotations should not be treated as *purely* factual statements, at least as a matter of law. This circumstantial and contextual method for determining whether language is factual enough to be susceptible to a truth or falsity test should be a threshold inquiry in cases involving alleged defamatory misquotation. If reasonable readers could disagree over whether a disputed quotation is factual, the presumption should be in favor of treating the quotation as nonfactual, protected expression. Such a test should precede the Supreme Court's material alteration test. Such a test might not have prevented the *Masson* case from going to trial, but its use would be much more reflective of *Sullivan's* conception of the First Amendment than the *Masson* ruling.

In *Masson*, the Supreme Court turned away from *Sullivan's* theory that self-government demands the utmost protection of expression in the public search for truth. The *Masson* Court refused to extend First Amendment protection to speech under the rationale that such protection might compromise the quality of public discourse by eliminating "the real meaning of quotations" and thus "any method of distinguishing between the statements of the subject and the interpretation of the author."[30] While safeguarding the quality of public discourse is, at least in theory, a useful goal, and may be a value of the First Amendment as theorized by Alexander Meiklejohn, it is not the value underpinning the central meaning of the First Amendment as articulated in *Sullivan*. In the end, the *Masson* decision and its turning away from *Sullivan's* broad protections for expression signal a turning away as well from the democratic theory at *Sullivan's* heart: the sovereignty of the citizen and the absolute necessity of robust public discourse to that sovereignty.

"The point of edifying philosophy," Richard Rorty wrote, "is to keep the conversation going rather than to find objective truth."[31] It is through such conversation, Rorty maintains, that we come to see our community "as *ours* rather than *nature's*, *shaped* rather than *found*, one among many which men have made."[32] The point of philosophy, or any human endeavor, he argues, is to find whatever truth is to be found in the free and vibrant communal search for knowledge. The point is to realize human freedom and "human solidarity" rather than "an already existing Truth."[33] Journalism is not philosophy, of course, but such a goal—the realization of human freedom and solidarity—seems fitting for a press committed to serving American democracy. The traditional report has long dominated American press expression and in that domination has provided little public space for the many alternative forms of press expression to flourish, including literary journalism. The Masson-Malcolm dispute revealed profound tensions between the traditional and literary traditions in American press expression of the twentieth century, tensions that have periodically led to attacks from the institutions representing the traditional report against those representing the literary report, as well as the literary report itself.

The press critic Jay Rosen has written that "journalism is best understood as one of the arts of democracy."[34] If the contemporary American press is to hold on to its claim to represent the Fourth Estate, if the American public and judicial system are to continue to understand the press as the necessary bulwark of democracy, then the American press and public must embrace the multitude of traditions and voices that together constitute American journalism. Sustaining the First Amendment and maintaining a vibrant public sphere where democracy has at least a chance of operating depend on what John Keane has called "pluralistic account[s] of public life."[35] If the press is to play a meaningful role in the public sphere, these accounts are best expressed by making room for press traditions beyond the traditional. One such tradition is that of literary journalism. Democracy demands that America let many flowers bloom in its news media.

According to Rosen, John Dewey's essential message about the press and the public and their role in American democracy should be the goal of contemporary journalism: "Build a better place for the public, and the public may one day find its place."[36] The more voices in American journalism, the stronger American democracy may become. The stronger American democracy is, the more likely it will be to sustain the constitutional freedoms that every American citizen enjoys. These freedoms include, of course, freedom of expression. A literary or narrative journalism—as well as a broader public conception of and discourse about what constitutes truthful historical, documentary, or journalistic accounts of the world around us—may help build this better place.

Appendix
The Disputed Quotations

Quotations taken from Janet Malcolm, In the Freud Archives
(1984; reprint, New York: New York Review Books, 1997).

"Maresfield Gardens [home of the Freud Archives] would have been a center of scholarship, but it would also have been a place of **sex, women, fun.** It would have been like the change in *The Wizard of Oz* from black and white into color." (36)

"Then I met a rather attractive older graduate student, and I had an affair with her. One day, she took me to some art event, and she was sorry afterward. She said, 'Well, it's very nice sleeping with you in your room, but you're the kind of person who should never leave the room—you're just a social embarrassment anywhere else, though you do fine in your own room.' And, you know, in their way, if not in so many words, [Kurt] Eissler and Anna Freud told me the same thing. They liked me well enough 'in my own room.' They loved to hear from me what creeps and dolts analysts are. **I was like an intellectual gigolo—you get your pleasure from him, but you don't take him out in public.**" (40–41)

"That remark about the sterility of psychoanalysis was something I tacked on at the last minute, and it was totally gratuitous. **I don't know why I put it in.**" (55)

"[Kurt Eissler, director of the Freud Archives] was always putting moral pressure on me. 'Do you want to poison Anna Freud's last days? Have you no heart? You're going to kill the poor old woman.' I said to him, 'What have I done? *You're* doing it. *You're* firing me. What am I supposed to do—be grateful to you?' 'You could be silent about it. You could swallow it. I know it is painful for you. But you could just live with it in silence.' 'Why should I do that?' 'Because it is the honorable thing to do.' **Well, he had the wrong man.**" (67)

"Wait till it reaches the best-seller list, and watch how the analysts will crawl," he crowed. "They move whichever way the wind blows. They will want me back, they will say that Masson is a great scholar, a major analyst—**after Freud, he's the greatest analyst who ever lived** . . . There is no possible refutation of this book. It's going to cause a revolution in psychoanalysis. Analysis stands or falls with me now." (153–54)

NOTES

Introduction: Journalism, Libel Law, and the Problem of Facts

1. Alex S. Jones, "Author Sues Magazine," *New York Times*, 2 December 1984, sec. 1, 39; *Masson v. New Yorker*, Complaint for Defamation and Invasion of Privacy no. 84-7548, filed in the U.S. District Court, Northern District of California, 29 November 1984. Copy received from the National Archives and Records Administration's San Bruno Archives in California.

2. Janet Malcolm, "The Annals of Scholarship: Trouble in the Archives—Part I," *New Yorker*, 5 December 1983, 59–152, and "Part II," 12 December 1983, 60–119.

3. *Masson v. New Yorker*, 686 F. Supp. 1396 (N.C. Cal. 1987) (granting summary judgment to defendants), *aff'd.*, 895 F.2d 1535 (9th Cir. 1989), *rev'd. and remanded*, 501 U.S. 496 (1991), 960 F.2d 896 (9th Cir. 1992) (affirming summary judgment for Knopf, remanding case for trial for Malcolm and the *New Yorker*), *aff'd.*, 85 F.3d 1394 (9th Cir., 1996). In June 1996 the Ninth U.S. Circuit Court of Appeals upheld the 1993 and 1994 trial verdicts which found in favor, respectively, of the *New Yorker* and Janet Malcolm.

4. *New York Times Co. v. Sullivan*, 376 U.S. 254, 279–80 (1964) ("The constitutional guarantees require, we think, a federal rule that prohibits a public official from recovering damages for a defamatory falsehood relating to his official conduct unless he proves that the statement was made with 'actual malice'—that is, with knowledge that it was false or with reckless disregard of whether it was false or not").

5. Jane Gross, "On Libel and the Literati: The New Yorker on Trial," *New York Times*, 5 May 1993, A1.

6. Malcolm, "The Annals of Scholarship: Trouble in the Archives—Part I," 59, and "Part II," 60.

7. Jeffrey Masson, telephone interview with author, 15 January 2005; Jane Gross, "Profile Writer Has Last Word in Defense against Libel Suit," *New York Times*, 25 May 1993, A14.

8. *Masson v. New Yorker*, Complaint.

9. Jane Gross, "Jurors Decide for Psychoanalyst but Split on Award in Libel Case," *New York Times*, 3 June 1993, A14.

10. *Masson v. New Yorker*, 686 F. Supp. 1396, 1407.

11. *Masson v. New Yorker*, 895 F.2d 1535, 1536.

12. *Masson v. New Yorker*, 501 U.S. 496, 525.

13. *Masson*, 960 F.2d 896, 898, 902.

14. "Retrial Is Set in Libel Case, but Without Magazine," *New York Times*, 10 September 1993, A20; Howard Mintz, "Judge Says New Yorker Libel Case Is Best Settled," *Recorder*, 4 August 1993, 3; Howard Mintz, "Judge Orders New Trial in Masson's Libel Case," *Recorder*, 10 September 1993, 3.

15. *Masson v. New Yorker*, Special Verdict no. C-84–7548 EFL, 2 November 1994, U.S. District Court, Northern District of California, 4–5.

16. *Masson v. New Yorker*, 85 F.3d 1394.

17. Jane Gross, "At Libel Trial, Speaking Style Becomes the Focus," *New York Times*, 19 May 1993, A16.

18. Ibid. Ralph Blumenthal, "Freud Archives Research Chief Removed in Dispute over Yale Talk," *New York Times*, 9 November 1981, B1; Eva Hoffman and Margot Slade, "Freud's Legacy: Totem and Taboo," *New York Times*, 15 November 1981, sec. 4, 7.

19. Gross, "At Libel Trial, Speaking Style Becomes the Focus," A16.

20. Ibid.

21. Janet Malcolm, afterword to *The Journalist and the Murderer* (New York: Vintage Books, 1990). See also Janet Malcolm, "The Morality of Journalism," *New York Review of Books*, 1 March 1990, 19.

22. Janet Malcolm, *In the Freud Archives* (New York: New York Review Books, 1997), 36.

23. *Masson*, 501 U.S. at 503.

24. Ibid., 503–4.

25. Roxanne Roberts and Annie Groer, "Writer's Notes Suddenly Appear," *Washington Post*, 26 August 1995, D1.

26. Jane Gross, "Psychoanalyst and Lawyer Duel over Nuances at a Libel Trial," *New York Times*, 13 May 1993, A20.

27. Federal Rules of Civil Procedure 56(c). See also Malcolm's discussion of this issue in afterword to *The Journalist and the Murderer*, 151n.

28. Malcolm, *The Journalist and the Murderer*, 153–55.

29. John C. Hartsock, *A History of American Literary Journalism: The Emergence of a Modern Narrative Form* (Amherst: University of Massachusetts Press, 2000), 55–57.

30. For discussions of defining characteristics of narrative journalism, see ibid. and Mark Kramer, "Breakable Rules for Literary Journalists," in *Literary Journalism: A New Collection of the Best American Nonfiction*, ed. Norman Sims and Mark Kramer (New York: Ballantine, 1995), 21–36.

31. This journalistic nonfiction form is known as literary journalism, narrative journalism, literary nonfiction, the art of fact, and the New Journalism—a broad but not exhaustive list. For useful definitions and discussions of these terms, see Mark Kramer, "Narrative Journalism Comes of Age," *Nieman Reports* (Fall 2000): 6, defining narrative journalism as the use of "storytelling techniques to convey news"; Kevin Kerrane, "Making Facts Dance," in *The Art of Fact: A Historical Anthology of Literary Journalism*, ed. Kevin Kerrane and Ben Yagoda (New York: Touchstone, 1997), 20, claiming that "the best characterization of literary journalism may ultimately be the definition that Ezra Pound gave for literature itself: 'news that stays news' "; Ben Yagoda, preface to Kerrane and Yagoda, *The Art of Fact*, 13–14, identifying literary journalism as "factual," "informed and animated by the central journalistic commitment to the truth," and "thoughtfully, artfully, and valuably innovative"; Chris Anderson, "Literary Nonfiction and Composition," in *Literary Nonfiction: Theory, Criticism, Pedagogy*, ed. Chris Anderson (Carbondale: Southern Illinois University Press, 1989), ix, x, identifying the "para-

doxical, threshold, problematic nature" of literary nonfiction as hybrid texts; and Phyllis Frus, *The Politics and Poetics of Journalistic Narrative: The Timely and the Timeless* (Cambridge: Cambridge University Press, 1994), ix, xvii, exploring the historical separation of fiction and journalism as narrative categories "and the various ways writers and texts on the border have muddied these neat distinctions and questioned their basis."

32. Hartsock, *A History of American Literary Journalism*, 1. Hartsock's full working definition of narrative literary journalism reads as follows: "[It is] a body of writing that . . . reads like a novel or short story except that it is true or makes a truth claim to phenomenal experience."

33. One author describes the debate in a particularly useful way: "Criticism of the new literary nonfiction came from both literary and journalistic quarters. Literary figures took it to task for remaining too journalistic, too tied to fact. As a way of expressing literary disapproval, the work was often dismissed as 'mere reportage.' At the same time journalistic figures faulted it for its literary aspirations, for appearing to take liberties with the facts or treating them in ways intended to create artistic or emotional effects." Ronald Weber, *The Literature of Fact: Literary Nonfiction in American Writing* (Athens: Ohio University Press, 1980), 27.

34. Peter Novick, *That Noble Dream: The "Objectivity Question" and the American Historical Profession* (Cambridge: Cambridge University Press, 1988), 543; David Paul Nord, "The Practice of Historical Research," in *Mass Communication Research and Theory*, ed. Guido H. Stempel III, David H. Weaver, and G. Cleveland Wilhoit (Boston: Allyn and Bacon, 2003), 362–63.

35. Nord, "The Practice of Historical Research," 363.

36. Tom Dickson, *Mass Media Education in Transition: Preparing for the 21st Century* (Mahwah, N.J.: Lawrence Erlbaum Associates, 2000), 3–24.

37. Jeremy Iggers, *Good News, Bad News: Journalism Ethics and the Public Interest* (Boulder: Westview Press, 1998), 66; Dan Schiller, *Objectivity and the News: The Public and the Rise of Commercial Journalism* (Philadelphia: University of Pennsylvania Press, 1981), 193.

38. Ben Yagoda, *About Town: "The New Yorker" and the World It Made* (New York: Scribner, 2000), 38–39.

39. Norman Sims, "Joseph Mitchell and *The New Yorker* Nonfiction Writers," in *Literary Journalism in the Twentieth Century*, ed. Norman Sims (New York: Oxford University Press, 1990), 83.

40. Yagoda, *About Town*, 401.

41. Brendan Gill, *Here at the New Yorker* (New York: Random House, 1975), 89–90.

42. Sims, "Joseph Mitchell and *The New Yorker* Nonfiction Writers," 85; Yagoda, *About Town*, 401; David Remnick, "Life and Letters: Reporting it All," *New Yorker*, 22 March 2004, http://www.newyorker.com/printables/fact/040329fa_fact1 (3 April 2005).

43. See Joanne Lipman, "At the New Yorker, Editor and a Writer Differ on the 'Facts': Author Alastair Reid Defends His Use of Composites," *Wall Street Journal*, 18 June 1984, 1: "Mr. Reid, who has been appearing in the New Yorker's prestigious pages since 1951, says he has spent his career creating composite tales and scenes, fabricating personae, rearranging events and creating conversations in a plethora of pieces presented as nonfiction. He insists his embellishments have made his articles that much more accurate, in spirit if not in fact. 'The implication that fact is precious isn't important,' Mr. Reid

says. 'Some people (at the New Yorker) write very factually. I don't write that way. . . . Facts are only a part of reality.' This is startling to hear from a writer at the New Yorker, often touted in journalistic circles as a magazine whose statements of fact can be taken without benefit of any grains of salt. The publication boasts an eight-member checking department that combs every article, perusing reams of evidence—often delivered by the shopping bagful—to verify every fact."

44. Yagoda, *About Town*, 401.

45. James W. Carey, "The Problem of Journalism History," *Journalism History* 1 (1974): 5.

46. David T. Z. Mindich, *Just the Facts: How "Objectivity" Came to Define American Journalism* (New York: New York University Press, 1998); Schiller, *Objectivity and the News*; Michael Schudson, *Discovering the News: A Social History of American Newspapers* (New York: Basic Books, 1978); Hartsock, *A History of American Literary Journalism*; Michael Schudson, "The Objectivity Norm in American Journalism," *Journalism* 2, no. 2 (2001): 149–70; Michael Schudson, *The Sociology of News* (New York: W. W. Norton, 2003).

47. Hartsock, *A History of American Literary Journalism*, 167.

48. Rodney A. Smolla, "Let the Author Beware: The Rejuvenation of the American Law of Libel," *University of Pennsylvania Law Review* (December 1983): 1; Norman Rosenberg, *Protecting the Best Men: An Interpretive History of the Law of Libel* (Chapel Hill: University of North Carolina Press, 1986), 252; Michael Schudson, "Watergate: A Study in Mythology," *Columbia Journalism Review* (May–June 1992): 32; Rodney A. Smolla, *Suing the Press* (New York: Oxford University Press, 1986), 9.

49. Peter Novick, *That Noble Dream: The "Objectivity Question" and the American Historical Profession* (Cambridge: Cambridge University Press, 1988), 567–68. For other enlightening discussions of the postmodern critique of objectivity, see Joyce Appleby, Lynn Hunt, and Margaret Jacobs, *Telling the Truth about History* (New York: W. W. Norton, 1994); Robert Berkhofer, *Beyond the Great Story: History as Text and Discourse* (Cambridge: Belknap Press, 1995); Georg G. Iggers, *Historiography in the Twentieth Century: From Scientific Objectivity to the Postmodern Challenge* (Middletown, Conn.: Wesleyan University Press, 1997); and James T. Kloppenberg, "Objectivity and Historicism: A Century of American Historical Writing," *American Historical Review* 94, no. 4 (1989): 1011–30.

50. Novick, *That Noble Dream*, 523.

51. William Safire, "Alone with 'Alone,' or What 'Is' Is," *New York Times Magazine*, 11 October 1998, 22–23.

52. *Masson*, 501 U.S. at 517.

53. *New York Times v. Sullivan*, 271.

54. Anthony Lewis, *Make No Law: The Sullivan Case and the First Amendment* (New York: Vintage Books, 1992), 156–57.

55. *New York Times v. Sullivan*, 271.

56. See *Rosenblatt v. Baer*, 383 U.S. 75, 86 (1966) (holding that public officials are "at the very least . . . those among the hierarchy of government employees who have, or appear to the public to have, substantial responsibility for or control over the conduct of governmental affairs); *Curtis Publishing Co. v. Butts*, 388 U.S. 130 (1967), and *Associated Press v. Walker*, 388 U.S. 130 (1967) (decided together in one opinion, holding that public figures must prove actual malice to prevail); *Time, Inc. v. Hill*, 385 U.S. 374 (1967) (holding that private plaintiffs in false-light invasion of privacy claims must

prove actual malice to prevail if the subject of the report is a matter of public concern); *Gertz v. Robert Welch, Inc.*, 418 U.S. 323 (1974) (holding that there are two kinds of public figures who, like public officials, must prove actual malice to prevail in libel suits: all-purpose public figures; and limited, or vortex, public figures. *Gertz* is also known for its holding that private citizens, when libeled, do not have to prove actual malice to prevail in libel suits but rather must show at least negligence); *Hutchinson v. Proxmire*, 443 U.S. 111 (1979) (holding that receiving public money by itself does not make a person a public figure if the person has been drawn involuntarily into a public controversy); *Wolston v. Reader's Digest Ass'n.*, 443 U.S. 157 (1979) (holding that involvement in a criminal proceeding does not by itself make a person a public figure if the person has been involuntarily drawn into a public controversy); *Philadelphia Newspapers, Inc. v. Hepps*, 475 U.S. 767, 769 (1986) (holding that when an allegedly libelous publication involves matters of public concern, a private plaintiff must prove falsity even when the fault level is negligence rather than actual malice); *Hustler Magazine, Inc. v. Falwell*, 485 U.S. 46 (1988) (holding that public figures claiming intentional infliction of emotional distress must prove publication of a false statement of fact with actual malice to prevail).

57. *Masson*, 501 U.S. at 517.
58. Kathy Roberts Forde, "How *Masson v. New Yorker* Has Shaped the Legal Landscape of Narrative Journalism," *Communication Law and Policy* 10 (Winter 2005): 101–33.
59. *Masson*, 501 U.S at 517, *quoting Heuer v. Kee*, 15 Cal. App. 2d 710, 714 (1936).
60. Ibid.
61. *New York Times v. Sullivan*, 270.
62. Lee C. Bollinger, "The End of *New York Times v. Sullivan*: Reflections on *Masson v. New Yorker Magazine*," *Supreme Court Review* (1991): 39.
63. John Dewey, *The Public and Its Problems* (New York: Henry Holt 1927); Walter Lippmann, *Public Opinion* (New York: Free Press, 1997); Walter Lippmann, *Liberty and the News* (New York: Harcourt, Brace, and Hone, 1920).
64. Robert B. Westbrook, *John Dewey and American Democracy* (Ithaca: Cornell University Press, 1991), 293–318.
65. Lippmann, *Public Opinion*, 226–28.
66. James Miller, *"Democracy Is in the Streets": From Port Huron to the Siege of Chicago* (New York: Simon and Schuster, 1987), 92–105; John Hellman, "Fact, Fable, and the New Journalist," in *Fables of Fact: The New Journalism as New Fiction* (Chicago: University of Illinois Press, 1981), 1–20.
67. John Dewey, *Democracy and Education* (New York: Macmillan, 1916); Lewis, *Make No Law*, 248.
68. Louis Menand, *The Metaphysical Club: A Story of Ideas in America* (New York: Farrar, Straus and Giroux, 2001).
69. Ibid., 441.
70. Nord, "The Practice of Historical Research," 363–64.
71. Janet Malcolm herself discusses the role of truth in court cases at length in her book *The Crime of Sheila McGough* (New York: Vintage Books, 2000), 4, 20, 67, 78–79. My own discussion depends in part on her insights.
72. Nord, "The Practice of Historical Research," 375–76.
73. See Novick, *That Noble Dream*, for a cogent and detailed historical discussion of this movement and its debates.

74. See, for example, Appleby, Hunt, and Jacobs, *Telling the Truth about History*, 254–87; Kloppenberg, "Objectivity and Historicism"; Douglas E. Litowitz, *Postmodern Philosophy and Law* (Lawrence: University Press of Kansas, 1997).

1. *Masson v. New Yorker* Goes to Trial

1. Jane Gross, "Jurors Decide for Psychoanalyst but Split on Award in Libel Case," *New York Times*, 3 June 1993, A1.

2. *Morning Edition*, episode 1095, broadcast 28 May 1993, National Public Radio, hosted by Bob Edwards; William Hamilton, "Write or Wronged? Masson v. Malcolm Goes to Jury," *Washington Post*, 28 May 1993, G1; Seth Mydans, "Second Trial of Libel Case Is Under Way," *New York Times*, 29 September 1994, B11.

3. Jane Gross, "On Libel and the Literati: The New Yorker on Trial," *New York Times*, 5 May 1993, A1.

4. Janet Malcolm, "The Annals of Scholarship: Trouble in the Archives," pts. 1 and 2, *New Yorker*, 5 December 1983, 59–152, and 12 December 1983, 60–119.

5. *Masson v. New Yorker*, 501 U.S. 496, 502, 505 (1991).

6. *Masson v. New Yorker*, 686 F. Supp. 1396, 1398 (N.D. Cal. 1987) (quoting declaration of Janet Malcolm in support of defendant's motion for summary judgment at 5: "I quoted Mr. Masson accurately, I presented him as he presented himself to me, and in writing my article/book I was consistently and solely guided by the ambition of making him as lifelike and real as possible so that my readers would get the same sense of him that I had received from actually knowing him. I invented nothing. I never harbored the least ill will toward Mr. Masson.").

7. The *New York Times*'s 2004 code of ethics states that quotations in newspaper articles should always be strictly verbatim: "Readers should be able to assume that every word between quotation marks is what the speaker or writer said. The Times does not 'clean up' quotations." "Guidelines for Integrity," *New York Times*, http://www.nytco.com/company-properties-times-integrity.html (5 November 2004). The *Washington Post*'s guidelines say the same: "When we quote someone in The Post, the quotation should be the words that were spoken. We should not alter a quotation to make it easier to understand or to correct the speaker's use of language. When necessary to make clear what someone is intending to say or to avoid embarrassing someone who has difficulty using the language, we may opt to avoid quotation and paraphrase what was said instead." Leonard Downie Jr., "A Note to Our Readers: The Guidelines We Use to Report the News," *Washington Post*, 7 March 2004, B1. See also M. L. Stein's discussion of quotation policies and practices in newsrooms around the United States in "9th Circuit: It's OK to Make Up Quotes," *Editor and Publisher*, 12 August, 1989, 16, 30.

8. *Masson*, 501 U.S. at 499.

9. *Masson*, 686 F. Supp. 1396 (granting summary judgment for defendants).

10. *Masson v. New Yorker*, 895 F.2d 1535 (9th Cir. 1989) (affirming the district court's grant of summary judgment for defendants).

11. *Masson*, 501 U.S. 496.

12. Robert S. Boynton, "Till Press Do Us Part," *Village Voice*, 29 November 1994, 31; Janet Malcolm, "The Morality of Journalism," *New York Review of Books*, 1 March 1990, 19.

13. A summary judgment is a court decision made in favor of one of the parties when the case contains no genuine controversy as to material facts and can thus be decided on

the basis of law. Such a decision obviates the need for a trial. In a study of media libel and privacy cases from 1980 to 2001, the Libel Defense Resource Center found that more than 75 percent of summary judgment motions were granted by state and federal trial courts. From 1997 to 2000 federal appellate courts upheld these grants of summary judgment in 85 percent of reported cases. Summary judgment is thus one of the media's strongest judicial tools for prevailing in a libel suit. Press release, Libel Defense Resource Center, 2001 Summary Judgment Study, 27 August 2001, http://www.ldrc .com/Press_Releases/bull2001–3.html (3 December 2005).

14. David Remnick, "The Assault on Freud: Jeffrey Masson and the Fight over Whether the Father of Analysis Was a Coward," *Washington Post,* 19 February 1984, F1.

15. See Ralph Blumenthal, "Did Freud's Isolation Lead Him to Reverse Theory on Neurosis?" *New York Times,* 25 August 1981, C1; Ralph Blumenthal, "Freud Archives Research Chief Removed in Dispute over Yale Talk," *New York Times,* 9 November 1981, B1; Eva Hoffman and Margot Slade, "Freud's Legacy: Totem and Taboo," *New York Times,* 15 November 1981, sec. 4, 7. See also Jeffrey Moussaieff Masson, introduction to *The Assault on Truth: Freud's Suppression of the Seduction Theory* (New York: Farrar, Straus and Giroux, 1984), xv–xxiii.

16. Jane Gross, "At Libel Trial, Speaking Style Becomes the Focus," *New York Times,* 19 May 1993, A16.

17. Janet Malcolm, *Psychoanalysis: The Impossible Profession* (New York: Alfred A. Knopf, 1981). See also Jane Gross, "New Yorker Writer Says a Disputed Paragraph Merged 3 Remarks," *New York Times,* 18 May 1993, A11.

18. Gross, "At Libel Trial."

19. Alex S. Jones, "Author Sues Magazine," *New York Times,* 2 December 1984, sec. 1, 39.

20. *Masson,* 501 U.S. 496, 506–7; Jane Gross, "In New Yorker Libel Trial, the Analyst Is Examined," *New York Times,* 11 May 1993, A12.

21. *Masson,* 501 U.S. 496, 507–8.

22. Jane Gross, "Jury Hears Final Arguments in Analyst's Libel Suit," *New York Times,* 28 May 1993, A10.

23. Janet Malcolm, *In the Freud Archives* (New York: New York Review of Books, 1997), 36, 38, 41.

24. Janet Malcolm, afterword to *The Journalist and the Murderer* (New York: Vintage Books, 1990), 155.

25. See Malcolm, "The Annals of Scholarship: Trouble in the Archives—Part I," 85 and 98; and William Hamilton, "The Writer He Says Done Him Wrong: Masson v. Malcolm: A Story of a Failed Relationship," *Washington Post,* 14 May 1993, B1.

26. *New York Times Co. v. Sullivan,* 376 U.S. 254, 279–80 (1964) ("The constitutional guarantees require, we think, a federal rule that prohibits a public official from recovering damages for a defamatory falsehood relating to his official conduct unless he proves that the statement was made with 'actual malice'—that is, with knowledge that it was false or with reckless disregard of whether it was false or not"). See W. Wat Hopkins, *Actual Malice: Twenty-five Years after Times v. Sullivan* (New York: Praeger, 1989), 47–74, for an excellent historical explanation of the term.

27. Anthony Lewis, *Make No Law: The Sullivan Case and the First Amendment* (New York: Vintage Books, 1992), 156–57.

28. See *Curtis Publishing Co. v. Butts,* 388 U.S. 130 (1967); *Associated Press v. Walker,* 388 U.S. 130 (1967) (decided together in one opinion, holding that public figures must

prove actual malice to prevail); and *Gertz v. Robert Welch, Inc.*, 418 U.S. 323 (1974) (holding that famous and notorious persons are public figures "for all purposes and in all contexts" and that a person who "voluntarily injects himself or is drawn into a particular public controversy" becomes "a public figure for a limited range of issues" [351]).

29. *Masson v. New Yorker*, 501 U.S. 496, 517.

30. William A. Henry III and Kathryn Jackson Fallon, '"He Said,' She Said," *Time*, 24 May 1993, 58–59. Abrams was not alone in characterizing the Masson-Malcolm dispute in these terms. Reporting for *Newsweek*, David Kaplan wrote, "That classic 'one of 'em must be lying' confrontation, of course, is the fulcrum of the trial." David A. Kaplan, "Annals of the Law of Libel," *Newsweek*, 17 May 1993, 56.

31. James Wagstaffe, e-mail to author, 27 January 2005.

32. Janet Malcolm, *The Crime of Sheila McGough* (New York: Vintage Books, 1999), 67.

33. Janet Malcolm, afterword to *The Journalist and the Murderer*, 153.

34. Malcolm, "The Annals of Scholarship—Part II," 114–15.

35. Ibid., 117.

36. "Jurors in a Libel Case Get Homework: Read," *New York Times*, 7 May 1993, A14.

37. Kaplan, "Annals of the Law of Libel," 56.

38. Ben Wildavsky, "Freud Scholar Opens Libel Trial in S.F.: New Yorker, Writer Accused of False Quotes," *San Francisco Chronicle*, 11 May 1993, A3; Gross, "In New Yorker Libel Trial, the Analyst Is Examined," A12.

39. Jeffrey Masson, telephone interview with author, 15 January 2005.

40. Malcolm, "The Annals of Scholarship: Trouble in the Archives—Part I," 39.

41. Malcolm, "The Annals of Scholarship: Trouble in the Archives—Part II," 112.

42. Masson, telephone interview with author, 15 January 2005.

43. Gross, "In New Yorker Libel Trial, the Analyst Is Examined," A12.

44. See Hamilton, "The Writer He Says Done Him Wrong," B1; Gross, "New Yorker Writer Says a Disputed Paragraph Merged 3 Remarks," A11.

45. David Gates with Lucille Beachy, "The Jeff and Janet Show," *Newsweek*, 31 May 1993, 59.

46. Jane Gross, "Tough Questioning of Libel Plaintiff," *New York Times*, 12 May 1993, A13; Ben Wildavsky, "Both Sides Bloodied in New Yorker Case: Writer and Accuser's Credibility Questioned," *San Francisco Chronicle*, 14 May 1993, A3.

47. Karl Olson, letter to the editor, "Wrong on Malcolm," *Manhattan Lawyer*, 12–18 September 1989, 16.

48. Howard Mintz, "Swearing Contest," *Recorder*, 17 May 1993, 1.

49. Gross, "Tough Questioning of Libel Plaintiff," A13.

50. Jane Gross, "Writer's Technique Put under Harsh Spotlight at New Yorker Trial," *New York Times*, 14 May 1993, A21; Hamilton, "The Writer He Says Done Him Wrong," B1; Gross, "New Yorker Writer Says a Disputed Paragraph Merged 3 Remarks," A11; Mintz, "Swearing Contest," 1; Howard Mintz, "Bad Memories Do Battle in New Yorker Suit," *Recorder*, 19 May 1993, 1.

51. Gross, "At Libel Trial, Speaking Style Becomes the Focus," A16; Ben Wildavsky, "New Yorker Libel Trial Focuses on Quote about Masson's Firing," *San Francisco Chronicle*, 19 May 1993, A5; Mintz, "Bad Memories Do Battle in New Yorker Suit," 1.

52. Ben Wildavsky, "Key Claim Rebutted by Editor in New Yorker Libel Lawsuit," *San Francisco Chronicle*, 20 May 1993, A4.

53. Jane Gross, "Editor Recalls Overriding Lawyer on a Quotation in Dispute," *New York Times*, 20 May 1993, A19.

54. Ibid.

55. Jane Gross, "Shawn Has a Say in New Yorker Trial," *New York Times*, 21 May 1993, A10; Ben Wildavsky, "Dead Editor of New Yorker 'Testifies' at Libel Trial," *San Francisco Chronicle*, 21 May 1993, A4.

56. Gwen Davis, "The Trials of Janet and Jeffrey," *Nation*, 28 November 1994, 645.

57. The former girlfriend was Denise Weinstein, and the anthropologist was Nancy Scheper-Hughes. Jane Gross, "New Yorker Articles on Analyst Harmed Their Relationship, His Ex-Lover Tells Jury," *New York Times*, 25 May 1993, A16; Ben Wildavsky, "Writer Didn't Take Notes, Says Witness in Libel Trial," *San Francisco Chronicle*, 25 May 1993, A6; Howard Mintz, "New Yorker Case Moves to Lawyer Credibility," *Recorder*, 28 May 1993, 3; Gross, "In New Yoker Libel Trial."

58. Ben Wildavsky, "Writer Denies Inventing Quotes," *San Francisco Chronicle*, 26 May 1993, A7; Howard Mintz, "Brosnahan Told Masson Not to Pursue Libel Suit," *Recorder*, 26 May 1993, 3.

59. Jane Gross, "Profile Writer Has Last Word in Defense against Libel Suit," *New York Times*, 26 May 1993, A14.

60. Ibid.

61. "Psychoanalyst Masson Sues the 'New Yorker' for Libel Segment," 12, show no. 1095, *Morning Edition*, National Public Radio, 28 May 1993, Sally Eisele, reporter.

62. William Hamilton, "Write or Wronged? Masson v. Malcolm Goes to Jury," *Washington Post*, 28 May 1993, G1; Jane Gross, "Jury Hears Final Arguments in Analyst's Libel Suit," *New York Times*, 28 May 1993, A10; Howard Mintz, "New Yorker Case Moves to Lawyer Credibility," 3; Ben Wildavsky, "New Yorker Case Goes to the Jury," *San Francisco Chronicle*, 28 May 1993, A 3.

63. Gates and Beachy, "The Jeff and Janet Show," 59.

64. Gross, "Jurors Decide for Psychoanalyst but Split on Award in Libel Case," A1; Jane Gross, "Impasse over Damages in New Yorker Libel Case," *New York Times*, 4 June 1993, A1; William Hamilton, "Libel Jury Deadlocked on Damages," *Washington Post*, 3 June 1993, C1; Ben Wildavsky, "S.F. Jury Finds Libel in New Yorker Case," *San Francisco Chronicle*, 3 June 1993, A1.

65. William Hamilton, "Libel Suit Ends in a Mistrial: Jury Finds in Masson's Favor before Deadlocking on Damages," *Washington Post*, 4 June 1993, C1; Ben Wildavsky, "Some Jurors Wanted to Give Masson $1: Panel Proposed Wide Range of Figures for Libel Damages," *San Francisco Chronicle*, 5 June 1993, A1.

66. *Masson v. New Yorker*, jury instructions no. C-84–7548, 8 June 1993, U.S. District Court, Northern District of California, 15.

67. Ben Wildavsky, "Mistrial in New Yorker Suit," *San Francisco Chronicle*, 4 June 1993, A1.

68. Jane Gross, "Reaching a Decision in the New Yorker Trial: A Juror's Account," *New York Times*, 5 June 1993, sec. 1, 7.

69. Curiously, Jane Gross's article does not indicate which of the three quotations recorded in Malcolm's typed notes the jury believed was not one of Malcolm's own observations about Masson. It is doubtful, however, that a juror could believe, given the profile of Masson that emerged in Malcolm's articles, that Malcolm would have observed that Masson was the "greatest analyst who ever lived."

70. Wildavsky, "Mistrial in New Yorker Suit," A1; Hamilton, "Libel Suit Ends in a Mistrial," C1; Gross, "Impasse over Damages in New Yorker Libel Trial," A1.

71. Gross, "Reaching a Decision in the New Yorker Trial"; Wildavsky, "Some Jurors Wanted to Give Masson $1," A1.

72. "Retrial Is Set in Libel Case, but without Magazine," *New York Times*, 10 September 1993, A20; Howard Mintz, "Judge Says New Yorker Libel Case Is Best Settled," *Recorder*, 4 August 1993, 3; Howard Mintz, "Judge Orders New Trial in Masson's Libel Case," *Recorder*, 10 September 1993, 3.

73. *Harte-Hankes Communications, Inc. v. Connaughton*, 491 U.S. 657 (1989).

74. *Masson v. New Yorker*, 960 F.2d 896, 898 (9th Cir., 1992), (stating that "the incremental harm doctrine measures the harm 'inflicted by the challenged statements beyond the harm imposed by the rest of the publication. If that harm is determined to be nominal or nonexistent, the statements are dismissed as not actionable,'" quoting *Herbert v. Lando*, 781 F.2d 298, 311 [2d Cir., 1986]).

75. *Masson*, 501 U.S. 496, 523 ("Here, we reject any suggestion that the incremental harm doctrine is compelled as a matter of First Amendment protection for speech").

76. *Masson*, 960 F.2d 896 ("we conclude that the incremental harm doctrine is not an element of California libel law").

2. Literary Journalism and the *New Yorker*

1. Ben Yagoda, *About Town: The New Yorker and the World It Made* (New York: Scribner, 2000), 38–39.

2. Ibid., 79.

3. Ibid., 77. The *New Yorker*'s legal files, found in the magazine's archives housed in the Manuscripts and Archives Division of the New York Public Library, show that the magazine copyrighted all department names and invested much time and many resources in protecting these copyrights from infringements, of which there were many. If imitation is the highest form of flattery, it is clear that publications across the country were flattering the *New Yorker* in the form of copyright infringement.

4. Norman Sims, "Joseph Mitchell and the *New Yorker* Nonfiction Writers," in *Literary Journalism in the Twentieth Century*, ed. Norman Sims (New York: Oxford University Press, 1990), 83.

5. Ibid., 84.

6. Chris Anderson, intro. to *Literary Nonfiction: Theory, Criticism, Pedagogy* (Carbondale: Southern Illinois University Press, 1989), ix, x.

7. Phyllis Frus, preface to *The Politics and Poetics of Journalistic Narrative: The Timely and the Timeless* (Cambridge: Cambridge University Press, 1994), ix, xvii.

8. Ben Yagoda, preface to *The Art of Fact: A Historical Anthology of Literary Journalism*, ed. Kevin Kerrane and Ben Yagoda (New York: Touchstone, 1997), 13–14.

9. Jane Gross, "Writer's Technique Put under Harsh Spotlight at New Yorker Trial," *New York Times*, 14 May 1993, A21. During testimony in the first trial of *Masson v. New Yorker*, Janet Malcolm said that she developed her techniques, particularly that of compression, by imitating these two revered *New Yorker* writers.

10. Yagoda, *About Town*, 325.

11. Sims, "Joseph Mitchell and the *New Yorker* Nonfiction Writers," 100–101.

12. Yagoda, *About Town*, 401.

13. Sims, "Joseph Mitchell and the *New Yorker* Nonfiction Writers," 85, quoting Joseph Mitchell, author's note to *Old Mr. Flood*, in *Up in the Old Hotel* (New York: Vintage Books, 1993), 373. It is interesting that in his author's note to *Up in the Old Hotel*, a collection of four books, Joseph Mitchell identifies the three stories in the original book *Old Mr. Flood* as fictional. Mitchell, *Up in the Old Hotel*, ix.

14. Yagoda, *About Town*, 401; David Remnick, "Life and Letters: Reporting It All," *New Yorker*, 22 March 2004, http://www.newyorker.com/printables/fact/040329fa_fact1, 3 April 2005. Describing Liebling's newspaper days, Remnick writes: "One of the commonplaces of feature writing at the time was a tendency to embroider. That is, there was a lot of making things up or, at the very least, helping things along. What is now a hanging offense was then a risible misdemeanor. Details were embellished, colors heightened, dialogue faked." According to Yagoda, the same could be said of some of Liebling's fact writing for the *New Yorker*.

15. Yagoda, *About Town*, 400–401.

16. Ibid., 402.

17. Mary F. Corey, *The World through a Monocle: The New Yorker at Midcentury* (Cambridge: Harvard University Press, 1999), 6.

18. Ibid., 21.

19. Yagoda, *About Town*, 366.

20. Ibid., 24. See also Louis Menand, "A Friend Writes: The Old *New Yorker*," in *American Studies* (New York: Farrar, Straus and Giroux, 2002), 125–45.

21. William Hamilton, "The Writer He Says Done Him Wrong," *Washington Post*, 14 May 1993, B1.

22. Janet Malcolm, "The Morality of Journalism," *New York Review of Books*, 1 March 1990, 19.

23. Ibid., 21; Janet Malcolm, afterword to *The Journalist and the Murderer* (New York: Vintage Books, 1990), 158.

24. Alex S. Jones, "Just How Sacrosanct Are the Words inside Quotation Marks?" *New York Times*, 20 January 1991, sec. 4, 6.

25. See, for example, James Atlas, "Stranger Than Fiction," *New York Times Magazine*, 23 June, 1991, sec. 6, 22, and the following *New York Times* articles: Deirdre Carmody, "Despite Malcolm Trial, Editors Elsewhere Vouch for Accuracy of Their Work," 30 May 1993, sec. 1, 26, and "Do Speakers Really Say What Is between Quotation Marks?" 21 June 21 1991, A12; Roger Cohen, "Writers Mobilizing against Restrictions on Using Quotations," 20 February 1991, C11; Fred. W. Friendly, "Was Trust Betrayed?" 25 February 1990, sec. 7, 1; Anna Quindlen, opinion column, "Public and Private: Quote Unquote," 19 May 1993, A19.

26. *Masson v. New Yorker*, 501 U.S. 496, 512 (1991).

27. Ibid., 513.

28. Ibid.

29. David T. Z. Mindich, *Just the Facts: How "Objectivity" Came to Define American Journalism* (New York: New York University Press, 1998), 1.

30. Dan Schiller, *Objectivity and the News: The Public and the Rise of Commercial Journalism* (Philadelphia: University of Pennsylvania Press, 1981); Michael Schudson, *Discovering the News: A Social History of American Newspapers* (New York: Basic Books, 1978).

31. Schiller, *Objectivity and the News*, 10.

32. Mindich, *Just the Facts*, 39.

33. Donald Shaw, "At the Crossroads: Change and Continuity in American Press News, 1820–1860," *Journalism History* 8 (1981): 41.

34. Ibid.

35. John C. Hartsock, *A History of American Literary Journalism: The Emergence of a Modern Narrative Form* (Amherst: University of Massachusetts Press, 2000), 124.

36. Thomas B. Connery, "A Third Way to Tell the Story: American Literary Journalism at the Turn of the Century," in Sims, *Literary Journalism in the Twentieth Century*, 4.

37. Dorothy Nelkin, *Selling Science: How the Press Covers Science and Technology*, rev. ed. (New York: W. H. Freeman, 1995), 86.

38. Mary O. Furner, *Advocacy and Objectivity: A Crisis in the Professionalization of American Social Science, 1865–1905* (Lexington: University Press of Kentucky, 1975), 1.

39. Nancy Cohen, *The Reconstruction of American Liberalism, 1865–1914* (Chapel Hill: University of North Carolina Press, 2002), 14–15, 159.

40. Louis Menand, *The Metaphysical Club: A Story of Ideas in America* (New York: Farrar, Straus and Giroux, 2001), 256–58.

41. Furner, *Advocacy and Objectivity*, 323.

42. Ibid.

43. Mary M. Cronin, "Trade Press Roles in Promoting Journalistic Professionalism, 1884–1917," *Journal of Mass Media Ethics* 8, no. 4 (1993): 227–28.

44. Norman L. Rosenberg, *Protecting the Best Men: An Interpretive History of the Law of Libel* (Chapel Hill: University of North Carolina Press, 1986), 226.

45. Tom Dickson, *Mass Media Education in Transition: Preparing for the 21st Century* (Mahwah, N.J.: Lawrence Erlbaum Associates, 2000), 3–24. See also Marion Tuttle Marzolf, *Civilizing Voices: American Press Criticism, 1880–1950* (New York: Longman, 1991), 53.

46. Schiller, *Objectivity and the News*, 193.

47. Mindich, *Just the Facts*, 10; Michael Schudson, *Discovering the News*, 77–80; David E. Shi, *Facing Facts: Realism in American Thought and Culture, 1850–1920* (New York: Oxford University Press, 1995), 66.

48. Marzolf, *Civilizing Voices*, 123.

49. Walter Lippmann, *Liberty and the News* (1920; reprint, New Brunswick, N.J.: Transaction, 1995); Walter Lippmann, "The Press and Public Opinion," *Political Science Quarterly* 42, no. 2 (1931): 161–70.

50. Richard Streckfuss, "Objectivity in Journalism: A Search and a Reassessment," *Journalism Quarterly* 67, no. 4 (1990): 974–80.

51. Jeremy Iggers, *Good News, Bad News: Journalism Ethics and the Public Interest* (Boulder: Westview Press, 1998), 66.

52. Ibid.

53. Bill Kovach and Tom Rosenstiel, *The Elements of Journalism: What Newspeople Should Know and the Public Should Expect* (New York: Crown, 2001), 72.

54. Ibid., 74.

55. See Michael Schudson, "The Objectivity Norm in American Journalism," *Journalism* 2, no. 2 (2001): 149–70, and *The Sociology of News* (New York: W. W. Norton, 2003), 82.

56. Schudson, "The Objectivity Norm," 161–63.

57. Ibid.

58. Ibid., 163.

59. For an excellent discussion of competing strains of journalism in the 1890s (the entertainment and information models) and their relationship to literary realism, see Karen Roggenkamp, *Narrating the News: New Journalism and Literary Genre in Late Nineteenth-Century American Newspapers and Fiction* (Kent: Kent State University Press, 2005).

60. Hartsock, *A History of American Literary Journalism*, 131.

61. Ibid., 57–59.

62. Ibid., 59.

63. Ibid., 57.

64. Hartsock, *A History of American Literary Journalism*, 23.

65. Schiller, *Objectivity and the News*, 2.

66. Ibid.

67. Hartsock, *A History of American Literary Journalism*, 78.

68. Ibid., 154.

69. "About Ourselves," *The Journalist* 3, no. 1 (1886), 8.

70. Lawrence W. Levine, *Highbrow/Lowbrow: The Emergence of Cultural Hierarchy in America* (Cambridge: Harvard University Press, 1988), 223–31.

71. Hartsock, *A History of American Literary Journalism*, 155.

72. Walter Lippmann, *Liberty and the News* (New York: Harcourt, Brace, and Hone, 1920), 5.

73. Schudson, *Discovering the News*, 151–55.

74. Hartsock, *A History of American Literary Journalism*, 167.

75. Ibid., 168–69.

76. Ibid., 171–72 .

77. Ibid., 187.

78. Schudson, *Discovering the News*, 187.

79. Ibid.

80. Ibid., 184.

81. Tom Wolfe, "Seizing the Power," in *The New Journalism* (London: Picador, 1975), 37–51. See also Ronald Weber, "Some Sort of Artistic Excitement," in *The Reporter as Artist: A Look at the New Journalism Controversy*, ed. Ronald Weber (New York: Hastings House, 1974), 13.

82. John Hellman, intro. to *Fables of Fact: The New Journalism as New Fiction* (Chicago: University of Illinois Press, 1981), 2.

83. Frus, *The Politics and Poetics of Journalistic Narrative*, 132.

84. John J. Pauly, "The Politics of the New Journalism," in *Literary Journalism in the Twentieth Century*, ed. Norman Sims (New York: Oxford University Press), 122.

85. Frus, *The Politics and Poetics of Journalistic Narrative*, 132.

86. Yagoda, *About Town*, 357.

87. Ibid., 357–58.

88. Malcolm, "The Morality of Journalism," 19.

89. *New York* was a new supplement to the *Sunday Herald Tribune* when it ran the infamous Wolfe articles in April 1965. Jim Bellows was editor of the newspaper, and Clay Felker edited the magazine. The magazine outlived the newspaper and is still being published today. Jim Bellows, *The Last Editor* (Kansas City: Andrews McMeel, 2002), 1–14.

90. Yagoda, *About Town*, 335.

91. Bellows, *The Last Editor*, 6. See also Marc Weingarten, *The Gang That Wouldn't Write Straight: Wolfe, Thompson, Didion, and the New Journalism Revolution* (New York: Crown, 2006).

92. Yagoda, *About Town*, 338–40.

93. Bellows, *The Last Editor*, 2, 7, 11.

94. Gardner Botsford, *A Life of Privilege, Mostly* (New York: St. Martin's Press, 2003), 231.

95. Tom Wolfe, "Tiny Mummies! The True Story of the Ruler of 43rd Street's Land of the Walking Dead!" and "Lost in the Whichy Thickets: *The New Yorker*," in *Hooking Up* (New York: Farrar Straus Giroux, 2000), 255–67 and 268–87, originally published in *New York* magazine, a Sunday supplement to the *New York Herald Tribune*, 11 and 18 April 1965.

96. Ved Mehta, *Remembering Mr. Shawn's New Yorker* (Woodstock, N.Y.: Overlook Press, 1998), 221–23; Yagoda, *About Town*, 337–38.

97. Wolfe, "Lost in the Whichy Thickets," 273.

98. Ibid., 274.

99. Yagoda, *About Town*, 336–41; Mehta, *Remembering Mr. Shawn's New Yorker*, 221–23.

100. Dwight Macdonald, "Parajournalism, or Tom Wolfe and His Magic Writing Machine," in *The Reporter as Artist: A Look at the New Journalism Controversy*, ed. Ronald Weber (New York: Hastings House, 1974), 223.

101. Yagoda, *About Town*, 357.

102. Wolfe, "Seizing the Power," 25.

103. Yagoda, *About Town*, 347–48.

104. Kathy Roberts Forde, "Discovering the Explanatory Report in American Newspapers," *Journalism Practice* 1, no. 2 (June 2007): 227–44.

105. Nieman Foundation, *Nieman Program on Narrative Journalism: Director's Corner* (2003), http://www.nieman.harvard.edu/narrative/about_narrative.html (9 December 2003).

106. Carl Sessions Stepp, "State of the American Newspaper: Then and Now," *American Journalism Review* (September 1999): 60–75.

107. *Masson v. New Yorker*, 895 F. 2d 1535 (9th Cir. 1989).

108. Ibid., 1559.

109. Ibid., 1561.

110. Ibid.

111. Schiller, *Objectivity and the News*, 196.

112. Kovach and Rosenstiel, *The Elements of Journalism*, 72.

113. *Masson v. New Yorker*, 501 U.S. 496, 513: "An acknowledgment that the work is so-called docudrama or historical fiction, or that it recreates conversations from memory, not from recordings, might indicate that the quotations should not be interpreted as the actual statements of the speaker to whom they are attributed. . . . A defendant may be able to argue to the jury that quotations should be viewed by the reader as non-literal or reconstructions, but we conclude that a trier of fact in this case could find that the reasonable reader would understand the quotations to be nearly verbatim reports of statements made by the subject."

114. Michael G. Killenberg and Rob Anderson, "What Is a Quote? Practical, Rhetorical, and Ethical Concerns for Journalists," *Journal of Mass Media Ethics* 8 (1993): 39.

115. Ibid., 38–39.

116. Ibid., 50.

117. Michael Hoyt. "Malcolm, Masson, and You," *Columbia Journalism Review* 29, no. 6

(1991): 43; see also Adrienne Lehrer, "Between Quotation Marks," *Journalism Quarterly* (May 1986): 902–6, 941.

118. See Elizabeth Fakazis, "Janet Malcolm: Constructing Boundaries of Journalism," *Journalism* 7, no. 1 (2006): 19–21. See also Peter Novick, *That Noble Dream: The "Objectivity Question" and the American Historical Profession* (Cambridge: Cambridge University Press, 1988).

119. Frus, preface to *The Politics and Poetics of Journalistic Narrative*, xiii.

3. The Historical Origins of the Masson-Malcolm Dispute

1. *Masson v. New Yorker*, 501 U.S. 496 (1991).
2. *New York Times v. Sullivan*, 376 U.S. 254 (1964).
3. *Masson*, 501 U.S. 496, 517.
4. Lee C. Bollinger, "The End of *New York Times v. Sullivan*: Reflections on *Masson v. New Yorker Magazine*," *Supreme Court Review* (1991): 39.
5. Leonard W. Levy, *Emergence of a Free Press* (Chicago: Ivan R. Dee, 1985), 8.
6. Ibid., 7.
7. Norman L. Rosenberg, *Protecting the Best Men: An Interpretive History of the Law of Libel* (Chapel Hill: University of North Carolina Press, 1986), 4.
8. Levy, *Emergence of a Free Press*, 12.
9. Rosenberg, *Protecting the Best Men*, 245.
10. *United States v. Hudson and Goodwin*, 11 U.S. 32 (1812).
11. *New York Times v. Sullivan*, 273.
12. Committee to Defend Martin Luther King and the Struggle for Freedom in the South, advertisement, "Heed Their Rising Voices," *New York Times*, 29 March 1960, L25.
13. Anthony Lewis, *Make No Law: The Sullivan Case and the First Amendment* (New York: Vintage Books, 1991), 5–8.
14. Ibid., 5–45 passim.
15. Ibid., 34.
16. See Robert D. Sack and Sandra S. Baron, *Sack on Defamation: Libel, Slander, and Related Problems*, 3rd ed., 2 vols. (New York: Practising Law Institute, 1999), §1.2.2, for a useful discussion of actual malice in *New York Times v. Sullivan*.
17. Ibid. See also W. Wat Hopkins, *Actual Malice: Twenty-five Years after Times v. Sullivan* (New York: Praeger, 1989), 3.
18. Hopkins, *Actual Malice*, 3.
19. *New York Times v. Sullivan*, 271.
20. Rosenberg, *Protecting the Best Men*, 155.
21. Ibid., 157.
22. Ibid., 177.
23. Ibid.
24. Ibid., 205.
25. Ibid., 205–6.
26. Ibid., 205.
27. Nancy Cohen, *The Reconstruction of American Liberalism: 1865–1914* (Chapel Hill: University of North Carolina Press, 2002), 5.
28. For rigorous and eminently readable accounts of this transformation, see Alan Brinkley, *Liberalism and Its Discontents* (Cambridge: Harvard University Press, 1998),

especially 37–62, "The Late New Deal and the Idea of the State." In this influential essay Brinkley suggests that the modern liberal concept of the state was shaped largely in response to the recession of the late 1930s and then to the experience of World War II. The main assumption of liberal thought of the day was that the U.S. economy was stagnant and the opportunity for expansion limited. The problem was how to keep the economy growing. Liberals saw two choices: (1) government spending to promote economic growth, which would require constant government surveillance and management of the economy; or (2) government spending to promote mass consumption. The second path was taken, and in its wake the state found it had to compensate for the social deficiencies of capitalism through social welfare and insurance, not management of capitalist institutions. Administered government came to be the hallmark of the American liberal state.

29. John Dewey, *The Public and Its Problems* (New York: Henry Holt, 1927); Walter Lippmann, *Public Opinion* (New York: Free Press, 1997); Walter Lippmann, *Liberty and the News* (New York: Harcourt, Brace, and Hone, 1920).

30. Lewis, *Make No Law*, 69.

31. Zechariah Chafee Jr., "Freedom of Speech in War Time," *Harvard Law Review* 32 (1918–19): 932–73.

32. Lewis, *Make No Law*, 75.

33. Chafee, "Freedom of Speech in War Time," 947.

34. Leonard Levy, *Legacy of Suppression: Freedom of Speech and Press in Early American History* (Cambridge: Belknap Press of Harvard University Press, 1960); *Emergence of a Free Press* (New York: Oxford University Press, 1985).

35. *Schenck v. United States*, 249 U.S. 47 (1919); *Frohwerk v. United States*, 249 U.S. 204 (1919); *Debs v. United States*, 249 U.S. 211 (1919).

36. *Masses Publishing Co. v. Patten*, 244 F. 535 (S.D.N.Y., 1917).

37. Ibid., 540.

38. Ibid.

39. Louis Menand, *The Metaphysical Club: A Story of Ideas in America* (New York: Farrar, Straus and Giroux, 2001), 428.

40. *Abrams v. United States*, 250 U.S. 616, 618 (1919).

41. Lewis, *Make No Law*, 69–75; Menand, *The Metaphysical Club*, 424–29.

42. *Abrams v. United States*, 630 (Justice Holmes dissenting).

43. Ibid.

44. Menand, *The Metaphysical Club*, 431.

45. *Gitlow v. New York*, 268 U.S. 652 (1925).

46. *Near v. Minnesota*, 283 U.S. 697 (1931).

47. *Whitney v. California*, 274 U.S. 357 (1927).

48. Lewis, *Make No Law*, 85.

49. Bradley C. Bobertz, "The Brandeis Gambit: The Making of America's 'First Freedom,' 1909–1931," *William & Mary Law Review* 40 (February 1999): 643.

50. Lewis, *Make No Law*, 86; see also Vincent Blasi, "The First Amendment and the Ideal of Civic Courage: The Brandeis Opinion in *Whitney v. California*," *William & Mary Law Review* 29 (Summer 1988): 684–89.

51. 274 U.S. at 375–76.

52. Blasi, "The First Amendment and the Ideal of Civic Courage," 683.

53. Menand, *The Metaphysical Club*, 431.

54. Ibid., xi.
55. Cohen, *The Reconstruction of American Liberalism*, 1–19. The historiography of American liberalism is broad and deep. Cohen's book is one of the more recent additions to this rich tradition of historical analysis.
56. U.S. Const., Fourteenth Amendment, sec. 1.
57. *Lochner v. New York*, 198 U.S. 45 (1905). For excellent discussions of the details of *Lochner* and Justice Oliver Wendell Holmes's dissent, see Menand, *The Metaphysical Club*, 421–22, and Lewis, *Make No Law*, 68n. For a discussion of Locke's conception of rights as a kind of property, see Cohen, *The Reconstruction of American Liberalism*, 6–7.
58. Cohen, *The Reconstruction of American Liberalism*, 239–40.
59. Walter Lippmann, *Liberty and the News* (1920; reprint, New Brunswick, N.J.: Transaction, 1995); Marion Tuttle Marzolf, *Civilizing Voices: American Press Criticism, 1880–1950* (New York: Longman, 1991), 123.
60. Bret Gary, *The Nervous Liberals: Propaganda Anxieties from World War I to the Cold War* (New York: Columbia University Press, 1999), 18–23.
61. Ronald Steel, foreword to *Liberty and the News*, by Walter Lippmann (Princeton, Princeton University Press, 2007), xviii.
62. Lippmann, *Public Opinion*, 10.
63. Ibid., 19.
64. Ibid.
65. John Dewey, "Public Opinion," *New Republic*, 3 May 1922, 215.
66. Lippmann, *Public Opinion*, 226.
67. Ibid., 228.
68. Ibid.
69. Lippmann, *Public Opinion*, 226.
70. John Durham Peters, "Democracy and American Mass Communication Theory: Dewey, Lippmann, Lazarsfeld," *Communication* 11 (1989): 210.
71. Lippmann, *Public Opinion*, 229.
72. In the three years that passed between Lippmann's publication of *Public Opinion* and his follow-up book, *The Phantom Public* (New York: Harcourt, Brace, 1925), his thinking had progressed to the point of a profound loss of faith in both scientific knowledge and democracy.
73. For a cogent discussion of the tenets of democratic realism, see Robert B. Westbrook, preface to *John Dewey and American Democracy* (Ithaca: Cornell University Press, 1991), xv–xvii.
74. See Robert D. Leigh, ed., Commission on Freedom of the Press, *A Free and Responsible Press: A General Report on Mass Communication* (Chicago: University of Chicago Press, 1947, 1974).
75. Peters, "Democracy and American Mass Communication Theory," 205.
76. Westbrook, *John Dewey and American Democracy*, xv.
77. Carl Bybee, "Can Democracy Survive in the Post-Factual Age? A Return to the Lippmann-Dewey Debate about the Politics of News," *Journalism Communication Monographs* 1 (Spring 1999): 34.
78. Dewey, *The Public and Its Problems*, 179–82.
79. Ibid., 208.
80. Ibid.
81. Ibid., 183.

82. Ibid.
83. Ibid., 184.
84. Ibid., 183–84.
85. Ibid., 184.
86. Ibid.
87. Peters, "Democracy and American Mass Communication Theory," 212.
88. Lippmann, *Liberty and the News*, 61.
89. Ibid., 66.
90. Ibid., 86.
91. Dewey, *The Public and Its Problems*, 167.
92. Ibid., 203.
93. Lewis, *Make No Law*, 154; Rosenberg, *Protecting the Best Men*, 238–39.
94. Rosenberg, *Protecting the Best Men*, 238.
95. Ibid.
96. Alexander Meiklejohn, *Free Speech and Its Relation to Self-Government* (New York: Harper and Brothers, 1948).
97. Ibid., 25–27.
98. Ibid., 37–39.
99. Alexander Meiklejohn, "The First Amendment Is an Absolute," *Supreme Court Review* 1961 (1961): 245.
100. Ibid., chap. 2, "Clear and Present Danger," 28–56 passim.
101. For example, see Robert C. Post, "Reconciling Theory and Doctrine in First Amendment Jurisprudence," *California Law Review* 88 (December 2000): 2353–74.
102. Meiklejohn, *Free Speech and Its Relation to Self-Government*, 87.
103. Ibid., 88.
104. Ibid., 25.
105. Ruth Walden, "A Government Action Approach to First Amendment Analysis," *Journalism Quarterly* 69 (Spring 1992): 65–66.
106. For an excellent discussion of Alexander Meiklejohn's collectivity theory of the First Amendment, see Robert C. Post, "Meiklejohn's Mistake: Individual Autonomy and the Reform of Public Discourse," *Colorado Law Review* 64 (Fall 1993): 1109–37.
107. Menand, *The Metaphysical Club*, 63, 430, 442.
108. Oliver Wendell Holmes Jr., *The Common Law* (1881), ed. Mark DeWolfe Howe (Boston: Little, Brown, 1963), and "The Path of the Law," *Harvard Law Review* 10 (1897): 991–1009.
109. Morton J. Horwitz, *The Transformation of American Law, 1870–1960: The Crisis of Legal Orthodoxy* (New York: Oxford University Press, 1992), 109.
110. Menand, *The Metaphysical Club*, 409.
111. *Abrams v. United States*, 630 (Justice Holmes dissenting).
112. Menand, *The Metaphysical Club*, 432–33.
113. *Abrams v. United States*, 630 (Justice Holmes dissenting).
114. Robert C. Post, "Reconciling Theory and Doctrine," 2360.
115. *Abrams v. United States*, 630 (Justice Holmes dissenting).
116. Westbrook, *John Dewey and American Democracy*, 41.
117. Bollinger, "The End of *New York Times v. Sullivan*," 41. First Amendment theorist Vincent Blasi offers an alternative value to self-governance as the basis for First Amendment protection of expression, one in line with realist democracy: the value

of checking governmental abuse of power. See Vincent Blasi, "The Checking Value in First Amendment Theory," *American Bar Foundation Research Journal* 3 (1977): 521–649.

118. *Masson v. New Yorker*, 686 F. Supp. 1396 (N.C. Cal. 1987) (granting summary judgment to defendants), *aff'd.*, 895 F.2d 1535 (9th Cir. 1989).

119. *Masson v. New Yorker*, 501 U.S. 496, 520.

120. Ibid.

121. Bollinger, "The End of *New York Times v. Sullivan*," 39.

122. Ibid.

123. *New York Times v. Sullivan*, 284, n. 23.

124. Ibid., 270.

125. Ibid., 271–72, quoting *N.A.A.C.P. v. Button*, 371 U.S. 415, 433 (1963).

126. Ibid., 279–80.

127. Ibid., 271, quoting *Cantwell v. Connecticut*, 310 U.S. 296, 310 (1940).

128. *Masson*, 501 U.S. 496, 517.

4. Libel at the *New Yorker*

1. Norman Rosenberg, *Protecting the Best Men: An Interpretive History of the Law of Libel* (Chapel Hill: University of North Carolina Press, 1986), 197–200.

2. Ibid., 199.

3. *New York Times Co. v. Sullivan*, 376 U.S. 254, 279–80 (1964) ("The constitutional guarantees require, we think, a federal rule that prohibits a public official from recovering damages for a defamatory falsehood relating to his official conduct unless he proves that the statement was made with 'actual malice'—that is, with knowledge that it was false or with reckless disregard of whether it was false or not").

4. Anthony Lewis, *Make No Law: The Sullivan Case and the First Amendment* (New York: Vintage Books, 1991), 157; W. Wat Hopkins, *Actual Malice: Twenty-five Years after Times v. Sullivan* (New York: Praeger, 1989), 49.

5. Harry Kalven Jr., "The New York Times Case: A Note on 'The Central Meaning of the First Amendment," *Supreme Court Review* (1964): 194–95; Lewis, *Make No Law*, 157.

6. See *Curtis Publishing Co. v. Butts*, 388 U.S. 130 (1967), and *Associated Press v. Walker*, 388 U.S. 130 (1967) (decided together in one opinion, holding that public figures must prove actual malice to prevail); *Gertz v. Robert Welch, Inc.*, 418 U.S. 323 (1974) (holding that famous and notorious persons are public figures "for all purposes and in all contexts"; that a person who "voluntarily injects himself or is drawn into a particular public controversy" becomes "a public figure for a limited range of issues" [351]; and that private persons must prove some level of fault to hold a media defendant liable for libel [347]); and *Philadelphia Newspapers, Inc. v. Hepps*, 475 U.S. 767, 769 (1986) (holding that private citizens involved in matters of public interest must prove falsity in order to prevail in a libel suit).

7. Rosenberg, *Protecting the Best Men*, 226.

8. Ibid., 208–15.

9. Lewis, *Make No Law*, 23.

10. Rosenberg, *Protecting the Best Men*, 225.

11. Ibid., 246–47; Susan Dente Ross and R. Kenton Bird, "The Ad That Changed Libel Law: Judicial Realism and Social Activism in *New York Times v. Sullivan*," *Communication*

Law and Policy 9 (2004): 521. In a concurrence to the majority opinion of *New York Times v. Sullivan*, 294–95, Justice Hugo Black wrote about other such speech-chilling uses of Alabama state libel law: "A second half-million-dollar libel verdict against the Times based on the same advertisement has already been awarded to another Commissioner. There a jury again gave the full amount claimed. There is no reason to believe that there are not more such huge verdicts lurking just around the corner for the Times or any other newspaper or broadcaster which might dare to criticize public officials. In fact, briefs before us show that in Alabama there are now pending eleven libel suits by local and state officials against the Times seeking $5,600,000, and five such suits against the Columbia Broadcasting System seeking $1,700,000."

12. Several of the most notable are Hopkins, *Actual Malice*; Leonard W. Levy, preface to *Emergence of a Free Press* (Chicago: Ivan R. Dee, 1985); Lewis, *Make No Law*; and Rosenberg, *Protecting the Best Men*.

13. *U.S. v. One Book Entitled Ulysses*, 72 F.2d 705 (C.C.A. 2d 1934); *U.S. v. 31 Photographs, Institute for Sex Research*, 156 F. Supp. 350 (S.D.N.Y. 1957).

14. Steven Brill, "The Way They Were," *American Lawyer* (June 1982): 1, 9.

15. Alexander Lindey, *Entertainment, Publishing, and the Arts: Agreements and the Law* (New York: C. Boardman, 1963–1977); reprinted as Alexander Lindey with Michael Landau, *Lindey on Entertainment, Publishing, and the Arts*, 3rd ed. (St Paul: West, 2004).

16. Alexander Lindey obituary, *New York Times*, 12 November 1981, D23. In addition to representing the *New Yorker*, Lindey also served as counsel for the American Newspaper Guild and the Newspaper Guild of New York.

17. Morris L. Ernst and Alexander Lindey, *Hold Your Tongue! Adventures in Libel and Slander* (1932; reprint, London: Methuen, 1936), 291.

18. *New Yorker* Records, Manuscripts and Archives Division, New York Public Library, Astor, Lenox and Tilden Foundations (hereafter NYR).

19. Ben Yagoda, *About Town: The New Yorker and the World It Made* (New York: Scribner, 2000), 79. For a discussion of the magazine's growth into a cultural icon, see Mary F. Corey, *The World through a Monocle: The New Yorker at Midcentury* (Cambridge: Harvard University Press, 1999).

20. R. Hawley Truax, Treasurer, *New Yorker*, to Robin Boyd, visiting professor, MIT, October 24, 1956, and Truax to Boyd, 19 November 1956, NYR, Box 1318, "Milton Greenstein/R. Hawley Truax," Folder 2, "Law-Notes on Libel, 1956–1967."

21. Yagoda, *About Town*, 78–79. Lewis Mumford was the *New Yorker* critic most responsible for the magazine's architectural criticism. He began writing such pieces for the *New Yorker* in 1931 in the "Skylines" column and continued until 1963.

22. J. A. Stevenson Jr., Esq., to James Thurber, n.d., NYR, Box 3, Folder "Thurber, James—Libel Case."

23. T-Square, "The Sky Line," *New Yorker*, 16 October 1926, 61.

24. Stevenson to Thurber, n.d.

25. Only four years after the Delmonico case, the Court of Appeals of New York decided an important libel case in which it affirmed that criticisms of matters of public interest "are not libelous, however severe in their terms, unless they are written maliciously." *Hoeppner v. Dunkirk Printing Company*, 254 N.Y. 95, 99 (Ct. App. 1930). Citing a libel case decided by the Supreme Court of Maine in 1896, *Bearce v. Bass*, 88 Me. 521 (S.C. Me., 1896), the court noted that "the architecture of public buildings" was one of many

"legitimate subjects of newspaper criticism." *Hoeppner*, 99. Although the *New Yorker* was clearly not a newspaper, the principle, of course, applied to its articles. Another opinion of the New York Court of Appeals, this one written in 1904, well before the *New Yorker's* Delmonico affair, explained the libel defense of fair comment or criticism as making a distinction between defamation and legitimate criticism: "It [criticism] never attacks the individual, but only his work"; see *Triggs v. Sun Printing & Publishing Assn.*, 179 N.Y. 144, 156 (Ct. App. 1904). The judge who refused to dismiss the Delmonico case missed this vital point. More generally, the common law privilege of fair comment, an import from English law, was firmly entrenched in American jurisprudence well before the Delmonico case. Robert Neal Webner, "The Fact-Opinion Distinction in First Amendment Libel Law: The Need for a Bright-Line Rule," *Georgetown Law Journal* 72 (1984): 1819–20.

26. *Severance v. F. R. Publishing Co.*, 222 N.Y.S. 898 (1927).
27. James Thurber, *The Years with Ross* (1957; reprint, New York: Perennial Classics, 2001), 181–82.
28. Truax to Boyd, 24 October and 19 November 1956. In the second letter Truax wrote, "The case was never tried on the merits, for it was while the case was awaiting trial that the matter was disposed of by settlement out of court." In the first letter he wrote, "We believed at the time, and have been borne out by court decisions in recent years, that the court's conclusion in this case was based on a misunderstanding of the law."
29. Although the state of New York developed a liberal privilege for the libel of public officials in *Bingham v. Gaynor*, 203 N.Y. 27 (1911)—that is, false statements made without malice and with belief in their truth were privileged—this privilege would not have extended to the alleged libel of an architect. See Clifton O. Lawhorne, *Defamation and Public Officials* (Carbondale: Southern Illinois University Press, 1971), 137.
30. Stevenson to Thurber, n.d.
31. Madeline E. DeFina, Attorney at Law (Brooklyn), to *New Yorker*, 8 April 1932, NYR, Box 1312, Folder 12, "Greenbaum, Wolff & Ernst, 1932–1937." The magazine used the legal services of Engelhard, Pollak, Pitcher & Stern to handle the DeFina complaint.
32. Alexander Woollcott, "In Behalf of an Absentee," *New Yorker*, 9 April 1932, 36–37.
33. "Cedarholm Suspect 'Fears' to Tell All," *New York Times*, 22 November 1930, 36.
34. Woollcott, "In Behalf of an Absentee."
35. Katharine White to Walter Pollak, Esq., 9 April 1932, NYR, Box 1312, Folder 12.
36. Wolcott Gibbs to Katharine White regarding telephone conversation with Lyman Sessen of Cullen & Dykman, 11 April 1932, NYR, Box 1312, Folder 12. The *New York Times* covered the Cedarholm-Hall affair quite thoroughly. See "To Sift Murder Hint in Cedarholm Case," 11 April 1930, 25; "Suspect Is Silent on Miss Cedarholm," 21 November 1930, 25; "Cedarholm Suspect 'Fears' to Tell All," 22 November 1930, 36; "Cedarholm Case Up Today," 10 September 1931, 17; "Hall Goes to Trial in Cedarholm Case," 29 September 1931, 7; "Hall Ready to Talk," 9 March 1932, 15.
37. Engelhard, Pollak, Pitcher & Stern to Madeline E. DeFina, 13 April 1932, NYR, Box 1312, Folder 12.
38. Pollak to *New Yorker*, 13 April 1932, NYR, Box 1312, Folder 12.
39. White to Ernst, 17 November 1932, NYR, Box 1312, Folder 12.
40. F. R. Bellamy to Mr. Hellman and Mr. Johnston, cc. Harold Ross, Katharine White, and Wolcott Gibbs, 9 May 1933, NYR, Box 1312, Folder 12.
41. Yagoda, *About Town*, 202–3.

42. Thomas Kunkel, *Genius in Disguise: Harold Ross of The New Yorker* (New York: Random House, 1995), 262–63.

43. Yagoda, *About Town*, 202.

44. J. O. Whedon to Alexander Lindey, 16 June 1936, NYR, Box 1312, Folder 12.

45. J. O. Whedon to Alexander Lindey, 13 February 1936, NYR, Box 1312, Folder 12.

46. Yagoda, *About Town*, 136–37.

47. St. Clair McKelway to J. O. Whedon, 14 June 1937, NYR, Box 1312, Folder 12.

48. Charles Brand to F. R. Publishing Corporation, 22 November 1932, NYR, Box 1312, Folder 12.

49. J. O. Whedon to Alexander Lindey of Greenbaum, Wolff & Ernst, 23 November 1937, NYR, Box 1312, Folder 12.

50. *New Yorker* to Charles Brand, 23 November 1937, NYR, Box 1312, Folder 12.

51. Harold L. Herzfelder, President, The Fan Company, to *New Yorker*, 25 February 1938, NYR, Box 1312, Folder 12.

52. Kristofer Allerfeldt, "Race and Restriction: Anti-Asian Immigration Pressures in the Pacific North-West of America during the Progressive Era, 1885–1924," *History* 88 (2003): 73; Nathan M. Becker, "The Anti-Japanese Boycott in the United States," *Far Eastern Survey*, 1 March 1939, 49.

53. Ik Shuman to Herzfelder, 3 March 1938, NYR, Box 1312, Folder 13, "Greenbaum, Wolff & Ernst, 1938–1941."

54. Annual Summary, Greenbaum, Wolff & Ernst to Raoul H. Fleischmann, *The New Yorker*, 4 June 1942, NYR, Box 1312, Folder 15, "Greenbaum, Wolff & Ernst, 1942."

55. *Sidis v. F-R Publishing Corporation*, 113 F. 2d 806 (C.C.A. 2d 1940), NYR, Box 1313, "Greenbaum, Wolff & Ernst," Folders 5–6, "Court Cases-*William Sidis v. The New Yorker*, 1940–1944." See Jared L. Manley (pseudonym of Barbara Linscott), "Where Are They Now? April Fool!" *New Yorker*, 14 August 1937, 26.

56. *Sidis v. F-R Publishing Corporation*, 34 F. Supp. 19 (S.D.N.Y. 1938), NYR, Box 1313, Folders 5–6.

57. 113 F. 2d 806, 811 (C.C.A. 2d 1940), NYR, Box 1313, Folders 5–6. The Second Circuit Court found "the facts necessary to support the third claim to be sufficiently different from those relied on to support the other claims so as to make the dismissal order appealable." Judge Clark, who wrote the opinion, dissented on this point, "for here a judgment against recovery for violation of privacy should be *res judicata* [an affirmative defense] against later claims of libel."

58. Ibid.

59. Office of the Clerk, Supreme Court of the United States, to Morris L. Ernst, Esq., 16 December 1940, NYR, Box 1313, Folders 5–6.

60. See NYR, Box 1313, Folders 5–6.

61. Summaries of law review articles on *Sidis* Courts of Appeals ruling, from *Columbia Law Review* (November 1940), *University of Pennsylvania Law Review* (December 1940), *New York University Law Quarterly Review* (November 1940), all in NYR, Box 1313, Folders 5–6.

62. *University of Pennsylvania Law Review* (December 1940): 251.

63. See NYR, Box 1313, Folders 5–6.

64. Alexander Lindey to Harold Ross, 24 July 1940, NYR, Box 1313, Folders 5–6. The "intimate details" of Sidis's private life were largely revealed in two paragraphs of the profile:

William James Sidis lives today, at the age of thirty-nine, in a hall bedroom of Boston's shabby south end. For a picture of him and his activities, this record is indebted to a young woman who recently succeeded in interviewing him there. She found him in a small room papered with a design of huge, pinkish flowers, considerably discolored. There was a large, untidy bed and an enormous wardrobe trunk, standing half open. A map of the United States hung on one wall. On a table beside the door was a pack of streetcar transfers neatly held together with an elastic. On a dresser were two photographs, one (surprisingly enough) of Sidis as the boy genius, the other of a sweet-faced girl with shell-rimmed glasses and elaborate marcel wave. There was also a desk with a tiny, ancient typewriter, a World Almanac, a dictionary, a few reference books, and a library book which the young man's visitor picked up. "Oh, gee," said Sidis, "that's just one of those crook stories." He directed her attention to the little typewriter. "You can pick it up with one finger," he said, and did so.

William Sidis at thirty-nine is a large, heavy man, with a prominent jaw, a thickish neck, and a reddish mustache. His light hair falls down over his brow as it did the night he lectured to the professors in Cambridge. His eyes have an expression which varies from the ingenuous to the wary. When he is wary, he has a kind of incongruous dignity which breaks down suddenly into the gleeful abandon of a child on holiday. He seems to have difficulty in finding the right words to express himself, but when he does, he speaks rapidly, nodding his head jerkily to emphasize his points, gesturing with his left hand, uttering occasionally a curious, gasping laugh. He seems to get a great and ironic enjoyment out of leading a life of wandering irresponsibility after a childhood of scrupulous regimentation. His visitor found in him a certain childlike charm.

Manley, "Where Are They Now? April Fool!" 25–26.

65. Alexander Lindey to Ik Shuman, 2 February 1943, NYR, Box 1313, Folder 6.
66. Ibid., Folders 5–6.
67. Alexander Lindey to T. M. Brassel, 21 December 1943, NYR, Box 1313, Folders 5–6.
68. Lindey to Shuman, 17 November 1943, NYR, Box 1313, Folders 5–6.
69. Shuman to Lindey, 18 November 1943, NYR, Box 1313, Folders 5–6.
70. *Sidis v. F-R Publishing Corporation*, Plaintiff's Bill of Particulars (no. L-71–153), filed in the U.S. District Court, Southern District of New York, 10 January 1944. Curiously, the bill of particulars lists the claims and statements in the disputed article that are true and asserts that everything else in the article is false. Sidis alleged "that the article . . . is false in its entirety in that it presents an entirely false picture of the plaintiff and that each and every part thereof contributes to said falsity."
71. Annual Summary of Services, Greenbaum, Wolff & Ernst, Alexander Lindey to Raoul H. Fleishmann, 1941–1942 Report, Memorandum C, NYR, Box 1314, "Greenbaum, Wolff & Ernst," Folder 1, "Services Rendered, Summaries of, 1938–1942."
72. Lindey to Brassel, 21 December 1943, NYR, Box 1313, Folders 5–6.
73. Annual Summary of Services, Greenbaum, Wolff & Ernst, Alexander Lindey to Raoul H. Fleishmann, 1939–1940 Report, NYR, Box 1314, Folder 1.
74. "Good Will Sidis," *Harvard Magazine* (March 1998), http://www.harvardmag.com/issues/ma98/pump.html (30 April 2005).
75. T. M. Brassel to Harold Ross, 18 August 1944, NYR, Box 1313, Folders 4–5; "Good Will Sidis."

76. Annual Summary of Services, Greenbaum, Wolff & Ernst, Alexander Lindey to Raoul H. Fleishmann, 1939–1940 Report, NYR, Box 1314, Folder 1.

77. Wolcott Gibbs and E. F. Kinkead, "Profiles: Lady of the Cats," *New Yorker*, 14 May 1938, 21.

78. Alexander Lindey to Ik Shuman, 8 July 1938, NYR, Box 1313, Folder 4, "Court Cases— Rita Ross v. The New Yorker, 1938–1943."

79. Rita Ross to Lindey, n.d., NYR, Box 1313, Folder 4.

80. Alexander Lindey to Ik Shuman, 18 August 1938, NYR, Box 1313, Folder 4.

81. Lindey to Shuman, 16 September 1938, NYR, Box 1313, Folder 4.

82. Shuman to Lindey, 29 November 1938, NYR, Box 1313, Folder 4.

83. Rita Ross to Lindey, quoted in Lindey to Shuman, 21 September 1939, NYR, Box 1313, Folder 4.

84. Bill of Particulars, Breach of Contract Claim, *Rita Ross v. New Yorker*, n.d., NYR, Box 1313, Folder 4.

85. Annual Summary of Services, Greenbaum, Wolff & Ernst, Alexander Lindey to Raoul H. Fleishmann, 1939–1940 Report, NYR, Box 1314, Folder 1.

86. Lindey to Shuman, 9 January 1939, NYR, Box 1313, Folder 4.

87. Eugene Kinkead to Ik Shuman, 10 January 1939, NYR, Box 1313, Folder 4.

88. Lindey to Shuman, 23 January 1939, NYR, Box 1313, Folder 4.

89. Lindey to Shuman, 23 March 1939, NYR, Box 1313, Folder 4.

90. Lindey to Shuman, 28 September 1939, NYR, Box 1313, Folder 4.

91. Ibid.

92. Lindey to Shuman, 6 November 1939, NYR, Box 1313, Folder 4.

93. Ibid. Shuman to Lindey, 8 November 1939, NYR, Box 1313, Folder 4.

94. Shuman to Lindey, 8 November 1939; Lindey to Shuman, 26 February 1940, NYR, Box 1313, Folder 4.

95. Lindey to Shuman, 19 September 1940, NYR, Box 1313, Folder 4.

96. Lindey to Shuman, quoting Rita Ross postcard to Lindey dated 3 February 1941, 14 February 1941, NYR, Box 1313, Folder 4.

97. Annual Summary of Services, Greenbaum, Wolff & Ernst, Alexander Lindey to Raoul H. Fleishmann, 1941–1942 Report, Memorandum C, NYR, Box 1314, Folder 1.

98. Harold Stern to Ik Shuman, 6 December 1943, NYR, Box 1313, Folder 4.

99. Richard Boyer, "Profiles: The Hot Bach III," *New Yorker*, 8 July 1944, 12, NYR, Box 1297, "Complaints by Readers—Court Cases," Folder 4, "*Schwartz, Julius "Yankee" v. F-R Corporation* (Settled), 1945."

100. Shwartz Complaint, Supreme Court of the State of New York, County of New York, 10 January 1945, NYR, Box 1297, Folder 4.

101. Theodora S. Zavin, Greenbaum, Wolff & Ernst, to F. S. Norman, The New Yorker, 1 October 1945, NYR, Box 1297, Folder 4.

102. The Office of Price Administration was a federal agency established during World War II to control inflation.

103. Theodora S. Zavin, Greenbaum, Wolff & Ernst, to F. S. Norman, The New Yorker.

104. R. H. Fleischmann to Mr. Norman, *New Yorker* interoffice memo, 14 November 1945, NYR, Box 1297, Folder 4.

105. Earl Schiek to Gentlemen at the *New Yorker*, 20 May 1948, NYR Box 1318, Folder 1.

106. "Apologia" printed at end of Thurber's fifth article in "Soapland" series, galley proofs, NYR, Box 1318, Folder 1. See also Thurber, *The Years with Ross*, 184.

107. Alexander Lindey to James Thurber, 7 July 1948, NYR, Box 1318, Folder 1.
108. Alexander Lindey to Hawley Truax, 7 June 1948, NYR, Box 1318, Folder 1.
109. Thurber, "Apologia."
110. Alexander Lindey to James Thurber, 7 July 1948, NYR, Box 1318, Folder 1.
111. Yagoda, *About Town*, 88–89. See also Thurber, *The Years with Ross*, 3–17.
112. James Thurber to Hawley Truax, 26 May 1948, NYR, Box 1318, Folder 1.
113. Ibid.
114. Ben Yagoda, *About Town*, 187–88, 203–5.
115. For another description of the *New Yorker*'s editorial processes, particularly under Ross, see Kunkel, *Genius in Disguise*, 265–67.
116. Yagoda, *About Town*, 200.
117. James Thurber to Hawley Truax, 26 May 1948, NYR, Box 1318, Folder 1.
118. Thurber, *The Years with Ross*, 184.
119. Walter Bernstein, "A Reporter at Large: Mingle!" *New Yorker*, 14 June 1950, 60.
120. *Fybish v. New Yorker*, transcript of verbal "opinion" delivered by Judge Streit, 13 May 1955, NYR, Box 1297, Folder 2.
121. Alexander Lindey to Lowenbraun & Lowell, 16 November 1950, NYR, Box 1297, Folder 2.
122. According to Brendan Gill's memoirs of his days as a writer and critic at the *New Yorker*, Hawley Truax served for many years as the only means of communication between editor Harold Ross and publisher Raoul Fleischmann. Brendan Gill, *Here at the New Yorker* (New York: Random House, 1975), 35.
123. Lindey to Milton Greenstein, 31 July 1951, NYR, Box 1297, Folder 2.
124. Lindey to Greenstein, 30 October 1951, NYR, Box 1297, Folder 2.
125. Lindey to Greenstein, 9 October 1952, NYR, Box 1297, Folder 2. Greenstein also served as a go-between for the editorial and business sides of the magazine. He was one of the few at the *New Yorker* who was able to move between the two famously separate departments. See Gigi Mahon, *The Last Days of The New Yorker* (New York: McGraw-Hill, 1988), 70.
126. Lindey to Greenstein, 13 January 1953, NYR, Box 1297, Folder 2.
127. *Fybish v. New Yorker*, transcript of verbal "opinion" delivered by Judge Streit.
128. William G. Klehm, counsel for Wells Church, to Raoul H. Fleischmann, president of The New Yorker Magazine, Inc., 4 March 1954, NYR, Box 1296, Folder 1.
129. Klehm to Hawley Truax, 4 March 1954, NYR, Box 1296, Folder 1.
130. Charles Wertenbaker to William Shawn, 17 May 1954, NYR, Box 1296, Folder 1.
131. Wertenbaker apparently was in the habit of signing all his correspondence and even contracts with a blue crayon. In a letter accompanying his note of apology for Church, sent first to the *New Yorker*, he wrote, "If he [i.e., Church's lawyer] objects to the signature in crayon, please tell him that I sign all my communications that way, including checks, leases, contracts, and my will; that a signature in ink would have lacked 'the characteristic of a personal communication'; that I consider his demand for an inky signature an unwarranted invasion of my privacy and an attempt to impose conformity, which as a citizen I feel bound to resist; and that I have just left for Johannesburg." Lindey included this excerpt from Wertenbaker's letter dated 8 September 1954 in his communication to Church's lawyer enclosing the final apology letter. It seems that Lindey included the second part of the excerpt, perhaps by mistake, against Milton Greenstein's wishes. Lindey to Klehm, with handwritten note by M.G. [Milton Greenstein], 13 September 1954, NYR, Box 1296, Folder 1.

132. Another libel suit filed in the early sixties, *Denham & Ballet Russe de Monte Carlo v. New Yorker*, involved a claim for a significant damage award, this time in the amount of $100,000. The alleged libel occurred in a 1960 *New Yorker* profile on the choreographer George Balanchine. The plaintiffs never pressed the case to trial. NYR, Box 1296, Folder 12.

133. Defendant's Trial Memorandum, draft, *Filler v. New Yorker*, 13 February 1958, NYR, Box 1297, Folder 13.

134. File memorandum re: *Filler-Whittey v. New Yorker*, Alexander Lindey, 16 September 1955, NYR, Box 1297, Folder 13.

135. Alexander Lindey to Milton Greenstein, 13 September 1955, NYR, Box 1297, Folder 13.

136. Alexander Lindey to John Sinai, Esq., Reno, Nevada, 2 October 1956, NYR, Box 1297, Folder 13.

137. Lindey to Greenstein, 27 September 1956, NYR, Box 1297, Folder 13.

138. Yagoda, *About Town*, 401; David Remnick, "Life and Letters: Reporting It All," *New Yorker*, 22 March 2004, http://www.newyorker.com/printables/fact/040329fa_fact1 (3 April 2005). Remnick wrote of Liebling's feature writing in his newspaper days: "One of the commonplaces of feature writing at the time was a tendency to embroider. That is, there was a lot of making things up or, as the very least, helping things along. What is now a hanging offense was then a risible misdemeanor. Details were embellished, colors heightened, dialogue faked." According to Yagoda, the same could be said of some of Liebling's fact writing for the *New Yorker*.

139. Lindey to Greenstein, 19 October 1962, NYR, Box 1296, Folder 13.

140. Ved Mehta, "Onward and Upward with the Arts: A Battle against the Bewitchment of our Intelligence," *New Yorker*, 9 December 1961, 59–158.

141. Ibid., 96. Mehta goes on to quote Gellner saying: "Muggeridge attacked royalty, and the B.B.C. immediately took him off the payroll. I attached the philosophical Establishment, and as long as the present philosophers remain in power, I will never have a position at an Oxford college." Muggeridge was a well-known print, radio, and television journalist and writer in England from the 1930s through the 1970s. See Roger Kimball, "Malcolm Muggeridge's Journey," *New Criterion* 21 (June 2003), http://www.newcriterion.com/archive/21/jun03/mugger.htm (10 April 2005).

142. Ernest Gellner to The Editors, *New Yorker*, 27 December 1961, NYR, Box 1296, Folder 4.

143. Draft letter, William Shawn to Ernest Gellner, 15 January 1962, NYR, Box 1296, Folder 4.

144. Ibid.

145. Lindey to Greenstein, 17 January 1962, NYR, Box 1296, Folder 4.

146. Ved Mehta, *Remembering Mr. Shawn's New Yorker* (Woodstock, N.Y.: Overlook Press, 1998), 143.

147. Alexander Lindey to David Fromkin, Esq. (Gellner's lawyer in New York), 24 January 1962, NYR, Box 1296, Folder 4.

148. Bertrand Russell, The Earl Russell, to Ernest Gellner, copy, 28 December 1961, NYR, Box 1296, Folder 4.

149. Ernest Gellner to Ayer (apparently A. J., or Freddie, Ayer), copy, 6 January 1962, NYR, Box 1296, Folder 4.

150. Mehta, *Remembering Mr. Shawn's New Yorker*, 143.

151. Gellner to Ayer.

152. George Woodward, London office, *New Yorker*, to Milton Greenstein, 6 April 1962, and Greenstein to Woodward, 10 April 1962, NYR, Box 1296, Folder 4.

153. Milton Greenstein to Ved Mehta, 10 October 1962, NYR, Box 1296, Folder 4.

154. Ved Mehta, "A Battle against the Bewitchment of Our Intelligence," in *Fly and the Fly-Bottle: Encounters with British Intellectuals* (Boston: Atlantic Monthly Press, 1963), 38.

155. Annual Summary of Services, Greenbaum, Wolff & Ernst, Alexander Lindey to Raoul Fleischmann, 8 June 1948, NYR, Box 1314, Folder 2. In another case of alleged libel, the *New Yorker* settled, for $500, with an aggrieved woman whose telephone number appeared on one of the magazine's cover cartoons, but only after she pressed her claim in court.

156. Annual Summary of Services, Memorandum C, Greenbaum, Wolff & Ernst, Alexander Lindey to Raoul Fleischmann, 4 June 1942, NYR, Box 1314, Folder 1.

157. Annual summary of Services, Greenbaum, Wolff & Ernst, Alexander Lindey to Raoul Fleischmann, 11 June 1940, NYR, Box 1314, Folder 1.

158. H. W. Ross to Mr. Mason, 9 May 1946, NYR, Box 1318, Folder 1.

159. H. W. Ross to Mr. Greenstein, 29 May 1946, NYR, Box 1318, Folder 1.

160. Alexander Lindey, "What Price Libel? Memorandum," 1 July 1964, NYR, Box 1318, Folder 2.

161. Ibid.

162. Ibid.

163. Ibid.

164. *Rushford v. New Yorker*, 846 F.2d 249 (4th Cir. 1988); *Levin v. McPhee, New Yorker, & Farrar, Straus & Giroux*, 119 F.3d 189 (2nd Cir. 1997); *Miracle v. New Yorker*, 190 F. Supp. 2d 1192 (D. Haw. 2001).

165. Anthony Lewis, "Stranger Than Fiction," op-ed, *New York Times*, 25 August 1995, A27.

166. James Atlas, "Stranger Than Fiction," *New York Times Magazine*, 23 June 1991, 22; Deirdre Carmody, "Despite Malcolm Trial, Editors Elsewhere Vouch for Accuracy of Their Work," *New York Times*, 30 May 1993, sec. 1, 26; Deirdre Carmody, "Do Speakers Really Say What Is between Quotation Marks?" *New York Times*, 21 June 1991, A12; Roger Cohen, "Writers Mobilizing against Restrictions on Using Quotations," *New York Times*, 20 February 1991, C11; Fred. W. Friendly, "Was Trust Betrayed?" *New York Times*, 25 February 1990, sec. 7, 1; Alex S. Jones, "Ideas and Trends: Just How Sacrosanct Are the Words inside Quotation Marks," *New York Times*, 20 January 1991, sec. 4, 6; Anna Quindlen, "Public and Private: Quote Unquote," *New York Times*, 19 May 1993, A19; Jane Gross, "Editor Recalls Overriding Lawyer on a Quotation in Dispute," *New York Times*, 20 May 1993, A19.

167. *Masson v. New Yorker*, 501 U.S. 496, 513 (1991).

168. *Masson v. New Yorker*, 960 F.2d 896, 902 (9th Cir. 1992).

5. *Masson v. New Yorker* in the Early Years

1. Rodney A. Smolla, "Let the Author Beware: The Rejuvenation of the American Law of Libel," *University of Pennsylvania Law Review* (December 1983): 1; Seth Goodchild, "Media Counteractions: Restoring the Balance to Modern Libel Law," *Georgetown Law Journal* (October 1986): 315; Michael F. Mayer, *The Libel Revolution: A New Look at Defamation and Privacy* (New York: Law Arts, 1987), 213.

2. Smolla, "Let the Author Beware," 11.

3. Ibid., 19–20. See also Mayer, *The Libel Revolution*, 213; Rodney A. Smolla, *Suing the Press* (New York: Oxford University Press, 1986), 24.

4. Randall P. Bezanson, Gilbert Cranberg, and John Soloski, *Libel Law and the Press: Myth and Reality* (New York: Free Press, 1987), 122.

5. Marc A. Franklin, "Suing Media for Libel: A Litigation Study," *American Bar Foundation Research Journal* (Summer 1981): 829.

6. *LDRC Bulletin*, no. 4, pt. 1 (Summer 1982): 3; *LDRC Bulletin*, no. 11 (Summer–Fall 1984): 2.

7. Michael Newcity, "Libel Law Then and Now: A Review Essay," *Wisconsin Law Review* (March 1989): 385–97. See also Randall P. Bezanson, "Libel Law and the Realities of Litigation: Setting the Record Straight," *Iowa Law Review* 71 (October 1985): 227.

8. Newcity, "Libel Law Then and Now," 397.

9. *Westmoreland v. CBS*, no. 82 Civ. 7913 (S.D.N.Y., suit withdrawn, 18 February 1985), reported in M. A. Farber, "A Joint Statement Ends Libel Action by Westmoreland," *New York Times*, 19 February 1985, A1.

10. *Tavoulareas v. Piro*, 759 F.2d 90, *vacated*, 763 F.2d 1472 (D.C. Cir. 1985) (*en banc*); Lee Levine, "Judge and Jury in the Law of Defamation: Putting the Horse behind the Cart," *American University Law Review* 35 (Fall 1985): 27; William A. Henry III, "Libel Law: Good Intentions Gone Awry," *Time*, 4 March 1985, 93; William A. Henry III, "It Was the Best I Could Get," *Time*, 4 March 1985, 70.

11. Norman Rosenberg, *Protecting the Best Men: An Interpretive History of the Law of Libel* (Chapel Hill: University of North Carolina Press, 1986), 252.

12. James Boylan, "Declarations of Independence," *Columbia Journalism Review* (November–December 1986): 41–42.

13. Michael Schudson, "Watergate: A Study in Mythology," *Columbia Journalism Review* (May–June 1992): 32.

14. Smolla, *Suing the Press*, 9.

15. Boylan, "Declarations of Independence," 41.

16. Michael Schudson, *Discovering the News: A Social History of American Newspapers* (New York: Basic Books, 1978), 175–77; quote on 176.

17. Ibid., 172–75.

18. Smolla, *Suing the Press*, 9.

19. Clifford Christians, "Enforcing Media Codes," *Journal of Mass Media Ethics* (Fall–Winter 1985–86): 15.

20. Casey Bukro, "The SPJ Code's Double-Edged Sword: Accountability, Credibility," *Journal of Mass Media Ethics* (Fall–Winter 1985–86): 11.

21. H. Eugene Goodwin, *Groping for Ethics in Journalism* (Ames: Iowa State University Press, 1983): 14–15.

22. Ibid., 16–17.

23. Philip Meyer, *Ethical Journalism* (New York: Longman, 1986), 168–72.

24. *Burnett v. National Enquirer, Inc.*, 144 Ca. App. 3d 991 (Cal. Ct. App. 1983).

25. Robert Lindsey, "Carol Burnett Given $1.6 Million in Suit against National Enquirer," *New York Times*, 27 March 1981, A1.

26. *Burnett v. National Enquirer, Inc.*, 1012.

27. UPI, "Burnett Libel Award Cut," *Los Angeles Times*, 20 July 1983, C17.

28. Jonathan Friendly, "In Libel Suits, Juries Exact Damaging Dues for Damaged Reputations," *New York Times*, 5 April 1981, sec. 4, 8.

29. *New York Times v. Sullivan*, 376 U.S. 254 (1964).

30. "A Five Year Legal Toothache," *Time*, 23 March 1981, 90; "Enquirer Belted," *Time*, 6 April 1981, 77; "The Libel Exception," *Nation*, 11 April 1981, 1; Eve Pell, "Libel As a Political Weapon," *Nation*, 6 June 1981, 681, 698–700.

31. Jonathan Friendly, "Double-Edge Challenge to Press Freedom," *New York Times*, 27 March 1981, A17.

32. Ibid.

33. Stuart Taylor Jr., "Washington Post Assessed $2 Million for Libel." *New York Times*, 31 July 1982, sec. 1, 1.

34. UPI, "Mobil President Sues Paper," *New York Times*, 27 November 1980, D5; AP, "Trial Opens in Mobil Libel Suit," *New York Times*, 8 July 1982, B16.

35. Stuart Taylor Jr., "Post Libel Verdict Worries the Press," *New York Times*, 1 August 1982, sec. 1, 20.

36. Stuart Taylor Jr., "Court Reinstates a Ruling of Libel of Mobil Oil Chief," *New York Times*, 10 April 1985, A1; *Tavoulareas v. Washington Post Co.*, 567 F. Supp. 651 (D.D.C. 1983); *Tavoulareas v. Piro*, 759 F.2d 90 (D.C. Cir. 1985).

37. *Tavoulareas v. Piro*, 759 F.2d 90, 120.

38. *Herbert v. Lando*, 441 U.S. 153 (1979).

39. *Tavoulareas v. Piro*, 759 F.2d 90, 145.

40. Ibid., 155.

41. Ibid., 166.

42. Anthony Lewis, "Getting Even," op-ed, *New York Times*, 11 April 1985, A27.

43. Eleanor Randolph, "Editors, Lawyers Say Libel Award against Post May Alter Journalism," *Washington Post*, 11 April 1985, A3.

44. *Tavoulareas v. Piro*, 817 F.2d 762, 766 (D.C. Cir. 1987) (en banc).

45. Ibid., 797.

46. Ibid.

47. Consider, for example, that the *New York Times* published approximately forty articles in this time period on the Tavoulareas case. Although the articles certainly did not demonize the *Washington Post*'s reporting, few would argue that such wide publicizing of the case and the charges against the *Post* would not have damaged, at least mildly, the newspaper's public image.

48. Mobil Corporation, "Are the Media Giving Us the Facts?" display ad, *New York Times*, 15 September 1983, sec. A, 27; Nicholas J. Jollymore, "Megaverdicts' Threat to Media Is No Myth," letter to the editor, *New York Times*, 1 October 1983, sec. 1, 26.

49. Mobil Corporation, "Are the Media Giving Us the Facts?"

50. Newcity, "Libel Law Then and Now," 364; *Westmoreland v. CBS*, reported in Farber, "A Joint Statement Ends Libel Action," A1; *Sharon v. Time*, no. 83 Civ. 4660 (S.D.N.Y., jury found in favor of *Time*, 24 January 1985), reported in David Margolick, "Sharon Case and the Law," *New York Times*, 25 January 1985, B4.

51. Newcity, "Libel Law Then and Now," 365.

52. Charles Mohr, "Westmoreland Denies He Underestimated Enemy," *New York Times*, 27 January 1982, A11.

53. "A General Surrenders," editorial, *New York Times*, 19 February 1985, A22.

54. Sally Bedell, "Westmoreland Files Libel Suit against CBS," *New York Times*, 14 September 1982, C9; M. A. Farber, "A Joint Statement Ends Libel Action"; Charles Mohr, "Westmoreland and Sharon: 2 Very Different Styles," *New York Times*, 18 November

1984, sec. 1, 45. A search of the *New York Times* Historical Index using the keywords "Westmoreland" and "CBS" finds that the paper has published a total of over two hundred items over the years about the Westmoreland-CBS dispute.

55. Sally Bedell, "CBS Follow-up on Vietnam Running into Snags," *New York Times*, 28 August 1982, sec. 1, 44.

56. Jonathan Friendly, "CBS Producer Defends Program on Vietnam," *New York Times*, 17 July 1982, sec. 1, 44.

57. Frank J. Prial, "CBS Vietnam Documentary Faulted," *New York Times*, 21 April 1983, C28.

58. Mary Thornton, "Libel Experts Warn of Repercussions: Westmoreland Case Could Inhibit Investigative Journalism," *Washington Post*, 19 February 1985, A11.

59. Jonathan Friendly, "20 Years After Key Libel Ruling, Debate Goes On," *New York Times*, 9 March 1984, A1.

60. Mohr, "Westmoreland and Sharon: 2 Very Different Styles."

61. "Sharon Files Suit against Magazine," *New York Times*, 1 March 1983, A8; David Margolick, "Sharon v. Time Inc.: Battleground Is the Courtroom," *New York Times*, 6 April 1984, B1.

62. Margolick, "Sharon Case and the Law."

63. Ibid.; *Sharon v. Time, Inc.*, 575 F. Supp. 1162, 1165–73 (S.D.N.Y. 1983).

64. Arnold H. Lubasch, "Time Cleared of Libeling Sharon but Jurors Criticize Its Reporting," *New York Times*, 25 January 1985, A1; Margolick, "Sharon Case and the Law."

65. "Beyond an Absence of Malice," editorial, *New York Times*, 25 January 1985, A26.

66. Sam Zagoria, "The Meaning of the Libel Trials," op-ed, *Washington Post*, 20 February 1985, A20.

67. Peter McGrath and Nancy Stadtman, "Absence of Malice," *Newsweek*, 4 February 1985, 52.

68. Zagoria, "The Meaning of Libel Trials."

69. Ibid.

70. Janet Cooke, "Jimmy's World," *Washington Post*, 28 September 1980, A1.

71. David L. Eason, "On Journalistic Authority: The Janet Cooke Scandal," *Critical Studies in Mass Communication* 3 (1986): 432.

72. "An Addict at 8," editorial, *Washington Post*, 30 September 1980, A18; "Telling the Story of a Child Addict," editorial, *Washington Post*, 1 October 1980, A16.

73. Cass Peterson, "Post Writer Wins Pulitzer for Story on Child Addict," *Washington Post*, 14 April 1981, A1.

74. David A. Maraniss, "Post Reporter's Pulitzer Prize Is Withdrawn," *Washington Post*, 16 April 1981, A1.

75. For an excellent review of this press commentary about the Cooke episode and press practices, see Eason, "On Journalistic Authority."

76. Thomas Griffith, "Credibility at Stake," *Time*, 11 March 1985, 57.

77. Alex S. Jones, "Public Views Newspapers with Mixture of Faith and Mistrust, Polls Find," *New York Times*, 13 April 1985, sec. 1, 8.

78. Alex S. Jones, "Polls Compare Journalists' and Public Views," *New York Times*, 30 October 1985, A13.

79. Alex S. Jones, "Journalists Disagree about Press Credibility," *New York Times*, 7 May 1985, A20.

80. Robert S. Boynton, "Till Press Do Us Part," *Village Voice*, 29 November 1994, 31.

81. Jeffrey Masson, telephone interview with author, 15 January 2005.

82. Jane Gross, "Profile Writer Has Last Word in Defense against Libel Suit," *New York Times*, 26 May 1993, A14.

83. Howard Mintz, "Brosnahan Told Masson Not to Pursue Libel Suit," *Recorder*, 26 May 1993, 3.

84. Gross, "Profile Writer Has Last Word."

85. Ben Wildavsky, "Writer Denies Inventing Quotes," *San Francisco Chronicle*, 26 May 1993, A7.

86. Mintz, "Brosnahan Told Masson," 3.

87. Ibid.

88. Jeffrey Masson, telephone interview with author, 15 January 2005.

89. Mintz, "Brosnahan Told Masson."

90. William Hamilton, "The Writer He Says Done Him Wrong," *Washington Post*, 14 May 1993, B1.

91. Ben Wildavsky, "Both Sides Bloodied in New Yorker Case," *San Francisco Chronicle*, 14 May 1993, A3.

92. Boynton, "Till Press Do Us Part," 36.

93. James Wagstaffe, telephone interview with author, 23 February 2005.

94. Boynton, "Till Press Do Us Part," 36.

95. Complaint for Defamation and Invasion of Privacy, *Masson v. New Yorker* (no. 84–7548), filed in the U.S. District Court Northern District of California, 29 November 1984. Copy received from the National Archives and Records Administration's San Bruno Archives in California.

96. *Masson v. New Yorker*, 686 F. Supp. 1396, 1397 (N.D. Cal. 1987).

97. Ibid.

98. *Masson*, 686 F. Supp. at 1398.

99. Ibid., 1397, quoting *Anderson v. Liberty Lobby, Inc.*, 477 U.S. 242, 106 S. Ct. 2505, 2513 (1986).

100. Ibid., 1398.

101. Bill Kovach and Tom Rosenstiel, *The Elements of Journalism: What Newspeople Should Know and the Public Should Expect* (New York: Crown, 2001), 43.

102. The Commission on the Freedom of the Press, *A Free and Responsible Press*, ed. Robert D. Leigh (1947; reprint, Chicago: University of Chicago Press, 1974), 23.

103. Committee of Concerned Journalists, *Journalism Principles: A Statement of Shared Purpose*, http://www.journalism.org/resources/guidelines/principles/purpose.asp (24 April 2004).

104. *Masson*, 686 F. Supp. at 1399.

105. *Bose Corporation v. Consumers Union*, 466 U.S. 485 (1984).

106. *Time, Inc. v. Pape*, 401 U.S. 279 (1971).

107. *Masson*, 686 F. Supp. at 1399.

108. Ibid., quoting *Bose*, 512–13; and *Time, Inc.*, 290.

109. Ibid., 1399.

110. Ibid., 1405.

111. Ibid.

112. Ibid.

113. Ibid., 1406.

114. Ibid. (emphasis added).

115. Ibid., 1407.
116. Janet Malcolm, "The Journalist and the Murderer," *New Yorker*, 13 March 1989, 59–152, and 20 March 1989, 60–119.
117. Janet Malcolm, *The Journalist and the Murderer* (New York: Vintage Books, 1990), 3.
118. "Journalists—and Con Artists," *New York Times*, 19 March 1989, sec. 4, 26.
119. Albert Scardino, "Ethics, Reporters, and The New Yorker," *New York Times*, 21 March 1989, C20.
120. Ibid.
121. "Journalists—and Con Artists," sec. 4, 26.
122. Gwen Davis, "The Trials of Janet and Jeffrey: Ignore that Woman behind the Curtain," *Nation*, 28 November 1994, 643.
123. *Masson v. New Yorker*, 895 F.2d 1535, 1554 (1989) (Judge Alex Kozinski dissenting, footnote 10).
124. Jeffrey Masson, interview with author, 15 January 2005.
125. Malcolm, *The Journalist and the Murderer*, 153.
126. Ibid., 154.
127. Fred W. Friendly, "Was Trust Betrayed?" *New York Times*, 25 February 1990, sec. 7, 1.
128. Ibid.
129. Janet Malcolm, letter to the editor, *New York Times*, 1 April 1990, sec. 7, 34.
130. *Masson v. New Yorker*, 895 F.2d 1535, 1536 (9th Cir. 1989).
131. Ibid., 1539.
132. Ibid.
133. Ibid., quoting *Hotchner v. Castillo-Puche*, 551 F.2d 910, 914 (2d Cir. 1977) (emphasis added).
134. Ibid., 1537.
135. Ibid., 1541 (emphasis added).
136. *Masson*, 686 F. Supp. at 1397, quoting *Anderson v. Liberty Lobby, Inc.*, 477 U.S. 242 (1986).
137. Committee of Concerned Journalists, *Journalism Principles*.
138. David A. Anderson, "Is Libel Law Worth Reforming?" In *Reforming Libel Law*, ed. John Soloski and Randall P. Bezanson (New York: Guilford Press, 1992), 6, 7.
139. *Masson*, 895 F.2d at 1558.
140. Ibid.
141. Ibid.
142. Ibid., 1559.
143. Ibid., quoting J. L. Hulteng, *The Messenger's Motives: Ethical Problems of the News Media* (Englewood Cliffs, N.J.: Prentice-Hall, 1976), 71.
144. Ibid., 1559 n.12.
145. Ibid., 1553.
146. Ibid.
147. Ibid., 1553–54.
148. Ibid., 1548.
149. Ibid., 1562.
150. Ibid.
151. Ibid.
152. Ibid.
153. Ibid.
154. Ibid., 1564.

155. A number of lawyers involved in the case on both sides, as well as Jeffrey Masson, believe that Judge Kozinski's dissent in the Ninth Circuit helped push the case onto the Supreme Court's docket. James Wagstaffe, counsel for the *New Yorker*, interview with author, 23 February 2005; Jeffrey Masson, interview with author, 15 January 2005; Charles O. Morgan, lead counsel for Jeffrey Masson, telephone interview with author, 14 January 2005; Paul Kleven, counsel for Jeffrey Masson, telephone interview with author, 13 December 2004.

156. Peter Novick, *That Noble Dream: The "Objectivity Question" and the American Historical Profession* (Cambridge: Cambridge University Press, 1988), 564.

157. National News Council, *After "Jimmy's World": Tightening Up in Editing* (New York: National News Council, 1981), 6.

158. *LDRC Bulletin*, no. 11 (Summer–Fall 1984): 2.

159. *LDRC Bulletin*, no. 17 (Spring 1986): 2. The average pre-*Sullivan* damage figure excludes the highest and lowest awards in the sample.

160. *Time, Inc. v. Hill*, 385 U.S. 374, 406 (1967) (Justice Harlan concurring in part and dissenting in part), quoted in Anthony Lewis, "*New York Times v. Sullivan* Reconsidered: Time to Return to 'The Central Meaning of the First Amendment,'" *Columbia Law Review* 83 (April 1983): 619.

161. Lewis, "*New York Times v. Sullivan* Reconsidered," 620.

162. *Masson*, 501 U.S. at 517 (1991).

163. *Time, Inc. v. Hill*, 406 (Justice Harlan concurring in part and dissenting in part).

6. Libel Law and the Postmodern Dilemma

1. *New York Times v. Sullivan*, 376 U.S. 254, 271 (1964).

2. *Milkovich v. Lorain Journal*, 497 U.S. 1 (1990).

3. *Masson v. New Yorker*, 501 U.S. 496 (1991).

4. See Robert D. Sack and Sandra S. Baron, *Sack on Defamation: Libel, Slander, and Related Problems*, 3rd ed., 2 vols. (New York: Practising Law Institute, 1999), §1.2.2, for a useful discussion of actual malice in *New York Times v. Sullivan*.

5. *New York Times v. Sullivan*, 279–80 ("A rule compelling the critic of official conduct to guarantee the truth of all his factual assertions—and to do so on pain of libel judgments virtually unlimited in amount—leads to a comparable 'self-censorship'").

6. *New York Times v. Sullivan*, 270.

7. Lee C. Bollinger, "The End of *New York Times v. Sullivan*: Reflections on *Masson v. New Yorker Magazine*," *Supreme Court Review* (1991): 39.

8. See *Roth v. United States*, 354 U.S. 476, 483 (1957) (holding that obscenity receives no First Amendment protection because it is expression "utterly without redeeming social importance"); and *Miller v. California*, 413 U.S. 15, 23 (1973) (holding that triable obscenity offenses must "be limited to works which, taken as a whole, appeal to the prurient interest in sex, which portray sexual conduct in a patently offensive way, and which, taken as a whole, do not have serious literary, artistic, political, or scientific value").

9. Bollinger, "The End of *New York Times v. Sullivan*," 39: "Here [in the Masson decision] for the first time, then, the Court refuses to extend First Amendment protection to speech because in its view to do so would undermine the character and quality of public discourse."

10. *Garrison v. Louisiana*, 379 U.S. 64, 75 (1964).

11. Bollinger, "The End of *New York Times v. Sullivan*," 39.

12. Douglas E. Litowitz, *Postmodern Philosophy and Law* (Lawrence: University Press of Kansas, 1997), 13.

13. W. Wat Hopkins, *Actual Malice: Twenty-five Years after Times v. Sullivan* (New York: Praeger, 1989), 49.

14. *New York Times v. Sullivan*, 271.

15. *Philadelphia Newspaper, Inc. v. Hepps*, 475 U.S. 767, 776 (1986).

16. Hopkins, *Actual Malice*, 164.

17. See Anthony Lewis, *Make No Law: The Sullivan Case and the First Amendment* (New York: Vintage Books, 1991).

18. In 1971, the U.S. Supreme Court ruled, in a plurality opinion, that private libel plaintiffs involved in issues of public concern also had to prove actual malice; *Rosenbloom v. Metromedia*, 403 U.S. 29, 44 (1971). This opinion stood for only a few years. In *Gertz v. Robert Welch, Inc.*, 418 U.S. 323, 346 (1974), the Court backpedaled, holding that such private person plaintiffs must prove some level of fault to be determined by the states, such as negligence, but not the high fault standard of actual malice.

19. *Herbert v. Lando*, 441 U.S. 153, 169 (1979), holding that the First Amendment does not protect media defendants from inquiry into the editorial process in libel cases. Such a privilege would, the Court wrote, "substantially enhance the [plaintiff's] burden of proving actual malice, contrary to the expectations of *New York Times*, *Butts*, and similar cases".

20. *Gertz v. Welch*, 418 U.S. 323 (1974).

21. See Litowitz, *Postmodern Philosophy and Law*, 13; and M. H. Abrams, *A Glossary of Literary Terms*, 7th ed. (Fort Worth: Harcourt Brace, 1999), 238–43, s.v. "poststructuralism."

22. *Garrison v. Louisiana*, 74.

23. Kyu Ho Youm, "The Plaintiff's Case," in *Communication and the Law*, ed. W. Wat Hopkins (Northport, Ala.: Vision Press, 2003), 96. See also Clive Walker, "International and Comparative Perspectives on Defamation, Free Speech,and Privacy: Reforming the Laws of Libel," *New York Law School Law Review* (2005/2006): 195–97.

24. *Garrison v. Louisiana*, 74.

25. *St. Amant v. Thompson*, 390 U.S. 727 (1968).

26. Ibid., 731. See Hopkins, *Actual Malice*, 120, explaining that the Court further ruled "that an assertion by a publisher that he believed in the truth of the publication, standing alone, would not automatically ensure a favorable verdict; that proof of good faith publication will ensure a favorable verdict for a defendant; and that failure to investigate, standing alone, is insufficient evidence of bad faith."

27. *St. Amant v. Thompson*, 732–33.

28. Ibid., 731.

29. Ibid., 732.

30. See *Rosenblatt v. Baer*, 383 U.S. 75, 86 (1966) (holding that public officials are "at the very least . . . those among the hierarchy of government employees who have, or appear to the public to have, substantial responsibility for or control over the conduct of governmental affairs"). See also *Curtis Publishing Co. v. Butts*, 388 U.S. 130 (1967), and *Associated Press v. Walker*, 388 U.S. 130 (1967) (decided together in one opinion, holding that public figures must prove actual malice to prevail); *Time, Inc. v. Hill*, 385 U.S. 374 (1967) (holding that private plaintiffs in false-light invasion of privacy claims must

prove actual malice to prevail if the subject of the report is a matter of public concern [390]); *Hutchinson v. Proxmire*, 443 U.S. 111 (1979) (holding that receiving public money by itself does not make a person a public figure if the person has been drawn involuntarily into a public controversy); *Wolston v. Reader's Digest Ass'n.*, 443 U.S. 157 (1979) (holding that involvement in a criminal proceeding does not by itself make a person a public figure if the person has been involuntarily drawn into a public controversy); and *Hustler Magazine, Inc. v. Falwell*, 485 U.S. 46 (1988) (holding that public figures claiming intentional infliction of emotional distress must prove publication of a false statement of fact with actual malice in order to prevail).

31. *Gertz v. Welch*, 344.
32. Ibid., 326.
33. Ibid., 347.
34. Norman L. Rosenberg, *Protecting the Best Men: An Interpretive History of the Law of Libel* (Chapel Hill: University of North Carolina Press, 1986), 254.
35. *Rosenbloom v. Metromedia, Inc.*, 403 U.S. 29, 43 (1971).
36. *Harte-Hanks Communications, Inc. v. Connaughton*, 491 U.S. 657 (1989).
37. Ibid., 660.
38. Ibid., 692.
39. Ibid., 683–85.
40. *Gertz v. Welch*, 339–40.
41. David A. Anderson, "Is Libel Law Worth Reforming?" in *Reforming Libel Law*, ed. John Soloski and Randall P. Bezanson (New York: Guilford Press, 1992), 12.
42. Anderson, "Is Libel Law Worth Reforming?" 12.
43. *Greenbelt Cooperative Publishing Association v. Bresler*, 398 U.S. 6 (1970).
44. Ibid., 7.
45. Ibid., 13–18.
46. Ibid., 13.
47. Ibid., 14.
48. *Time, Inc. v. Pape*, 401 U.S. 279 (1971).
49. Ibid., 290.
50. *National Association of Letter Carriers, AFL-CIO v. Austin*, 418 U.S. 264 (1974).
51. Ibid., 267.
52. A demurrer is a pleading which states that the facts alleged in a complaint, while perhaps true, are not sufficient to allow the plaintiff to establish a claim for relief and for the defendant to produce an answer. In most states this kind of pleading is now called a motion to dismiss. *Black's Law Dictionary*, 7th ed., ed. Bryan A. Garner (St. Paul: West Group, 1999), 444–45.
53. *National Association of Letter Carriers v. Austin*, 269.
54. Ibid., 272–73.
55. Ibid., 270.
56. Ibid., 287 (Justice Douglas concurring at 287–88).
57. Ibid., 284.
58. *Cantrell v. Forest City Publishing Co.*, 419 U.S. 245 (1974).
59. Ibid., 248.
60. Ibid., 253.
61. Ibid., 253.
62. *Bose Corp. v. Consumers Union of United States, Inc.*, 466 U.S. 485 (1984).

63. Ibid., 487.

64. Ibid., 513.

65. Ibid., 514.

66. Ibid., 512, quoting *Time, Inc. v. Pape*, 401 U.S. at 290 (1971).

67. *Philadelphia Newspapers, Inc. v. Hepps*, 769.

68. Ibid., 776.

69. *Hustler Magazine, Inc. v. Falwell*, 48.

70. Ibid., 50.

71. Ibid., 50.

72. Ibid.

73. Ibid., 54, 57.

74. *Milkovich v. Lorain Journal Co.*, 19.

75. *Hustler Magazine, Inc. v. Falwell*, 54–55.

76. *Milkovich v. Lorain Journal Co.*, 18.

77. Ibid., 19.

78. Ibid., 19.

79. Ibid., 17.

80. Ibid., 4.

81. Ibid., 17.

82. Ibid., 20.

83. Ibid., 19.

84. Martin F. Hansen, "Fact, Opinion, and Consensus: The Verifiability of Allegedly Defamatory Speech," *George Washington Law Review* 62 (1993): 46.

85. Ibid., 68.

86. *Ollman v. Evans*, 750 F.2d 970 (D.C. Cir. 1984) (*en banc*), *cert. denied*, 471 U.S. 1127 (1985).

87. Other tests include the Restatement (Second) of Torts §566 (1977) "pure" opinion analysis, which asserts that an opinion is not "pure" when it implies a false and defamatory fact unknown to the audience. Such an opinion would be actionable. Another test, developed in *Hotchner v. Castillo-Puche*, 551 F.2d 910, 913 (2d Cir.), defined protected opinion as "an assertion that canot be proved false." See Hansen, "Fact, Opinion, and Consensus," 48–49.

88. *Ollman v. Evans*, 979.

89. Ibid.

90. Ibid., 978.

91. *Milkovich v. Lorain Journal*, 24 (Justice Brennan dissenting).

92. Ibid., 28.

93. Ibid., 32.

94. Ibid.

95. Hansen, "Fact, Opinion, and Consensus," 46.

96. *Milkovich v. Lorain Journal*, 28.

97. Ibid., 22.

98. Janet Malcolm, "The Annals of Scholarship: Trouble in the Archives," *New Yorker*, 5 December 1983, 59–152, and 12 December 1983, 60–119.

99. *Masson*, 501 U.S. at 510.

100. Ibid., 511.

101. Ibid., 512.

102. Ibid., 513.

103. Ibid.

104. Ibid.

105. See ethical codes in Jay Black, Bob Steele, and Ralph Barney, *Doing Ethics in Journalism: A Handbook with Case Studies*, 3rd ed. (New York: Allyn and Bacon, 1999), 6–11; and Committee of Concerned Journalists, *Journalism Principles: A Statement of Shared Purpose*, Project for Excellence in Journalism, Washington, D.C., 2004, http://www.jour nalism.org/resources/guidelines/principles/purpose.asp (23 March 2005). The closest such codes come to discussing a social contract is to assert that journalists should distinguish between advocacy and news reporting by labeling all analysis and commentary. Of course, such labeling makes little sense in the context of magazine essays such as Janet Malcolm's, which are commonly understood to be a blend of traditional reporting with analysis and commentary.

106. In Black, Steele, and Barney, *Doing Ethics in Journalism*, 25.

107. *Masson*, 501 U.S. at 513.

108. Ibid., 514.

109. Ibid.

110. Ibid.

111. Ibid., 514–15.

112. Ibid., 511.

113. See Deirdre Carmody, "Do Speakers Really Say What Is between Quotation Marks?" *New York Times*, June 21, 1991, A12, quoting a *Times* editor as saying, "We believe that the material between quotation marks must be an absolutely literal rendition of what the quoted person said. . . . We believe that if there is any reason to alter it for clarity or grammatical improvement, then the quotation marks come off and we resort to paraphrase and fragmentary quotes." The *New York Times* still ascribes to the same exacting standards in the reporting of quotations:

> Readers should be able to assume that every word between quotation marks is what the speaker or writer said. The *Times* does not "clean up" quotations. If a subject's grammar or taste is unsuitable, quotation marks should be removed and the awkward passage paraphrased. Unless the writer has detailed notes or a recording, it is usually wise to paraphrase long comments, since they may turn up worded differently on television or in other publications. "Approximate" quotations can undermine readers' trust in The *Times*.
>
> The writer should, of course, omit extraneous syllables like "um" and may judiciously delete false starts. If any further omission is necessary, close the quotation, insert new attribution and begin another quotation. (The *Times* does adjust spelling, punctuation, capitalization and abbreviations within a quotation for consistent style.) Detailed guidance is in the stylebook entry headed "quotations." In every case, writer and editor must both be satisfied that the intent of the subject has been preserved.

New York Times Company, "Quotations," in *Guidelines on Integrity*, 2005, http://www .nytco.com/company-properties-times-integrity.html (23 March 2005).

114. Carmody, "Do Speakers Really Say What Is between Quotation Marks?"

115. *Masson*, 501 U.S. at 516.

116. Ibid.

117. Ibid., 517, quoting *Heuer v. Kee*, 15 Cal. App. 2d 710, 714 (1936).

118. Ibid..
119. Ibid., 520.
120. Ibid.
121. Ibid., 518, quoting *Time, Inc. v. Pape*, 285.
122. Ibid., 521.
123. Ibid., 525.
124. Lee C. Bollinger, "The End of *New York Times v. Sullivan*: Reflections on *Masson v. New Yorker Magazine*," *Supreme Court Review* (1991): 31.
125. Ibid.
126. Ibid., 31–32.
127. Harold L. Nelson and Dwight L. Teeter, *Law of Mass Communications: Freedom and Control of Print and Broadcast Media* (Mineola, N.Y.: Foundation Press, 1969), 141.
128. William G. Hale, *The Law of the Press: Text-Statutes-Cases*, 3rd ed. (St. Paul: West Publishing, 1948), 110.
129. *Cantrell v. Forest Hill Publishing*, 419 U.S. 245 (1974).
130. Judith Lichtenberg, "In Defence of Objectivity Revisited," *Mass Media and Society*, 2nd ed., ed. James Curran and Michael Gurevitch (London: Arnold, 1996), 225–42, 236.
131. Ibid., 237.
132. Litowitz, *Postmodern Philosophy and Law*, 38.
133. See ibid., 13, discussing the postmodern notion of truth.
134. Alexander Meiklejohn, *Free Speech and Its Relation to Self-Government* (New York: Harper and Brothers, 1948), 25.

7. The End of the Line for *Masson*

1. Craig Seligman, "Janet Malcolm," *Salon*, 29 February 2000, http://dir.salon.com/people/bc/2000/02/29/malcolm/index.html (25 April 2005).
2. Janet Malcolm, *The Journalist and the Murderer* (New York: Vintage Books, 1990), 3.
3. Janet Malcolm, *The Silent Woman: Sylvia Plath and Ted Hughes* (New York: Vintage Books, 1994), 9.
4. Ibid.
5. Ibid., 176.
6. Janet Malcolm, *The Crime of Sheila McGough* (New York: Vintage Books, 2000), 4.
7. Ibid., 78–79.
8. *Masson v. New Yorker*, 501 U.S. 496, 525 (1991).
9. *Masson v. New Yorker*, 960 F.2d 896 (9th Cir. 1992).
10. Ibid., 898.
11. Ibid., 902.
12. Ibid.
13. Ibid., 902.
14. Ibid., 901.
15. See Janet Malcolm, *In the Freud Archives* (New York: New York Review Books, 1997), 31–45.
16. *Masson*, 501 U.S. at 514.
17. *Masson*, 960 F.2d at 901, footnote 5.

18. Ibid., 903.
19. Lee C. Bollinger, "The End of *New York Times v. Sullivan*: Reflections on *Masson v. New Yorker Magazine*," *Supreme Court Review* (1991): 39.
20. Ben Wildavsky, "Mistrial in New Yorker Suit," *San Francisco Chronicle*, 4 June 1993, A1; William Hamilton, "Libel Suit Ends in Mistrial," *Washington Post*, 4 June 1993, C1; Jane Gross, "Impasse over Damages in New Yorker Libel Trial," *New York Times*, 4 June 1993, A1.
21. *Masson*, 501 U.S. at 517.
22. Ibid., 520.
23. *Masson v. New Yorker*, Special Verdict no. C-84–7548 EFL, 3 June 1993, U.S. District Court, Northern District of California, 4–5.
24. *Masson v. New Yorker*, Jury Instructions no. C-84–7548, 8 June 1993, U.S. District Court, Northern District of California, 15.
25. Ibid., 22.
26. Ibid., 23.
27. *Harte-Hanks Communications, Inc. v. Connaughton*, 491 U.S. 657, 663 (1989), quoting *Curtis Publishing Co. v. Butts*, 388 U.S., at 155 (opinion of Justice Harlan).
28. Ibid., 692.
29. James Wagstaffe, telephone interview with author, 23 February 2005.
30. These books include *The Assault on Truth: Freud's Suppression of the Seduction Theory* (New York: Farrar, Straus and Giroux, 1984); *The Complete Letters of Sigmund Freud to Wilhelm Fliess, 1887–1904* (Cambridge: Belknap Press of Harvard University Press, 1985); *Final Analysis: The Making and Unmaking of a Psychoanalyst* (Reading, Mass.: Addison-Wesley, 1990); *My Father's Guru: A Journey through Spirituality and Disillusion* (Reading, Mass.: Addison-Wesley, 1993). *Against Therapy* (Monroe, Me.: Common Courage Press, 1994) was published the year of the second trial. In the years that followed, Masson, a committed vegetarian, made a successful career publishing books such as *When Elephants Weep: The Emotional Lives of Animals* (New York: Delacorte Press, 1995); *Dogs Never Lie about Love* (New York: Crown, 1997); *The Emperor's Embrace: Reflections on Animal Families and Fatherhood* (New York: Pocket Books, 1999); *The Nine Emotional Lives of Cats* (New York: Ballantine Books, 2002); and *The Pig Who Sang to the Moon: The Emotional World of Farm Animals* (New York: Ballantine Books, 2003).
31. Gwen Davis, "The Trials of Janet and Jeffrey," *Nation*, 28 November 1994, 645.
32. Jeffrey Masson, telephone interview with author, 15 January 2005.
33. Jane Gross, "On Libel and the Literati: The New Yorker on Trial," *New York Times*, 5 May 1993.
34. Ibid.
35. Ibid.
36. Ibid.
37. Jane Gross, "Writer's Techniques Put under Harsh Spotlight at New Yorker Trial," *New York Times*, 14 May 1993, A21.
38. Ibid.
39. Ibid., 154.
40. Ibid., 155.
41. Anna Quindlen, "Quote, Unquote," *New York Times*, 19 May 1993, A19.
42. Jane Gross, "Shawn Has a Say in New Yorker Trial," *New York Times*, 21 May 1993, A10.

43. Deirdre Carmody, "Despite Malcolm Trial, Editors Elsewhere Vouch for Accuracy of Their Work," *New York Times*, 30 May 1993, sec. 1, 26.
44. Jane Gross, "U.S. Judge Weighs Retrial of New Yorker Libel Case," *New York Times*, 3 July 1993, sec. 1, 45; Howard Mintz, "Judge Says New Yorker Libel Case Is Best Settled," *Recorder*, 4 August 1993, 3.
45. "Retrial Is Set in Libel Case, but Without Magazine," *New York Times*, 10 September 1993, A20.
46. Seth Mydans, "Second Trial of Libel Case Is Under Way," *New York Times*, 29 September 1994, B11.
47. Robert S. Boynton, "Till Press Do Us Part," *Village Voice*, 29 November 1994, 32.
48. *Masson v. New Yorker*, 832 F. Supp. 1350, 1377 (N.D. Cal. 1993).
49. "Retrial Is Set in Libel Case."
50. Mydans, "Second Trial of Libel Case Is Under Way," B11.
51. Howard Mintz, "Defense Verdict May Finally Have Ended New Yorker Libel Case," *Recorder*, 3 November 1994, 1.
52. David Margolick, "Psychoanalyst Loses Libel Suit against a New Yorker Reporter," *New York Times*, 3 November 1994, A1.
53. William Hamilton, "Write or Wronged? Masson v. Malcolm Goes to Jury," *Washington Post*, 28 May 1993, G1.
54. Steven Rubenstein, "New Yorker Trial—Lots of Sex, No Fun," *San Francisco Chronicle*, 21 May 1993, A4.
55. Jane Gross, "At Libel Trial, Speaking Style Becomes the Focus," *New York Times*, 19 May 1993, A16.
56. Jane Gross, "New Yorker Writer Says a Disputed Paragraph Merged 3 Remarks," *New York Times*, 18 May, 1993, A11.
57. Ibid.
58. Howard Mintz, "Swearing Contest," *Recorder*, 17 May 1993, 1.
59. Davis, "The Trials of Janet and Jeffrey"; Robert S. Boynton, "Till Press Do Us Part," *Village Voice*, 29 November 1994, 32.
60. David Margolick, "Psychoanalyst Loses Libel Suit against a New Yorker Reporter," *New York Times*, 3 November 1994, A1.
61. Charles O. Morgan, lead counsel for Jeffrey Masson, telephone interview with author, 14 January 2005.
62. Paul Kleven, counsel for Jeffrey Masson, telephone interview with author, 13 December 2004.
63. James Wagstaffe, telephone interview with author, 23 February 2005.
64. Seth Mydans, "2d Trial in Libel Case Opens with Blocks and Interview Tape," *New York Times*, 4 October 1994, A19; Susan Cohen, "The Libel Suit That Wouldn't Die," *Washington Post*, 4 October 1994, E1.
65. Mydans, "2d Trial in Libel Case Opens," A19.
66. Margolick, "Psychoanalyst Loses Libel Suit."
67. Davis, "The Trials of Janet and Jeffrey," 644.
68. Boynton, "Till Press Do Us Part," 36.
69. Ibid., 37.
70. Masson, telephone interview with author, 15 January 2005.
71. Margolick, "Psychoanalyst Loses Libel Suit," A1.

72. Ibid; *Masson v. New Yorker*, Special Verdict no. C-84–7548 EFL, 2 November 1994, U.S. District Court, Northern District of California, 4–5.

73. Margolick, "Psychoanalyst Loses Libel Suit"; Susan Cohen, "Writer Wins in Masson Libel Retrial," *Washington Post*, 3 November 1994, D1.

74. Maura Dolan, "New Yorker Writer Cleared of Libeling Psychoanalyst," *Los Angeles Times*, 3 November 1994, A1.

75. Margolick, "Psychoanalyst Loses Libel Suit."

76. M. L. Stein, "Hiring of Jeffrey Masson Produces Scathing Reaction in Student Newsletter," *Editor & Publisher*, 3 December 1994, 12, 37; David Margolick, "Analyst Steps into New Press Storm," *New York Times*, 8 December 1994, A18; Cohen, "Writer Wins in Masson Libel Retrial," D1.

77. Jeffrey Moussaieff Masson, curriculum vitae, http://www.jeffreymasson.com/cv.html (22 April 2005).

78. *Masson v. New Yorker*, 85 F.3d 1394 (9th Cir., 1996).

79. Anthony Lewis, "Stranger Than Fiction," op-ed, *New York Times*, 25 August 1995, A27.

80. Roxanne Roberts and Annie Groer, "Writer's Notes Suddenly Appear," *Washington Post*, 26 August 1995, D1; David Stout, "Malcolm's Lost Notes and a Child at Play," *New York Times*, 30 August 1995, C9.

81. Lewis, "Stranger Than Fiction," A27.

82. Jeffrey Moussaieff Masson, "Let's Have a Look at Janet Malcolm's Notes," letter to the editor, *New York Times*, 23 September 1995, sec. 1, 22.

83. Seligman, "Janet Malcolm."

84. James Wood, "Interview: A Woman of Letters," *Guardian Weekend*, 15 October 1994, T34.

85. Masson, telephone interview with author, 15 January 2005.

86. Ibid.

87. Ibid.

88. *Philadelphia Newspapers v. Hepps*, 475 U.S. 767, 776 (1986).

89. *Masson v. New Yorker*, 501 U.S. at 517, quoting R. Sack, *Libel, Slander, and Related Problems* (1980, 138.

90. Bollinger, "The End of *New York Times v. Sullivan*," 31.

Conclusion: The Meanings of the Masson-Malcolm Dispute

1. *New York Times v. Sullivan*, 376 U.S. 254, 271 (1964).

2. Joyce Appleby, Lynn Hunt, and Margaret Jacobs, *Telling the Truth about History* (New York: W. W. Norton, 1994), 285.

3. To review various scholars' critical consideration of the pragmatic conception of truth as a possible way out of postmodern language dilemmas, see Appleby, Hunt, and Jacobs, *Telling the Truth About History*; Judith Lichtenberg, "In Defence of Objectivity Revisited," *Mass Media and Society*, 2nd ed., ed. James Curran and Michael Gurevitch (London: Arnold, 1996), 225–42; Douglas E. Litowitz, *Postmodern Philosophy & Law* (Lawrence: University Press of Kansas, 1997), 174–75; Peter Novick, *That Noble Dream: The "Objectivity Question" and the American Historical Profession* (Cambridge: Cambridge University Press, 1988), 567–73, 626–27; John E. Toews, "Intellectual His-

tory After the Linguistic Turn: The Autonomy of Meaning and the Irreducibility of Experience," *American Historical Review*, 92, no. 4 (1987): 904.

4. Michael Schudson, *Discovering the News: A Social History of American Newspapers* (New York: Basic Books, 1978), 5.

5. Michael Schudson, *The Sociology of News* (New York: W. W. Norton, 2003), 83–84.

6. Jeffrey Masson, telephone interview with author, 15 January 2005.

7. *Masson v. New Yorker*, 895 F.2d 1535, 1562 (1989).

8. *Masson v. New Yorker*, 501 U.S. 496, 513 (1991).

9. Masson, telephone interview with author, 15 January 2005.

10. *Masson*, 501 U.S. at 512–13.

11. The Supreme Court opinion in *Masson v. New Yorker* displayed a notable uneasiness with the meaning of quotation marks and quotations. On the one hand, the Court said that "the reasonable reader" would understand the disputed quotations in Janet Malcolm's profile "to be nearly verbatim reports" of Masson's statements (ibid., 513). On the other, the Court acknowledged that even with a tape recording of a speaker's statements, "the full and exact statement will be reported in only rare circumstances. The existence of both a speaker and a reporter; the translation between two media, speech and the printed word; the addition of punctuation; and the practical necessity to edit and make intelligible a speaker's perhaps rambling comments, all make it misleading to suggest that a quotation will be reconstructed with complete accuracy" (ibid., 515). Even given such contingencies, the Court apparently believed that reconstructed quotations should always be "nearly verbatim."

12. Ibid., 513.

13. Ben Wildavsky, "Dead Editor of New Yorker 'Testifies' at Libel Trial," *San Francisco Chronicle*, 21 May 1993, A4.

14. Jeremy Iggers, *Good News, Bad News: Journalism Ethics and the Public Interest* (Boulder: Westview Press, 1998), 73.

15. David Harvey, *The Condition of Postmodernity: An Enquiry into the Origins of Cultural Change* (Cambridge: Blackwell, 1990), 9.

16. Peter Novick, *That Noble Dream: The "Objectivity Question" and the American Historical Profession* (Cambridge: Cambridge University Press, 1988), 572.

17. Ibid., 564.

18. Appleby, Hunt, and Jacobs, *Telling the Truth about History*, 268, 285.

19. James T. Kloppenberg, "Pragmatism: An Old Name for Some New Ways of Thinking," *Journal of American History* (June 1996): 136.

20. Appleby, Hunt, and Jacobs, *Telling the Truth about History*, 255–56.

21. Ibid., 262.

22. Hayden White, *Tropics of Discourse: Essays in Cultural Criticism* (Baltimore: Johns Hopkins University Press, 1978), 123. See also Robert F. Berkhofer, Jr., *Beyond the Great Story: History as Text and Discourse* (Cambridge: Belknap Press of Harvard University Press, 1995).

23. Ibid., 125.

24. Mark Kramer has identified many such standards for reporting and writing literary journalism in "Breakable Rules for Literary Journalists," in *Literary Journalism: A New Collection of the Best American Nonfiction*, ed. Norman Sims and Mark Kramer (New York: Ballantine, 1995), 23–27.

25. *Masson*, 501 U.S. at 520. See also Lee C. Bollinger, "The End of *New York Times v. Sulli-*

van: Reflections on *Masson v. New Yorker Magazine*," *Supreme Court Review* (1991): 39–41.

26. Norman Rosenberg, *Protecting the Best Men: An Interpretive History of the Law of Libel* (Chapel Hill: University of North Carolina Press, 1986), 225.
27. Quoted in Anthony Lewis, *Make No Law: The Sullivan Case and the First Amendment* (New York: Vintage Books, 1992), 154.
28. *Milkovich v. Lorain Journal*, 497 U.S. 1, 20 (1990).
29. *Ollman v. Evans*, 750 F.2d 970 (D.C. Cir. 1984).
30. *Masson*, 501 U.S. at 520. See also Bollinger, "The End of *New York Times v. Sullivan*," 39.
31. Richard Rorty, *Philosophy and the Mirror of Nature* (Princeton: Princeton University Press, 1979), 377.
32. Richard Rorty, *Consequences of Pragmatism: Essays, 1972–1980* (Minneapolis: University of Minnesota Press, 1982), 166.
33. Richard Rorty, *Contingency, Irony, and Solidarity* (Cambridge: Cambridge University Press, 1989), xvi.
34. Jay Rosen, *What Are Journalists For?* (New Haven: Yale University Press, 1999), 295.
35. John Keane, "Structural Transformations of the Public Sphere," in *The Media, Journalism, and Democracy*, ed. Margaret Scammell and Holli Semetko (Hanover, N.H.: Ashgate Press, 2000), 70.
36. Rosen, What Are Journalists For? 293–94.

SELECTED BIBLIOGRAPHY

Primary Sources

THE *NEW YORKER* RECORDS

Manuscripts and Archives Division, the New York Public Library, Astor, Lenox and Tilden Foundations.

INTERVIEWS

Author's telephone interview with Jeffrey Masson, tape recording (Auckland, New Zealand, and Durham, N.C., 15 January 2005).
Author's telephone interview with James Wagstaffe, counsel for the *New Yorker*, tape recording (San Francisco, Calif., and Durham, N.C., 23 February 2005).
Author's telephone interview with Charles O. Morgan, lead counsel for Jeffrey Masson, tape recording (San Francisco, Calif., and Durham, N.C., 14 January 2005).
Author's telephone interview with Paul Kleven, counsel for Jeffrey Masson, tape recording (San Francisco, Calif., and Durham, N.C., 13 December 2004).

ETHICAL CODES AND STATEMENTS OF PRINCIPLE

New York Times Company, "Quotations," *Guidelines on Integrity. New York Times*, 2005. http://www.nytco.com/company-properties-times-integrity.html (23 March 2005).
Committee of Concerned Journalists, *Journalism Principles: A Statement of Shared Purpose.* Washington, D.C.: Project for Excellence in Journalism, 2004. http://www.journal ism.org/resources/guidelines/principles/purpose.asp (23 March 2005).

LEGAL CASES AND DOCUMENTS

Masson Cases
Masson v. New Yorker, 686 F. Supp. 1396 (N.D. Cal. 1987) (*granting* summary judgment to defendants).
——895 F.2d 1535 (9th Cir. 1989), *aff'd.*
——501 U.S. 496 (1991), *rev'd. and remanded.*

——960 F.2d 896 (9th Cir. 1992) (*affirming* summary judgment for Knopf, *remanding* case for trial for Malcolm and the *New Yorker*).

——85 F.3d 1394 (9th Cir., 1996) (jury verdict in favor of Malcolm *aff'd.*).

Other Masson Legal Documents

Masson v. New Yorker, Complaint for Defamation and Invasion of Privacy (no. 84–7548), filed in the U.S. District Court, Northern District of California, 29 November 1984. Copy received from the National Archives and Records Administration's San Bruno Archives in California.

Masson v. New Yorker, Jury Instructions (no. C-84–7548), 8 June 1993, U.S. District Court, Northern District of California.

Masson v. New Yorker, Special Verdict (no. C-84–7548 EFL), 3 June 1993, U.S. District Court, Northern District of California.

Supreme Court Cases

Abrams v. United States, 250 U.S. 616 (1919).

Associated Press v. Walker, 388 U.S. 130 (1967).

Bose Corp. v. Consumers Union of United States, Inc., 466 U.S. 485 (1984).

Cantrell v. Forest City Publishing Co., 419 U.S. 245 (1974).

Curtis Publishing Co. v. Butts, 388 U.S. 130 (1967).

Debs v. United States, 249 U.S. 211 (1919).

Frohwerk v. United States, 249 U.S. 204 (1919).

Garrison v. Louisiana, 379 U.S. 64 (1964).

Gertz v. Robert Welch, Inc., 418 U.S. 323 (1974).

Gitlow v. New York, 268 U.S. 652 (1925).

Greenbelt Cooperative Publishing Association v. Bresler, 398 U.S. 6 (1970).

Harte-Hanks Communications, Inc. v. Connaughton, 491 U.S. 657 (1989).

Herbert v. Lando, 441 U.S. 153 (1979).

Hustler Magazine, Inc. v. Falwell, 485 U.S. 46 (1988).

Hutchinson v. Proxmire, 443 U.S. 111 (1979).

Lochner v. New York, 198 U.S. 45 (1905).

Masson v. New Yorker, 501 U.S. 496 (1991).

Milkovich v. Lorain Journal, 497 U.S. 1 (1990).

National Association of Letter Carriers, AFL-CIO v. Austin, 418 U.S. 264 (1974).

Near v. Minnesota, 283 U.S. 697 (1931).

New York Times v. Sullivan, 376 U.S. 254 (1964).

Philadelphia Newspapers, Inc. v. Hepps, 475 U.S. 767 (1986).

Rosenblatt v. Baer, 383 U.S. 75 (1966).

Schenck v. United States, 249 U.S. 47 (1919).

St. Amant v. Thompson, 390 U.S. 727 (1968).

Time, Inc. v. Hill, 385 U.S. 374 (1967).

Time, Inc. v. Pape, 401 U.S. 279 (1971).

United States v. Hudson & Goodwin, 7 Cranch 32 (1812).

Wolston v. Reader's Digest Ass'n., 443 U.S. 157 (1979).

Other Legal Cases

Bearce v. Bass, 88 Me. 521 (S.C. Me., 1896).

Burnett v. National Enquirer, Inc., 144 Cal. App. 3d 991, 1012 (Cal. Ct. App. 1983).

Hoeppner v. Dunkirk Printing Company, 254 N.Y. 95, 99 (Ct. App. 1930).

Levin v. McPhee, New Yorker, & Farrar, Straus & Giroux, 119 F.3d 189 (2nd Cir. 1997).

Masses Publishing Co. v. Patten, 244 F. 535 (S.D.N.Y., 1917).

Miracle v. New Yorker, 190 F. Supp. 2d 1192 (D. Haw. 2001).

Rushford v. New Yorker, 846 F.2d 249 (4th Cir. 1988).

Sharon v. Time, no. 83 Civ. 4660 (S.D.N.Y., jury found in favor of Time, 24 January 1985) (reported in David Margolick, "Sharon Case and the Law." *New York Times*, 25 January 1985, B4).

Sidis v. F-R Publishing Corporation, 34 F. Supp. 19 (S.D.N.Y. 1938); *Sidis v. F-R Publishing Corporation*, 113 F. 2d 806 (C.C.A. 2d 1940).

Tavoulareas v. Piro, 245 U.S. App. D.C. 70, 120 (1985); *Tavoulareas v. Piro*, 817 F.2d 762, 766 (D.C. Cir. 1987).

Triggs v. Sun Printing & Publishing Assn., 179 N.Y. 144, 156 (Ct. App. 1904).

Westmoreland v. CBS, no. 82 Civ. 7913 (S.D.N.Y., suit withdrawn, 18 February 1985) (reported in M. A. Farber, "A Joint Statement Ends Libel Action by Westmoreland." *New York Times*, 19 February 1985, A1).

BOOKS AND ARTICLES BY JANET MALCOLM

"The Annals of Scholarship: Trouble in the Archives—Part I." *New Yorker*, 5 December 1983, 59–152.

"The Annals of Scholarship: Trouble in the Archives—Part II." *New Yorker*, 12 December 1983, 60–119.

The Crime of Sheila McGough. New York: Vintage Books, 1999.

In the Freud Archives. New York: New York Review of Books, 1997.

The Journalist and the Murderer. New York: Vintage Books, 1990.

"The Morality of Journalism." *New York Review of Books*, 1 March 1990, 19.

Psychoanalysis: The Impossible Profession. New York: Alfred A. Knopf, 1981.

The Silent Woman: Sylvia Plath and Ted Hughes. New York: Vintage Books, 1994.

MEMOIRS AND OTHER WORKS OF *NEW YORKER* WRITERS AND EDITORS

Adler, Renata. *Gone: The Last Days of the New Yorker*. New York: Simon and Schuster, 1999.

Botsford, Gardner. *A Life of Privilege, Mostly*. New York: St. Martin's, 2003.

Gill, Brendan. *Here at the New Yorker*. New York: Random House, 1975.

Grant, Jane. *Ross, The New Yorker, and Me*. New York: Reynal, 1968.

Mehta, Ved. *Remembering Mr. Shawn's New Yorker*. Woodstock, N.Y.: Overlook, 1998.

Mitchell, Joseph. Author's Note. In *Up in the Old Hotel*, ix–xiii. New York: Vintage Books, 1993.

Ross, Lillian. *Here But Not Here: My Life with William Shawn and The New Yorker*. Washington, D.C.: Counterpoint, 2001.

Thurber, James. *The Years with Ross*. 1957. Reprint, New York: Harper Perennial Classics, 2001.

Secondary Sources

Anderson, Chris. "Literary Nonfiction and Composition." In *Literary Nonfiction: Theory, Criticism, Pedagogy,* ed. Chris Anderson, ix–xxvi. Carbondale: Southern Illinois University Press, 1989.

Anderson, David A. "Is Libel Law Worth Reforming?" In *Reforming Libel Law,* ed. John Soloski and Randall P. Bezanson, 1–67. New York: Guilford Press, 1992.

Appleby, Joyce, Lynn Hunt, and Margaret Jacobs. *Telling the Truth about History.* New York: W. W. Norton, 1994.

Barnhurst, Kevin G., and John Nerone. *The Form of News: A History.* New York: Guilford Press, 2001.

Bellows, Jim. *The Last Editor.* Kansas City: Andrews McMeel, 2002.

Berkhofer, Robert F. Jr. *Beyond the Great Story: History as Text and Discourse.* Cambridge: Belknap Press of Harvard University Press, 1995.

Berner, Thomas R. "Literary Newswriting: The Death of an Oxymoron." *Journalism Monographs* 99 (1986): 1–33.

Bezanson, Randall P. *How Free Can the Press Be?* Chicago: University of Illinois Press, 2003.

———. "Libel Law and the Realities of Litigation: Setting the Record Straight." *Iowa Law Review* 71 (October 1985): 226–33.

Black, Jay, Bob Steele, and Ralph Barney. *Doing Ethics in Journalism: A Handbook with Case Studies.* 3rd ed. Boston: Allyn and Bacon, 1999.

Black's Law Dictionary. 7th ed. Ed. Bryan A. Garner. St. Paul: West Group, 1999.

Blanchard, Margaret A. "Filling in the Void: Speech and Press in State Courts Prior to *Gitlow*." In *The First Amendment Reconsidered: New Perspectives on the Meaning of Freedom of Speech and Press,* ed. Bill F. Chamberlin and Charlene J. Brown, 14–59. New York: Longman, 1982.

Blasi, Vincent. "The Checking Value in First Amendment Theory." *American Foundation Research Journal* 3 (1977): 521–649.

———. "The First Amendment and the Ideal of Civic Courage: The Brandeis Opinion in *Whitney v. California*." *William & Mary Law Review* 29 (Summer 1988): 653–97.

Bobertz, Bradley C. "The Brandeis Gambit: The Making of America's 'First Freedom,' 1909–1931." *William & Mary Law Review* 40 (February 1999): 557–651.

Bollinger, Lee C. "The End of *New York Times v. Sullivan*: Reflections on *Masson v. New Yorker Magazine*." *Supreme Court Review* (1991): 1–47.

Boynton, H. W. "Journalism and Literature." In *Journalism and Literature and Other Essays,* 3–23. Boston: Houghton, Mifflin, 1904.

Brinkley, Alan. "The Late New Deal and the Idea of the State." In *Liberalism and Its Discontents,* 37–62. Cambridge: Harvard University Press, 1998.

Bukro, Casey. "The SPJ Code's Double-Edged Sword: Accountability, Credibility." *Journal of Mass Media Ethics* (Fall–Winter 1985–86): 10–13.

Bybee, Carl. "Can Democracy Survive in the Post-Factual Age? A Return to the Lippmann-Dewey Debate about the Politics of News." *Journalism Communication Monographs* 1 (Spring 1999): 29–62.

Calhoun, Craig. "Introduction: Habermas and the Public Sphere." In *Habermas and the Public Sphere,* ed. Craig Calhoun, 1–48. Cambridge: MIT Press, 1992.

Calvert, Clay. "Awareness of Meaning in Libel Law: An Interdisciplinary Communication and Law Critique." *University of Illinois Law Review* 16 (1995): 111–40.

Carey, James W. "The Problem of Journalism History." *Journalism History* 1 (1974): 3–5, 27.

Chafee, Zechariah Jr. "Freedom of Speech in War Time." *Harvard Law Review* 32 (1918–19): 932–73.

Chance, Sandra F. "The Media in the New Millennium: Exploring Myths and Misconceptions before Shooting the Messenger." *Florida Journal of Law and Public Policy* 10 (1998): 157–72.

Christians, Clifford. "Enforcing Media Codes." *Journal of Mass Media Ethics* (Fall–Winter 1985–86): 14–21.

Cohen, Nancy. *The Reconstruction of American Liberalism, 1865–1914*. Chapel Hill: University of North Carolina Press, 2002.

Commission on the Freedom of the Press. *A Free and Responsible Press*, ed. Robert D. Leigh. 1947. Chicago: University of Chicago Press, 1974.

Connery, Thomas B. "Discovering a Literary Form." In *A Sourcebook of American Literary Journalism*, ed. Thomas B. Connery, 3–37. New York: Greenwood Press, 1992.

———. "A Third Way to Tell the Story: American Literary Journalism at the Turn of the Century." In *Literary Journalism in the Twentieth Century*, ed. Norman Sims, 3–20. New York: Oxford University Press, 1990.

Corey, Mary F. *The World through a Monocle: The New Yorker at Midcentury*. Cambridge: Harvard University Press, 1999.

Cowan, Geoffrey. "The Legal and Ethical Limitations of Factual Misrepresentation." In *The Future of Fact*, ed. Jeffrey J. Strange and Elihu Katz, 155–64. Thousand Oaks, Calif.: Sage Publications, 1998.

Cronin, Mary M. "Trade Press Roles in Promoting Journalistic Professionalism, 1884–1917," *Journal of Mass Media Ethics* 8, no. 4 (1993): 227–38.

Dawley, Alan. *Changing the World: American Progressives in War and Revolution*. Princeton: Princeton University Press, 2003.

Dennis, Everette E., and William L. Rivers. *Other Voices: The New Journalism in America*. San Francisco: Canfield Press, 1974.

Dewey, John. *Democracy and Education*. New York: Macmillan, 1916.

———. *The Public and Its Problems*. New York: Henry Holt, 1927.

———. "Public Opinion." *New Republic*, 3 May 1922, 286–38.

Dickson, Tom. *Mass Media Education in Transition: Preparing for the 21st Century*. Mahwah, N.J.: Lawrence Erlbaum Associates, 2000.

Douglas, George H. *The Golden Age of the Newspaper*. Westport, Conn.: Greenwood Press, 1999.

Drechsel, Robert E. "Media Ethics and Media Law: The Transformation of Moral Obligation into Legal Principle." *Notre Dame Journal of Law, Ethics, and Public Policy* 6 (1992): 5–32.

Eason, David. "The New Journalism and the Image-World." In *Literary Journalism in the Twentieth Century*, ed. Norman Sims, 191–205. New York: Oxford University Press, 1990.

———. "On Journalistic Authority: The Janet Cooke Scandal." *Critical Studies in Mass Communication* 3 (1986): 429–47.

Ernst, Morris L., and Alexander Lindey. *Hold Your Tongue! Adventures in Libel and Slander* (London: Methuen, 1936).

Fakazis, Elizabeth. "Janet Malcolm: Constructing Boundaries of Journalism." *Journalism* 7, no. 1 (2006): 5–24.

Fitzpatrick, Peter, and Alan Hunt, eds. *Critical Legal Studies*. London: Basil Blackwell, 1987.

Forde, Kathy Roberts. "Discovering the Explanatory Report in American Newspapers." *Journalism Practice* 1, no. 2 (June 2007): 227–44.

——. "How *Masson v. New Yorker* Has Shaped the Legal Landscape of Narrative Journalism." *Communication Law and Policy* 10 (Winter 2005): 101–33.

Franklin, Mark A. "Suing Media for Libel: A Litigation Study." *American Bar Foundation Research Journal* (Summer 1981): 795–831.

Frus, Phyllis. *The Politics and Poetics of Journalistic Narrative: The Timely and the Timeless*. Cambridge: Cambridge University Press, 1994.

Furner, Mary O. *Advocacy and Objectivity: A Crisis in the Professionalization of American Social Science, 1865–1905*. Lexington: University Press of Kentucky, 1975.

Goodchild, Seth. "Media Counteractions: Restoring the Balance to Modern Libel Law." *Georgetown Law Journal* (October 1986): 315–59.

Goodwin, H. Eugene. *Groping for Ethics in Journalism*. Ames: Iowa State University Press, 1983.

Gray, James. "The Journalist as Literary Man." In *American Non-Fiction: 1900–1950*, ed. May Brodbeck, James Gray, and Walter Metzger, 95–147. Chicago: Henry Regnery, 1952.

Habermas, Jürgen. *The Structural Transformation of the Public Sphere: An Inquiry into a Category of Bourgeois Society*. Trans. Thomas Burger. Cambridge: MIT Press, 1989.

Hale, William G. *The Law of the Press: Text, Statutes, Cases*, 3rd ed. St. Paul: West Publishing, 1948.

Hansen, Martin F. "Fact, Opinion, and Consensus: The Verifiability of Allegedly Defamatory Speech." *George Washington Law Review* 62 (1993): 43–99.

Hartsock, John C. *A History of American Literary Journalism: The Emergence of a Modern Narrative Form*. Amherst: University of Massachusetts Press, 2000.

Hellman, John. "Introduction: Fact, Fable, and the New Journalist." In *Fables of Fact: The New Journalism as New Fiction*, 1–20. Chicago: University of Illinois Press, 1981.

Hollowell, John. *Fact and Fiction: The New Journalism and the Nonfiction Novel*. Chapel Hill: University of North Carolina Press, 1977.

Holmes, Oliver Wendell Jr. *The Common Law*. 1881. Ed. Mark DeWolfe Howe. Boston: Little, Brown, 1963.

——. "The Path of the Law." *Harvard Law Review* 10 (1897): 991–1009.

Hopkins, W. Wat. *Actual Malice: Twenty-five Years after Times v. Sullivan*. New York: Praeger, 1989.

Horwitz, Morton J. *The Transformation of American Law, 1870–1960: The Crisis of Legal Orthodoxy*. New York: Oxford University Press, 1992.

Hoyt, Michael. "Malcolm, Masson, and You." *Columbia Journalism Review* 29, no. 6 (1991): 38–44.

Iggers, Georg G. *Historiography in the Twentieth Century: From Scientific Objectivity to the Postmodern Challenge*. Middletown, Ct.: Wesleyan University Press, 1997.

Iggers, Jeremy. *Good News, Bad News: Journalism Ethics and the Public Interest*. Boulder: Westview Press, 1998.

Kahn, Ronald. *The Supreme Court and Constitutional Theory, 1953–1993*. Lawrence: University Press of Kansas, 1994.

Kaltenbach, Richard T. "Fabricated Quotes and the Actual Malice Standard: *Masson v. New Yorker Magazine*." *Catholic University Law Review* 41 (1992): 745–77.

Keane, John. "Structural Transformations of the Public Sphere." In *The Media, Journalism, and Democracy*, ed. Margaret Scammell and Holli Semetko, 53–74. Hanover, N.H.: Ashgate, 2000.

Kenner, Hugh. "The Politics of the Plain Style." In *Literary Journalism in the Twentieth Century*, ed. Norman Sims, 183–90. New York: Oxford University Press, 1990.

Kerrane, Kevin. "Making Facts Dance." In *The Art of Fact: A Historical Anthology of Literary Journalism*, ed. Kevin Kerrane and Ben Yagoda, 17–20. New York: Touchstone, 1997.

Killenberg, G. Michael, and Rob Anderson. "What Is a Quote? Practical, Rhetorical, and Ethical Concerns for Journalists." *Journal of Mass Media Ethics* 8, no. 1 (1993): 37–54.

Kim, Gyong Ho. "Evidentiary Behaviors Constituting Reckless Disregard for the Truth." *Communications and the Law* 20 (1998): 39–62.

Kimball, Roger. "Malcolm Muggeridge's Journey." *New Criterion* 21 (June 2003). http://www.newcriterion.com/archive/21/jun03/mugger.htm (10 April 2005).

Kinkopf, Neil J. "Malice in Wonderland: Fictionalized Quotations and the Constitutionally Compelled Substantial Truth Doctrine." *Case Western Reserve Law Review* 41 (1991): 1271–1310.

Kloppenberg, James T. "Objectivity and Historicism: A Century of American Historical Writing." *American Historical Review* 94, no. 4 (1989): 1011–30.

Kovach, Bill, and Tom Rosenstiel. *The Elements of Journalism: What Newspeople Should Know and the Public Should Expect.* New York: Crown Publishers, 2001.

Kramer, Mark. "Breakable Rules for Literary Journalists." In *Literary Journalism: A New Collection of the Best American Nonfiction*, ed. Norman Sims and Mark Kramer, 21–36. New York: Ballantine, 1995.

——. "Narrative Journalism Comes of Age." *Nieman Reports* (Fall 2000): 5–8.

Lehrer, Adrienne. "Between Quotation Marks." *Journalism Quarterly* (May 1986): 902–6, 941.

——. "The (In)accuracy of Quotation." *Editor and Publisher*, 25 January 1992, 44, 30–31.

Lentz, Richard. "The Search for Strategic Silence: Discovering What Journalism Leaves Out." *American Journalism* (Winter 1991): 10–26.

Lessner, Jonathan I. "*Masson v. New Yorker Magazine, Inc.*: 'Sex, Women, Fun, and Altered Quotations.'" *University of Miami Law Review* 45 (1990): 159–200.

Levine, Lawrence W. *Highbrow/Lowbrow: The Emergence of Cultural Hierarchy in America.* Cambridge: Harvard University Press, 1988.

Levine, Lee. "Judge and Jury in the Law of Defamation: Putting the Horse behind the Cart." *American University Law Review* 35 (Fall 1985): 3–92.

Levy, Leonard W. *Emergence of a Free Press.* Chicago: Ivan R. Dee, 1985.

Lewis, Anthony. *Make No Law: The Sullivan Case and the First Amendment.* New York: Vintage Books, 1992.

——. "*New York Times v. Sullivan* Reconsidered: Time to Return to 'The Central Meaning of the First Amendment.'" *Columbia Law Review* 83 (April 1983): 603–25.

Libel Defense Resource Center, Press Release, 2001 Summary Judgment Study, 27 August 2001.http://www.ldrc.com/Press_Releases/bull2001–3.html (3 December 2005).

——. *LDRC Bulletin*, no. 4, pt. 1 (Summer 1982).

——. *LDRC Bulletin*, no. 11 (Summer–Fall 1984).

——. *LDRC Bulletin*, no. 17 (Spring 1986).

——. "Media Defendants' Win Rate Higher . . . but So Are Damage Awards." Press Release for *2002 Report on Trials and Damages*, *LDRC Bulletin*, no. 1 (2002).

Lichtenberg, Judith. "In Defence of Objectivity Revisited." In *Mass Media and Society*, ed. James Curran and Michael Gurevitch, 225–42. 2nd ed. London: Arnold, 1996.

Lindey, Alexander. *Entertainment, Publishing, and the Arts: Agreements and the Law*. New York: C. Boardman, 1963–1977. Reprinted as Alexander Lindey with Michael Landau, *Lindey on Entertainment, Publishing, and the Arts*, 3rd ed. St Paul: West, 2004.

Lippmann, Walter. *Liberty and the News*. 1920. New Brunswick, N.J.: Transaction, 1995.

———. *The Phantom Public*. New York: Harcourt, Brace, 1925.

———. "The Press and Public Opinion." *Political Science Quarterly* 42, no. 2 (1931): 161–70.

———. *Public Opinion*. New York: Free Press, 1997.

Litowitz, Douglas E. *Postmodern Philosophy and Law*. Lawrence: University Press of Kansas, 1997.

Macdonald, Dwight. "Parajournalism, or Tom Wolfe and His Magic Writing Machine." In *The Reporter as Artist: A Look at the New Journalism Controversy*, ed. Ronald Weber, 223–33. New York: Hastings House, 1974.

Mahon, Gigi. *The Last Days of the New Yorker*. New York: McGraw-Hill, 1988.

Marzolf, Marion Tuttle. *Civilizing Voices: American Press Criticism, 1880–1950*. New York: Longman, 1991.

Masson, Jeffrey Moussaeiff. Introduction to *The Assault on Truth: Freud's Suppression of the Seduction Theory*, xv–xxiii. New York: Farrar, Straus and Giroux, 1984.

Mayer, Michael F. *The Libel Revolution: A New Look at Defamation and Privacy*. New York: Law Arts Publishers, 1987.

Mehta, Ved. "A Battle against the Bewitchment of Our Intelligence." In *Fly and the Fly-Bottle: Encounters with British Intellectuals*, 1–45. Boston: Atlantic Monthly Press, 1963.

Meiklejohn, Alexander. *Free Speech and Its Relation to Self-Government*. New York: Harper and Brothers, 1948.

———. *Political Freedom: The Constitutional Powers of the People*. New York: Oxford University Press, 1965.

Menand, Louis. "A Friend Writes: The Old *New Yorker*." In *American Studies*, 125–45. New York: Farrar, Straus and Giroux, 2002.

———. *The Metaphysical Club: A Story of Ideas in America*. New York: Farrar, Straus and Giroux, 2001.

Meyer, Philip. *Ethical Journalism*. New York: Longman, 1986.

Miller, James. *Democracy Is in the Streets: From Port Huron to the Siege of Chicago*. New York: Simon and Schuster, 1987.

Mindich, David T. Z. *Just the Facts: How "Objectivity" Came to Define American Journalism*. New York: New York University Press, 1998.

Mitchell, Joseph. *Up in the Old Hotel*. New York: Vintage Books, 1993.

Morning Edition. Episode 1095, broadcast 28 May 1993 by National Public Radio, hosted by Bob Edwards.

Murchison, Brian C., John Soloski, Randall P. Bezanson, Gilbert Cranberg, and Roselle L. Wissler. "*Sullivan*'s Paradox: The Emergence of Judicial Standards of Journalism." *North Carolina Law Review* 73 (1994): 7–113.

National News Council. *After "Jimmy's World": Tightening Up in Editing*. New York: National News Council, 1981.

Nelkin, Dorothy. *Selling Science: How the Press Covers Science and Technology*. Revised ed. New York: W. H. Freeman, 1995.

Nelson, Harold L., and Dwight L. Teeter. *Law of Mass Communications: Freedom and Control of Print and Broadcast Media.* Mineola, N.Y.: Foundation Press,, 1969.

Neuwirth, Robert. "Shop Talk at Thirty: The Journalist and the Joyrider." *Editor and Publisher,* 31 July 1993, 44.

Newcity, Michael. "Libel Law Then and Now: A Review Essay." *Wisconsin Law Review* (March 1989): 359–402.

Nieman Foundation, *Nieman Program on Narrative Journalism: Director's Corner.* 2003. http://www.nieman.harvard.edu/narrative/about_narrative.html (9 December 2003).

Nord, David Paul. "The Practice of Historical Research." In *Mass Communication Research and Theory,* ed. Guido H. Stempel III, David H. Weaver, and G. Cleveland Wilhoit, 362–85. Boston: Allyn and Bacon, 2003.

Novick, Peter. *That Noble Dream: The "Objectivity Question" and the American Historical Profession.* Cambridge: Cambridge University Press, 1988.

Pauly, John. J. "The Politics of the New Journalism." In *Literary Journalism in the Twentieth Century,* ed. Norman Sims, 110–29. New York: Oxford University Press, 1990.

Peters, John Durham. "Democracy and American Mass Communication Theory: Dewey, Lippmann, Lazarsfeld." *Communication* 11 (1989): 199–220.

Podhoretz, Norman. "The Article as Art." In *The Reporter as Artist: A Look at the New Journalism Controversy,* ed. Ronald Weber, 125–36. New York: Hastings House, 1974.

Polk, Katherine. "Inferring Actual Malice from Altered Quotations, *Masson v. New Yorker Magazine, Inc.,* 111 S. Ct. 2419 (1991)." *Harvard Journal of Law and Public Policy* 15 (1992): 255–66.

Post, Robert C. "Meiklejohn's Mistake: Individual Autonomy and the Reform of Public Discourse." *Colorado Law Review* 64 (Fall 1993): 1109–37.

———. "Reconciling Theory and Doctrine in First Amendment Jurisprudence." *California Law Review* 88 (December 2000): 2353–74.

Powe, Lucas A. Jr. *The Warren Court and American Politics.* Cambridge: Belknap Press of Harvard University Press, 2000.

Raskin, Jamin R. *Overruling Democracy: The Supreme Court vs. The American People.* New York: Routledge, 2003.

Remnick, David. "Life and Letters: Reporting it All." *New Yorker,* 22 March 2004. http://www.newyorker.com/printables/fact/040329fa_fact1 (3 April 2005).

Roggenkamp, Karen. *Narrating the News: New Journalism and Literary Genre in Late Nineteenth-Century American Newspapers and Fiction.* Kent, Ohio: Kent State University Press, 2005.

Rosen, Jay. *What Are Journalists For?* New Haven: Yale University Press, 1999.

Rosenberg, Norman L. *Protecting the Best Men: An Interpretive History of the Law of Libel.* Chapel Hill: University of North Carolina Press, 1986.

Sack, Robert D., and Sandra S. Baron. *Sack on Defamation: Libel, Slander, and Related Problems.* 3rd ed. 2 vols. New York: Practising Law Institute, 1999.

Schiller, Dan. *Objectivity and the News: The Public and the Rise of Commercial Journalism.* Philadelphia: University of Pennsylvania Press, 1981.

Schudson, Michael. *Discovering the News: A Social History of American Newspapers.* New York: Basic Books, 1978.

———. *The Good Citizen: A History of American Civic Life.* New York: Free Press, 1998.

——. "The Objectivity Norm in American Journalism." *Journalism* 2, no. 2 (2001): 149–70.

——. *The Power of News*. Cambridge: Harvard University Press, 1995.

——. *The Sociology of News*. New York: W. W. Norton, 2003.

Schwartz, Bernard. *The Ascent of Pragmatism: The Burger Court in Action*. Reading, Mass.: Addison-Wesley, 1990.

Shaw, Donald. "At the Crossroads: Change and Continuity in American Press News 1820–1860." *Journalism History* 8, no. 2 (Summer 1981): 38–50.

Shi, David E. *Facing Facts: Realism in American Thought and Culture, 1850–1920*. New York: Oxford University Press, 1995.

Sims, Norman. Introduction to "The Art of Literary Journalism." In *Literary Journalism: A New Collection of the Best American Nonfiction*, 3–19. New York: Ballantine, 1995.

——. "Joseph Mitchell and *The New Yorker* Nonfiction Writers." In *Literary Journalism in the Twentieth Century*, ed. Norman Sims, 82–109. New York: Oxford University Press, 1990.

Smolla, Rodney A. "Let the Author Beware: The Rejuvenation of the American Law of Libel." *University of Pennsylvania Law Review* (December 1983): 1–94.

——. *Suing the Press*. New York: Oxford University Press, 1986.

Steel, Ronald. Foreword to *Liberty and the News*, by Walter Lippmann. Princeton, Princeton University Press, 2007.

Stephens, Mitchell. *A History of News: From the Drum to the Satellite*. New York: Viking, 1988.

Stepp, Carl Sessions. "State of the American Newspaper: Then and Now." *American Journalism Review* (September 1999): 60–75.

Streckfuss, Richard. "Objectivity in Journalism: A Search and a Reassessment." *Journalism Quarterly* 67, no. 4 (1990): 973–83.

Toews, John E. "Intellectual History After the Linguistic Turn: The Autonomy of Meaning and the Irreducibility of Experience." *American Historical Review* 92, no. 4 (1987): 879–907.

Tuchman, Gaye. *Making News: A Study in the Construction of Reality*. New York: Free Press, 1978.

Walden, Ruth. "A Government Action Approach to First Amendment Analysis." *Journalism Quarterly* 69 (Spring 1992): 65–88.

Walker, Clive. "International and Comparative Perspectives on Defamation, Free Speech, and Privacy: Reforming the Laws of Libel. " *New York Law School Law Review* (2005/2006): 195–97.

Watson, John C. "*Times v. Sullivan*: Landmark or Land Mine on the Road to Ethical Journalism." *Journal of Mass Media Ethics* 17, no. 1 (2002): 3–19.

Weber, Ronald. *The Literature of Fact: Literary Nonfiction in American Writing*. Athens: Ohio University Press, 1980.

——. "Some Sort of Artistic Excitement." In *The Reporter as Artist: A Look at the New Journalism Controversy*, ed. Ronald Weber, 13–23. New York: Hastings House, 1974.

Westbrook, Robert B. *John Dewey and American Democracy*. Ithaca: Cornell University Press, 1991.

White, Hayden. *Tropics of Discourse: Essays in Cultural Criticism*. Baltimore: Johns Hopkins University Press, 1978.

Winfield, Richard N. "Altered Quotes: Holding the Line on the First Amendment." *Editor and Publisher*, 6 April 1991, 24, 26.

Wolfe, Tom. "Seizing the Power." In *The New Journalism*, ed. Tom Wolfe and E. W. Johnson, 23–36. New York: Harper and Rowe, 1973.

Yagoda, Ben. *About Town: "The New Yorker" and the World It Made*. New York: Scribner, 2000.

———. Preface to *The Art of Fact: A Historical Anthology of Literary Journalism*, ed. Kevin Kerrane and Ben Yagoda, 13–16. New York: Touchstone, 1997.

Youm, Kyu Ho. "The Plaintiff's Case." In *Communication and the Law*, ed. W. Wat Hopkins, 93–112. Northport, Ala.: Vision Press, 2003.

Ziff, Larzer. *The American 1890s: Life and Times of a Lost Generation*. New York: Viking, 1966.

INDEX

KATHY ROBERTS FORDE is an assistant professor in the School of Journalism and Mass Communication at the University of Minnesota, Twin Cities, where she teaches journalism history, media law, and literary journalism.